THE SOCIAL ECONOMY

The Social Economy

PEOPLE TRANSFORMING MODERN BUSINESS

SEVERYN T. BRUYN

Boston College

A WILEY-INTERSCIENCE PUBLICATION

JOHN WILEY & SONS, New York · Chichester · Brisbane · Toronto

Library of Congress Cataloging in Publication Data:

Bruyn, Severyn Ten Haut, 1927–
   The social economy.

   "A Wiley-Interscience publication."
   Includes indexes.
    1. Industry–Social aspects–United States.
2. Industry and state–United States. 3. International business enterprises–Social aspects. I. Title.

HD60.5.U5B78   658.4'08   77-14597
ISBN 0-471-01985-2

Printed in the United States of America

10 9 8 7 6 5 4 3 2 1

PERSONAL NOTE

When I first started studying this area many years ago, I recommended to students in my courses that they make social profiles of business corporations. I suggested a few guidelines and then encouraged them to develop an outline of their own. In one case, a student decided to include the names of major stockholders of the corporation he was studying. He had a difficult time finding out the names, however, and finally came to me for help.[1] I went to the Business Library to pursue the matter of stock ownership myself and asked the librarian for assistance. The librarian did not know how to locate corporate owners and referred me to a member of the Business School faculty for help. The faculty member did not know either, but the curious point was that he found the project quite improper. He felt it was a private matter. I said, "But this company is one of the largest and oldest in the country! It's like a public institution!" His incensed reply and the heated exchange that followed need not be recorded here. The issue was a matter of what was public and what was private. The corporation was not seen as a public enterprise. It was none of my business! I did not realize then that this was the beginning of a deep and developing involvement with the subject.

As I continued to pursue this inquiry, it became increasingly clear to me how much the field of sociology had ignored the social nature of the economy as a major area of study. It was not a domain of knowledge like the community, the family, race relations, or stratification. Clearly the tradition in sociology for the study of occupations and industrial relations did not include the systematic study of social economy. There were no definitive studies on the *social nature of property*, the *social organization of wholesaling, commerce, trade associations, or types of economic exchange.* There was no special field of study called the *sociology of taxation;* no substantial research on the *sociology of money;* no solid pieces of research on the varieties of *private and social ownership,* on the operations of *retail establishments such as grocery, drug, and clothing stores.*

v

There were no creditable *sociological studies of banking.* The general field of social economy simply did not exist as an important tradition of sociology, in spite of the fact that it was a major area of interest of the great German sociologist, Max Weber.

The direction of research in sociology today is often limited by the framework of established fields in the profession. But one can carry his investigations beyond the established framework if it becomes necessary to answer important questions. This is what happened in my case.

I had begun studies in the field of criminology, doing fieldwork in prisons, searching for the causes of crime. The search for causes then led me back to the community. I directed a program in community development tied to a program in academic studies. It soon became apparent, however, that the roots of social problems were much more complex than our program staff and researchers could discern or community groups could treat at the local level. Many of the basic problems of the community were traceable to the structure of the larger society. The local organizations such as the church, the retail store, the factory, the fraternal club, the welfare agency, the Boy Scouts, were all tied significantly to national affiliates, which in turn determined local policy either by bureaucratic mandate or by their national norms and customs of organization. It was then that I began to see the great significance of the economic order in society.

This new line of inquiry meant that I had to change my schedule of readings and my focus of research. I had to become more a part of the economic order that I was studying. When I was younger, I worked on an assembly line in an American Can factory. I also worked as a laborer in an International Harvester plant and with other big companies. I now visited trade conferences, talked with corporate executives and local business people, volunteered for part-time jobs, and finally was led to visit business operations in other nations. I visited the settings of multinational corporations in Central America, Mexico, and Puerto Rico, and lived for a summer on the plantations of the United Fruit Company in Honduras and Guatemala. To see the round of life in international commerce and industry, I not only needed to talk with executives in their offices in foreign capitals but also needed to go into the hills to talk with people who were affected by the corporations. I visited Cuba to gain a sense of the reasons for revolution and what happens in the aftermath. This all now seems like a large order of inquiry when I look back on it, but the project grew gradually for me. I began to see the necessity of building a theoretical orientation for new studies in the discipline of social economy.

Over the years the many insoluble problems I confronted in my investigation made it essential that I obtain a more complete picture. I suggested to students that they work as participant observers in stores, factories, and white collar jobs to become more involved in their own study of economic life.[2] Their own recordings on the quality of daily worklife showed it to be pretty dismal; this fact led me to develop a theory of value and direction in economic life. Daily work seemed to be only a routine without any relation to the larger scope and purpose of things. It soon became clear to us how we were in a special position to see the connections between the parts and the whole in our seminar, a perspective not normally contained in the occupational world of any single person.

For example, when I worked as a part-time gas station attendant on one of my forays into the field, I found that the larger picture of corporate life was simply not a part of that world. It was a unique world with a special language that we used to talk about auto repair, special stereotypes that guided our conversations about the customers, special times allotted to give directions to motorists lost on the road, special courtesies we gave to kids whose bikes broke down, special allowances to friends to use station equipment for personal repair jobs, and a special humor about how hard we all worked on the job. We did not discuss stockholder issues of the company or the involvement of our company in South Africa and the Middle East oil disputes. These larger social issues of the corporation for which we worked were simply not an important part of our daily life. We could not care less whether the corporation was contributing to Apartheid in Africa or widening the gap between wealth and poverty in the Arab countries. The same was true of other life-worlds in which I became a part. As I learned from lengthy conversations, there was a special routine to being small business men and women. We were concerned about creating adequate parking facilities for customers; we were upset about national discount chains underselling us; and we were angry at the big corporation that had failed to honor a promise not to sell our product line to a neighborhood competitor. But there was no nationwide effort to alter the power of big national chain corporations. We did not discuss how the growth of such "concentrations of power" might affect political life in the United States.

There was also a special world for the big business executives with whom I talked at length. Here was a concern for markets and technology. Most executives were quick to discuss the good and bad side of business, but on the whole they believed that business contributed to the social good. A few businessmen talked about the inevitability of socialism in this country. By socialism they meant increasing government controls and power. Business was becoming trapped by the government, but there was no time for "executive thinking" about alternative social systems of business that would remove the need for government controls. The *social organization* of the economy was not a part of the language and thought of business life. Instead, the issues were economic and were discussed in such terms as inflation and the gross national product.

In this process, I found myself looking at the economy differently. When I wandered about shopping centers, I was no longer simply looking for low prices or the most durable products in my role as customer. I was looking for the way stores were socially related to their national affiliates and also socially related to one another. I would go into Woolworth's, purchase a key chain, and then explain my interests in the social economy to the manager. We would then talk about the kind of individual decisions that his superiors permitted him to make at the store level on matters of pricing, employment, and accounting. I would go into the A&P to buy groceries and then talk with the manager about the extent to which he could purchase goods independently and arrange his own displays. Though it had never occurred to me before, I became interested in the extent to which authority was decentralized in large corporations.

I designed a research project for students so they could talk with store owners in Newton (a well-to-do white suburb of Boston) and in Roxbury (a poor black neighborhood in Boston), hoping to observe differences in business styles and community control. We learned many facts about these communities. Prices were higher in the black neighborhood, and black business people could not obtain fair insurance coverage. But we also learned what business failure meant personally to people. It changed our conception of business life.

The failure rate of small businesses is very high in all communities for many reasons, including being in the shadow of corporate growth. As I thought about our personal discoveries in the two business communities, the image of a vast forest came to mind. I suddenly remembered as a boy arguing about whether falling trees in a forest made a sound if there was no one around to hear them. A parallel was coming to mind in the thousands of business failures that must have occurred beyond our study of the two business communities. We knew that business failures affected people personally and socially. They sometimes became family tragedies. Yet they were never heard in the vast forest of business. It was clear that the social dimension of business was not conceived to be part of the economic order. The business order and the social order were separated. The modern image of business operations is drawn from the metaphor of nature and animalkind rather than from society and humankind.

The notes I took through interviews, participant observation, conferences, and trips abroad are an implicit part of this writing, and my experiences are a significant part of the motivation for writing this book. They were part of my reason for developing a theoretical orientation that could stimulate thinking about the social economy in all its dimensions. The social organization of the economy could not be discussed in everyday life as easily as the social organization of the government, the community, and the family. Yet in our seminars on campus we saw that the economy was constituted by social relations, and that the problems these relations engendered were affecting the government, the community, and the family. The fact that the public could not consider the organization of the business economy to be an issue affecting the nation increased my concern that contemporary foundations for the study of social economy should begin to be formulated.

Through my studies and personal experiences in this country and overseas, I became more aware of a great social change taking place in the organization of the American economy. It has become increasingly clear to me over the years that powerful and subtle changes are occurring that are leading us toward a new society.

The theory of social economy that began to emerge in this search then became partly a critique of the life-worlds I witnessed in the field. It also became a critique of the disciplines that study the production and distribution of goods. The dominant position of economics as the special language for interpreting the macro system of business, for example, has seemed to me to carry a mythos about it that blinds us to the social and political realities of the economic system. The picture of the economy and the treatment of its problems outlined by John Maynard Keynes seemed a "total picture" to many academics with whom I have talked. And yet it has been abundantly clear that the social organization of the economy is significantly missing from Keynesian theory. I am convinced this social organization is fundamental to understanding the direction in which we are all heading.

Social economy is a field of study designed to answer the questions that traditional economics does not. It is a discipline that looks at the organization of economic enterprise on a human scale. It emphasizes the social and personal dimensions of economic life. It examines the connections between the small and the big organizations of the economy and their effect on people. It studies the relationship that may exist between the personal troubles we have and the structure of the economic order. It seeks to bridge the gap between scientific studies and social policy. It aims thereby to bring some measure of human understanding to the study of the economy and some degree of social control over the great economic forces of society.

Scientific studies of the local gas station or factory in this view remain important by themselves, but they gain significance as their findings connect with the larger picture. We want to know how the freedom of people in the locality is affected by the larger economic system and how valuable local workers are in that system. At the same time, studies of the national or world economy are important by themselves, but they gain in significance as they stimulate policies that respect the quality of working life among people in the local community.

The purpose of this work in the final analysis is to help build a human perspective into the scientific study of the economy. Scientific inquiry may then not only contribute to our general knowledge but also guide social policy and human development in society.

---

1. Part of the difficulty was in the fact that corporate owners may conceal their identity with "street names" or "nominees" like Byeco, Cadco, Gepco, and Ninco. The Bank of America, for example, has 111 front names. In the pursuit of corporate owners, Senator Lee Metcalf (Montana) discovered a private group called the American Society of Corporate

Secretaries that had a code-list revealing original owners, but its distribution was limited to private members. Senator Metcalf managed to obtain a copy of the code-list and published it in the *Congressional Record,* June 24, 1971, Vol. 117, No. 98, Part II. Since that time, however, many "street names" have been changed.

2. I suggested that students read Sidney and Beatrice Webb, *Methods of Social Study* (London: Cambridge University Press, 1975; original publication, 1932).

PREFACE

It has become increasingly apparent to me over the years that we live with a picture of the economy that misdirects scientific research and public policy. Our picture is based partly on the classical imagery of political economy in the last century and partly on the vocabulary of the sophisticated economics in this century. We tend to look today at the economy as a system of "natural forces" operating independently of ourselves, and we talk about the economy as a private system of free enterprises operating in a free market. We learn about the economy in such sophisticated terms as the "gross national product," "levels of unemployment," "stock market quotations," "profit and loss," "supply and demand," and "consumer price index." These are scientific terms, and they partly define our public image of the economy. They are indeed helpful measures, but nevertheless they fail to provide us with a sufficient understanding of how the economy really works. We miss seeing the social foundation of the economy that is so fundamental to its very existence.

The problem of public imagery is far-reaching. When we picture the business system as "the private sector," consisting of enterprises that are economically motivated, we ignore the vast network of social activity that really governs the entire operation of the economy. When corporate business is defined as "private," it soon becomes shrouded in secrecy. Corporate secrecy is made legal, and the social dimensions of economic life elude us still further, officially hidden from our view. Our public concept of the economy then becomes largely a fiction.

Our public concept of the economy overlooks the social domain and fails to direct scientific studies toward critical issues. The critical issues cannot be approached merely through the classical imagery of the nineteenth century or even through the sophisticated techniques of modern economics. Studying the economy as though it were operating under the laws of supply and demand may offer suggestions on how the government could control the prime interest rates or the amount of money in circulation, but it fails to focus attention on how the economy is composed of people who create that supply and demand through their private organizations. Studying the economy as though it were a "system of prices" or in terms of "marginal utility" may tell us how scientific variables function in the system but it does not tell us how to act within it to help solve its human problems. Studying the economy as though it were a "market system" may provide interesting statistics about cycles of inflation and depression, but it does not tell us how a nonmarket system of organizations helps to cause those cycles and how they may be treated through the reformation of that system without government controls.

An alternative way of looking at the economy is to see it as an institutional order of associations and values created by people. We can then describe it as a network of partnerships, corporations, unions, trade federations, cooperatives, and consumer organizations managed by human beings. We can then see how people determine policy through corporate rules, government regulations, voluntary contracts, legal requirements, social expectations, public opinion, and informal agreements. The modern economy is then seen to be socially designed.

My purpose here is not to outline a systematic view of the field of social economy but simply to provide an orientation for studies of the American economy. A basic question in the years ahead hopefully will be: What constitutes the field of social economy? The theoretical orientation expressed here is intended in part to contribute to the answer to that question. It is intended to stimulate thinking and research in this neglected area of sociology.

THE ORGANIZATION OF THE BOOK

The book is organized in four parts: The Corporate Economy, The Federal Economy, The International Economy and The Social Economy. These four parts constitute the main themes characterizing studies in the book.

The first chapter begins with a corporate history. It discusses the critical importance of writing a history of society that includes the economy as well as the government. Special attention is given to the outlooks of corporate lawyers, executives, workers, and researchers. I argue that a "social consciousness" has been developing among all classes of people who have worked with the corporation. People have been gradually changing the traditional business orientation of "self-interest" and "profits" to include public responsibility and accountability. The business system has been shifting significantly toward a social orientation while maintaining its basic economic orientation. It is this theme that occupies much of our attention in the remainder of the book.

I explore the scientific implications of this shift toward a social orientation in the second chapter. The purpose is to find new professional grounds for corporate research in the light of what we know about the social direction of corporations. The discussion, therefore, is of special interest to professional researchers, and the general reader may want to skip to the next chapter.

In Chapter Three we look at the social problems, created by the business system, that the government must solve. Government departments and regulatory agencies must be created to deal with such problems as environmental pollution, economic concentration, inflation, labor exploitation, land speculation, inadequate supply of farm products, deceptive advertising, and unemployment. At the same time we also see how such problems have been solved by business itself as it has developed systems of social accountability and self-regulation: private tribunals, review boards, codetermination of labor and management, consumer councils, land trusts, and community development corporations. We argue that under the right conditions the enterprise system can treat its own problems without government regulatory agencies.

In Chapter Four we look in some detail at a proposal to treat the problem of corporate monopoly and concentration. I suggest the potential for decentralizing corporate authority and developing local responsibility through the auspicies of a chartering agency. We see here how local subsidiaries can increase their local accountability and how self-managing enterprises can be developed through federal chartering of the very large corporations.

The social and political implications of decentralizing authority in the big corporations then lead us to examine the concept of the private federation. In Chapter Five I discuss the history of the federation and then point to its development in the modern period, noting how federations have emerged in every sphere of modern life, including education, religion and government as well as in the economy. In the economy they exist as nonprofit corporations, helping to solve social problems in the business system. We see how union federations, business federations, and cooperative federations have been developing a social foundation to the institutional economy. They now offer a place in the national economy for devising solutions to the problems of the "macro system," becoming part of the self-monitoring and self-governing system of alternatives, reducing the need for more government agencies.

This institutional alternative of social (nonstatist) federations is examined from an international perspective in Chapter Six. We look at the development of nongovernmental federations in other societies and interpret "the movement" at the world level. We are interested especially in the trend toward increasing worker responsibilities in the *production sector* of the economy through union federations, the trend toward increasing managerial responsibilities in the *distribution sector* through trade and employer federations, and the trend toward increasing consumer responsibilities in the *consumption sector* through cooperatives and consumer federations.

The theoretical implications of these international trends are discussed in Chapter Seven. We examine the direction of this development in the more technical terms of the behavioral sciences. Here we look at the importance of balancing the power of these production-distribution-consumption federations to reduce the need for state intervention and control.

Our attention turns in Chapter Eight to the international world of business. We look at social models of economic development with reference to multinational corporations. Here we look at the way "social indicators" can be formulated to measure how global business helps or hinders the development of a self-governing nation, and discuss a model of self-governance among developing nations in relation to business.

With this technical discussion in mind, we then look at social policies for the democratic development of economic systems among nations. We examine social policy applied at local, national, and international levels of economy. The question here is how policies at each level may help social development. We examine certain policies which should reduce the need for the nation-state to serve as the sole agent of human development in the world economy.

In the concluding chapter I summarize the basic ideas in the book from the perspective of social planning. We begin with basic assertions underlying social economy as a field of knowledge and indicate how they point toward principles of decentralized development. These principles are applied in Chapter Ten to interpret the experience of top-down state planning in Western European countries. I note certain problems of *state planning,* which then sharpens our discussion of alternative modes of *social planning* in the special context of American society.

The Appendix provides examples of the "impact" of corporations on social and political life. It is a case study of two American companies seeking to begin copper mining on the island of Puerto Rico and is based on reports from one of my field investigations. It illustrates very concretely both the problems and their solutions that were discussed in the main body of the book. Some readers therefore may choose to begin the book at the end in order to observe what can happen when business corporations enter into the political economy of a developing country.

The book indicates a social foundation for research and a social direction to national economic policy. It speaks especially to leaders in labor, business, law, and science, but its call for leadership is not limited to these fields. The responsibility to help build a social economy falls equally upon all of us.

Many people have contributed to the writing of this book by responding to inquiries made in the course of my field work, and I thank them all. Others helped me to clarify some of the ideas contained in the book: Professor George Lodge, Harvard Graduate School of Business Administration, Professor David Garson, Department of Political Science, Tufts University; Professor Irving Louis Horowitz, Department of Sociology and Political Science, Rutgers University; Professor William Foote Whyte, Department of Industrial and Labor Relations, Cornell University; Dr. Denis Goulet, Overseas Development Corporation; Dr. Norman Faramelli, Associate Director, Boston Industrial Mission; Dr. Charles Savage, Senior Research Analyst, Commerce and Labor Committee, Massachusetts Statehouse; Professor Michael Useem, Department of Sociology, Boston University; Mr. David Ackerman, Vice President, AMAX Corporation; Mr. Gerald Harris, Retired Regional Director, United Auto Workers; Professor Rafael Corrada, Professor of Social Planning, University of Puerto Rico; Professor Max Stackhouse, Andover Newton Theological Seminary; Dr. Roland Warren, Professor of Community Planning, Florence Heller School, Brandeis University; various faculty members of the Boston College School of Management, including Associate Director Richard Maffei, Professors Ed Huse and Walter Klein; many members of the local Association for Self-Management, including Dr. David Ellerman, economist; Dr. Joan Rothchild, political scientist; Mr. John Blanchard, American Friends Service Committee; and Ms. Mindy Reiser, Graduate Student at Brandeis University. Professor Robert Frederick, Professor of Business Administration, University of Pittsburgh, read the whole manuscript and made very helpful comments on each chapter.

Finally, I want to thank members of my department for their patience at different stages of writing when the project took time away from department activities. I also appreciate the interest of Professor Everett Hughes in coteaching a course on American corporations with me very early in my work. I learned much from his insistence on field work for students studying "on-going institutions." At different times, simple conversations over coffee with department colleagues stimulated important thoughts about this area of research. And our department secretaries were especially helpful to me: Mrs. Lorraine Bone, Mrs. Alice Close, and Mrs. Shirley Urban.

My wife, Louise, is of course without parallel in her perceptive reading and helpful comments on chapters in rough draft.

SEVERYN T. BRUYN

Chestnut Hill, Massachusetts
June 1977

CONTENTS

THE SOCIAL ECONOMY

Introduction

Social Economy
As A Field of Knowledge

Social economy is a field of knowledge rooted within the disciplines of sociology and economics with significant links to other disciplines. It represents an important convergence in subject matter that has been developing from a wide range of scientific fields and public policy programs. It focuses on the economy as an institutional order within society and has links to such fields as industrial psychology, occupational sociology, business administration, labor studies, scientific management, public administration, environmental studies, and consumer research. They are all functionally related to the field of social economy within the larger subject of society.

Many of these specialized disciplines are now challenged by the changing structure of society, and this fact gives impetus to the development of social economy as an integrating field of knowledge. Industrial sociology, for example, must explain the fact that a postindustrial service economy is developing alongside traditional industrial organization. It must broaden its theoretical base to explain this transition from industrial life. Scientific management is coming to terms with the growing power of labor organizations in capitalist societies. Labor is gaining managerial significance in ways that require a new integral outlook in the field of management. Industrial psychology is having to take greater account of the effect of business systems on personality in different social settings as business expands its operations domestically and internationally. Industrial management in capitalist societies is having to recognize the developing field of socialist management as different types of nations increase their trade relations. Socialist management is having to come to terms with capitalist economics as leaders perceive it to be effective and applicable in socialist organization.

1

Business administration has to account for socialist administration as it shows evidence of viability in the cultural life of modern nations. In this mix of specialized fields of theory and practice there is need for an integral perspective. Social economy is the link between these separate areas of investigation. It takes account of the strains and provides a general scientific outlook integral to them. Its strength lies in its potential to provide insight into the relationships among special areas of study developing in both capitalist and socialist nations.

The term "social economy" has alternated with "political economy" in different nations to refer to that field of knowledge which signifies linkages between the economy and society. In France, for example, following the tradition that began with Montchretien and Rousseau, the term "political economy" has been used consistently up to the present period. But in other European countries the term "social economy" was more prevalent. The term "social economy" was widely used in Poland in the late nineteenth century and early twentieth century. In Italy, Luigi Cossa published *Economia Sociale* in 1891. In Germany, in 1895, Heinrich Dietzel wrote *Theoretische Sozialoekonomik.* England followed the French tradition, beginning with James Stuart's *Inquiry Into the Principles of Political Economy* in 1767. In this tradition Marx and Engels used the term to describe the social relations of production and distribution of goods. Since then, the term "political economy" has been commonly used in western literature.[1]

The term "economics" has its own history. It was only after Alfred Marshall published his influential *Principles of Economics* in 1890 that the term began to be used frequently in English-speaking countries. It came to replace the term "political economy" in the twentieth century. Since the time of Marshall, then, the terms "economics" and "political economy" have come to represent different scientific traditions.

The separate intellectual traditions of economics and political economy have much to offer one another, as scholars in both traditions suggest. The Polish socialist Oskar Lange has said that Marxian economics would be a poor basis for running a central bank or anticipating the effects of a change in the rate of discount, even though it provides the basis for anticipating the dissolution of capitalist economies. MIT economist Paul Samuelson has said that Marx's economic tools constitute a sterile analysis of both capitalism and socialism, "but try to convince a billion people of that."[2]

In this period of transition for modern society, "social economy" is a most accurate and appropriate term to characterize the study of economy and society. "Political economy" continues to be a vital term to describe certain key features of the economy, but today it refers to specific aspects of a larger field of knowledge. It can now be seen as the study of power in the relationship of the economy to the society. Political economy is a special dimension of the general field of social economy.

The contemporary disciplines of sociology and economics can find common ground in the concept of social economy. This concept suggests an order of study and thought that takes account of the older tradition of political economy and adds a twentieth century perspective of the social sciences. It assumes that political institutions and the political factor in general constitute only one major characteristic of society. The economic order has a political character; it also has a relationship to the state that is fundamental to observe and study. But the political concept cannot represent all the multifaceted relations of the economy in the context of society. The field of political economy remains a perfect reference for scholars studying power inherent in the relations of the economy and the state within the context of society.

The scientific concepts that are used in the study of society need to express accurately and completely the total human reality. The "social concept" has an efficacy of its own in this respect. It is basic and inclusive of many other institutional relationships. Karl Marx often interchanged the concept of being "social" with that of being "human." Max Weber defined "social" as being oriented to others in action. This orientation could be based on many motives: religious, educational, economic, personal, or political. The usages of Marx and Weber thus include a variety of nonpolitical relationships in the study of economy and society.

The political concept by itself restricts studies to the phenomenon of power and the formal government of the state. It is implicitly assumed in the theory of political economy that all human relationships are based on power. Although this is true, it is not true exclusively, and therefore the assertion by itself becomes deceptive. Power is a complicated concept that has not yet been fully distinguished in relation to other great concepts such as "status," "community," "love," "truth," and "value." Some theorists claim truth to be the basis of power, whereas others claim that power can be realized only in community. Some scholars claim that all relationships are based, in the final analysis, on love. Many different basic concepts explain human behavior in the context of society. Certain ones have priority over politics and power in explaining the complicated context of economic life in society. The social concept, therefore, is closer to comprehending the relationship of people within the economic order of society and therefore in this respect has the greater efficacy. Power is examined as one fundamental component of social relations within the economy.

In the light of these basic assumptions, then, a broad scope of studies is possible. The social relationship of the economy to such modern institutional settings as education and religion can be explored more easily when their own cultural systems are taken into account. The relationship of power to such constituents of society as spiritual values and artistic works can more easily be investigated when it is not automatically assumed that power and politics supersede the investigation of all other human factors. These are questions that can be pursued openly in the study of social economy.

The premises of social economy as a field of knowledge are deeply embedded in the intellectual traditions of Western thought. The framework for study in social economy had its origins in the work of both sociologists and economists. The social concept—the idea of sociality—is complex, extending from Saint-Simon, Karl Marx, Auguste Comte, Emile Durkheim, Max Weber, into modern sociological thought and studies.

On the one hand, the social concept refers to the subjective aspects of relationships among people in society. People interpret daily interactions in personal terms. On the other hand, it has an objective dimension understood in the theoretical interpretations of these interactions. Social scientists attempt to categorize subjective interaction and study it objectively on verifiable grounds. These categorizations are then quite various and complex.

The economic concept—the idea of economy—finds origins in the work of Aristotle. The meaning of economy, however, is also complex, extending through Adam Smith, David Ricardo, and Alfred Marshall into modern economic thought and studies. On the one hand, it refers to the objective meaning found in the production of material gain having measurable utility. On the other hand, it has a subjective dimension when the terms that define it operationally are understood in their cultural and historical context.

Social economy is a convenient phrase to express the purposes of this book. As a field of knowledge, social economy, maintains a scientific framework that can account for institutions changing in the context of history. It is this framework that challenged such different theorists as Karl Marx and Max Weber. Scientific interests guided their separate efforts to study economic life in society. Like Marx and Weber, social scientists paradoxically stand apart from ideological expressions of economic order. They study them both subjectively and objectively and seek to explain the differences among them.

Social economy seeks to understand the subjective dimensions of ideology and at the same time to account objectively for the larger reality. The scientist begins in this case with the premise that all economies are to some extent social and require study. The social economist, therefore, sets forth theories relying upon empirical studies interpreted within a cross-cultural perspective. He or she proposes theories recognizing the value-premises inherent within them and their relationship to both history and contemporary society.

Important value-premises within the field of social economy are found in its defining terms and its scientific framework. Some of these can be suggested here in an introductory way. First, the social concept stresses the importance of studying human relationships in economic organization. It imparts an importance to the observation of social interaction in the economic life of society. The researcher takes an interest in investigating the kind of social relationships existing within the productive and commercial systems of exchange within society. Second, the study of social economy applies to all societies. Important values are found in concepts that are universally applicable. Social economy seeks to be scientific (nonideological) in the spirit of both the Marxian and Weberian traditions. Third, the study of social economy recognizes ideology as a force of human development. It takes ideology seriously as a contextual force that shapes the foundations of economic life and is also shaped by it. The relationship between ideology and economic life is of special interest to both research and theory. The social economist in different political contexts recognizes that any investigation expresses ideological features, even when they are unintended. Fourth, this ideological accounting includes continuous critical review of the theoretical premises of the field itself as well as the impact of its inquiry on the organization of society. Social economy as a field of inquiry reflects upon itself in society.

The growth of political and economic relationships between capitalist and socialist nations gives cause for the development of social economy as a scientific discipline on international grounds. The growing political contacts of the United States with Russia and China and the new developments in trade among socialist and capitalist nations mark the beginning of a new period of world history. They provide a rationale for creating a professional discipline to study the social complexity of economic enterprise in all modern societies. A discipline of social economy that crosses national boundaries will have the political foundations necessary to take account of both ideology and the economic organization of life in different social contexts.

There is a further reason for the development of social economy as a field of knowledge in this modern period. In the face of vastly changing technology, the development of new modes of production, unprecedented population growth, rapid world transport, and instant communications, all nations are facing social crises in a new setting. They are forced by circumstances to find a rationale for existing in a complex world order. They are forced to construct new grounds for their socioeconomic relations with other nations as well as within their own national boundaries. This requires the creation of scientific foundations for the study of types of economic development that break with the past, finding new patterns of living together in a socioeconomic network. Nations must find new grounds for creating forms of social economy to guide their common development toward the twenty-first century.

This process involves new studies of social development. Developing nations in Africa, Asia, and Latin America are creating their own directions in their own unique environments. There are clear indications of stagnation in traditionalism, tribalism, imperialism, and old patterns of exploitation, but there are also important signs of social innovation, creative national policy, and new world standards of justice and freedom in many new nations. Nations are no longer guided by reference to past ideologies of capitalism and socialism. They are finding it necessary to study and create new patterns of social economy.

The intellectual traditions of both Karl Marx and John Maynard Keynes are in trouble as guides to development in their respective cultures.[3] These two major intellectual traditions are no longer sufficient to guide policy making in socialist and capitalist nations. They are being transcended in the practical life of all modern governments. Nations are making their own histories and turning the keys to unlock their own futures. As doors open to change, new ideas about how people can live together socially and economically are emerging. These new ideas help explain and direct the transition toward a "post-modern" period. But they still face the conflict of old ideologies and require both international organization and conceptual foundations for the study of social economy.

Changes in national policies are communicated quickly in the news media for mass consumption, but they must also be interpreted by scientists dealing with a new combination of scientific categories. Many new ideas about living together are explained scientifically by the various categories in the field of social economy. Social economy shows promise of helping to explain, as well as to act within, the transition toward new societies developing in a world context.

A THEORETICAL PERSPECTIVE: THE AMERICAN ECONOMY IN TRANSITION

Our task now is to describe a special orientation to the study of the corporation and modern business in American society. Research into the social transition of the business system is being carried out in many directions but the perspective of social economy offers a special theoretical approach. We know that business has social foundations and that it affects people at every level of society. The task now is to develop a set of ideas within this perspective that will yield useful propositions and new facts through field research. I believe this can be done without taking the idea of social economy as dogma.

At the outset we can say that there seems to be no overarching idea at this stage of knowledge that is capable of explaining all change in society. Social economy is wide ranging, but it cannot explain all the ends and means of human development. It is thus distinguished from certain modes of socialist thought. The sources of change are not all social and economic. The basic notion of social economy informs our analysis, but it does not provide us with ultimate ends. The notion of social economy has policy and action implications, but it does not supply us with a metaphysics guiding all human action. It has epistemological overtones, but it does not subsume the meaning of all values and explain the origin of all things.

We can also say that the concept of the individual is not sufficient without the contrasting concept of community. The individual person is vital to our perspective of social economy, but we see at the same time the modern forms of society in capitalism and socialism curbing individuality. They contain forms of community that restrict individual freedom. The individual person, therefore, remains a vital starting point, but we know it is through the transforming powers of the larger community that we are enabled to live more fully as individuals. The study of the social economy is therefore central to our understanding of the importance of the individual in this larger context.

We take the corporation as important to study within the social economy because of its central position in the larger society. The corporation affects all of us. It extends beyond capitalist societies into socialist societies. It remains a viable unit capable of destructive or creative action. Its power to direct production and at the same time to dominate people through its hierarchies of supervision and rationality is a modern phenomenon of the big nation. The corporation is fundamental to understand in the resolution of problems that extend to all other major institutions of society.

This theoretical perspective goes further in that it confronts the issues of the state and the problem of power within the corporate system. It builds on the work of scholars who have already touched on this subject and yet have remained relatively separate from one another in their analysis of society. Karl Marx, Max Weber, and Emile Durkheim are three scholars whose works are essential to our concept of economy and society.

The work of Karl Marx points to a dialectical process in which we find the business society undergoing a transformation. The process is not always within our control, but we understand it best when we consider seriously the economic formation of society. Marx developed his thought from the dialectical tradition of Georg Friedrich Hegel, who saw the rational spirit of people emerging in history. But Marx saw that spirit emerging from within the evolving political economy. For Marx the capitalist order was repressing the human spirit, restraining rationality and giving us false images of reality. The system was prey to its own contradictions and was doomed to collapse before the rise of a new social order.

Marx was seeking the basis for being human and natural at the same time in society. He was examining the contradictions of capitalist society with a view of its anarchic foundations. These foundations led to instabilities and human oppression under the auspices of the state. Marx saw the state as having developed an authoritarian bureaucracy that had become sacred to people in society. It was imprisoning the people's soul:

Bureaucracy possesses the state's essence, the spiritual essence of society, as its private property. The general spirit of bureaucracy is the official *secret,* the mystery sustained within bureaucracy itself by hierarchy and maintained on the outside as a closed corporation. Conducting the affairs of the state in public, even political consciousness, thus appears to the bureaucracy as high treason against its mystery. Authority is thus the principle of its knowledge, and the deification of authoritarianism is its credo. . . . For the individual bureaucrat the state's purpose becomes his private purpose of hunting for higher positions and making a career for himself. In one respect he views actual life as something material, *for the spirit of this life has its separate existence* in bureaucracy. . . . Bureaucracy has therefore to make life as materialistic as possible. . . . The bureaucrat sees the world as a mere object to be managed by him.[4]

For Marx, an ultimate aim of socialism was the elimination of the state with its bureaucracy through the creation of a new social economic order. Marx said very clearly in his *Critique of the Gotha Program:* "Freedom consists in converting the state from an organ standing above society into one completely subordinated to it."[5]

Emile Durkheim, the French sociologist, was also concerned about the power of the state, but he saw the rise of the corporation as equally significant to the future of society. He saw the instabilities of the capitalist order leading society toward anarchistic conditions. In the preface to *The Division of Labor in Society,* he repeatedly insists on the juridical and moral breakdown (anomie) of social life under the business system. Occupational ethics, he said, could exist only "in the most rudimentary state" in this type of economic order.

At the end of the nineteenth century, Durkheim saw the future unfolding in the race for power between the corporation and the state. He saw society becoming composed of a vast system of corporations that appeared to transcend the state in their importance. He also saw the state as the only major collective entity surviving the tempest of change in the nineteenth century. The state tended "to assume functions for which it was unfitted and which it has not been able to discharge satisfactorily." In all of this lay the great social problems. Suicide was only one problem among many that he linked to the instability of the capitalist society.

For Durkheim, the solution to these problems lay at least in part in the creation of a moral order of occupational communities that could be represented in a national assembly. The occupational communities would maintain an independence from the state and serve as part of the *collective conscience,* that is, the moral community within society. It was essential that these occupational communities would be decentralized. The problem was how decentralization could best take place. Too rapid decentralization might disturb that collective conscience. The question was how to decentralize power in such a way that the unity of a nation could be preserved while diversity was developed within the economic order:

The only decentralization which would make possible the multiplication of the centers of communal life without weakening national unity is what might be called *occupational decentralization.* . . . This has been understood by the ever growing number of authors and statesmen, who wish to make the occupational group the base of our political organization, that is, divide the electoral college, not by sections of territory but by corporations.[6]

Durkheim hoped that representative assemblies of occupational corporations could set the conditions for a new morality within the economic order of business that would at least reduce its tendency to perpetuate anomie in the normative life of society.

For Max Weber, the primary problem of modern society was bureaucratic dominance. Bureaucracy had become the primary form of organizational life in the rational order of modern society. The source of bureaucratic superiority lay in the technical knowledge needed for the development of modern economic organization. It made no great difference to Weber whether the economic system was organized on a capitalist or a socialist basis. Modern development had created the need for a stable, strict, intensive, and dependable administration. It was fatefully coming to dominate humankind. The bureaucratic society of the future could be like an "iron cage." The development of socialism only accentuated the problem. The only solution for Weber was to decentralize authority. It was the only hope of escaping that dreaded trend of bureaucracy:

Only by reversion in every field—political, religious, economic, etc.—to small-scale organization would it be possible to any considerable extent to escape its influence.[7]

Each major theorist thus provides us with certain ingredients for our theoretical perspective. Marx causes us to look at the irrationality in capitalism and supplies us with insight into how a false consciousness of freedom can arise to justify a system doomed to collapse. Weber tells us about the rationality within capitalism and warns us of the worsening trends of bureaucracy in socialism. Durkheim makes us aware of how a moral order exists in every society and suggests the basis for its transition to a new reliable order of economic life.

Certain factors are missing in these three intellectual traditions. The three scholars did not explain how to eliminate corporate and state bureaucracy under either capitalism or socialism. They pointed to the problem but did not explicate the solution. They were all aware of the need to decentralize and develop human resources within society, but they never explained how the process might be studied and implemented on a practical basis. This is where our study begins.

THE BASIC ORIENTATION

Our main task here is to formulate a way of looking at the economy in the United States that yields insight into the nature of its governance and at the same time offers some direction to its social development. To do this requires that we formulate concepts to guide historical and social studies. Here we cannot discuss the "systematics" of social economy as a field of knowledge, but we can take steps in this direction by viewing the American economy as a social phenomenon.

The focus of this study, then, is on the social organization of the American economy, and its purpose is to suggest key concepts for designing research. We want to offer some direction to professional studies on the social governance and development of the American economy.

Two theoretical concepts are important to note at the outset. One is social governance and the other is social development. *Social governance* refers to the way people manage their own affairs at all levels of the economy, including the workplace, the firm, the industry, and finally the entire economy as a human institution. *Social development* refers to the way people cultivate human resources at all levels of the economic order. Both concepts involve, ultimately, looking at how both material and human resources are created together in the context of society. No single theory in sociology and economics has focused systematically on these two concepts, although many studies point in this direction.

Social governance refers to the way people manage their economic affairs in all institutions. It includes the state as one institution helping or hindering in this process, but it does not find its principal meaning there. Its primary concern is with the way people manage economic activities without state controls. The fact that economic governance is "social" means simply that we manage things in conjunction with others.

Social development is closely related to the notion of social governance. It refers to an increase in the application of human resources in economic affairs. Therefore, it implies an increase in the capacity to manage economic activities with some measure of autonomy. Social development is the development of human authority and responsibility, which reduces the necessity for the formal government or state to assume the management of economic life. "Development" implies a broadening of the organized base of leadership among people working at different levels of the economy. It signifies an increase in personal and social accountability for one's actions in the workplace and the marketplace. It implies an enhancement of the quality of worklife in all its aspects, from the factory to the administrative office to the household economy. It means an increase in the level of self-determination and freedom in one's place of work. It generally means some deepening in human sensitivity and strengthening of needed skills of the increasing number of people engaged in the corporate economy. It points toward a higher degree of self-knowledge and self-reliance of people at every level of worklife. Development implies a broadening of social consciousness among everyone, including managers, white collar workers, laborers, lawyers, and researchers. It means, in its broad scope, the creative enhancement of life itself in the economic order of society.

Social development thus leads toward social governance when there is a reduction in the need for state bureaucracy and federal agencies controlling economic organization. Development means a decrease in external authority and external controls over human conduct. At the same time it implies an increase in the inner resources of authority, in responsibility, and in the power of people in all walks of life to control their own economic activities. Social development implies, in the final analysis, an increase in individual self-determination within the economic order of society.

SCIENTIFIC AND POLICY ORIENTATIONS: FACT AND VALUE

The study of social economy involves both a scientific and a policy orientation. These two orientations are in tension with one another in the pursuit of social knowledge. Social knowledge always involves at once both facts and values. Scientific studies emphasize the pursuit of facts, but they are always based on certain values. Policy studies emphasize the pursuit of value, but they are always based on facts. The special concepts guiding this study can perhaps illustrate the subtlety of this dimension of social economy as a field of knowledge.

The concept of social governance is both a fact and a value of all human organization. It yields two subconcepts we will later describe as self-governance and mutual governance. These concepts in turn show both a factual and a value orientation.

Self-governance can be an idea approved by some people and frowned upon by others in particular circumstances. But for our purposes of scientific research the idea may be defined in more specific terms as a theory leading to research models. Its broad reference as an idea can be translated into scientific models where specific traits are investigated. Suppose an economist and a sociologist study a business firm for its capacity to optimize its material and human resources. The firm could aim for higher profits as one criterion of self-governance related to its material resources. It could aim for democratic self-management as a criterion of self-governance related to its human resources. Efforts to maximize either profits or democratic self-management may result in retarding or advancing the firm as a viable self-governing entity in the economic order of society. This fact can be objectively recorded and studied.

Social development is also both a fact and a value. It refers to purposeful social change and ultimately to the unfolding of human resources in the economy. It is also a very broad concept that requires scientific models for definitive study at different levels of economic life. Its broad reference has a value in orienting theorists to a general field of study where it requires "progressive specification" of its meaning. We need to know more exactly what we mean when we talk about development of human "authority," "responsibility," "imagination," and "sensitivity" in the social organization of the economy. The concept of development is, therefore, like self-governance, a variable factor that must be studied objectively within the social economy.

The general phrase *social economy* is also an expression of both fact and value. It is a fact that every economy has a social foundation. All economic activities at some point are rooted in social relationships. People are oriented toward one another as well as themselves in developing resources. An economy can thus be studied scientifically as a social fact, and in the process it reveals human values, as we shall see.

The study of the economy as a social fact changes our ordinary perspective of it in a business society. It assumes, for example, that the problems of business are not all economic in origin; they are also social. We then see that *business problems* may also be *social problems* and furthermore that economic problems have social causes.

To treat the social causes of economic problems, then, people must guide, redirect, and reconstruct the organization of the economy. We are thus led to the policy implications of the values hidden in this original scientific perspective on the economy as a social fact.

Scientific studies here are based on the observation of the economy as a social phenomenon. The ultimate criteria of truth are the established standards in the social sciences. Policy studies focus on a problem in the governance of the economy. They are designed to gather facts that clarify the practical means of overcoming the problem.

Historical and theoretical studies are also relevant here to understand the governance of the economy. Historical studies offer an opportunity to look at the pattern of human events over time and assess the direction of development. In the light of history, theoretical studies offer the opportunity to formulate propositions guiding both scientific and policy research. Historical and theoretical studies generally provide a background and a vision to research in social economy.

This text expresses historical, scientific, policy, and theoretical orientations to the study of social economy. These perspectives must be balanced if we are to provide an adequate picture of the field. Furthermore, the tension between them keeps us aware of the awesome gap between what we know to be a fact about the social economy and what we believe needs to be done to solve its problems.

NOTES

1. Oskar Lange, *Political Economy* (New York: Macmillan, 1963), pp. 13-14.

2. Paul Samuelson, *Economics* (New York: McGraw-Hill, 1961), p. 836.

3. Robert L. Heilbroner, *Between Capitalism and Socialism, Essays in Political Economics* (New York: Vantage Books, 1970).

4. Lloyd Easton and Kurt H. Guddat (eds) *Writings of the Young Marx on Philosophy and Society,* (New York: Doubleday, 1967), pp. 184, 185, quoted in: Daniel Bell, *The Coming of Post-Industrial Society: A Venture in Social Forecasting* (New York: Basic Books, 1973), p. 83.

5. Karl Marx, *Critique of the Gotha Programme* (New York: International Publishers, 1938), p. 17.

6. Emile Durkheim, *Suicide: A Study in Sociology* (Glencoe, Ill.: The Free Press, 1951), p. 390.

7. Max Weber, in Guenther Roth and Claus Wittich (eds), *Economy and Society: An Outline of Interpretive Sociology* (New York: Bedminster Press, 1968), p. 224.

The Corporate Economy

KARL MARX. Life is not determined by consciousness, but consciousness by life. In the first method of approach the starting point is consciousness taken as the living individual; in the second it is the real living individuals themselves, as they are in actual life, and consciousness is considered solely as *their* consciousness.

EMILE DURKHEIM. We repeatedly insist in the course of this book upon the state of juridical and moral anomy in which economic life actually is found. Indeed, in the economic order, occupational ethics exist only in the most rudimentary state.

MAX WEBER. Action will be said to be "economically oriented" so far as, according to its subjective meaning, it is concerned with the satisfaction of "utilities." "Economic action" is a peaceful use of the actor's control over resources, which is primarily economically oriented, by deliberate planning, to economic ends. An "economic system" is an autocephalous system of economic action. An "economic organization" is a continuously organized system of economic action.

ONE

THE SOCIAL HISTORY OF THE BUSINESS CORPORATION

The British historian A. L. Rowse challenges us to begin thinking and writing about a new type of history.[1] He speaks of recording the "social history" of *society* rather than the "political history" of a *nation*. The history of a society, he says, is more than just the formal record of its politics and government. It is the formal and interpretive record of its economic life, industries, agriculture, educational organizations, religious groups, ethnic patterns, class structure, and family life as well as its politics and government life. History at its best is a total record of society.

But a social history is not easy to write. There are few guidelines and social scientists are not providing enough of them. Historians claim they do not have adequate criteria to write the interpretive record of "society." Decisions must be made about how much space should be given to different institutions of society and how to judge the relationships among them. Historians do not have sufficient knowledge about how a total society operates to give such a history its proper "balance." Without adequate guidelines, social history remains largely an ideal.

With the challenge of Rowse before us, we focus here on the social history of the business corporation. Corporate history is often omitted from standard high school and college textbooks. But corporate history is, of course, part of the large complicated history of which Rowse speaks. From a Marxian perspective, corporate history is more important than the history of formal politics. It is associated with the economic foundations of society and therefore represents the location of real power. It is thereby also the source of significant social change and development.

We limit ourselves in this chapter to a brief historical sketch and a sociological interpretation of it. We focus on major occupational groups working for the corporation—corporate executives, lawyers, laborers, and researchers. We want to see how they have changed in their relationship to the corporation over time.

My basic hypothesis is that the social consciousness of all these groups has increased significantly over this period. A greater degree of common identity has developed between groups, reducing the degree of hostile conflict; new systems of social accountability have emerged where none had existed before; and a greater awareness of social responsibility for corporate actions has appeared in the context of society.[2]

This does not mean that the business system today is any more stable than in past years or that basic problems in the structure of the economy have been solved. It simply means that some measure of social development is visible within the complex whole.

In this short history we are exploring the meaning of certain theoretical propositions of Marx and Durkheim. In the Marxian tradition, for example, we are interested in looking at the role of labor and the development of a social consciousness in the working class. Marx proposed that labor would break through the corporate self-interest ideology and eventually transform the economic foundations of society toward social and human ends. In the Durkheimian tradition, however, we examine the social consciousness of four occupational groups within the corporation. In this respect, we focus in effect on the formation and reformation of a "collective conscience" symbolically uniting occupational communities.

Our hypothesis on the development of a social consciousness within the corporate economy finally leads us to examine the larger historic changes in the structure of occupational groups and the purposes of corporations in the economy.[3] We seek a basis for determining guidelines for social research related to policies of development and governance of corporate life in the United States.

AN HISTORICAL PERSPECTIVE

The Early European Background

Henry Maine traces the origins of the corporation to the Roman Empire, where property rights within the extended family require the formation of a legal contract among its members. If the father died, for example, the rights and obligations of family members (including the slaves) had to be formally reconstituted in order to control the distribution of property and perpetuate the existence of the family unit. In place of the "status relation" that previously controlled family organization, a new legal "contract relation" was created.[4]

Property became corporate and communal, its ownership determined by family and kinship relations. The property contract was designed to perpetuate family possessions beyond the lifetime of any single member. Corporate property gained a quality of "immortality." The concepts of "perpetuity" and the "formal contract," introduced at that time, together constituted an essential beginning for the corporate idea in Western society.

The Roman family, however, was not an economic entity whose primary purpose was to accumulate property. The business corporation as we know it today is more closely associated with the late medieval period, when commercial enterprise began to appear independent of state administration. The sixteenth and seventeenth centuries saw the formation of trading companies, plantation enterprises, mines, insurance companies, and banks whose economic existence was considered "immortal." These new economic entities added other new dimensions to the corporate concept—shareholders, transferable shares, mergers, and a profit motive. The corporation whose primary purpose was to produce material wealth emerged slowly as the capitalist system evolved in Europe.

The business corporation was not an "ideal" of early capitalist thought. On the contrary, the "corporation" was repudiated by major political economists of the time. Adam Smith believed that corporations were ineffective and monopolistic and not to be a part of the ideal design of free enterprise. The market economy rested upon the free operation of small business units. Smith warned repeatedly against the "exclusive privileges" of large corporations. He insisted that the state eliminate corporate privileges so that free enterprise could develop.

The rise of industry, however, soon put an end to the Smithian concept of small business. The need for large capital resources encouraged the growth of large corporations; the introduction of new accounting practices and the reduction of government strictures on corporate charters made it possible. Governments needed the large corporation if they were to compete successfully in the modern world.

The close association of the corporation with governments in the rise of capitalism raised important questions for scholars about the nature of the corporation in the modern world. The question of whether the corporation originated outside the state in the form of a cooperative association or within it by sovereign authority became a matter of historical contention. The early history of corporations in both England and Continental Europe shows them working closely with the state, to their mutual benefit. The colonial companies envisaged by Queen Elizabeth were understood to be branches of the royal government. The British East India Company and the South Sea Company were operated for profit and political purposes at the same time.

It is clear that the state needed to bring the larger corporations under its control at certain junctures of history—for revenue, for national development and expansion, for protection against their growing power within society. Therefore, it becomes an academic debate whether the modern corporation originated when the state played a key role in shaping its course or whether it originated before the state became a significant factor.[5]

The political role of the corporation in English society was to have a significant effect on development of the corporation in America. Sixty years before the American Revolution, the South Sea Corporation had produced an enormous speculative inflation, and on its collapse the English Parliament passed legislation that severely limited the further development of corporations in England. The legislation remained effective in England for the remainder of the eighteenth century. The English monarchy gradually assumed authority for the creation of corporations. In 1766, Blackstone explicitly stated that in England the formation of corporations required the King's consent. In 1780—at the time of the American Revolution—England's Comyns stated concisely: "A corporation is a Franchise of the King."[6]

The Early American Background

It is clear that in early American society, the corporation was looked upon with great suspicion by the emerging government. At first, corporations could be formed for only very limited purposes in transportation, banking, or insurance, where large fixed capital was required. In the early decades of the nineteenth century, corporations were surrounded with all manner of restrictions. Statutory limits were placed upon their size, capital, scope of powers, and location, and upon the indebtedness of incorporators.

A company called Maine Flour Mills was incorporated in Massachusetts in 1818. Its total property value was limited to $50,000, of which no more than $30,000 could exist in land. The purchase of land was restricted to Kennebec County. The Company was required to have its corporate name printed on every barrel of flour it produced. If it failed to do so, it was subject to a $2.00 penalty for each unprinted barrel.

Justice John Marshall's description of the corporation in the Dartmouth College case (1819) set the legal guidelines for understanding the nature of the corporation.

A corporation is an artificial being, invisible, intangible, and existing only in the contemplation of the law. Being the mere creature of the law, it possesses only those properties which the character of its creation confers on it, either expressively, or as incidental to its very existence. These are such as are supposed best calculated to effect the object for which it was created. Among the most important are immortality, and, if the expression be allowed, individuality; properties by which a perpetual succession of many persons are considered the same, and may act as a single individual. They enable a corporation to manage its own affairs, and to hold property without the perplexing intricacies, the hazardous and endless necessity, of perpetual conveyances for the purpose of transmitting it from hand to hand. It is chiefly for the purpose of clothing bodies of men, in succession, with these qualities and these capacities, that corporations were invented and are in use. . . .[7]

It was a decision born in the English tradition of law and tempered by the American colonial experience with English "oppression." The colonial "charter" to incorporate the colonies was originally a contract between the King of England and the colonists as well as a contract among the colonists themselves. The Supreme Court said in effect that the Sovereign State of New Hampshire replaced the King but was bound under the U.S. Constitution not to interfere with the internal government of Dartmouth College. Only the members of that internal corporate government could change its character.

This legal principle was then extended to business corporations. The decision created legal grounds for maintaining separation between the affairs of state and the affairs of business. It clearly had great social consequences. At the same time the decision was limited in its expression of social consciousness. The legal definition rings with the historic individualism that was emerging in the early nineteenth century. The corporation was a "mere creature of law"—as though there were no social factors involved in its formation, no significant social organization, no social or environmental effects to be considered, no social relationship to employees or to the community. The most important features of the corporation were its "immortality" and "individuality." The corporation was conceived as an individual person; there was no legal recognition of how "corporateness" is a fundamentally different reality.

It was left to the law itself, then, to restrain the growing power of the corporation. These legal restraints were retained by the separate states through a major part of the nineteenth century. Justice Louis Brandeis describes the limits on assets toward the end of the century.

Until 1881, the maximum for business corporation in New York was $2,000,000; and until 1890, $5,000,000. In Massachusetts the limit was at first $200,000 for some businesses and as little as $5,000 for others. Until 1871 the maximum for mechanical and manufacturing corporations was $500,000; and until 1899, $1,000,000. The limit of $100,000 was retained for some businesses until 1903.[8]

These limitations, however, did not last much past the end of the century. The power of the growing number of corporations to influence political decisions and beliefs is clearly evident in the history of American corporate law.

Businessmen were willing to pressure and to pay congressmen to write "liberal laws." Businessmen wanted the freedom to exploit resources and to operate independently of state restrictions. They took the view that the issuance of "special charters" that placed limits on business activities was bad for the economy. A general corporation law, they urged, should be created for corporations to function freely in every state.

States competed for the privilege of hosting the large corporation. Their weapon against each other was the provision of a corporate charter with the least restrictions on business activity. By 1875, permission to incorporate for "any lawful purpose" was common. The individual states were prey to corporate power as interstate competition grew.

In 1875 New Jersey provided a general corporation act that gave wider powers to incorporators than ever before. Corporations migrated in droves to New Jersey, and other states suffered from the loss of revenue. In 1890 New York revised its statutes to permit intercorporate stockholding, but that was not enough to stop the New Jersey migration. In 1892 the Governor of New York was forced to approve a special charter for General Electric to keep it from leaving the state. That special charter was modeled after the New Jersey Act. By 1901 New York had to revise its law to make it competitive with New Jersey, and by 1903 Massachusetts had done the same.[9]

The public "conscience" was roused by corporate "trusts," but it was not strong enough to restrain the power of the new corporations through state law. The New Jersey law was revised with new constraints under the governorship of Woodrow Wilson. Delaware, however, was the next state to win the competition for the most "liberal" charter law, and today it remains the most popular state for the legal residence of American corporations. No public conscience expressed through individual states could compete with the power of the corporation whose operations were nationwide.

Delaware's popularity rests in its competitive advantage over other states in its special charter rulings. For example, there are no limitations on the diversity of capital structure in a corporation—allowing executives more freedom to build their conglomerate organization. Directors do not need to be shareholders or residents of the state. Dividends may be paid more freely from current earnings or surplus. Officers and directors can be indemnified against expenses in defense of lawsuits to which they were parties; the corporation will pay all legal costs of corporate officers.

By the turn of the twentieth century, no state charters placed major restrictions on corporate activity. Thereafter corporations were relatively free to develop their own course. No limits were set on their size. They were no longer required to have a singular purpose. Any number of corporations could gather under one corporate charter. The power to hold stock in other corporations, not previously conferred or implied in the law, became permissible across the land. The time limits of corporate franchises, previously limited to 20 or 30 years, were eliminated. The enforcement power in the legal doctrine known as *ultra vires*—which held the corporation legally responsible for acts committed in violation of its charter limitations—had effectively disappeared.

At this point it seems clear from a Marxian perspective how the corporation has achieved the power to influence the state on behalf of its own economic interests. We are no longer in the handicraft and petty bourgeois period of American history. Before the end of the nineteenth century we entered a period of corporate capitalism. The state has released its original power to control economic development through its legal restraints on the charter of the corporation. The federal government has begun to introduce a measure of antitrust legislation, but it has conceded to the corporation the power to conduct operations at the national level in its own economic self-interest. The development of a dominant social interest in the well-being of society, according to Marx, now rests with the laboring class.

This issue lies in the background of our remaining historical account of the later stages of corporate capitalism in American society.

THE DEVELOPMENT OF A SOCIAL CONSCIOUSNESS: OCCUPATIONAL GROUPS

Marx anticipated a significant and rapid increase in social consciousness among laborers in the nineteenth century. By social consciousness he meant an identity with human interdependence within the political economy. He meant also an awareness of the exploitative nature of the capitalist system and an interest in overcoming it. This awareness and interest in overcoming economic exploitation has been very evident among laborers, but it has also been a complicated variable in American history. The social consciousness of laborers has changed its intensity and character over time. It has not increased steadily and expanded rapidly in the direction that Marx anticipated.

The greater complication here, however, is that an increase in social consciousness is evident among all other major occupational groups, including corporate lawyers, executives, and researchers. Furthermore, having become conscious of the exclusive and exploitative economic interests of the corporation, these groups have shown an interest in overcoming them. They have also shown an increased awareness of the needs of others affected by the corporation in the larger society. Let us look in more detail at dimensions of this growth in social consciousness among each of these occupational groups.

The Lawyer: The Legal Dimension

The fact that "economic interests" influenced the states to provide liberal corporate characters is generally recognized in the legal profession. Dean R. S.

Stevens, for example, candidly explains that "states cannot afford to retain conservative corporation laws lest they lose the incorporation of those businesses which are to be conducted entirely within their borders."[10] But what follows historically is that lawyers have shown an interest in challenging the idea that profits ought to be the primary motive in determining the corporation's course of conduct. Many lawyers have sought to make social motives a legitimate part of corporate enterprise. This effort has a long tradition in the legal profession.

The legal concept of the corporation as a purely economic entity whose goal is to make profits had precedence in English law. In 1883 an English court decision (*Hutton* v *West Cork Railway Corporation*) held that the business corporation existed only as a profit-making enterprise. In other words, it could distribute profits only to its stockholder-owners. The English case was legal ammunition for stockholders in the United States, who raised a clamor over the distribution of profits in the public interest. They considered it "socialization" and opposed to their legitimate self-interests as "owners."

New Jersey began socializing corporate law in the 1930s and continued to do so during the succeeding decades. By 1950 the New Jersey legislature had passed a law stating that it was "public policy" for corporations to be empowered to contribute moneys to improve the social and economic conditions of society. In other words, the corporation could take account of the social needs of others in society and so orient its course and policy in addition to the purely economic interests of its owners.

In the following year in the same state, the case for legislation permitting corporate executives to make social policy was strengthened in a new legal decision. It allowed A. P. Smith Manufacturing Company to make a grant of $1500 to Princeton University.[11] Corporate directors and management wanted to make the gift available to Princeton regardless of stockholder interest in dividend returns. Stockholders resisted the management policy in court. They based their opposition in this test case on the fact that A. P. Smith had been incorporated in 1896 for the specific purpose of engaging "in industry for purposes of profit." They argued that the diversion of any company income from general funds for the maintenance of private education was a misappropriation of money. The gift was an *ultra vires* act—that is, it violated the property and contract rights of the stockholders.

Management lawyers argued, however, that the New Jersey statutes, originally passed in the 1930s, permitted corporations to cooperate with other corporations in the creation and maintenance of community funds or philanthropic activities. Corporation lawyers argued that the directors were therefore permitted to expend these funds in ways they deemed would contribute to both the "public interest" and the "corporate interest."

Judge J. C. Stein decided in favor of the corporation's gift to Princeton on the grounds that the two institutions were highly interdependent and complementary. He said that college-trained men and women were a reservoir from which industry could draw in its own corporate interests. Furthermore, the pattern of corporate gift-giving was an alternative to state support of the university:

The only hope for the survival of the privately supported American college and universities lies in the willingness of corporate wealth to furnish in moderation some support to institutions which are so essential to public welfare, and therefore, of necessity, to corporate welfare.[12]

The trend toward social consciousness in the legal profession did not always originate from ideals. In many cases it was encouraged by outside pressures. A new level of social consciousness among lawyers, for example, was developed from practical motives during the Great Depression. Federal disclosure statutes such as the Securities Act of 1933 and the Securities Exchange Act of 1934 were part of a growing national concern about the effects of corporate behavior. The concern led toward a broader public accountability of corporate activities. These acts were designed especially to promote a greater social responsibility in decision-making by requiring that the performance record of corporate management be made known to investors who proposed to buy or sell company shares. They were intended to protect investors from being deceived about the value of securities issued and traded in public markets. Businesses were required to file and distribute financial information and other corporate data to keep stock market operations functioning in the public interest.

Most observers acknowledge that the laws have succeeded in inhibiting gross forms of misconduct. They have avoided the grosser deceptions on the stock market. But the movement toward social consciousness did not end there. The Securities Exchange Act was later to become the focus of legal attack on grounds that it protected private interests that interfered with the public interest.

The principal focus of social concern became Rule 14a-8 of the 1934 Securities Exchange Act, which allowed management to disregard shareholder proposals to take "corrective actions" at the annual meetings of corporations. The Act had specified the conditions under which *management could refuse to introduce proposals* from their stockholders. Management, for example, was given the right to refuse proposals that were (1) not proper subject for action by security holders under state law. (2) submitted primarily for the purpose of promoting general social, economic, or political causes not related to the company's business or within its control, and (3) related to the company's ordinary business operations. Rule 14a-8 clearly protected management from the shareholders so that the companies could continue to function in their own economic self-interest. Recently, this rule has been the focus of many legal cases involving stockholders who contend that their companies are not functioning in the public interest.[13]

The increase in social consciousness is associated with an increase in demand for "accountability." Many court cases requiring corporate accountability have involved the 14th Amendment of the U. S. Constitution. This amendment bars all state action that arbitrarily or unfairly favors one person over another or deprives anyone of liberty or property "without due process of law." Chief Justice Fred M. Vinson observed in 1948 that the amendment applies only to states and not to the "merely private conduct" of corporations. Nevertheless, judges have been steadily building up a body of law that broadens the scope of the 14th Amendment to apply to business. They are subjecting companies to the same "due process" imposed on states. In other words, Supreme Court decisions have been leading toward the principle that private enterprise must conform to constitutional standards. The idea of social justice and corporate democracy has been introduced into the business system.[14]

The recent legal requirement that corporations disclose political gifts is part of the same movement toward social consciousness and accountability. Related developments include recent legal proposals to require that large banks reveal how they allocate credit, that the Federal Reserve System's key Open Market Committee disclose its monthly decisions on monetary policy as soon as they are made, and that a labor union representative serve on the Federal Reserve Board. Such proposals are all indications of a steady broadening of social consciousness and accountability to new sectors of the economy. The most recent significant trend among lawyers is to create "public interest law."[15]

Legal scholars have proposed wide-ranging theories regarding the proper role of the corporation in the context of society. These theories vary on a continuum based on the amount of legal control deemed correct for the state to exercise over the corporation and the degree to which the corporation is expected to operate in the public interest. They can be summarized as follows:

(1) The "enabling act" concept, which suggests that corporate privileges should be made freely available with a minimum of restrictions. It represents the prevailing practice in the law today. (2) The "interposition" concept based upon the importance of legislative safeguards. The law should be interposed at critical junctures in corporate operations where past experience has shown that difficulties arise. (3) The "prescription" concept, which supports legislation on the kind of corporate contracts that will protect investors and creditors. The purpose of such laws is to create public confidence in the corporate system and make it more effective in society. (4) The "public interest" concept, which holds that the corporation should be limited to operating primarily in the interest of the larger society while taking fair account of the interests of investors, creditors, customers, and employees. It is argued that corporate executives following this concept would not be under obligation to maximize profit but would operate their corporation in the general interest of society.[16]

The first theory tends to represent the mainstream of thought and practice in corporate law today, while the last is finding growing support in the legal profession. These theories, in effect, express part of the "collective conscience" of the legal profession with respect to the corporation. The recent trends in the law suggest that legal theory has been moving steadily from the first to the last category of "public interest" in the last decade.

The vanguard of this public-interest theory has been a group of writers who might be called the legal institutionalist school: Adolf Berle, Gardiner Means, Kingman Brewster, Scott Buchanan, and recently Ralph Nader. We want to return to their work after we point to more traces of the developing consciousness of the corporation in society.

The Executive: The Business Dimension

The growth in social awareness among business executives has a long and complicated history, but a few events can illustrate its development.

Early in the history of General Electric, for example, Gerald Swope was conscious of the problem of "social accountability." In 1926 he outlined a private employment compensation plan for General Electric employees. He insisted that industry had an obligation to "maintain stability" in society. In 1931 he called for a more active role on the part of trade associations to create a system of pensions and employment insurance. The system would be paid by workers and companies, and a federal supervisory body would function to oversee it in the public interest. In 1934 he persuaded the Assistant Comptroller of G. E. to crusade in various states for the adoption of unemployment compensation laws. He called for "a new constitution for industry designed to stabilize production and consumption, to minimize unemployment, and to solve adequately the problem of security for the workers and their families in illness, disability, involuntary idleness, old age and death." Subsequently his plan received the full support of the United States Chamber of Commerce.

In the 1930s, business fell into its greatest economic depression. The social consciousness of many business executives like Gerald Swope expanded radically in the crisis. They hoped to develop a still broader base for fixing the social responsibility of business in society. The National Recovery Administration (NRA) was introduced to give trade associations a broad social role in determining codes of conduct. The new expanded role for business, however, was short-lived. The Supreme Court found the NRA unconstitutional.

Following this court decision (*Schechter Poultry Corp.* v *U. S.,* 1935), the new socially defined role of trade associations as a protector of the public interest narrowed again to the pursuit of their own private interests. The structure of the business corporation during this period remained relatively unchanged.

A later president of General Electric, C. E. Wilson, defended the business corporation based upon profit:

There is nothing antisocial in profit. I think the truth of the matter is that—given access to all as buyers and sellers—the profit earned by the wise businessman is a measure of the service he has rendered to his market, in terms of a value placed on those services by the buyers, individually and collectively.[17]

While the profit-oriented structure of the corporation did not change, the attitudes and outlook of a larger number of business executives did. Encouraged by a 1935 amendment to the Internal Revenue Code that provided deductions for charitable contributions, and later court decisions that were favorable toward this avenue to social accountability, many executives began to expand the purposes of the corporation.

Company foundations were organized with sizeable endowments for the purpose of contributing to enterprises with social, spiritual, educational, scientific, and community-oriented goals. These foundations increased from 20 in 1939 to over 1500 in 1962. Some corporations organized "contribution committees" with full-time employees devoted to gift activities. In 1965 a survey of 139 companies showed that 15 to 20 percent of them employed a formula determining how much they should give to social and charitable enterprises.

The significance of this shift in monetary outflow to nonprofit purposes lies in the fact that it changes the definition of the corporation in the mind of the business executive. Leading executives today recognize this difference in their policy statements.

The Committee for Economic Development (CED), for example, is composed of leading business people in the nation. Its Research and Policy Committee published a statement in June, 1971 dealing with the social responsibilities of business enterprises in contemporary American society. Its purpose was to "address ourselves predominantly to the *social* rather than the *economic* aspects of business" and "to consider the structure of corporations as it affects social responsiveness and accountability."

The philosophy expressed in the statement indicates a new breadth to social consciousness among business executives. Note some of the following statements:

1. Business functions by public consent, and its basic purpose is to serve constructively the needs of society—to the satisfaction of society.
2. The discontinuity between what we have accomplished as producers and consumers and what we want in the way of a good society has engendered strong social pressures to close the gap—to improve the way the overall American system is working so that a better quality of life can be achieved for the entire citizenry within a well-functioning community.
3. The American business corporation, like the society in which it has its being, is a dynamic and changing institution.
4. Current profitability, once regarded as the dominant if not exclusive objec-

tive, is now often seen more as a vital means and powerful motivative force for achieving broader ends, rather than as an end in itself.

5. Increasing attention is also being given to broadening the composition and enhancing the effectiveness of boards of directors. . . . There is obviously under way a quest for better ways of integrating the various interests of major constituencies into the governance structure and process and of relating the entire enterprise to society.

6. In a broad sense, therefore, these developments are designed to make the corporation more responsive to its constituencies and to the larger society. . . . Thus, the modern manager sees the corporation as a social as well as an economic organization, functioning in the whole of society rather than just in the marketplace.

7. In the laissez-faire system, it was the *unseen hand* that was counted on to lead the pursuit of selfish private interests into realization of the public good. In the alternative system suggested here, it is the *visible hand* that is expected to achieve the same result.[18]

The *visible hand* is measured in terms of social performance. Social criteria for judging performance were offered by the Committee. These criteria include the following:

Education. Direct financial aid to schools, including scholarships . . . support for increases in school budgets . . . donation of equipment . . . aid in counseling . . .

Employment. Active recruitment of the disadvantaged . . . provision of daycare centers . . . retraining of workers . . .

Civil Rights. Encouraging adoption of open-housing ordinances, building plants in ghettos, financing minority enterprise . . .

Urban Renewal. Building low-income housing, improving transportation systems . . .

Pollution Abatement. Cooperating with municipalities in joint treatment facilities, recycling and reusing disposable materials . . .

Culture and the Arts. Direct financial support to art institutions, sponsoring artistic talent . . .

Medical Care. Helping plan community health activities, designing low-cost medical-care facilities . . .[19]

The foregoing list is an abridgement of the Committee's list, but it is a significant part of the report. It is useful in developing a model of social measurement (along with the economic measurement) of corporate performance.

Business conferences on "social responsibility" have become more numerous in the last decade. In the 1960s Joseph C. Wilson, Xerox Corporation president, described the corporation as a social entity and claimed that "economic gain" was no longer the sole motivating force of the business executive. In 1970 at a White House Conference on the Industrial World ahead, other corporate executives took cognizance of the need for social responsibility. Arjay Miller, Dean of the Graduate School of Business at Stanford University and former president of Ford Motor Company, urged American business managers to weave "social" (as well as profit) goals into the fabric of their companies. Managers should be required to meet social objectives, he said, the way they now meet profit goals. Typical of such social objectives included quotas for hiring members of minority groups and for the purchase of goods and services from minority-owned firms.[20]

The growing power of labor unions in the United States has altered the attitude of the business executive toward the system of labor-management itself. Some businesspersons claim that the system is no longer working in the interest of society and that a new system must be created. James P. McFarland, Chairman of the Board of General Mills, Inc., had this to say:

The corporation of 1990 will in all probability have an employer–employee relationship with its personnel that is dramatically different than that of today. The changes may occur in ways which are not only different but to some extent contradictory.[21]

Carl A. Gerstacker, Chairman of the Board, The Dow Chemical Company, spoke extensively on a number of key issues including the labor-management system. He introduced the concept of "corporate democracy" and said:

The adversary system of labor vs. management has about run its course. As an adversary system it is often destructive rather than constructive, counterproductive rather than productive, tyrannical rather than democratic. . . . Most of the time its failures . . . cause far more injury to third parties (the consumer, the supplier) than they ever do to the participants. . . . We must move from an adversary system to some new system devised to accommodate to each other's needs without a constant power struggle. . . . I would suggest that because of the scope, complexity, and potential benefit to be accrued that a special governmental commission might fruitfully explore the vast possibilities of this subject. And I would suggest that far-sighted unionists themselves ought to take the lead in fomenting the new and bloodless revolution that we need, and that I firmly believe will take place.[22]

Gerstacker's recommendation for a change in the "adversary system" of labor and management indicates an awareness that may yield new forms of "accountability." This matter is treated later in more detail.[23]

The Worker: The Labor Dimension

In the early 1830s, Workingmen's Parties were organized in U.S. cities and states. Labor leaders tried to persuade workers to join city councils and state congresses and through politics to influence legislation favorable to them. Their efforts were largely futile. It was not until the 1870s that national unions would rise with the purpose of social reform. Our discussion of that growth in consciousness and purpose can only be interpretive and illustrative.[24]

The Knights of Labor was one of the early unions whose main goal was the social reform of labor practices. Initially a secret organization, it surfaced in 1878 as an early expression of industrial unionism. The Knights stood for "radical measures" of social change: the abolishment of child labor, a graduated income tax, an eight-hour day, government supervision of railways and the telegraph system. Failing to achieve these ends in their day, they pressed for an even more fundamental change. They proposed the creation of a commonwealth of producer cooperatives.

Between 1885 and 1886 the Knights' membership rose from 100,000 to over 700,000. Union leaders strove to democratize their national organization into local assemblies and district assemblies, culminating finally in a general assembly of workers. These were early efforts to develop a base for "corporate democracy."

But its leadership could not be sustained in the face of corporate resistance. By 1890 it had lost its power, and large-scale industrial unionism was not destined to appear again for a half century.

The decline of the Knights of Labor led to the rise of the American Federation of Labor, which was based upon craft unionism. Under the leadership of Samuel Gompers, the AFL supported social reforms, but its primary goal was economic: higher wages and shorter hours. It became, in effect, a "countercorporation" standing in opposition to business in a struggle for limited power.

The AFL grew slowly. It fought heavy battles, like the Homestead Strike, and lost. The power of corporate management to muster private police forces and call the government to its defense was disillusioning for the rank and file. It seemed that the response of the "working man" had to go deeper. The corporate struggle had to be translated into a broad-scale social struggle.

Some of the rank and file turned against the philosophy of capitalism and embraced socialism, forming the Socialist Labor Party in 1876. The party soon became deeply divided over the question of whether to use force to achieve its ends. A faction supporting forceful measures became engaged in a series of struggles that ended in the Haymarket Riot. The violence of that event shook the country but did not stop the movement toward an expanding social consciousness of the laborer.

In 1895, Daniel de Leon, having failed to organize a socialist faction within the AFL, set up a rival organization called the Social Trade and Labor Alliance. In 1901 one division of the Alliance joined with Eugene Debs to create the Socialist Party. The efforts to find an ideological position for labor continued. A third socialist organization, the Industrial Workers of the World, arose in 1905.

The socialist movement gained momentum. Eugene Debs ran for President of the United States and won almost a million votes.

Then came World War I. Socialist leaders opposed the U. S. position in the war with Germany, calling it a conflict between imperial powers. Leaders of the IWW and Debs' socialists went to prison for their beliefs. The Great War united the country against an external threat and slowed socialist efforts among labor leaders to change the corporate system. Gompers and the AFL, however, had supported the war. This part of the labor movement then continued to gain in collective power as a combatant of management.[25]

Labor found a new stimulus under the New Deal. The National Recovery Act affirmed the right of workers to organize and bargain collectively. Under the National Labor Relations Act, affirmed by the Supreme Court in 1937, the employer could no longer refuse to meet with representatives of employees. With this government support, the consciousness of laborers broadened and solidified. Their right to exist as a collective group within the corporation was sanctioned. Management had to be accountable to them, and they in turn had to be accountable to management through the labor contract. Their numbers increased fourfold by World War II.

The gains for labor were significant in the degree to which unions achieved a relatively powerful position in the corporate economy. At the same time, the broad social vision of early labor leaders of creating a commonwealth of producer cooperatives and a socialist society had narrowed to the special interests of the trade union itself. Labor consciousness had broadened and then focused on "their own kind" in the same sense that the consciousness of business executives had broadened and then focused in the organization of trade associations. The efforts of labor leaders now centered on obtaining job security, wages, and benefits for their union members.

In their struggle with management, labor unions began to model themselves after the business corporation. They retained democratic beliefs but at the same time began to assume a business orientation. Many union leaders adopted the model of a "command system" under which executives operate within the corporation. Unions in general assumed a practical orientation in the United States.

The Scientist: The Research Dimension

It has been the purpose of corporate research to gather valid, reliable data about the behavior of the corporation. This aim, however, has not left researchers themselves unaffected by their work. In the space of about seventy years of study, the effect of corporate research has been to make researchers more aware of the complex web of interdependence in the corporate system.

Corporate research began with a focus on the physiological effects of labor. It gradually broadened its area of interest over the years to a psychology, then to a social psychology, and finally to a sociology of work. Put another way, corporate research began with a scientific interest in how the individual functions in an economic context of work. Over the years it assumed a wider scope of social consciousness. The individual became observed as an interdependent part of work teams, factory systems, communities, national and multinational corporations.[26]

The earliest scientific studies were directed by corporate management and designed for largely economic and profit motives. Investigators studied problems of worker fatigue, accidents, and diseases, but their primary purpose was to learn how to increase individual productivity. L. J. Henderson's Fatigue Laboratory at Harvard was an early example of this research orientation. A conscious designing of the structure of work for profit motives began under the leadership of Frederick Taylor. Taylor convinced Bethlehem Steel that he could increase the amount of tonnage that each worker could handle per day by analyzing work movements such as the simple act of shoveling coal. In his studies, he suceeded in increasing productivity, and "time and motion studies" were born.

Industrial psychology, which began to develop in the 1920s, broadened the scope of scientific inquiry from matters of physiological fatigue to psychologically induced fatigue. Researchers sought to understand human frustration, worker morale, and human motivation. Their studies began to break through the purely economic image of the worker as an isolated individual working only in his or her own self-interest. However, the social psychology of industry during the next three decades remained primarily within the economic orientation of the corporation.

The significant change in focus from the individual to the social group began with the Elton Mayo studies in the 1930s. Mayo and his associates studied the life of the worker in a more complicated social context. Mayo had begun his research in a Philadelphia spinning mill in the 1920s. There he had experimentally introduced different physical stimuli into the environment of the worker for the purpose of observing their effects on individual productivity. However, at a second location, the Hawthorne Electric Plant, he experimented with "social variables," which eventually led to a critique of the "economic man" theory supporting the corporate system. It was in these now famous Hawthorne experiments that the researchers found that workers were not governed by physical conditions or economic motives alone.

The workers at the Hawthorne plant put together relay circuits while undergoing experimental changes in their environment. Their pay was lowered and raised; their lighting on the job was reduced and increased; their rest periods were reduced and increased in number. The results were surprising. In each case, when Mayo added or subtracted desirable conditions, the productivity of the workers increased! It did not make sense that the workers should produce better under unpleasant conditions, especially under a reduced income. The results were beyond the classic meaning of work.

It was finally realized that the workers were gaining a sense of recognition and purpose in their work under the conditions of a social experiment. They were no longer simply cogs in the industrial machine. They were working for social purposes beyond the material incentives or physical conditions of work. In effect, they were being recognized as part of a cooperative effort to discover what it means to work as a human being.

Mayo questioned the prevailing corporate myth of individualism and economic incentive. He described the myth as the "rabble hypothesis" and summed it up as follows:

1. Natural society consists of a horde of unorganized individuals.
2. Every individual acts in a manner calculated to secure his self-preservation or self-interest.
3. Every individual thinks logically, to the best of his ability, in the service of this aim.[27]

The experiments at the Hawthorne Plant did not substantiate these beliefs in economic individualism. Mayo was developing a social consciousness of the interdependent variables of work in the corporation.

Mayo's research was a major turning point in corporate studies. Researchers then moved to expand their social framework for interpreting corporate behavior. Our references to that expansion of consciousness can be only illustrative and synoptic.

In the 1940s researchers began to observe primary groups of workers in departments of factories and plants. They broadened the framework to study managerial behavior (in contrast to worker behavior) in the setting of a single corporation. Then they added the local community within which corporate behavior was to be understood. In the 1950s the union came under considerable study both as a local and a national organization. The factory system was studied. Absentee ownership came into the social spectrum of study as the local factory finally proved inadequate as a system-framework for explaining the course of social behavior within itself. In a study of a shoe factory in Newburyport, Massachusetts, for example, W. Lloyd Warner found that a local strike could not be explained solely within the context of either the factory or the local community. Decisions affecting Newburyport were being made from New York offices, and the strike could be explained only in terms of an intercity corporate network of control.

Social scientists became aware of the risks of managerial bias, and the conduct of research under the auspices of either side became a methodological problem. Corporate researchers at midcentury began to question the ethics of studying the corporation from only the standpoint of management. Some began to see themselves as a tool of management rather than as social scientists seeking the total picture. They began therefore to approach both labor and management together before making studies and also to share their findings with both groups rather than management alone. A sense of social accountability to both labor and management was developing among researchers.[28]

A shift in the identification of the corporate researcher toward the interests of labor, however, was not total. It was not an exclusive or primary identification with a larger social purpose as might be found in Marxist studies. It was rather a shift toward a new consciousness of the workers as human beings in the context of the private aims of the corporation. The studies of Douglas Mc-Gregor, Frederick Herzberg, and Rensis Likert especially show a broader consciousness of the worker while remaining largely within the traditional framework of the business corporation.

Douglas McGregor, for example, began in the 1950s to attack managerial assumptions about workers' motivation and character. He described these assumptions as "Theory X." According to Theory X, "The average human being has an inherent dislike of work and will avoid it if he can." McGregor said most managers assume that "people must be coerced, controlled, directed, threatened with punishment" to work. Managers assumed that "the average human being prefers to be directed, wishes to avoid responsibility, has relatively little ambition, wants security above all." McGregor disclaimed such assumptions. He substituted Theory Y, which reversed the assumptions of Theory X. Theory Y assumed that workers wanted to exercise self-direction and seek responsibility in work. Theory Y assumed workers had a high degree of imagination and creativity that simply needed to be released under the right conditions.[29]

McGregor himself, of course, believed in Theory Y. He and other researchers were humanizing research and at the same time socializing the work process.[30]

In the next decade, researchers continued to expand their framework of study. (See Figure 1.) The macro system of the economy began to be examined more seriously from a sociological viewpoint. Radical studies emerged on issues of corporate imperialism and corporate concentration of power.[31] These studies continued into the 1970s, at which time a new international focus developed. New questions were raised about corporate structure and the behavior of the multinational corporation operating on a global level. The issues of corporate imperialism in Marxist studies were translated into issues of social accountability and responsibility on the international scene. Specific questions on "ethical conduct," "disclosure of information," "world charters" were raised and discussed in the management and business schools of major United States universities.[32]

A gradual development of social consciousness in research theory and a growing sense of social accountability among corporate researchers is evident as a trend in this historical period. Corporate research began at the turn of the century with a focus on "physiological man." It expanded to "economic man" and developed further to "social man" without excluding earlier perspectives.[33] It expanded still further in studies of increasing social complexity—first assembly

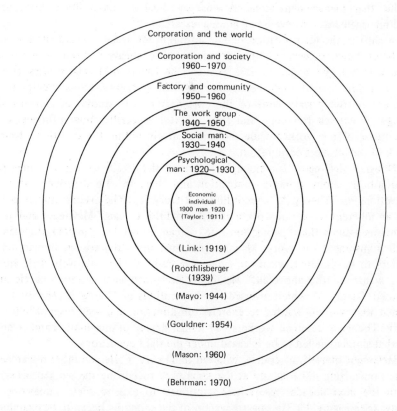

Figure 1. Expanding social consciousness in corporate studies. Sources: Frederick Taylor, *The Principles of Scientific Management* (New York: Harpers, 1911); Henry Link, *Employment Psychology* (New York: Macmillan, 1919); F. J. Roethlisberger and W. J. Dickson, *Management and the Worker* (Cambridge: Harvard Univ. Press, 1939); Elton Mayo and George F. F. Lombard, *Teamwork in the Aircraft Industry of Southern California* (Harvard Business Research Studies, No. 32, 1944); Alvin Gouldner, *Patterns of Industrial Bureaucracy* (Glencoe, Ill.: Free Press, 1934); Edward S. Mason (ed), *The Corporation in Modern Society* (Cambridge: Harvard Univ. Press, 1960); Jack N. Behrman, *National Tensions Over the Multinational Enterprise* (Englewood Cliffs, N. J.: Prentice-Hall, 1970).

lines, then factory systems, then the factory in society, and finally multinational corporations.

Lawyers, executives, laborers, researchers—all have broadened their identities as occupational communities and deepened their sensitivity to people working in the larger complex of the corporate system. But they are not the only occupational groups that can be identified, and they do not tell the whole story of cor-

porate development. New occupational groups have risen to places of significance, and the corporation itself has changed something of its character as an
overall entity in American society. These historical facts are essential for us to
grasp before we proceed toward more detailed studies of the corporation in its
complex settings.

CHANGES IN OCCUPATIONAL GROUPS

The major occupational groups called *labor* and *management* are still important
today, but they do not define the whole matrix of employees in the corporate
economy. A vast middle layer of white collar employees, for example, do not
fit into these two categories. White collar workers constitute the fastest growing
group of corporate employees in society, and their number should by all counts
continue to increase in the future. This white collar group includes many professional people who work for business corporations.

Here we find the professional motives of accountants, physicians, chemists,
biologists, physicists, engineers, nurses, lawyers, artists, and architects, conflicting at many points with the profit motive of the corporation. The conflict results in various forms of accommodation and compromise. But it also results in
changes that alter the structure and the conduct of the business corporation.
The corporate accountant, for example, may insist on institutionalizing procedures in bookkeeping that run contrary to the economic interests of management.
The corporate medical staff may insist on the budgeting of funds to maintain the
health and safety of the employees in spite of an attempt to restrict such expenditures in the interest of profit. The engineer may insist on using quality materials in products that make them last longer in spite of a managerial interest in
obsolescence and higher long-run market sales. The professions have many noneconomic purposes, which include the advancement of truth, art, science, health,
safety, and social well-being. The increase in the number of professional people,
therefore, has a bearing on the historic drift toward a social consciousness as
opposed to a purely economic orientation of the business corporation.

CHANGES IN THE CHARACTER OF THE
CORPORATE SYSTEM IN SOCIETY

Add to this shift in the occupational character of the labor force a shift in the
nature of corporations themselves, and we see an epoch-making change occurring
within the corporate economy today. The new nonindustrial corporations in recreation, real estate, transportation, retail services, insurance, and tourist accommodations altogether change the primary relationship of the corporate enterprise

with its employees toward a relationship with consumers and customers. Many corporations have set up customer service departments and consumer councils. This direct relationship with the customer, then, has a socializing effect on the corporation that is different from the historic case of labor and the industrial corporation. It brings into focus the needs of the consumer.

The shift from corporate manufacturing and the industrial economy toward the "service economy" is related to the shift in the character of the labor force. Daniel Bell points out that shortly after the turn of the century, only three in every ten workers in the nation were employed in the service sector and seven out of ten were in the production of goods. By 1968 the proportions had shifted to *six out of every ten in the service sector,* with no sign of the trend stopping. The service economy includes corporate trade, utilities, professional services, and domestic services, as well as government services. This rising service sector has now superseded the goods-producing sector (construction, mining, manufacturing, agriculture, forestry, and fishing) in its proportion of the total labor force.[34]

Bell notes that in the service sector the greatest growth has occurred in the government, where one out of every six workers is employed. The next most rapid growth is in general services, which include private educational institutions. Bell argues in effect that industrial corporations no longer characterize the main body of corporate work. The overall purposes of the American corporation are shifting from primarily economic interests toward a variety of other interests.

Part of this shift has been due to the growth of the nonprofit corporation. In 1929 the nonprofit sector accounted for 12.5 percent of all goods and services purchased. By 1963 it stood above 27 percent and was rising.[35] This growth is significant because many nonprofit corporations are closely involved in the direction of the purely business sector. This includes business and trade associations, trade unions, and cooperatives with social aims.

The rise of trade unions helped change the character of the economic motive by introducing a social factor into the internal decision-making of the corporation. Business can no longer consider labor simply a marketable item in the pursuit of profit. Similar changes in the character of the economic motive can be seen with the rise of the trade association and the cooperative. We shall deal with them in more detail later. In addition, we find nonprofit corporations operating in the fields of health, education, and research in ways that significantly affect the social direction of the profit-centered business. In sum, the rise of nonprofit corporations has helped to shape the direction, the identity, and the style of life of the business corporation.

We can now begin to see the business corporation in an environment of nonprofit corporations, including the corporate church, university, hospital, and thousands of voluntary associations such as the YMCA, Kiwanis Club, and Rotary International. These varied forms of nonprofit corporations criss-cross in their membership and their activities with the business corporation in ways that significantly affect its direction. The business corporation is only one part of a larger corporate economy.

The corporate economy today has a manifest dimension and a latent dimension. The manifest dimension is the business enterprise whose primary interest is in profits. The latent dimension is the corporate enterprise whose primary interest may be fraternal, religious, recreational, educational, health, etc. The intricate relationships between the corporate life of the manifest and latent economies has yet to be studied. But this relationship has been a basic part of the development of a social consciousness in corporate business.

The trade union is a nonprofit corporation and part of the latent economy. Its policies bear directly upon the development of the business corporation. In spite of the burgeoning white collar class that has not been unionized, organized labor today is numerically the most powerful mass organization in the United States. It holds a central place in the social development of the economic order.

The occupational shift toward white collar employees and a service economy, however, tells us that unions may find their strength largely within the goods-producing sector and the industrial corporation. The service sector involves unions as only one type of nonprofit corporation. Many other types of nonprofit corporations such as the American Bar Association, the American Hospital Association, the American Education Association, and the Cooperative League of the USA, also have a "mass organization." They each have a local organization linked vertically to their national organization. They each represent important parts of the nonprofit corporate economy.

A CRITICAL REVIEW OF SOCIAL HISTORY

A social history of the business corporation includes much more than I have covered in this brief discourse. The special emphasis I have given to the "social consciousness" of the lawyer, executive, laborer, and scientist, narrows the selection of facts even while it covers a broad scope of corporate history. The focus is intended here to offer a key hypothesis about historical development and thus to open a line of historical and scientific inquiry.

A rounded social interpretation of corporate history includes a description of the changes in the size of corporations and the social ecology of different corporate sectors, including banking, manufacturing, retailing, and wholesaling. It includes a general review of changes in corporate administrative systems. It involves additional social concepts. In addition to "social consciousness," for example, we would need a concept of social dominance and exploitation. Guided by these concepts we would then look systematically at the record of corporate conflict, monopoly, deception, greed, and failure. One historical section might focus only on the violent conflicts between labor and management. Still another section might focus on "economic contradictions" and their effects within the larger corporate system. We would then learn much more about how social consciousness among occupational groups could have increased over time. Indeed, a focus on "conflict" in the social history of the corporation would also inform us more about the struggle ahead in developing the social foundations of the economy.[36]

Our purpose here, however, is not to predict the future. It is rather to indicate the possible lines of corporate research within the framework of social economy. These lines of research then offer a scientific basis for making social policy that shapes the development of economic life in the United States.

NOTES

1. A. L. Rowse, *The Use of History* (New York: Macmillan, 1948), p. 64ff.

2. I treat technical aspects of this hypothesis in the next chapter on research models of the corporation. Here the concept of social consciousness in its general meaning of an awareness of human interdependence suits our purpose. It guides our selection of historical facts. As we proceed, other concepts such as identity, perception, responsiveness, and accountability become important parts of a research model for this hypothesis. These terms are oriented toward a research model in Chapter 2.

3. This line of inquiry is pursued partly in the tradition set by the American historian Frederick Turner Jackson. Jackson presented a paper at the World's Columbian Exposition in 1893 called "The Significance of the Frontier in American History" that stimulated some controversy among historians. Turner viewed the "frontier," not as a line between the east and the west, but as a "process" that changed constantly, depending on land resources and the backgrounds and beliefs of people who move into a geographical area. It was an interpretation of historical development that raised issues among historians but never led toward social scientific studies for its clarification and validation. Here we suggest that the connections can be made between an historical interpretation and scientific research today. We are talking about the social frontier of the American economy.

4. Sir Henry Sumner Maine, *Ancient Law* (London: Oxford University Press, 1931).

5. The key distinctions on the "natural history" of the corporation are made by Otto von Gierke, *Das Deutsche Genossenschaftsrecht* (4 vols. Berlin: 1868–1913, Vol. IV unfinished). Gierke distinguishes between the corporation conceived on the one hand as a collective personality originating in cooperative fellowship and on the other hand as an artificial creation of the sovereign, conceived as a fictitious person. Sections of the last volume were translated by Ernest Barker in 1934 and printed in paperback by Beacon Press in 1959. Cf. Otto Gierke, *Political Theories of the Middle Age,* translated by Frederic William Maitland (Cambridge: University Press, 1927).

6. Quoted by Adolf Berle, "Historical Inheritance of American Corporations," in Ralph J. Baker and William Cary (eds), *Corporations, Cases and Materials* (Brooklyn: The Foundation Press, 1959), p. 2. The regulatory mechanism of the European States over corporations was extensive in the seventeenth and eighteenth centuries. Cf. Frederich Nussbaum, *A History of the Economic Institutions of Modern Europe* (F. S. Crofts, 1935), p. 68.ff.

7. *Dartmouth College* v *Woodard*, 4 Wheaton 518 (1819).

8. *Liggott Co.* v *Lee,* Supreme Court of the United States, 1933, Brandeis opinion. Quoted in Baker and Cary, op. cit., p. 7.

9. Baker and Cary, op. cit., p. 8.

10. R. S. Stevens, "Uniform Corporation Laws Through Interstate Commerce Compacts and Federal Legislation," *Michigan Law Review,* 34 (1936): 1063, 1067–1070.

11. *A. P. Smith Manufacturing Company* v *Barlow et al.* (May 19, 1953). New Jersey Sp. Ct. Chancery Division, *Atlantic Reporter,* 197: 186–96. For a discussion of this case, see Clarence C. Walton, *Corporate Social Responsibilities* (Belmont, Cal. Wadsworth, 1968), p. 48.

12. Quoted in William J. Baumol, "Enlightened Self-Interest and Corporate Philanthropy," in *A New Rationale for Corporate Social Policy,* Committee for Economic Development, Supplementary Paper No. 31, p. 7.

13. Donald Schwartz, "The Public-Interest Proxy Contest," *Michigan Law Review,* 69 (January, 1971): 421–538.

14. The case of the Dow Chemical Company is one example of a social decision made by a federal court of appeals on the application of Rule 14a-8. In the Dow case, the Medical Committee for Human Rights obtained shares of Dow common stock and offered a stockholder proposal in a management's proxy statement. It asked the board of directors to consider the advisability of an amendment to the corporation's charter that would prohibit the sale of napalm unless assurance was provided that it would not be used against human beings. Dow declined to include the proposal, claiming it interfered with "ordinary business" and involved a "political cause." The SEC upheld the judgment of the company. The Medical Committee then appealed the case to the federal court. The court indicated that it disagreed with the Commission on the merits of the case. It said that the exclusion of the Medical Committee's proposal was inconsistent with the purpose of the statute to promote corporate democracy, that is, "to assure to corporate shareholders the ability to exercise their right—some would say their duty—to control the important decisions which affect them in their capacity as stockholders and owners of the corporation." *Medical Committee for Human Rights* v *Securities and Exchange Commission,* 432, F. 2d, 659 (D. C. Cir., 1970).

15. Note the perspectives developing in James W. McKie (ed), *Social Responsibility and the Business Predicament* (Washington, D.C.: The Brookings Institution, 1974).

16. This is my summary of an article by Wilber G. Katz, "The Philosophy of Mid-century Corporation Statutes," *Law and Contemporary Problems,* School of Law, Duke University, Vol. 23, No. 2 (Spring 1958).

17. C. E. Wilson, *Hearings on Profits (Flanders Subcommittee)* Eightieth Congress, Washington, D. C., 1949, p. 475.

18. Committee for Economic Development, *Social Responsibilities of Business Corporations,* June 1971.

19. Ibid., pp. 37–40. Critical dissent was expressed by other business people on the CED. A most significant point of dissent came from Philip Sporn, who argued that businessmen should be looking at their social responsibilities in the area of their own business instead of giving more money to schools and charity. For example, the automobile industry should be putting their money into devices to protect the environment from pollution and toward improving the transportation system. p. 62ff.

20. Arjay Miller, "The Social Responsibility of Business," Stanford University News Service, February 7, 1972.

21. James P. McFarland, "The Corporation in 1990," Department of Public Relations, The Dow Chemical Company, Midland, Michigan, February 8, 1972.

22. Speech at The Whitehouse Conference on the Industrial World Ahead, A Look at Business in the 1990s, Washington, D. C., February 1972.

23. History and science meet here in the development of this concept. The idea of "accountability" is today being defined in more scientific terms with the development of the social audit for the business corporation. Social concepts generally have their origins in history as an idea expressed by people in everyday life; they may express a change in popular thought or point to the significance of a new series of events. Thus the idea of the "Protestant work ethic," "corporation," "business" originated in history and later became refined into more definitive concepts. The social historian is concerned about the accuracy of an idea like the Protestant work ethic to explain a series of historical events, but the social scientist is concerned more with its precision as a concept for research. In this sense of precision, we discuss the idea of social consciousness and accountability as scientific concepts in the next chapter on research models.

24. For studies of early labor history, see: John R. Commons et al., *History of Labour in the United States* (New York: Macmillan, 1918); Selig Perlman, *A History of Trade Unionism in the United States* (New York: Macmillan, 1922).

25. The development of a social consciousness within each of these occupational groups should *not* be seen in isolation. Pressures from the labor movement helped change the attitudes of business executives. In this period of struggle with labor, management began introducing profit-sharing schemes, stock-ownership plans, insurance programs, pensions, and personnel departments that had never existed before. The growing social consciousness of business executives is closely related to the growing power of organized labor.

26. Miller and Form describe four stages of corporate research: (1) viewing the worker as a biological machine (1900–1920), (2) viewing the worker as an individual personality (1920–1940), (3) viewing the worker as a group member (1940–1960), (4) viewing the worker as a sociopolitical man (1960–present). Delbert C. Miller and William H. Form, *Industrial Sociology* (New York: Harper & Row, 1964), pp. 643–86.

27. Elton Mayo, *The Human Problems of an Industrial Civilization* (New York: Macmillan, 1933), p. 40.

28. Some studies then began to bring management into serious question. Alvin Gouldner studied corporate bureaucracy with an eye to how management became "punishment-centered" and how a "representative-centered" bureaucracy was in many ways more effective and humane. Later, from a Marxist perspective, Robert Blauner studied the problems of alienation among workers in different sociotechnical systems. Cf. Alvin Gouldner, *Patterns of Industrial Bureaucracy* (Glencoe, Ill.: The Free Press, 1954); Robert Blauner, *Alienation and Freedom: The Factory Worker and His Industry* (Chicago: University of Chicago Press, 1964).

29. Douglas McGregor, *The Human Side of Enterprise* (New York: McGraw-Hill, 1960).

30. In the decades since, literally hundreds of studies have focused upon administrative and bureaucratic problems of the corporation. Huse and Bowditch summarize these studies in three different research types: (1) the "structural-design approach," which is concerned with bureaucratic hierarchy built around such subsystems as marketing, production, and finance; (2) the "work-flow approach," which is concerned with the way materials and information flow across the corporate organization and the way information-systems are developed; and (3) the "human approach," which is concerned with the social processes of

leadership, individual behavior, and group dynamics. E. F. Huse and J. L. Bowditch, *Behavior in Organizations* (Reading, Mass.: Wesley, 1973).

31. Milton Mankoff, *The Poverty of Progress* (New York: Holt, Rinehart and Winston, 1972); Richard Edwards, Michael Reich, and Thomas Weiskopf, *The Capitalist System* (Englewood Cliffs, N. J.: Prentice-Hall, 1972); Maurice Zeitlin (ed), *American Society, Inc: Studies of the Social Structure and Political Economy of the United States* (Chicago: Markham, 1970).

32. Richard Eells, "Corporate Sovereignty: A Charter for the Seven Seas," *Columbia Journal of World Business,* 4 (July/August, 1970: 66–70; Stephen Hymer, "The Multinational Corporation and the Law of Uneven Development," in J. N. Bhagwati (ed), *Economics and World Order* (New York: World Law Fund, (1970); Raymond Vernon, "Future of the Multinational Enterprise," in Charles P. Kindleberger (ed), *The International Corporation* (Cambridge: M.I.T. Press, 1970).

33. The term "man" reflects its general usage by researchers. Today we are conscious of the sexist nature of a term using the single male gender to define a group that includes both male and female.

34. Daniel Bell, *The Coming of Post-Industrial Society: A Venture in Social Forecasting* (New York: Basic Books, 1973), p. 130ff.

35. Eli Ginzberg et al., *The Pluralistic Economy* (New York: McGraw-Hill, 1965), p. 86, quoted in Bell, *ibid.,* p. 147.

36. The apparent trend toward social consciousness in occupational sectors should not lead us to believe that it will continue into the future. All possibilities of development are open, and a whole range of courses of action is conceivable. For example, the corporate system could move toward a major collapse in the coming decades because of internal or external pressures. The nation could be confronted with a new form of dictatorship. The corporate system, on the other hand, could remain quiescent without much change visible for a long time. At the other extreme, with leadership, the corporate system could move toward new creative forms of social development and governance within the economy. This is the direction toward which we focus social research in succeeding chapters of this book. See Severyn T. Bruyn, "Notes on the Contradictions of Capitalism: Macro-System Guidelines for Studies of the Social Economy," *Sociological Inquiry,* Vol. 42, No. 2 (Spring, 1972): 123–143; also, "The Dialectical Society," *Cultural Hermeneutics,* 2 (1974): 167–209.

TWO

MODELS OF THE CORPORATION

The study of the business corporation is undergoing formalization within the behavioral sciences. Formalization is a technical process of making explicit a set of logical assertions about a phenomenon under scientific investigation. The significant fact about the formalization of corporate studies is that it is revealing a complex set of assertions about the social nature of business in society. These assertions are that the corporation is more than an economic entity and that it is engaged in more than "doing business" in communities. The corporation is a social entity considerably more complex than originally conceived. Furthermore, the formalization of corporate studies has begun to raise fundamental questions about the nature of the whole corporate system in society today.

Berger, Cohen, Snell, and Zelditch describe types of formalization in the modeling of small-group research that can also be very appropriate to modeling corporate research.[1] It is partly in this formal tradition of modeling research that the assertions about the nature of the business corporation are being expressed and studied. But to formulate models and evaluate studies with accuracy requires a more comprehensive theory about corporate life, one that extends beyond the framework of business and economics. Furthermore, formalization of analytic models leads to the formulation not only of empirical models for research purposes but also of normative models for guiding policy and practice. In this transition between types of models it is essential to grasp the totality of corporate life. This is important in part to see the full implications of scientific work leading to the formulation of policy. A theoretical framework and rationale is needed for studying corporations from all angles.

We shall examine the theoretical framework within which major assertions have been made about the business corporation. We are interested in building a rationale for future studies that is broadly based in human reality. It is not simply the models themselves that we are examining, but the *range* of theoretical assertions that corporate research must take into account in formulating an accurate model. We begin with assertions associated with the more formal studies and conclude with the more interpretive assertions that the formalization process cannot fully grasp. It is the complicated schema of corporate life that concerns us as the corporation becomes the most significant unit of operation in the life of both socialist and capitalist nations today.

The generic categories within which the entire range of assertions are made about corporate life are economic, social, and cultural. It is within these three categories that we assume the corporation is understood in terms most basic to its existence in society. We note that the economic category is largely defined by assertions that the corporation operates primarily on a profit motive. The profit motive is complex, as we shall see in models that have already been formulated. Profit making, for example, has a social context that leads us to examine the nonprofit corporation as an entity standing midway between the social and the economic categories. The social category is partly defined by assertions that the corporation operates on a political motive. We shall see that the political motive is also complex. It is understood in concepts of social power expressed through autocratic, constitutional, and democratic types of corporate organization. The social category also contains assertions that the corporation is a system of exchange relations in which investments and returns of all sorts are made. This notion is related to the idea that the corporation is an ecological unit in an interdependent system of communities. Finally, the cultural category is defined by the assertion that the corporation is a symbolic entity with moral, religious, and aesthetic characteristics. These are interpretive characteristics and not easily subjected to formalized research, but they are still a highly significant part of the total schema of corporate life. They must be understood in developing a rationale for future studies.

My assumption in proposing an analytic framework is that all assertions about the nature of corporate life must be considered even though they may not always be evident in everyday life. The social and cultural factors in business life are often latent. They are not observed as readily as economic factors. It is not my purpose to "prove" the significance of social and cultural factors, but to indicate the rationale through which their significance can be comprehended in future corporate research.

We begin with the economic category and the profit motive as the most widely accepted assertion explaining corporate behavior. We then introduce social factors that are gaining recognition for their significance in the modeling process.

THE ECONOMIC CATEGORY

The Profit Model

Profit is the basic index by which the performance of a business firm and its departments or subsidiaries is judged. It is the factor that is believed to determine the chances of a firm to attract new capital and thereby survive and develop, as well as the chances of managers to retain their jobs and be promoted.

The place of profit in the total goal structure of the corporation, however, is a theoretical issue. For example, Neil Chamberlain contends that the goal of business planning is not profit maximization but a "specific rate of return on net worth, total assets, or sales."[2] The profit standard for each corporation is based on past performance and what other, comparable firms have done. Chamberlain sees profit maximization as a long-range goal rather than a short-range goal. It follows that, from the standpoint of comparative evaluation within the dominant norms of the business field, the short-range goal is "satisfactory profits."

One Goal versus Many Goals

Marris and Williamson have independently suggested formal models designed to show systematically how managers behave within the basic context of profit making. In the tradition of formalization, they seek to "render a more precise meaning" to the profit motive.

Marris has proposed that a variety of utility values exist within the motivational life of the manager. These include salary, power, status, turnover, capital, share of the market, and public image as well as profits. In addition, Marris proposes a summative principle inclusive of them all. The most fundamental principle explaining behavior is a desire for *corporate growth,* especially as measured through diversification or activities. The Marris model of course assumes a reasonable degree of security for the managers, especially from the fear of general dismissal as in the case of a stockholders' raid. (To avoid a raid, managers generally try to keep the rate of return of productive assets high and avoid excessive retention of profits or excessive liquidity.) Once security is clear for the managers, their aim is to achieve a satisfactory growth rate measured by a rate of diversification and average profit margin.[3]

A model proposed by Cyert and March assumes that many groups within the corporation compete and bargain in a goal-setting process. Goals cannot be described in terms of a "preference order" but rather are best seen as a result of a socioeconomic process. In business corporations there are normally five goals that affect corporate behavior: (1) a production goal, (2) an inventory goal, (3) a sales goal, (4) a market-share goal, and (5) a profit goal. Each goal has its own motivational structure. Different sets of managers compete for the achievement of these goals in the framework of the corporation.[4]

Table 1 Motive-Value Structure

Motive-Values	Individual		Managerial Set	
	Owner	Manager	Top Executives	Dept. Officers
Profit				
Prestige				
Power				
Job security				
Stability				
Survival				
Employee welfare				
Growth				
Efficiency				
Dividends				
Cost reduction				
Department goals				
Sales				
Production				
Quantity				
Quality				
Inventory				
Market share				
Charity				

Rating: Strong, moderate, weak.

Maximize versus Optimize

Williamson, in the same vein, assumes that the valuation that executives place on various factors in policy making depends not merely on the firm's productivity or diversification but on the manner in which these factors enhance the goals of lower level managers. Top executives have a preference for expenditures oriented toward building managerial staff and the special material advantages accruing to them. Within this preference framework, managers have an overall preference for profits. The problem of research in this case is to measure the variable strength of preferences that together represent an effort to maximize utility in corporate life. But if all preferences represent "utility," then optimizing profits may be the best way on the whole to describe management policy.[5]

The study of motive-values operating within the business enterprise is complex. Research modeling must take account of the complicated roles of managers within the entire corporate setting. The context of decision-making can include maximizing many different interests and values within the economically motivated firm. Some of the motives found in past studies are listed in Table 1.

If the motive-values in specific corporate contexts are standardized, they can be studied as norms through systematic interviews, questionnaire surveys, and participant observation on a systematic basis. They can be rated quantitatively in surveys encompassing managerial sets in different businesses. They may also be studied through objective criteria, leading observers to judgments of "strong," "moderate," or "weak" as suggested in the table.

The assumption is that executives want to optimize profits as a general norm of business but that they do so within a set of social norms related to many variable motive-values, including prestige, job security, power, labor, and welfare. Profits are affected by overstockpiling because of fears of the market, purchasing company planes for private use, padding expense accounts to treat political friends, and so forth. Community contexts within which motives arise constitute a socioeconomic "field force" within which the behavior of the corporation can be examined.

A theoretical problem in modeling corporate studies involves distinguishing the relationship between the subjective motives of executives and the objective social context in which they operate. Objective social variables that can affect the motivation of executives include the type of departmental organization in which they work, the ethnic and racial composition of the business, the size of the city in which the business is located, the demography of the business community, the type of business services provided, the age of the company, and many other comparable variables. In this sense, the social structure of the industry becomes vitally important to explaining business behavior. A study of 10,000 firms in Poughkeepsie, New York, for example, revealed that 30 percent failed in their first year. In a study by Hutchison and Newcomer, it was found that only 22 percent survived for 10 years.[6] The reason for high or low rates of success are complex, but given a steady state economy they can be based as much on social factors as on economic factors. Businesses may fail because of the "tax climate" in a state, or succeed because a war is declared and their special products are needed. Social and political variables, therefore, are an important part of the study of executive behavior. The profit motive may not always be the primary basis for explaining corporate behavior.

Social factors enter visibly into the motive system of the nonprofit corporation. The nonprofit corporation is socially oriented but it must operate on economic incentives. It is therefore an important bridge between the economic and social categories that explain corporate life in the United States.

The Nonprofit Model

The nonprofit corporation differs from the normal business corporation primarily in that (1) it is limited in the amount of profits it can make in certain states (e.g., 6 percent), (2) it must reinvest its profits within a brief period (e.g., within one year), (3) it must refrain from supporting political activities, (4) its profits may be returned to its investors or its members only in the form of salaries.[7]

Nonprofit corporations range in type from churches to hospitals to fraternal associations. But the nonprofit corporation most closely associated with business and commerce is the cooperative. The cooperative is a business owned by its customers or its employees. There are retail co-ops, consumer co-ops, farm co-ops and producer co-ops. Cooperatives are in all major fields of business and industry: communications, insurance, transport, housing, foods, fuels. They vary in type from the economically oriented National Cooperative Refining Association in McPherson, Kansas, to the religiously oriented farm community in Koinonia, Georgia.

For modeling purposes, a continuum can be drawn with social and economic interests as endpoints. At the economic end of the continuum there are cooperatives organized primarily for competition and profit (redistributed to member-customers). At the social end there are cooperatives organized primarily for fraternal, religious, or community interests. In the middle of the continuum are those cooperative businesses that fulfill both the social and economic interests of members.

The *community development corporation* stands in the middle of the continuum. Its purpose is to promote the general welfare of citizens in a specific locality while at the same time maintaining an interest in economic growth and revenue on their behalf. Community development corporations have been organized in various parts of the United States. Two examples are FIGHTON in Rochester, New York and Progress Enterprises in Philadelphia, Pennsylvania.

The continuum concept, then, can be the basis for modeling the motive-value structure of nonprofit corporations. The variety of interests that can guide the policy of community development corporations is indicated in the following list.

The Community Development Corporation: Motive Structure

I   Community Development Goals (Examples)
  A. Physical improvements
    1. Parks and recreation centers
    2. Street lighting
  B. Family development
    1. Delinquency and drug prevention programs
    2. Psychodrama clinics and family counseling
  C. Adequate local market and housing
    1. Local shopping center
    2. Local apartment complex

    D. Consumer research
      1. Health and safety programs
      2. Quality control: local inspection programs of water and food

II Economic Goals (Examples)
    A. Balanced budget (set rate of return on investments)
    B. Research and development
    C. New investments
    D. Business interests (market share, inventory gains, sales opportunities, etc.)

The difference between nonprofit and profit corporations is difficult to assess in specific cases. They often look alike in the marketplace and have a similar type of organization. In fact, some states refuse to make a precise legal distinction between them in their statutes. But the distinction becomes important analytically in the modeling of research. In the nonprofit corporation the economic factor may not be conceived to be any more significant than the social factor. The legal purposes and the conscious motives of its executives are social as well as economic. In place of maximizing profit, executives consider maximizing social development in its various forms of expression. The nature of social development however, is a scientific problem not treated by economics and generally ignored in the field of business administration.

THE SOCIAL CATEGORY

The scientific problem of the social category has concerned the organizational life of the corporation. Social research on the business corporation might best be typified in organizational models that link their basic research problems to concepts of bureaucracy (Weber) and alienation (Marx). The underlying theme has been to overcome bureaucracy and alienation through experimental studies in different organizational settings.

This tradition of studying social development in the corporation began with Elton Mayo's research at the Hawthorne Electric Plant in the 1930s. It has been carried further in the research of such men as Charles Walker on the organization of the automobile assembly line, Dorwin Cartwright and Alvin Zander on group dynamics, Chris Argyris on organizational effectiveness and interpersonal competence, Rensis Likert and Douglas McGregor on human patterns of management, Louis Davis on redesigning jobs, F. E. Emery and Eric Trist on sociotechnical systems of work, and many others. These social scientists have built creative models for studying the metaeconomic organization of the corporation.

But the social assertion that the corporation is a political organization may be the most challenging to future studies. The assertion that the corporation is a polity has special significance to an analytic framework that treats both the problem of alienation and the problem of bureaucracy in the larger corporate context of society.

The Political Model

Questions of corporate power in business have already been raised within the fields of economics and sociology but studies that link these two disciplines have not been made. The separate "languages" of sociology and economics are important to keep in mind because they inhibit, as well as release, our understanding of corporate reality. Consider the following two interpretations of corporate power, one by a noted economist and the other by a noted sociologist.

Carl Kaysen writes:

How does the giant corporation manifest its power? Most directly, in economic terms, the noteworthy dimensions of choice open to it include prices and price-cost relations, investment, location, research and innovation and product character and selling effort. Management choice in each of these dimensions has significance for the particular markets in which the firm operates, and with respect to some of them, may have broader significance for the company as a whole.[8]

C. Wright Mills observes:

Corporations command raw materials, and the patents on inventions with which to turn them into finished products. They command the most expensive, and therefore what must be the finest, legal minds in the world, to invent and to refine their defenses and their strategies. They employ man as producer and they make that which he buys as consumer. They clothe him and feed him and invest his money. They make that with which he fights the wars and they finance the ballyhoo of advertisement and the obscurantist bunk of public relations that surround him during the wars and between them. Their private decisions, responsibly made in the interests of the feudal-like world of private property and income, determine the size and shape of the national economy, the level of employment, the purchasing power of the consumer, the prices that are advertised, the investments that are channeled. Not "Wall Street financiers" or bankers, but large owners and executives in their self-financing corporations hold the keys of economic power. Not the politicians of the visible government, but the chief executives who sit in the political directorate, by fact and by proxy, hold the power and the means of defending the privileges of their corporate world. If they do not reign, they do govern at many of the vital points of everyday life in America, and no powers effectively and consistently countervail against them, nor have they as corporate-made men developed any effectively restraining conscience.[9]

From an economic perspective, Carl Kaysen restricts the concept of power to the system of pricing, investment, and so on. From a social perspective, C. Wright Mills broadens the concept to the larger society. Mills refers to the power of the corporation to "command" the best lawyers and, in effect, to "purchase" consumers. One interpretation originates in the rhetoric of the "objective categories" of economic study. The other originates in the rhetoric of social standards. The rhetoric of Mills begins from a perception of standards not wholly recognized in the culture of business. It is an angry rhetoric, but it takes account of values that become explicit when the full power of the corporation in society is understood. The full power of the corporation is understood when political factors are added. Let us see how they are first added to "economics."

Theory and method in economics reflect the norms of modern business and commerce. The scientific study of power in economics is essentially guided by the normative values of corporate capitalism, which places high priority on power defined in monetary and market terms and not directly in political terms. A principal focus for the study of corporate power is *economic concentration* and monopoly. At least a half-dozen "variables" have been employed by economists to measure economic concentration, including total assets, net capital assets, sales, value added by manufacture, value of shipments, income, and employment.

Operational measures of economic concentration, however, may proliferate endlessly without treating the larger social problem of corporate power. Corporate power is both an objective and a subjective phenomenon in the context of society. It is felt and experienced as well as objectively observed. It has an intersubjective texture that goes unstudied in the research on economic concentration. The social definition of power in this sense has yet to be clearly defined. But it is central to the formation of an analytic framework for corporate studies and therefore deserves our attention.

Let us assume that power in the social category is related to the human experience of choices and values in the corporate production of goods and services. The social scientific question is how the concept of power is related to the concepts of choice and value in the modeling of corporate studies.

Model Definitions of Power

If we take W. A. Gamson's definition of power as "the ability of a system to utilize and mobilize resources for the development of collective goods,"[10] we can begin to formulate the basis for examining corporate power both subjectively and objectively. We can study corporate power, including economic concentration, in relation to the human experience of mobilizing resources for the production of collective goods.

Let us assume that the concept of "resources" includes primarily human (social) factors without excluding material (economic) factors. Human resources include the intelligence, knowledge, skills, and sensitivity of people working to develop collective goods. Let us assume that the concept of "goods" involves primarily material (economic) factors, recognizing that they also have some inherent collective value in society. The definition of corporate power can then be translated as follows: the ability to mobilize and utilize *human resources* for the development of goods having *collective value.* We assume that the ability to merely produce material goods without them being valued is not a sign of power.

In the theory of Talcott Parsons, the concept of polity applies to the study of corporate systems. It supplies us with a social orientation to power in the Weberian tradition.[11] Parsons' concept of choices through "pattern variables" suggests that choices exist in all social action. This gives us an added subjective element of choice in defining power.[12] We assume further that choices are made on the basis of consent and some kind of authority. Consent and authority may not always be conscious on the part of participants, but they are always "constituents" in the exercise of power through social action.

These added elements allow us to define power as the ability of the corporation to utilize and mobilize human resources with consent and authority for the development of collective goods. The extent to which a corporation expresses power is then dependent partly upon how well it carries the authority to do so through consent, which is explicit or implicit in its production of collective goods. Furthermore, part of the corporation's power exists in its authority to create goods of collective value. Since values are found in the final analysis in the context of the whole society, goods can then be evaluated in that context.

This may seem to be a rather complex set of assertions about the nature of power, but social power is plainly a conglomerate variable. The terms of this perspective on power are consonant with the terms of both Marxian and Weberian definitions even though each retains a special accent. In the Weberian tradition, power is the capacity to realize individual or corporate will and compel conformity. The power to compel conformity must be based on some accepted authority such as reason, tradition, or charismatic leadership. In the Marxian tradition, however, if the corporate will is not located in the whole of society, it is most likely a form of domination by implicit consent. Put another way, *power is the capacity to realize human values through social authority within the economic order of society.* Power in the final analysis is the ability to produce goods through the general will and authority of participants in the context of society.

The legal phrase that refers to the general will and authority of citizens in American society is the "public interest." The public interest is a term that represents the highest interest values of society. It has a subjective reference in the terms of everyday life and an objective reference in the legal system.

Economic concentration of power succeeds in the corporate interest only to the extent that it approaches a general interest within society. To the extent that it legally violates the public interest, it loses power. Corporate monopoly, then, subtracts from the capacity of the corporation to produce goods with authority within society. The economic definition of total assets, sales, and values of shipments are operational criteria of the Antitrust Division in the U. S. Department of Justice measuring the degree to which the corporation has functioned in the public interest as opposed to its own self-interest. The corporation that expresses a legal monopoly fails to express justice as a value of the whole society.

This definition of power within the social category broadens our analytic framework, however, to include a larger set of terms leading to further study of the corporation. The kind of authority and power that the corporation expresses as a political body (mobilizing human resources for the production of goods) is a special problem of social research. But the study of the corporation as a political body requires a special set of modeling criteria.

The Corporation as a Political Body: Model Criteria

The corporation can exercise power in society in ways that make its political role more significant than its economic role. The corporation is manifestly dependent on the state by authority of its charter, but its latent power to dominate the state is another matter. It has been described as a "private government" that rivals the state in its capacity to mobilize resources and command authority in the social system of which it is a part. It would be difficult to interpret the Du Pont Corporation as dependent on the State of Delaware or United Brands as dependent on the State of Honduras. The corporation is a latent "political body" existing among other socially recognized political bodies. The political organization of the corporation requires study in its own right.

Earl Latham describes five essential elements of political bodies that can be conceived as the basic part of a political model:[13]

1. The allocation of powers and functions within the system.
2. The symbolic form for legitimating decisions.
3. The command structure.
4. The system of rewards and punishments.
5. The juridical system.

There are very few social studies of "the allocation of powers and functions" within the business corporation in its conglomerate form.[14] The concept of the corporation as a polity is not part of the analytic language of economics nor the language of everyday discourse. Therefore, we can at best only illustrate the viability of Latham's political model in the corporate system.

The organization of companies within conglomerates like LTV or the General Host Corporation become analogous to a federal system of polity but without federal principles guiding their administration. The "symbolic form" legitimating management operations is often called "line and staff" within a command system. The "command system" of the large corporation has been crudely compared to that of a feudal monarchy or the modern military, even though it has its own independent characteristics of being based upon a rational order of rules. The comparison does hold in the sense that power is officially dispensed from the top of the organizational hierarchy to the bottom. Corporate democracy is not typically an "intention" of business administration. The top officers retain authority by virtue of latent choice. There is agreement among employees as "subjects" rather than as "citizens" of the system.[15]

The command structure of the corporation at the turn of the century wielded a more dominant form of power over its personnel (private detectives, police forces, labor market monopolies) than is typical today. Power through various forms of domination still exists, but it is rationalized and transformed into corporate bureaucracy. The use of private police today is more for security purposes than enforcement of work. The strike-breaking process, furthermore, has become a function of the state court system and the state police.

Juridical systems exist within the corporate order, but they are largely unstudied. In 1958, the U. S. Chamber of Commerce conducted a survey of 634 trade associations and found that 195 were engaged in some form of commercial arbitration. Some associations heard and settled controversies between members and customers as well as among themselves. At least 133 associations reported cooperating in some form of arbitration. Some decisions were reported to have compulsory requirements placed on disputing parties.

A concept of justice that reflects Latham's criterion of rewards and punishments is thus operant in the private corporate order. Theorists, therefore, may model a normative concept of justice and study its approximation to reality in the practices of corporations and their trade associations. Furthermore, justice norms exist between the corporation and government agencies. This relationship too can be studied for the degree to which the model fits reality.

In many cases, the large size of the corporate polity makes the problems of rendering fair judgments from the state polity (e.g., the Department of Justice) virtually impossible. In 1939, for example, the General Motors Acceptance Corporation controlled the financing of approximately 50 percent of total car sales. Even though GMAC and GM were found guilty of violating the antitrust laws, they were not compelled to separate their corporate functions and compete with one another. General Motors was finally fined $20,000. The yearly budget for advertising alone in General Motors was at the time reported around $100,000.[16]

Prices on the market can be conceived as "political decisions" within the corporation as much as economic decisions. Administrative pricing was a part of the private polity well before "price control" was established by the U. S. government. The hearings of the Senate Subcommittee on Antitrust and Monopoly of the Senate Judiciary Committee, for example, demonstrate that pricing in large corporations is generally determined through a corporate hierarchy of politically oriented committees.

The Senate Subcommittee took General Motors as a prime example of the way a large corporation sets prices. After GM had obtained a profit of over a billion dollars (after taxes), the Subcommittee inquired into the process by which GM set prices. The Subcommittee found that pricing in GM followed a standard that had remained the same for 20 years. The planned "yield" was 15 to 20 percent on the net capital employed. Even though the yield from 1948 to 1955 far exceeded their standard, prices were not lowered. Furthermore, workers were laid off.

The GM decision appears on the surface to be solely an economic decision. General Motors executives argued that the sales of the corporation might decline in the future and the decision not to lower prices was made to protect the corporation from future losses. Such a decision on the amount of profit making, however, is heavy with political (power) factors, both manifest and latent.

A decision about the rate of return on investment must take account of the entire corporate constituency. This includes stockholders, labor unions, consumers, the government, suppliers, and business customers. It is a decision having important "political consequences" in each constituency. The decision affects the amount of dividends, the amount of wages, the level of prices, the public image of the corporation, the amount of gift giving, the extent to which money can be spent on research and development, new safety devices, and pollution control, as well as the level of prices. A balance of power exists among these constituencies which must be reckoned in the decision. An antipollution device, for example, may cost more than it is worth in economic terms, but the company may be forced to install it because of the pressures of a federal agency or consumer organization.

In addition to the economic factor, then, the political factor is part of the explanation of prices. If a labor union is well organized, it can affect prices through its pressure for higher wages. If the stockholders are well organized in their own interest, they can affect prices through the demand for higher dividends. The economic factor is still there, but it may not be prominent in the explanation of why prices have changed over a specific period of time. The dominant factor may be a change in the nature of authority and the balance of power in the newly organized constituency of the corporation.

The operation of the corporate polity has yet to be carefully modeled as part of an analytic framework for studying corporate life. The polity of any association is various and complex so that many concepts may serve as points of departure for new studies. The concept of a political "constitution," for example, has its own rich potential for modeling corporate studies.

The Constitutional Model. The corporation is related to the law in both its latent and manifest dimensions. The manifest dimension is found in state statutes and the charter of the corporation. The latent dimension may be found in the social "constitution" of the corporation. These manifest and latent dimensions are the bases for developing a sociolegal model of the business corporation.

The legal charter of a business corporation in American society is a compact between (1) the state and the corporation, (2) the corporation and stockholders, and (3) the stockholders themselves. In one legal tradition, the corporation is said to be chartered, not from sovereign concession, but from the promoter's initiative and with sovereign permission. This tradition asserts that it is in the nature of the corporation to be independent of the state.

Corporate law is explicit in the statutes of all fifty states. The Delaware statute, for example, gives only certain express powers to the shareholders: the power to elect the directors; the power to enact by-laws (the certificate of incorporation may confer that power on directors); the power to approve directors' resolutions proposing charter amendments, reduction of capital, merger, consolidation, sale or lease of all corporate property and its dissolution; the power to appoint an auditor or remove a director guilty of misconduct. This is the manifest dimension of corporate constitutionality.

This dimension can by no means account for the unwritten norms and the common law surrounding the social constitution of the corporation. A social constitution is a body of fundamental principles that determine corporate authority and power relations. It may be written or unwritten. Every major nonprofit corporation has a written constitution and by-laws. The profit corporation, on the other hand, normally has a charter but no written constitution.

A constitution consists simply of the basic assumptions of corporate polity; it is the way in which the corporation exercises formal authority; it is the anatomy of a social organization. A formal constitution shifts attention toward human rights granted within a system of authority.

The following areas are typically treated in a formal constitution:

1. The purposes and order of associational life.
2. The distribution of power.
3. The accountability of governors or the governed.
4. The protection of private rights.

The study of the constitution of a business corporation begins analytically and empirically and leads logically toward normative designs. The normative design begins to be clarified with an analysis of existing practices that are not all manifest or public. The relationships of the General Motors Corporation to its constituencies, for example, are not fully manifest. The state charter does not account for them. General Motors has a complicated constituency throughout the length and breadth of American society as well as around the world. It has written and unwritten business practices established with customers, dealers, suppliers, buyers, employees, and subsidiaries. The social scientific study of these existing practices provides an empirical base for studying GM's "operating" constitution. This empirical study then leads logically toward formalizing a constitution in the normative sense.

A formal constitution in the normative sense is designed to guide business practice in its own interest and the public interest. The normative constitution is realistically designed to take account of those established customs, conventions, folkways, and human rights that have already been determined empirically to function in the interest of constituencies and the public.

The business corporation in the U. S. is said to be closer politically to the English model of a cabinet–parliamentary election chain of accountability than the American model, which involves the separation of powers. An analysis takes this into account. An empirical study documents it or refutes it in different case studies. A normative model then takes account of the findings and raises questions about how the corporation can express its power most fully in the public interest.

A constitution for a corporation the size of General Motors introduces questions about the distribution of power based upon a federal concept of polity. It requires a model of federalism conceived apart from state administration and control and applied to the corporate order. It requires a design of polity in the private sector that can function in the public interest.

Basically, a constitution answers questions about the protection of private rights within the corporation: free inquiry, free speech, freedom to publish. Secondly, it answers questions about the civil rights of both employees and customers of the corporation. Finally, it answers questions about the inner core bureaucracy and its relationship to the periphery of subsidiaries, suppliers, buyers, holding companies, and local communities.[17]

The study of the constitutional order of corporations can begin with firms that have practiced some degree of corporate democracy over the years. The Lincoln Electric Company in Cleveland, Ohio made an early attempt at it. It has an advisory board of elected representatives from each department that has met twice monthly since 1914. It began paying life insurance for all employees in 1945. Employee income has been geared to a cost-of-living index since 1923. It has had a stock purchase plan since 1925. Since 1934 its profit-sharing plan has paid out more than $100 million. Constituent relations have been relatively stable over these years while management has sought at times to practice a degree of corporate democracy.

Democratic models of the business corporation, however, require separate consideration. They are a type of political model defined by a conventional value pattern. They are normatively oriented to the expression of democratic values in ways comparable to that of workers councils in the socialist tradition. A model for corporate democracy in a nonstatist economy, however, may develop its own unique characteristics.

The Democratic Model. A number of companies in England are demonstrating that it is possible to introduce a form of social democracy into the life of the corporation while still accounting for, and even enhancing, economic values. They have shown that it is possible to write a constitution, permit lower level employee participation in higher levels of decision-making, and still be a very profitable and productive organization.

The following brief descriptions are suggestive of three types of "democratic organization" in English companies related to a continuum of increasing work authority in each respective company.[18]

CASES OF CORPORATE DEMOCRACY

The *Glacier Metal Company* employs about 5,000 people. The managerial authority to make final decisions is retained by top officers but employees participate in formulating policy which managers are expected to follow. The relationship is several steps more advanced in participatory authority for workers than is expressed in the traditional labor-management pattern.

The written constitution of the Company describes the "legislative" system of elected Work Councils in each of the Company's units. Each "main layer" in the factory's organizational hierarchy has representation on the Council. The Council consists of the area chief-executive, one senior and two middle-level staff, three clerical staff, and seven shop stewards representing the rank and file. The Councils meet monthly and any member can request a subject be placed on the agenda. Any employee can attend meetings as a spectator. The Councils make policy, write Company documents as well as "standing orders" guiding daily work practices. The constitution stipulates that no policy change shall be made within this framework unless all agree to it unanimously. The Councils discuss matters of direct concern to workers—wage systems, factory closure, night shifts —but major top policy decisions are made independently by the Board of Directors.

The Board of Directors authorizes capital expenditures, decides dividends, appoints the Managing Director, decides director's fees, confirms senior appointments. In other words, the distinction between management and ownership has been retained in practice at the executive level. Rank and file show little interest in the annual report, accounts or investment decisions even though employees are permitted to participate in the full range of decision-making.

The *John Lewis Partnership* involves still a higher degree of participation among employees. The house journal states that "the supreme purpose of the whole organization is to secure the fairest possible sharing by all members of all the advantages of ownership, gain, knowledge, and power." All shares in the Partnership are held by a Trust and all distributed profits are shared by the partner-employees. All employees are equal in the sense that all share the rewards from profits. The distribution of rewards, however, is according to a hierarchical level of pay related to job responsibility.

Rank and file are represented on Councils. The Central Council has rights which allow it certain sanctions against the Chairman and the Board if major disagreement were to arise. It appoints three Trustees of the Constitution who become directors and it also nominates five other directors. The Central Council has 140 members, three fourths of whom are elected and the rest appointed by the Chairman of the Partnership including senior management. Candidates for the Council come from all ranks but they are more likely to be of managerial status. Between 1957 and 1968 the proportion of managerial rank councillors varied from 61% to 70%. Branch Councils are more representative of the *rank and file*, who compose about one half of the elected membership.

The Branch Councils administer welfare funds and sponsor resolutions to the Central Council. The resolutions become recommendations to management. About six to seven resolutions a year are made and a third of them are accepted. The representative bodies act as close consultative bodies rather than in a final-decision-making role but the degree of participation is clearly greater than in the orthodox case of company management.

The *Scott Bader Commonwealth* is a plastic resin manufacturing company in Wallaston, Northants, employing about 350 persons. It has made a most significant advance in corporate democracy. All the shares are held communally and membership is open to all employees after a probationary period of one year. The main legislative body is the General Meeting which meets quarterly. Each member of the Commonwealth has one vote. It has final approval over the conduct of the business, the right of approval of any investment over £ 10,000 before it is made, and approval of the disposal of the surplus profits after viewing the recommendation of the Community Council and Board of Directors.

The Community Council is the main administrative body composed of 12 persons of whom nine are elected; two are nominated by the Board; and one, representing the local community, is nominated by the Council and approved by the Board. The Council is concerned with welfare facilities and rules of membership.

An additional representative body is noteworthy. This is a special Panel of Representatives (twelve members) who are chosen at random from the Commonwealth to decide whether "the conditions and atmosphere that exists in the firm justify them in recording a vote of confidence in the Board of Directors."

All employees have one vote at the General Meeting. They all enjoy a high degree of security on the job since only gross misconduct and incompetence is taken as grounds for dismissal. At the same time, an appeal system operates in case an employee feels treated unfairly. Members have the right to raise critical questions in the Company newspaper and management is obliged to answer. Furthermore, members have the right to inspect accounts and have considerable access to information about the affairs of business.

The constitution lays down a ratio between the highest and lowest salary which is not to exceed 7:1. All employees are salaried and have a guaranteed minimum wage.

Experiments in corporate democracy frequently reveal that workers themselves place limits on the degree and kind of their own participatory authority. On the one hand, many workers have shown more interest in authority on their "job" than authority over the higher decisions such as making corporate investments. On the other hand, workers have also expressed a feeling of inferiority in their ability to make decisions in spheres of work in which they have no competence. The English socialist G. D. H. Cole once noted that there is a "training for subservience" for the worker in the capitalist system that carries over to block efforts to democratize industrial organization.

The practical and economic limits to sharing authority in the political order of the corporation can be studied in models of corporate democracy. The study includes (1) the limits in individual ability to learn skills essential to all jobs, (2) the economic costs involved in learning new jobs, (3) motivational limits in relocating employees to different jobs in which they indicate less interest, (4) the economic costs in taking time for social decision-making, and (5) the survival requirements of the corporation in a competitive system that makes high productivity a necessity for survival.

A general model of corporate democracy can be devised to specify the kinds of social authority that exist in different settings. Different categories of analysis can be defined that apply directly to the *governance* of the corporation and to *decision-making* relationships that correspond to areas of governance. (See Table 2.)

For example, governance in corporate life is related to problems of social administration, education, welfare, personnel relations, and economic performance. *Social administration* decisions have to do with nonprofit activities (with a profit impact) that take place within the corporation, such as the operation of the cafeteria, planning vacation schedules, parking agreements, retirement plans, transportation to and from work, employee sports and recreation. *Education* decisions involve the personal development and enlightenment of all employees—job training, the process of job transfer, work discipline and rules, sensitivity training programs, health and safety programs, adult education. *Welfare* decisions concern employee benefits such as profit-sharing, social insurance, travel allowances, and stock options. *Personnel relations* decisions are those affecting human relations, including grievance committees, conflict-resolution tribunals, absenteeism, and wage differentials. *Economic performance* decisions are decisions made to promote productivity and efficiency within the corporation, including time and motion studies, technical research and development, investments, and incentive pay.[19]

Table 2   Categories of Governance and Decision-Making

	Categories of Governance					
Categories of Decision-Making	Social Administration	Education	Welfare	Personnel	Economic Performance	
	Company Sports*	Sensitivity Groups*	Health Plan*	Wages*	Investments*	

Management

Authoritative

1. Gives orders
2. Gives advice
3. Gives information

Legalistic

4. Accepts requests and adjusts complaints
5. Negotiates

Workers

Authoritative

1. Follows orders
2. Accepts advice
3. Acts as expected

Legalistic

4. Make requests and complaints
5. Seeks to bargain

Democratic

6. Asks for joint consultation
7. Participates equally in decisions with workers
8. Participates through chosen representative
9. Informal consensus

*Sample area to be studied.

Democratic

6. Participates on the basis of co-influence
7. Participates with direct democratic authority
8. Participates with representative authority
9. Informal consensus

Table 3 Patterns of Power and Equity in the Corporation

	Income	Knowledge	Expertise	Justice	Communications	Benefits
Measures of equity Among Employees	Dollars[a]	Tests[a]	Tests[a]	Rights and Practices[b]	Rights and Practices[b]	Types of Privilege[b]
Exact						
Approximate						
Very little						
Minimum						

[a] Quantitative Measures
[b] Qualitative Measures

Governing powers can be categorized according to social relations that are typical of labor and management in the corporation. For example, an *authoritative* pattern exists in the act of giving orders, advice, and information to workers, which the latter are expected to follow according to managerial expectations. A *legalistic* pattern exists where negotiation and bargaining are institutionalized in union-management practices. A *democratic* pattern exists where management and workers join in making decisions through requests submitted and received by either side and by formal patterns of joint decision-making in which employees are given full authority.[20]

These categories can be cross-referenced and studied comparatively within companies for their social and economic effects. For example, specific measures of decision-making can be studied in corporate activities involving company recreation and sports, sensitivity groups, health plans, wages, investments. Each activity can be examined for the effects of democratic participation on the departmental life of a corporation.

The degree to which power is shared in a corporation is difficult to model and measure. The sharing of power cannot be evaluated solely by measuring the formal decision-making processes within a corporation. Different expressions of power among employees are related to such categories as *income, knowledge, expertise,* and access to systems of *justice* and *communication,* as well as special *benefits* offered in the corporation. (See Table 3.) An employee who has considerably more income than another employee can gain power partly through enhanced status and partly through the ability to use the income for special interests. An employee who has more general knowledge about the total operation of the corporation, ranging from stock operations to the procedures for making labor contracts, is in a better political position than others to exercise power. An employee who has rare expertise needed by the corporation is in a position to exercise powerful influence. An employee who has a union to defend his or her rights in a grievance committee is much more powerful than one who has no rights and no union to obtain justice. Employees who have access to communication systems such as the company newspaper, local radio station, memoranda distributed to personnel, have more power than those without such access. Employees who have special benefits in stock options, insurance plans, travel allowances, use of plant machinery, company planes, have more power than those who do not have such benefits. Those employees who have official voting rights in particular areas of governance have more power than those without such rights.

The degree of equity that exists within each category can be measured and compared among companies. Income can be easily compared in dollars and cents; general knowledge and scarce expertise can be measured by tests and by conducting interviews among employee groups; formal rights to fair hearings and to communication systems can be specified and observed along with actual practices in each company; special benefits provided by the corporation, such as moving costs and travel allowances, can be specified and compared among employee groups.

Each corporation differs in the extent to which particular categories of governance and authority apply. Preliminary investigations are needed to prepare research models with an eye to both uniqueness and comparative evaluation among companies.

The local retail outlet is vertically related to its parent body and horizontally related to other agencies within its community setting. This introduces another pattern of corporate relationships that can be examined within the democratic model. Different local outlets of parent companies have different degrees of autonomy within the larger sphere of socioeconomic action. These degrees of autonomy can be categorized for study. (The franchise system in American business contains a reservoir of different formal-contract relations between local and national business from which to draw typologies.) At the same time, the local chamber of commerce and local government are constitutionally related to their parent bodies in ways that affect the local retail outlet. A decision by the state chamber of commerce and state agencies to promote industry, for example, can change the local patterns of exchange. These vertical and horizontal relationships can be modeled according to their authoritative-legalistic-democratic patterns of decision-making. They can be studied for their impact on both corporate and community life.

Normative models of the business corporation that have been legally formulated in other nations should be studied for their applicability to the American context. A few years ago, for example, George Goyder came to the Jenkins Committee on Company Law in England and proposed a plan he called "The Participating Company." The plan had significance because it extended the concept of corporate democracy to a wider political context of responsibility. It introduced the notion of a social audit in relation to three constituencies: the workers, consumers, and the community. Part of the plan read as follows:

Amend the Companies Act to make employees members of the corporation with the same rights as shareholders except that they need not be issued shares. Amend the Memorandum and Articles of Association of the companies to include a general purpose clause which states explicitly the responsibility of the company to itself, to the shareholders, employees, consumers, and the community. The Board of Trade would be empowered to appoint one or more "Trustees of the Company." Their function would be to arbitrate any dispute referred to them by the directors as to the interpretation of the Memorandum's provisions. Their decision would be final. Three new directors would be added to the Board by election at the annual meeting: one from a list submitted by the appropriate *consumers' advisory service;* one from a list provided by the *workers' council;* one from a list provided by the *local authority* in the case of a local board, and by the president of the Board of Trade in the case of a national or international board. These special directors would be required to report to the annual meeting on their area of responsibility and their reports would be published and circulated with the chairman's speech. They would also have the right, individually, to make representations to the trustees.

Once in every three years the trustees would appoint experts to conduct a *social audit* and report to the annual meeting on how well the company had discharged its responsibilities to the workers, consumers, and the community.

The Board of Trade would be given the power to declare any company a Participating Corporation when it determined the company to be a monopoly or oligopoly defined by the Monopoly and Restrictive Practices Act. The ruling would become effective on the approval of Parliament.[21]

The Exchange Model

The distinction between profit and nonprofit corporations is increasingly significant in the light of the exchange system becoming evident among all corporations. For example, the issue of close relationships between business and government corporations has been raised in political debate. The power of a corporation like International Telephone and Telegraph to provide large funds to "lobby" Congress (including luncheons, travel expenses, limousines, airplanes, honorariums) or to support a nonprofit corporation like the Republican Party is expressed within an exchange system. It is a system that is more than economic, and its field of operation is international.

A theory of exchange asserts that the reciprocity among corporations is social and political as well as economic. It assumes that an exchange system can exist among all profit and nonprofit corporations without always being evident to participants. The field of corporate exchange, for example, includes such different associations as businesses, management schools, universities, churches, Rotary Clubs, unions, and trade associations. These associations are all corporately organized though not all in what we call the manifest or profit economy. The university corporation, for example, assumes the financial costs of training employees for the business corporation without charging it any official fees. It supplies the teachers, the textbooks, the curriculum. In "exchange," universities theoretically have the freedom to shape the outlook of company personnel in the educational process. The church corporation maintains major investments in business corporations through stock ownership and other means. It provides its own investment committees and economic analysts for this purpose. In return, it supplies part of the justification for maintaining the structure of business as it now exists. Similarly, the secondary school, the community council, the private foundation, the social work agency, the hospital, the Kiwanis club, are all nonprofit corporations that as part of the vast socioeconomic exchange system help support profit corporations in the United States.

The nonprofit corporation by itself limits political gifts, excessive profits, the length of time earnings may be retained, and political lobbying. It is one type of corporation that modeling must take into account in the study of exchange relations. The nonprofit model reveals insight into how the tendencies of the business corporation toward monopoly and economic exploitation are restrained by its own charter-constitution. It also gives insight into how a corporation adds value to the cultural life of society. But most important, the exchange system that the nonprofit corporation has with profit corporations reveals the power in their relationship. It is a power that can variously justify, support, refute, protest, reform, or radically change the profit system. Let us look at this matter more closely.

Profit and nonprofit corporations are part of a vast exchange network in more ways than can be suggested here, but these ways can be illustrated in the modeling of one case. We can take the church as one case of a nonprofit corporation that exists in a complicated exchange relationship with the business corporation.

The System of Exchange Between the Church and Business

The church exists within the *latent economy*, while the business enterprise exists within the *manifest economy* in American society. Put another way, the church does not exist primarily to make a profit but it nevertheless has large investments in profit corporations that help it survive. The modeling of corporate research can take account of church investments and returns as a form of exchange between two types of economies. The latent and manifest economies stand in close relationship in support of each other through a system of monetary exchange and a partially overlapping set of beliefs.

Church decisions to invest in corporate stock are often made separately from any direct religious purpose. Business people generally serve on lay committees of the church, and they emphasize the economic factor in looking for high dividend returns and safe investments. Designing a study of these church investments in stock, would involve at best an interpretation of the beliefs existing in both the church and the business. Here we can only suggest directions for formal study without engaging in any examination of religious beliefs or what might be called a "theology of investment."

On the one hand, the church invests its money to express its religious purposes *directly* in ministerial salaries, social services, and educational activities; on the other hand, it invests in stocks and other properties to fulfill its purposes *indirectly* through monetary returns. The one may be called a "direct" and the other an "indirect" exchange relation with people, both involving church property. The "direct" exchange theoretically borders on the concept of *Gemein-schaft* where no formal exchange exists. Exchange is replaced by an informal reciprocity and sharing in community life.

A direct investment relationship would be in the costs of church buildings and their maintenance, the provision of ministerial service, and religious education. Examples of direct investments are many. Protestants, for example, have invested deeply in the educationally oriented publishing business. The Methodist publishing house, Abingdon Press, does a business of $40 million annually. Other publishers include Westminster Press (Presbyterian), Beacon Press (partially divested from the Unitarian-Universalist), and Concordia Press (Lutheran). Churches have acquired large tracts of land in rural areas for summer camps closely related to their religious purposes. They have also acquired and constructed retirement homes for the elderly in direct connection with their religious-educational purposes. The Beatitudes, for example, is a large retirement home in Phoenix, Arizona, sponsored by the United Church of Christ. It contains 500 units and represents an investment of about $5 million.[22]

The church is also engaged in investments for profit, suggesting an exchange relationship with the "manifest economy." It is an indirect exchange because the purposes of the church are not fulfilled directly by the investment but rather indirectly through the receipt of dividends, which are in turn directly invested for religious purposes.

The Corporate Information Center of the National Council of Churches studied ten denominations with investment portfolios totaling $1.5 billion. In particular, the Center reported heavy investments in 29 corporations holding military contracts with the defense department. In general, the nation's three major religions—Protestant, Catholic, and Jewish—are estimated to have about $22 billion invested in the stock market on a national, regional, and local basis.[23]

Metropolitan churches have large commercial holdings. The Trinity Episcopal Church located on Wall Street in New York has commercial assets of more than $50 million. It owns 18 major business buildings in the city, including the 17-story Standard and Poor Building. Its commercial real estate holdings are assessed at $32 million. St. Paul's Episcopal Church in Richmond, Virginia, operates a 200-car commercial parking garage whose profits are about $2700 a month.

The First Baptist, Second Presbyterian, and First Christian Churches of Bloomington, Illinois, purchased the Billman Hotel of Dayton, Ohio, for $3.5 million in 1954. They leased it back to the original owner for $250,000 a year and received a net annual income without cost of maintenance. In 1963, the churches sold the same property back to the original owners for a tax-free capital gain exceeding $1 million.[24]

Churches have invested in every type of business in the United States. The Southern Baptist Convention owns properties leased to such concerns as Bemis

Bais, The Borden Company, Dunlop, Firestone, Mack Truck, and others. The Cathedral of Tomorrow in Akron, Ohio, owns a shopping center, a 13-story apartment house, the Nassau Plastics and Wire Company of Brooklyn, the United Electronics Company, and the Real Form Girdle Company of Brooklyn. The Jesuits are reported to be one of the largest stockholders in Republic and National Steel Companies; they are also among the most important owners of Boeing, Lockheed, Douglas, and Curtis. They also have a controlling interest in the Phillips Oil Company. As a fraternal group related to the Church, the Knights of Columbus owns extensive real estate, including the land under Yankee Stadium, which provides a lease return of $182,000 per year. They also own the $1.8 million steel tube mill of the Bridgeport Brass Company, the St. Louis Frontenac Apartments, and the site of the $5 million Sheraton Hotel in New Haven.

Tax exemptions for the church are involved in both direct and indirect forms of investment, although the pattern is not always consistent. The nonprofit church publishing house business has complete federal income tax exemption. The publishing plants themselves are also generally immune from local property taxes. No federal income tax is due on St. Paul's commercial parking garage. The Knights of Columbus pay no income taxes on the commercial income derived from their properties. Trinity Church, however, does pay real estate taxes on its commercial properties, while its direct investment in church buildings is exempt.

The theoretical distinction between direct and indirect investments is important to the modeling process, so the point should be restated for clarity. Direct investments mean financial disbursements for the specific purpose of expressing the values of the church. These values may be embodied in the form of religious retreat centers, educational buildings, retirement homes, or church edifices themselves. Here the message of the church is intended to be conveyed in the form of religious activities or educational programs.

Indirect investments mean financial disbursements for the specific purpose of receiving monetary return. Church investment in securities, stocks, and profit-making enterprises are intended for profit. The indirect returns are conceived in their eventual church use for religious purposes. A socioeconomic study of economic investments and returns within these separate social categories could be devised as shown in Table 4.

The study of investments and monetary returns of the church invites new hypotheses about corporate life. The variable forms of investment are related to social factors such as church size, church organization, church class structure, composition of church investment committees. Sample hypotheses associated with this type of model construction are: 1) The highest monetary returns for the church are in companies primarily engaged in military production, 2) the ratio of direct investment (relative to total expenditures) is higher among lower class churches than upper class churches.

Table 4   Corporate Investments of the Church

Type	Real Estate	I	R	Securities	I	R	Total I	Total R
Direct	Church property	$	$	Educational enterprise	$	$	$	$
Indirect	Commercial property	$	$	Industrial enterprise	$	$	$	$

I = investments; R = returns.

The theory of direct and indirect investments is important to modeling the exchange pattern that has developed between the church and business. The theoretical issues center around purposes and consequences of each type of investment. For example, questions have been raised about whether both the tax-exempt status of the church and its large stock investments function to "exempt" the state and the corporation from theological criticism and social protest. In the Marxian outlook on the relationship, the church becomes an "opiate" that dulls the consciousness of people to the exploitative nature of business. In the Weberian outlook, it could be interpreted along practical lines that stock investments obligate the church toward greater social responsibility. The church could take social action through stockholder inquiries to correct malpractices of the corporation.

Direct investments in church buildings, religious retreat camps, or other like-minded nonprofit enterprises are beginning to be studied for their "consistency" with theological and doctrinal concerns. Certain social motives are seen consistent with these religious concerns—community development, fellowship, self-realization, elimination of poverty areas, social welfare. The capacity of a socially oriented nonprofit corporation to orient its conduct to religious intent may then be studied. Such studies, however, must be assessed theologically and doctrinally as well as sociologically. There is a difference between the socially oriented study of the church's corporate life and the less measurable and more fundamental values defined in doctrine and church belief.

The Ecological Model

The theory of social ecology assumes that all human groups are symbiotically related in spatial communities. Corporations are no exception. Beneath the beliefs in corporate autonomy and competition lies a system of mutual sustenance in which profit and nonprofit corporations are found to be symbiotically interdependent. On the negative side, this can be noted in the fact that if one major corporation goes bankrupt it takes a dozen parasitic corporations down with it. On the positive side, new technology can create a new breed of corporations developing a new major sector of the economy. Whole trade areas can be observed to be delicately balanced in a spatiotemporal system of contractual and commercial interdependence.

An ecological model guides researchers to assert the nature of this symbiotic relationship in the context of the corporate community. The key concepts of the ecological model—succession, concentration, invasion, density, segregation, centralization, transition zones—are all applicable to the explanation of corporate life. They help explicate the movement of factories, retail stores, wholesale distributors, and realtors in urban space. The ecological model in its general application requires researchers to observe the size, shape, and type of corporations that become spatially distributed in local and regional systems within the national community. Each ecological concept serves as a basis for modeling corporate studies.

The original biological meaning of "succession," for example, can be applied metaphorically to the study of corporate life. The concept of succession can be illustrated in the environmental changes that take place in a small lake or pond. Let us say that a pond has underwater plants growing near the floor. As these plants die, they sink to the bottom of the pond. The sinking plants slow down water currents. More sand and mud begin to settle around them. Gradually, the water becomes shallower. Plants that grow with their roots underground and their leaves above water begin to grow in the area. As more plants grow, more materials settle to the bottom until the water becomes shallow. The shallow water allows sedges, wild iris, and new grasses to grow until the pond entirely disappears. The succession of environmental changes is complete. The environment has been transformed in the process of succession.

The same concept can be formalized as a model for studying the corporate environment. There are signs in the ecology of the corporate system, for example, that the size and shape of business corporations are changing in the context of the national community. A succession of corporate types appears to be reshaping the economic landscape. While the size of corporations is increasing, the internal structure is changing. The corporate pattern appears to be moving from small vertical structures to large horizontal structures. (A horizontal corporation is one engaged in many diversified activities, while a vertical corporation is engaged in a single product line, including raw production, processing, shipping, wholesaling, jobbing, and retailing.) The question today is whether a succession of corporate types is actually changing the quality of the environment and creating an entirely new landscape. And if so, what is causing it?

A model can be constructed to illustrate the hypothetical direction of ecological change in a continuum of successive corporate types. At one end of the continuum, a perfect monopoly of market control exists in 1000 product lines, with one corporation existing for each product. This makes 1000 corporations in 1000 different product lines. Now let us assume that the size of these corpora-

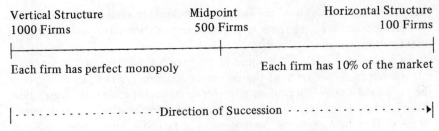

Continuum by Degree or Market Control and Type of
Vertical-Horizontal Structure

Figure 2

tions increases while the number of them decreases. The number of products produced by each corporation increases while the market control decreases. In the final accounting, 100 firms exist, each with only 10 percent of the market in each of the 1000 product lines. At the far left of the continuum the firms are vertically structured and at the far right they are horizontally structured (see Figure 2).

The theory is that the large-scale diversified (horizontal) type of corporation is successively replacing the small (vertically inclined) corporation in the economic system. The direction of succession is toward the right of the continuum. The shift in corporate type is more visible in certain economic sectors than others, but the issue in the ecological metaphor is whether the succession is interrupting the free flow of currents feeding the pond. Can new companies develop freely in the changed corporate environment? In what spatial areas is this change most visible? The question is whether the change in the landscape is desirable for those who live in the corporate community.

One theory for the shift in size and type of corporation toward the right of the continuum is that the symbiotic relationship of the corporation with the federal government has changed the original environment of corporate life. The hypothesis is that the policies of government agencies such as the Antitrust Division and the Federal Trade Commission have unintentionally driven corporations to structure themselves to the far right. This is because regulatory and judicial powers of the federal government require businesses with monopolistic vertical structures to reconstitute themselves. In order to keep growing, the corporation has been required to diversify. Federal agencies have punished the growth of vertical firms but not horizontal firms. They have not punished growth itself. Hence, the growth toward the right.

The history of United Brands (formerly the United Fruit Company) is an example of this change in corporate type. The Company began in 1899 when separate efforts to produce and transport bananas from Central America were combined into one business. In 1900 the Company had about 75 percent of the market and about twenty small competitors. Between 1910 and 1930, the competitors made inroads on the market, but the Company maintained about 60 percent of the market. The Company began to add new companies such as A & W Root Beer, Baskin Robbins, and Clemente Jacques. By 1958 the market percentage in bananas had not changed significantly. Since the Company continued to maintain a vertical monopoly over production, shipping, and finally, retail jobbing, the U. S. Justice Department required that it separate its control over jobbing in the retail market. The Department also filed a consent decree in the Federal Court of Appeals requiring the Company to create a new competitor. The legal battle continued in the courts until November, 1970. At that time, the Del Monte Company was given the opportunity to purchase all of the United Fruit holdings in Guatemala. In 1969 the Company was purchased by a corporation called AMK. It is important to note that AMK had begun as a machinery company called American Seal-Kap and then gradually added other companies including John Morrell & Co., the nation's fourth largest meatpacker. In sum, the United Fruit Company had begun as a vertical corporation but was gradually reshaped in effect by government policy into a horizontal corporation. Its market percentage was reduced, and it no longer exists as a separate corporation. It is simply a company division of AMK, which is a conglomerate of companies retaining limited market percentages within its many product lines.

The ecological model places the analysis of the corporation squarely in the scientific tradition rather than in the normative tradition of modeling. The social ecology of the corporation asserts that the system has natural ingredients and tendencies even when socially conceived. This type of model is also consonant with the capitalist tradition in the sense that it asserts that the business corporation operates as part of a natural system allocating goods in the market. In our illustration, however, we have added the U. S. Department of Justice to the market as part of the ecological system. This broadens the field of study. Social ecology takes account of all units that are mutually interdependent in a spatial area. The actions and reactions of the government cannot be ignored as part of the ecological community. It simply means adding another highly significant agency to the total symbiotic complex. It adds complexity, to be sure, but it also creates a firmer foundation for modeling studies in the ecological framework.

THE CULTURAL CATEGORY

The concept of culture refers to the material and social design for living in society. Culture is expressed through a whole range of human activities and beliefs, including the corporate life. It includes the patterns of political economy, religion, art, literature, architecture, folkways, technology, and the entire symbolic life of society.

The business corporation is not a total way of life even though we may see strains in that direction. The corporation is disposed to become a cultural design for living partly because people spend half their waking hours working in it. By applying culturally oriented models in research, therefore, we can see what is happening to the corporation as it leans toward becoming an integral unit of society and what is happening to people as they attempt to maintain their own integrity within it.

We can assert here that the corporation is an expression of the totality of society and study it on these grounds. The corporation can be viewed as a cultural microcosm of the larger society and interpreted through a number of independent disciplines such as aesthetics, theology, jurisprudence, and linguistics. In these disciplines the symbolic life of the corporation would be interpreted by universal standards applied, respectively, in the domains of art, religion, law, and language. Standards of evaluation about symbolic life could thus be formulated independently of sociology. The study of corporate language, for example, would be made in terms of expression of phonemes and morphemes in office discourse, the semantic expression of metonomy, synecdoche, litote, etc. in corporate communications. The corporation, studied culturally, generates a whole variety of symbolic forms.

The corporation is an organization expressing all the basic aspects of modern civilization. The nonprofit corporation, for example, includes religion (the corporate church), education (the corporate university), politics (the Democratic Party), and art (the private orchestra and art museum) as well as many other fields and areas of life. In view of the close relationship between the nonprofit and profit corporations today, it behooves us to look briefly at this cultural dimension. Here we look at the moral, religious, and aesthetic aspects of the profit corporation.

Emile Durkheim offers an opening for us in the study of the business corporation within a cultural framework. He was a sociocultural theorist whose work in many ways bridged the fields of sociology and anthropology. He found the moral and religious expressions within society important to study objectively. He believed that society must be looked upon as an "object" in the tradition of the natural sciences, but his studies showed that an "object" of society was the moral life. His work therefore became a creative paradox. He sought to remain outside society as a scientist studying its systems of belief while increasingly over his lifetime he came to see the necessity of a common faith, a *conscience collective* within society. The capitalist society was no exception.

Durkheim distinguished the capitalist society in history from earlier traditional and primitive types of societies. The earlier societies were more unified by a collective conscience. Earlier societies had very little diversity, a very slight division of labor, and a very high degree of common identity among their members. The capitalist society, on the other hand, was highly diverse and based on what he called an "organic solidarity." It was grounded in formal contract and rational agreement rather than on common sentiment. The identities of people were channeled toward many different corporate groups rather than focused directly and intensely on the society as a whole. These groups in effect stood as intermediaries between people and the formation of the state as the modern embodiment of unifying beliefs about the society. The capitalist society, therefore, did not express a high degree of solidarity and moral unity as did past societies, but it did yield a high degree of freedom and individuality.

The main problem of the capitalist society was that it did not have an adequately integrated moral order. Durkheim claimed that its "social bonds" were weak. Weak social bonds meant a high rate of suicide and crime. Durkheim's own study of suicide showed a high correlation of suicide rates with conditions of weak bondedness and a low level of solidarity. People committing suicide had tended to become separated from supportive groups that would otherwise have helped them overcome personal crises. They lacked a stable moral community.

The business society was, in effect, generating conditions of *anomie* or normative instability. It was producing weak moral bonds, which led to high rates of crime, suicide, and other social problems. The capitalist economy was producing a high level of social disorganization even while it produced a high level of material goods for society.

But Durkheim believed he could see the emergence of "occupational communities" within this loosely structured capitalist society. Here a moral order might be formed in a manner that would treat the social problems of society stemming from a state of anomie. At the same time, Durkheim was cautious about returning to a high degree of moral unity because that condition also generated its own problems, including what he called "altruistic suicide." An overintegrated society with a high sense of unity had its own problems. People came to identify too strongly with it and thus failed to see the larger order of things. Instead, Durkheim pointed to an intermediate order of human bondedness in society that was neither too weak nor too strong. In capitalist society this meant the development of a new moral and political order within the organic life of the economy.

In this tradition of Durkheim, then, we will look first at a research model that may guide historical and contemporary studies on the growing moral order of corporate life. We then look at the corporation symbolically as an expression of the religious life of the society. Finally, we look at the corporation for its potential to express art in society. These assertions of the corporation as a moral, religious, and artistic body are all important to comprehend the nature of the corporation as a civil agent of modern society.

The Corporation as a Moral Order

I noted in the first chapter that major occupational groups such as corporate lawyers, executives, laborers, and researchers were developing a "social consciousness" over time. They are showing signs of becoming increasingly aware of their own collective identity in relation to the corporation in society. Furthermore, they seek in various ways to overcome an exclusive emphasis on private profit-making in the business corporation. This was suggested as a hypothesis that could be investigated in a social history of the corporation.

The hypothesis offers one perspective on corporate history, but a more precise definition of social consciousness is needed for scientific studies. It needs to be "operational" for designing empirical research. Social consciousness is at present a complex philosophical term with many dimensions to its meaning.

The term "social consciousness" means generally an awareness of human interdependence in society. An increase in this consciousness suggests that people are perceiving more about the complex relationships between themselves and others. It also suggests an increasingly broader common identity among people.

Let us define this notion now in more precise terms. We will also add a concept of social responsibility to round out a model measuring the "collective conscience" of the occupational communities in the corporate system. Following Durkheim's theory, we can then study the degree of human community emerging among laborers in unions, executives in trade associations, engineers and accountants in professional associations, farmers in farm organizations, as well as many other "occupational communities" existing in the corporate economy.

Definition of Social Consciousness and Responsibility

Let us begin by suggesting that the concept of social consciousness has depth and breadth and can be studied as a scientific paradigm.

We assume that the *depth* of consciousness can be studied by measuring the degree of personal identity that occupational groups have with each other in the corporate system. This depth can be observed on a continuum that begins with very little identity of one group with another (total detachment). At the other end of the continuum is a high degree of identity (total involvement). We now have one measure of the degree of social solidarity of different occupational groups with each other in the corporate system.

In the theoretical tradition of Durkheim, we can speculate that overidentity or underidentity could result in trends toward deviancy and contradictory behavior. We would assume that a midpoint on the continuum of personal identity would show a moderate degree of social bondedness. This midpoint should be difficult to achieve under present conditions. Here one group would perceive people in other occupational groups as human beings like themselves.[25]

The *breadth* of consciousness, on the other hand, can be studied by the degree to which corporate groups have an accurate "rational perception" about themselves. By this I mean an awareness of the complex interdependent relationships between such groups as labor, management, office workers, and customers. Breadth of consciousness refers to the accurate social perception of the varied legal, political, economic, and organizational factors that affect the relationship between occupational groups. It contrasts with "depth," which is a measure of the degree of personal identity between groups.[26] We will discuss more on this later.

A concept of "social responsibility" adds a moral imperative to social consciousness. Social responsibility can be defined as the capacity of occupational groups to respond to problems between themselves and other groups with some measure of fairness and equity. We will divide this concept into two subconcepts called social responsiveness and social accountability. *Social responsiveness* refers to the degree of interest that groups have in acting with understanding and equity toward one another. *Social accountability,* on the other hand, refers to the requirements that corporate groups respond justly through some legal institution.

Legal institutions have emerged in great numbers in corporate history to require occupational groups to become more responsible to one another in society. These institutions include employment compensation, pension plans, auditing systems, conciliation boards, and tribunals. They are, in effect, ways to monitor social conduct and assess social responsibility. They ensure the fact that occupational groups will act toward one another with some measure of understanding and equity.

The concept of social responsibility thus has a subjective reference in the notion of responsiveness, a readiness to act with understanding and equity; at the same time, it has an objective reference in the notion of accountability, a means whereby equitable action is observed to take place. (See Table 5.)

We have now narrowed the meaning of these concepts from their broad usage toward that which the sociologist Herbert Blumer calls "sensitizing concepts." They are more specifically defined than for their general use in everyday speech. The concept of human identity can be quantified and measured on a continuum; the other concepts can be likewise defined operationally for more precise research. It is then possible to take these concepts as the basis for further historical and contemporary research on the moral order of corporate life.[27]

A note of caution on the use of these concepts is appropriate here. From a scientific perspective, the notion of a possible increase in social consciousness and social responsibility over time does not refer to some ideal standard of the future. The concepts of "consciousness" and "responsibility" are not measured in relation to what "could be" in a social vision. They are not measured by what "ought to be" in some higher moral imperative. If these standards were applied, we might find very little consciousness and responsibility today in the business system. Instead, the concepts are measured as "facts" in their comparative expression between periods of American history and between occupational groups today.[28]

Table 5   Measures of Social Solidarity

Social Interdependence	Occupational Communities: Constituencies				
	Lawyer	Executive	Laborer	Researcher	Others
Consciousness					
(a) Personal identity (subjective)					
(b) Rational perception (objective)					
Responsibility					
(a) Responsiveness (subjective					
(b) Accountability (objective)					

Historical and Contemporary Research

Our hypothesis is that occupational groups in the nineteenth century showed a relatively low degree of social consciousness compared to what they express today. But this consciousness has varied considerably and has not shown a linear development in all cases. We can only hint here how this hypothesis could be further studied given the paradigm of social consciousness and responsibility.

We can speculate, for example, that Justice John Marshall's famous declaration that the corporation was "an artificial being, invisible, intangible, and existing only in the contemplation of the law" was symbolic of legal thought in early times for lawyers associated with the corporation. Marshall was intending to separate the concept of the corporation as an entity from the state as an entity. However, Marshall's legal concept of the nature of the corporation was quite limited *relative* to legal concepts of today. The legal liabilities and civil relations of the corporations with respect to employees, customers, the public, and the environment is a far cry from what was originally perceived in the early nineteenth century. The rudiments of twentieth century problems with employees and customers existed at that time, but they were "invisible" and "intangible" to Marshall's corporate law. This suggests that Marshall's own personal identity with the people affected by the corporation was highly limited *from a legal standpoint.* It means also that lawyers in that day would receive a low score on legal responsiveness and accountability to corporate constituencies like laborers and customers. It is simply an early stage in the development of corporate law.

Corporate lawyers today are beginning to conceive of a "social law" existing within corporate life outside the jurisdiction of the state. Social law refers to the norms governing the conduct of employees. It stands apart from state "inter-position" and yet it is important to the effective operations of the corporation. Infractions of social law-norms may require "due process" within the internal order of the corporation itself.[29]

Corporate executives were another occupational group in the nineteenth century who expressed a low degree of responsiveness and accountability to the labor force relative to today. Labor was looked upon impersonally as an item to be bought in the marketplace. This "market perception" of labor may remain in some measure today in the minds of many executives, but its character has no doubt changed. It is hypothetically less strong and is qualified by the experiences of collective bargaining.

Corporate researchers are still another occupational group that showed a lower degree of social consciousness and responsibility in their early days than is generally expressed in the literature on research today. The historical development, however, is not easily defined. When Frederick W. Taylor first questioned the way work was organized, it was a shock to business executives. Work had been thought to be only a part of "nature" or "tradition." Taylor's concept was a breakthrough in social consciousness relative to nineteenth century thought. After the socialist revolution in Russia, Lenin even recognized the social value of Taylor's work in the United States. It meant that people could design jobs according to their own social purposes. Taylor's work, however, began with *no* significant identification with the needs of workers. His occupational concern in research was directed to the need for increasing production for the corporation. Early corporate researchers in the United States simply accepted the profit motive and the bureaucratic organization of work without question.

Today corporate researchers can look back upon many of these early forms of corporate organization as forms of patriarchy. They are only one type of organization among many others including the democratically oriented administration of the corporation. The researchers' *perception* of the complicated factors between themselves and other groups has therefore increased over the years. Their *identity* has broadened to include labor. But the process is not finished, as we indicate later.

This paradigm of a "collective conscience" forming among occupational groups in history can also be applied to the corporate system today. Contemporary corporate groups have different degrees of consciousness and responsibility relative to each other. The relationship between laborers and stockholders, for example, would likely show a low degree of consciousness and responsibility. Stockholders in the main would have little *personal identity* with the life and needs of laborers in the companies they own. The role of the stockholder in large corporations has become relatively separate from any social identity with the needs of "their employees." The concern is instead with the exchange value of the stock and the stability of the stock market.

Future empirical research may supply answers to questions raised about the contemporary scene. We do not know to what extent each variable is related to the other, much less the degree of their expression among corporate groups today. We would ask: To what extent do mechanisms of accountability increase the identity of groups with one another? Does increasing personal identity between groups mean that the degree of responsiveness will increase in correlative terms? These are complex variables surrounding the study of autonomous groups in the corporate system.

The moral order of corporate life is still in transition and shows many of the instabilities that Durkheim saw inherent in the business society at the turn of the century. At the same time, the signs of a growing social consciousness are important to investigate for their course of development in the future of the corporate economy.

The Corporation as a Religious Body

Emile Durkheim once defined religion as a "unified system of beliefs and practices relative to sacred things, uniting into a single moral community all those who adhere to those beliefs and practices."[30] It is important to stress that Durkheim perceived a sacred-moral propensity in the modern division of labor that could lead in many different directions.

While it is not a corporate intention to create a "religion" in the life of employees, the structure of daily work requires the kind of personal investment in time and energy that induces a quality of religious life. The habits of people working five days a week at their job create a life style that can structure more of the "faith" by which people live than one day a week at the church or synagogue. The system of office privileges, the tax protections, travel allowance, bonuses, insurance policies for the family, become part of the survival requirements of modern life. The set of beliefs surrounding the survival of the business system represents a religious order in everyday life.

The depth of the business commitment in the life of the individual in the system is generally unrecognized. Leaders in the church and the synagogue do not as a rule look carefully at the implications of a business environment that protects, supports, and provides continuity in the life of loved ones. The popular definition of religion as constituted in "the church" bars public awareness of its potential significance in the context of society. Yet the assertion that the corporation is a religious body is as important analytically as the assertion that it is a political body.

Clifford Geertz sets forth more specific criteria of religion:

(1) a system of symbols which acts to (2) establish powerful, pervasive, and long-lasting moods and motivations in men by (3) formulating conceptions of a general order of existence and (4) clothing these conceptions with such an aura of factuality that (5) the moods and motivations seem uniquely realistic.[31]

The criteria of Geertz and Durkheim may well serve as a theoretical background to the study of corporate life. The set of beliefs that dominates the modern corporation creates "powerful, pervasive and long-lasting moods." The beliefs guide the fundamental decisions of people in daily life. An example of corporate belief: "men are motivated fundamentally by the desire for money because it is natural." Another: "The business system cultivates moral character because it holds individual values supreme."

There are many sacred parts to the corporate mythology that bind people together and at the same time create other negations and "devil systems." It would be "wrong" to place the interests of a "competitor" ahead of one's own interests in an economic exchange. It could be "right" to condemn all communists as part of a system bent on overthrowing the government by force. A corporate belief assumes a reality. It becomes a "fact of life."

Furthermore, corporate beliefs acquire a quality of "ultimacy." That is, they function as though they are the final and only solution to recurrent problems of human existence such as poverty and suffering. It is as though they were the only foundation for achieving freedom and happiness. The corporate system becomes the strategy toward these ends—with its own rites and ceremonies. The corporation can then become essential to the solution of the major problems of life.

The religious dimensions go still further into business life because the resolution of the most complex problems of collective existence has a mysterious element to it. Since no single individual can know the answers to existential problems with certainty (at least according to the standards of truth in the system), they must be taken on faith. The problem of poverty might be grappled with differently in an alternative system. A federal pattern of CDCs could be a means to eliminate poverty and fulfill the great values of individuality and freedom. But its effectiveness cannot be known until it is tried at the national level. The alternative at the level of the whole society cannot be easily confirmed or denied by science. Beliefs in the corporate system therefore are a means of transcending that unknowingness which encompasses individuals in their search for existential solutions.

The existential problems remain. In Sartre's classic words, "There is no exit." There is perpetual alienation. The "organization man" stands on the brink of communism and chooses the profit-oriented corporation.[32]

Durkheim's analysis found common ground with socialists, but it was not in socialism that Durkheim searched for the moral integration of society. For Durkheim, the socialists were in the same camp as the economic liberals. They both foundered on the problem of morality. Neither saw the religious and moral significance of the corporation in society. The "liberals" segregated their religion in the church; the socialists denied its validity.[33]

Durkheim's theory claims implicitly that corporations express a moral element, and it is on that assertion that a theory of religious symbolism emanating from the corporation is developed. The assertion of a religious dimension to business corporations cannot be easily denied either by people who work within them or by the social scientist who studies them. Such a denial only hides it from consciousness. It becomes a part of the symbolic life of people but unrecognized for its capacity to control institutional behavior. Without critical consciousness in the citizenry, it can rise like a specter in a great mythology of the corporate state that haunts people by legitimating totalitarian control. Or it can loom forth to control "facts of life," as suggested by Geertz's criteria of religion. Without consciousness of the religious factor, people sacrifice their lives readily in the belief that the corporate mythology is an ultimate system of values.

Durkheim envisioned a moral community developing through corporate associations. It was only the direction and growth of that moral association that remained a mystery to him. It still remains a mystery, but answers are forthcoming partly through the critical study of the moral community that is now developing in the corporate world of both capitalist and socialist nations.

The Corporation as an Art Form

Many corporate executives have demonstrated an interest in the art world through their own private art collections, their philanthropic gifts to art foundations, their special attention to decor, the display of expensive art objects in executive suites, and the special accent on corporate gifts to art centers. Richard Eells provides evidence for a growing interest in art among business executives including a rapidly rising proportion of corporate gifts to the field of art.[34]

This pattern of relationships is one of the signs that executives see the business corporation and their life-work in more than economic terms. It is even feasible to suggest that the self-image of some executives may contain a vestigial quality of the renaissance. Executives may increasingly see their work as an expression of art in the tradition of that renaissance image.

The art world, in the past, has been clearly separated from the world of the laborer and the white collar worker in the corporation. The executive role has been relatively open and flexible while the worker's role on the assembly line has been narrowly defined. It has been only recently that unions and management have been giving attention to changing the routine and drudgery of the worker through job redesign. The redesigning of jobs has introduced flexibility and diversity in the work experience. The process of job redesign may well lead toward the introduction of new meanings to work itself. Some part of these new meanings may be drawn from the field of art.

D. W. Gottschalk describes a framework within which art may be understood in society. He bases his framework on the meaning of the "aesthetic experience," which he defines as "the full apprehension of the intrinsic being and value of an art object." The aesthetic experience involves the total person encountering the total object. Fundamental qualities of personality are involved in this experience. They are the senses, intelligence, imagination, intuition, and feeling. A work of art is understood on the basis of the enhancement of these personal qualities through a four-dimensional field of perception: (1) material, (2) function, (3) form, (4) expression. These four dimensions are the prisms through which the art object is interpreted. A work of art is interpreted with respect to how it creates an aesthetic experience for the artist and the participating audience.[35]

If the corporation were viewed as a work of art, these four dimensions would become the basis for interpreting how it may be (or may not be) an aesthetic experience for the "whole person" working in it. It may be argued that an individual working full time in a corporation strains toward wholeness, that is, toward living fully as a person. The study of corporate work involves the degree to which the employee—salesperson, executive, typist, factory worker—experiences intrinsic fulfillment in his or her perception of the job. Based on the criteria of the aesthetic model, the perception would be based upon: the *sensation* of the corporate environment, the *intuition* of the order and arrangement of the work situation, the engagement of the *intellect* in the work tasks, the *feelings* that attend working with the products, the *imagination* that is cultivated in the work activity.

The employee is an artist in the sense that he or she creates beauty, form, rhythm, color, and shapes of some sort even in routine activities with other people in the office. The worker or manager is engaged in a creative process that is sensitively expressed to some extent every minute of the day. A study of the fullness of that work experience and the sensitive control over the work is part of the research attention directed by the aesthetic model.

CONCLUSION

The business corporation can best be understood in economic, social, and cultural categories. It can then be modeled according to its orientation to profits, polity (constitutional, democratic), interdependence (exchange, ecology), and symbolic life (moral, religious, aesthetic) in society. It is through the assertions contained in these great categories that the complex schema of corporate life can be understood and studied as a basic part of everyday life.

Although the economic category fails by itself to provide a wholly adequate account of the meaning of the corporation, the combination of categories together accomplish that task. They reflect the human reality of the corporation. To render a precise meaning to the economic factor in the making of corporate profits, for example, is important but not sufficient to explain the power and authority of the corporation in society. The premises underlying the theoretical schema for modeling social scientific research are that the corporation is engaged in more than making profits and doing business. The rationale for corporate studies carries assertions beyond the purely economic category. Indeed, it is within the social category that corporate studies are finding a new significance.

The relation between the social and economic categories has not yet been fully explored. From an analytical standpoint, for example, the corporation can be observed primarily as a social entity. The assertion is that the corporation operates as a social (not primarily an economic) system. In the Weberian sense, the corporation is social because it must "take account of the behavior of others" and thereby be oriented in its course. Its economic interests are then definable secondarily as part of the many socially oriented criteria by which managers take account of corporate performance.

The terms are reversed, however, in everyday life in business law and corporate policy. The corporation is observed primarily as an economic entity and secondarily as a social entity. In broad terms, it is possible to hypothesize that the different emphases on the social assertion and the economic assertion may be changing significantly in daily life. The social assertion may become increasingly important in the future as part of corporate policy. This becomes a major scientific concern in modeling corporate studies. The question is whether the social category holds the key to accurate prediction, description, and explanation of corporate behavior and performance in the future.

It can be hypothesized that a greater social consciousness in corporate life may then lead to basic changes in the organization of the corporation. It may provide a legitimate basis for corporate reorganization and ultimately define it in everyday life as a social entity. If the corporation is eventually viewed as a social entity in legal terms, a fundamental change will have occurred within the corporate system. Indeed, at this point the symbolic and cultural nature of the corporation begins to assume greater public significance. The great symbols of justice, freedom, and democracy, for example, begin to take on new importance in the daily operations of business. The corporation then may be observed for its deeper cultural complexity as one of the major human designs of the post-modern world.

The modeling of corporate studies in these varied ways thus leads not only toward the explication of corporate behavior in more precise terms for predictive purposes. It leads also toward a clarification of the significance of the corporation in the context of the whole society. The social scientist may then play a vital role in both formalizing knowledge about the corporation and helping to define its critical shape in society.

NOTES

1. These authors divide formalization into three types: the explication model, the representation model, and the theoretical-construct model. The explication model has its goal as the "rendering of a precise meaning, the one or more basic concepts." The concepts may or may not be embedded within a substantive theory. The representational model is one that signifies in a precise and formally simple manner "a recurrent but specific instance of an observed social phenomenon." In this case, the theorist brings together a variety of observed characteristics of the phenomenon. The theoretical-construct model involves formalizing a particular theory that is used to account for specific social behavior or activity. The theorist aims to derive and predict an actual observed process as a consequence of the explanatory theory. See: Joseph Berger, Bernard Cohen, J. Snell, and M. Zelditch, *Types of Formalization in Small Groups Research* (Boston: Houghton-Mifflin, 1962).

2. Neil W. Chamberlain, *The Firm: Microeconomic Planning and Action* (New York: McGraw-Hill, 1962); cf. W. J. Baumol, *Business Behavior, Value, and Growth* (New York: Macmillan, 1959).

3. R. A. Marris, "A Model of the 'Managerial' Enterprise," *Quarterly Journal of Economics,* 77 (1963): 185–209.

4. R. M. Cyert and J. G. March, *A Behavioral Theory of the Firm* (Englewood Cliffs, N. J.: Prentice-Hall, 1963).

5. O. E. Williamson, *The Economics of Discretionary Behavior: Managerial Objectives in a Theory of the Firm* (Englewood Cliffs, N. J.: Prentice-Hall, 1964).

6. R. G. and A. R. Hutchison and Mabel Newcomer, "A Study in Business Mortality," *American Economics Review,* 28 (1938): 497–514.

7. Harold L. Oleck, *Non-Profit Corporations and Associations* (Englewood Cliffs, N. J.: Prentice-Hall, 1956).

8. Carl Kaysen, "The Corporation: How Much Power? What Scope?" in Edward S. Mason (ed), *The Corporation in Modern Society* (Cambridge: Harvard University Press, 1966), pp. 91-92.

9. C. Wright Mills, *The Power Elite* (New York: Oxford University Press, 1956), pp. 124-125.

10. William Gamson, *Power and Discontent* (Homewood, Ill.: Dorsey Press, 1968).

11. Note Parsons' concept of power as "generalized capacity to secure the performance of binding obligations [with] presumption of negative situational sanctions." Our contention is, however, that power may be exercised through sheer influence without negative sanctions determining choice. See: Talcott Parsons, *Sociological Theory and Modern Society* (New York: The Free Press, 1967), p. 308.

12. Talcott Parsons, *The Social System* (Glencoe, Ill.: The Free Press, 1951), p. 60.

13. Earl Latham. "The Body Politic of the Corporation," in Edward S. Mason (ed), *The Corporation in Modern Society* (Cambridge: Harvard University Press, 1960).

14. One of those studies is Alfred D. Chandler, *Strategy and Structure* (New York: Doubleday, 1966). The philosophy behind current corporate models for allocating power is discussed by Richard Eells, *The Meaning of Modern Business* (New York: Columbia University Press, 1960).

15. The "subjects" of a monarchy have no manifest choice in the selection of their king. The choice is "latent," that is, it does not exist in overt action. Nor is there a choice *not* to choose the king. The king retains his authority by "consent" through a legitimating belief in

"divine right." Likewise, the president of a corporation gains his or her authority through a legitimating belief in "family inheritance" or "wealth" by purchase of the corporation. The *choice* of the employee is, therefore, *latent* in the corporate system. It does not exist overtly or consciously even though it exists potentially.

16. Senate Report, 1879. The case is noted in Earl Latham, op. cit., p. 236.

17. Richard Eells, *The Government of Corporations* (Glencoe, Ill.: The Free Press, 1962).

18. This summary is drawn from Carole Pateman, *Participation and Democratic Theory* (Cambridge: University Press, 1970); Fred H. Blum, *Work and Community* (London: Routledge & Kegan Paul, 1968); Elliot Jaques, *The Changing Culture of a Factory* (London: Tavistock, 1951);

19. Peter Drucker describes six categories of governance-functions divided according to degrees of relevance to economic productivity and performance. Peter Drucker, *The New Society* (New York: Harpers, 1950).

20. These categories of decision-making were adapted from a chart by Delbert C. Miller and William Form, *Industrial Sociology* (New York: Harper, 1964), p. 763.

21. Richard A. Sabatine, "The Responsible Corporation," *The American Journal of Economics and Sociology*, 1966, p. 256ff. Cf. George Goyder, *The Future of Private Enterprise* (Oxford: Basil Blacknell, 1954).

22. Martin Larson and C. Stanley Lowell, *Praise The Lord for Tax Exemption* (Washington: Robert B. Luce, 1969), pp. 213, 222-225.

23. "Corporate Responsibility and Religious Institutions," *Information and Action Documents*, April 19, 1971.

24. Larson, op. cit., pp. 213-214, 216-217, 219-220. The facts on church ownership in the following paragraph are also drawn from this book. Cf. Martin Larson, *Church Wealth and Income* (New York: Philosophical Library, 1965).

25. The researcher may note the connection of this variable with the Marxian concept of a class "which claims no traditional status but only a human status." Also, in the tradition of George Herbert Mead, the depth of social consciousness suggests measuring the ability to "take the role of the other" symbolically in the corporate system. Finally, people are not solely "engineers," or "executives," or the "clerical force" but individuals who can think independently of their corporate roles. If operationalized, this concept then would measure the capacity to identify with the human status, the social role, and the potential for individuality among people in different occupational groups. This type of *social identity* should result in a medium point on a continuum. The continuum should in other cases point to strong negative and positive degrees of stereotyping toward other groups.

26. The precise definition and quantification of *social perception* depends partly on the focus of the research design. The researcher may want to measure this variable in connection with such perceptions as (1) alienation in the workplace and the organization of industry, (2) domination and exploitation in human organization, and (3) principles of social justice and freedom operating within the political economy.

27. These variables help to "progressively specify" Durkheim's concept of social solidarity. Table 5 simply illustrates their position relative to one another.

28. If "social consciousness" is combined here with a concept of "social responsibility," our historical hypothesis suggests that a measure of moral progress has occurred during this time span. I am not attempting to treat the larger issue of moral progress, but this scientific method implies that moral concepts are researchable in history. Moral concepts such as "social responsibility," "social justice," "freedom," and so forth can be tested on factual

grounds for their development in history. Their meaning may change somewhat to fit scientific requirements. Scientific research generally functions at a more precise level of understanding than is the case for moral concepts. Scientists look at the "types" of an abstract concept and its empirical reference in history. But the whole concept can be approximated through "typifications" of its philosophical meaning. The study of "moral development" is feasible within the confines of precise definition and availability of data. It is an important form of research because it provides a greater comprehension of how the moral dimension of human beings functions in history.

29. Georges Gurvitch, *The Sociology of Law* (London: Routledge and Kegan Paul, 1973).

30. Emile Durkheim, *The Elementary Forms of Religious Life* (Glencoe, Ill.: The Free Press, 1947 [1912]), p. 47.

31. Clifford Geertz, in Michael Banton (ed), *Anthropological Approaches to the Study of Religion* (New York: Frederick Praeger, 1966), p. 4.

32. This suggests that the "organization man" syndrome described by William H. Whyte may be only a special account of a problem that penetrates much deeper into the workings of the cultural system. The solution to the social dilemma for Whyte was to "fight the organization" and be an "individual." This may be interpreted in broad scope as part of a cultural phenomenon. Whyte's solution can be seen as made within the ethos of individualism. The "solution" offered may no longer have viable foundations in the modern corporate system. The return to individualism is not viable without a corporate alternative.

The problem can be percieved partly in the sacredness surrounding the corporation itself with its special structures and attendant beliefs. The real solution may lie only in changing the structure of the corporation and ultimately its set of beliefs. The whole system may be calling for a new social foundation that makes possible a creative life for people working within it. See: William H. Whyte, Jr., *The Organization Man* (New York: Simon & Schuster, 1956).

33. For an analysis of Durkheim's position on this matter, see Theodore Steeman, "Durkheim's Professional Ethics," *Journal for the Scientific Study of Religion,* Vol. II, No. 2, Spring, 1963.

34. Richard Eells, *The Corporation and the Arts* (New York: Macmillan, 1967).

35. D. W. Gottschalk, *Art and the Social Order* (Chicago: The University of Chicago Press, 1947).

THREE

THE INSTITUTIONAL ECONOMY:
Social Problems and Economic Alternatives

Social economy is a way of looking at how people develop resources together in society. It is a way of seeing how we produce, distribute, and consume goods in our own best interest. It is a perspective on organizing production to meet human needs, develop human resources, and fulfill important human values.

This perspective changes our image of the capitalist economy. It is no longer merely a mechanism measured by sets of statistical indicators, nor merely understood in terms of business cycles, stock market behavior, consumer price indexes, inflationary spirals, and economic growth. The economy is instead a way of enhancing human life in society. The emphasis on mechanism and statistical indicators becomes part of a larger picture.

Our purpose here is to reveal the human factor in this larger picture of economic life. It requires new indicators of social organization and human resources. In addition to current studies that measure productivity, we need social studies that tell us how well people have organized themselves for production. In addition to a system of economic accounts to assess the growth of goods and capital, we need a system of social accounts to assess the quality of that growth, including the balance of rural and urban economic development and the way enterprises have enhanced the quality of work life.

The gap between economic and social measures of development has become increasingly evident. A Council of Economic Advisors has been established nationally to make an economic accounting to the U.S. Congress, but no Council of Social Advisors exists to make a social accounting of the economy. A system of economic accounts exists to measure economic development in terms of the Gross National Product, but no system of social accounts exists to measure social development within economic life. Major national associations exist to study changes in the stock market, but no major national associations exist to study changes in work systems and their effects on workers. Major national groups gather data on shifts of capital investment, but no major national groups exist to gather data on shifts in corporate interests and organization in different industries. No institutional base exists to encourage public studies on the corporate organization of the economy and how it may develop human resources at the national level.

New methods for studying the economy at the national level could be established, and a system of social accounts could be created. Social accounts are important to understanding how the economy may be organized in the best interest of its participants. Such accounts can also be the basis for making sensible and significant changes in corporate organization to enhance human development. These changes begin with publicly supported professional studies directed to all levels of economic life from assembly lines to large-scale commercial activity. The introduction of new social research into the order of economic life then leads toward a sound basis for seeing how the corporate system functions as a self-determining and self-governing institution in society.

Public studies of the national economy need to take *social account* of work systems, factory systems, banking systems, and retail systems. Such studies could offer the opportunity to examine how the economy can develop social resources as well as material resources. We could then begin to see the possibilities for combining the human factor with the economic factor in making national policies.

Here we suggest that changing the corporate system requires social research involving both professional people who can study the economy technically and working people who can study their work life. Both types of studies are important to comprehend the complexity of the self-regulating forces within the economic system.

GENERAL METHOD

The field of community development in sociology can serve as a model here for introducing studies of corporate policy and development. This field of study assumes that both professional scientists and lay citizens have an important role in diagnosing community problems but that only the local citizenry can make the changes necessary to improve the quality of community life. Professionals can supply important technical information, but in the final analysis citizens must make the essential changes themselves. In this tradition of community study, we now look at changes in corporate policy and development that are self-directed. Professional researchers can help labor and management make their own studies, but these researchers cannot make the actual changes themselves. Labor and management together must do this. At best, in this situation all the employees of a corporation jointly study the social problems in their work environment. They study these problems like corporate citizens who then must take the necessary steps to improve the quality of life in their own corporation.

Let us look briefly at the idea of professional and employee studies. Then we can look in more detail at the problem area of the economy that require both types of studies to effect the changes needed today in the corporate life of the economy at the national level.

Professional Studies

Business corporations show more complexities in the context of society than economics alone can explain. To explain how corporations cause social problems, we need a broader base of professional studies in the social sciences. In addition to measures of economic performance of business corporations we need measures of social performance. Corporations can then monitor themselves through a system of social accounts measuring levels of "accountability" much as they do through a system of economic accounts measuring levels of production.

Social accounting has already begun in the field of economics. It has begun to examine what are called "social costs," "externalities," and "market failures."[2] Such studies have shown that the "optimizing behavior" (profit seeking) of individual businesses often proves to be "suboptimal" (undesirable) for the system of which they are a part. These economic studies are constructed from standard economic models of firm behavior. That is, the effects of pollution, congestion, and racial discrimination are studied now by traditional economic models. They are applied to these public issues in the same way they were applied in the past to the economic problem of "consumer surplus."

Some economists have begun to offer proposals for changing the "operating mechanisms" of the capitalist society in the light of their research findings. The key concept underlying these professional economic studies is that the corporation is a multipurposed organization within the larger system. The behavior of both the corporation and the society in this professional perspective is to be explained in terms of "combinations of goal achievements based on the technological potential and changing preferences over time."[3] This notion brings a social focus into economic studies and leads us toward the human factor.

Economic studies of the firm are generally based upon the concept of a self-regulating market. This concept by itself is of course naive and has been effectively attacked in many works, including Karl Polanyi's classic *The Great Transformation*. But this economic concept can now be seen as part of a more complicated situation. The market is one part of a complex social system that can itself be seen as relatively self-regulating. The self-regulating market still plays an important role in this picture but not central to explaining what happens within the social system. The social economy has its own self-governing mechanisms, as we shall see in the remaining chapters.

Self-governance is an idea that grows from the basic traditions of American society. It refers to the capacity of the economy to stand apart from government controls while at the same time contributing to the development of the society. The self-governing economy is seen in this case as an autonomous institution that is also an integral part of society. It is not conceived as an integral part of the federal government, however, even though a relationship develops with it as another institution in society.

This notion of self-governance is very important to follow because it provides the basis for professional studies as well as links with employee (lay) studies. The idea of self-governance defines different levels of independent regulatory activity within the economy. We look first at the capacity of the economy as a whole to manage its own affairs; then we look at its parts in the same light. Economic enterprises or corporations, for example, can be seen as self-governing units. We expect business firms to manage their own affairs. It follows that the capacity of business firms as a whole to manage their own activities contributes toward the self-governance of the economy *as an institution*. Self-governing economic enterprises are, then, one measure of the power of the economy to regulate itself. We can, therefore, observe the way business firms govern themselves as a means of contributing to the self-regulation of the economy as a human institution.

Still further, we are interested in the extent to which employees within separate enterprises manage their own affairs at each level of administration. The subsidiary of the large corporation develops a degree of capability for self-management, for example, in the larger conglomerate system. The subsidiary may manage its own financial accounts, arrange its own decor, and set prices, as well as hire and fire its employees. Even further within the organization of the subsidiary, divisions and subdivisions of administration show various degrees of self-management. The sales division, for example, must manage its own affairs. The subdivision of the assembly line in the production division must also handle its own affairs. Finally, individuals in the workplace are self-managers. They must learn to control their own sphere of work within an optimum degree of autonomy and self-direction.

We are now looking at the whole organization of the economy and its parts as a way of allowing people to manage their own affairs with a minimum degree of outside interference while they contribute toward the larger needs of people in the economic system. The self-regulating market is taken as part of the larger social whole of self-regulation involving industries, economic enterprises, and their subdivisions.

Self-governance, then, is a model or standard for making professional studies that complements employee studies. It becomes the basis by which social and economic "well-being" can be evaluated technically in its larger institutional scope. The model permits the traditional values of economic growth and productivity to be integrated with values of enterprise self-management.

Employee Research: Corporate Self-Studies

Professional studies are not sufficient in themselves to bring about real changes in the corporate system. In fact, professional studies tend to defeat many of their own ends. Many professional economists make special reports to Congressional subcommittees, which in turn lead to legislation that augment government agencies and adefeat the model of market self-regulation. The alternative is to study the system from within itself and locate the social basis for generating change.

People who work in the system can gather their own facts about their own spheres of work. This method of study actually leads to more effective change than any professional study could bring about. In the field of community development it has become clear that social problems are best studied and resolved by the people who are affected by them. People who study their own social problems know best how to treat them.

This employee self-study process involves the following steps in a corporation: (1) The opportunity is made available for employees to make studies on their own account. (2) Employees identify the boundaries of the system to be studied. (3) They help set the goals and the values guiding the study. (4) They diagnose what is wrong with the system based upon the gathered facts and the values they have determined to be important. (5) They think of their own practical solutions and alternatives and list the steps necessary to achieve them. (6) They are then in the position to take action themselves to achieve the goals they set for themselves.

Our examination of the institutional economy is then based on the assumption that real change comes from people in the business and labor community where self-studies can be made. Here we shall offer a picture of goals, facts, problems, and alternative solutions at the level of the economy as a whole. But only with the recognition that the real picture emerges from the process itself.

SOCIAL GOALS: The Quality of Life

Government agencies and private planning groups make an effort to set goals for the American economy. These goals then provide the basis for legislation as well as for government agencies to study how well the economy is doing from year to year.[4]

Government goals focus on economic growth and stability as measures of economic well-being. The key statistical index is found in the Gross National Product (GNP). The GNP is a quantitative measure of the greatest importance to economists who determine policy at the national level. It measures the quantity flow of annual production and constitutes the standard by which economic growth and stability are evaluated. The GNP represents the annual aggregate of real output in the economy and provides the basis for judging whether other goals can be achieved for the economy.

Other goals include "cutting inflation" as well as reducing levels of unemployment and poverty. These are generally secondary goals, however, relative to the achievement of economic growth and stability. The basic economic goal is to increase productivity and thus to make the total pie bigger so that everyone gets more. The main focus is not on more equitable cuts of the pie but on more pie for everyone. The irony is that unemployment and welfare continue to exist even when there are major increases in productivity.

Since we are looking at the social economy, our goals are not set solely in the tradition of economics. We are interested rather in seeing how economic goals combine with social goals calling for the development of human resources. Our assumption is that the integration of social and economic goals may enhance the overall development of the American economy conceived as a human institution; that economic and social goals are not necessarily in basic opposition although they may appear to be. They can be complementary and are always closely interdependent. The achievement of economic goals is in part based on the achievement of social goals. A social goal such as the elimination of unemployment or the welfare system, for example, can be conceived as the best way to achieve the economic goal of greater productivity.

Social goals are concerned with the development of human life and resources in the organization of the economy. The achievement of these goals means broadening the base of human authority and leadership within the corporate system, and increasing the level of imagination, sensitivity, strength, and responsibility among people who work in the economic order. Social goals also mean the enrichment and enlargement of human experience in the work life of the corporate economy. They are further concerned with the enhancement of the natural order of life. They focus on the development of the ecological order with which the corporate system is interdependent. These goals are intimately related to the way we are organized to produce and distribute goods and services.

Traditional economists have emphasized certain values over others and here lies the core of public debate. They have considered corporate "efficiency" and "rationality" to be important, *but they have not considered social justice and equity in the economy to be equally important.* They have accepted freedom of enterprise as essential, *but they have not seen the development of the community as equally essential.* The public task now is to diagnose the problems of the economic order in the light of the broader scheme of human values. The public questions are complicated, but they include the issue of whether the traditional goals of productivity, efficiency, and rationality can be brought together with the social goals of life-enhancement through the development of human resources. The issue is whether the economic order can now be seen as an integral part of the development of society.

DIAGNOSIS: A Major Contradiction Between Goals and Structure

The economy has always been pictured in American society as operating relatively independent of the government. The tradition of "laissez-faire" refers to an economy relatively free of government controls. However, the dramatic fact of this century is that the economy has continued to lose ground to the government. It shows every sign of continuing in the same direction indefinitely. The federal and state governments are not only growing more rapidly than the economy but are also increasing their control over it.

In fiscal terms, the total federal government spending has grown from 3.7 percent to 21 percent of the GNP. Since 1942, about half of the expansion has occurred in national defense programs. Rates of growth, however, tell us that federal expenditures have far outdistanced private investment and consumer expenditures. Between 1930 and 1968, federal expenditures had a rate of growth eight times the gross private domestic investment rates. (Defense expenditures have increased at a rate nearly 17 times greater than consumer expenditures and 10 times greater than the gross private domestic investment.) The federal expenditure rate of growth is more than 6 times the GNP rate. The rate of government outlay, not including defense spending in 1968, was 37 times that for 1930.[5] (See Table 6.)

While statistics are important measures of government size relative to the economy, more important is the growth in control over economic affairs by government agencies. This control cannot be detailed here, but the following summary offers examples:

1. Government agencies that regulate aggregate demand, such as the Federal Reserve Board and the Federal Housing Authority.
2. Agencies that seek to equalize supply and demand, such as the Bureau of Mines, the Interstate Oil Compact, and the Department of Agriculture.
3. Agencies that seek to regulate economic activities directly, such as the Interstate Commerce Commission, the Civil Aeronautics Board, and the Federal Power Commission.
4. Agencies in direct production, such as the TVA and the Atomic Energy Commission.
5. Agencies, such as Vocational Rehabilitation, Public Aid, and Welfare, that support groups disadvantaged by the private economy.

Table 6

Fiscal Categories	1930	1968	Rate of Growth
Gross National Product	$90.4 billion	$860.6 billion	850%
Private Expenditures			
a. Personal consumption expenditures	$69.9 billion	$533.8 billion	660%
b. Gross private domestic investment	$10.3 billion	$127.7 billion	1100%
Federal Expenditures			
a. Total	$ 3.32 billion	$178.9 billion	5300%
b. Federal defense expenditures	.734 billion	$ 80.5 billion	11,000%

Sources: *Historical Statistics of the United States* (1960), p. 719. *Statistical Abstracts of the United States* (1969), pp. 310; 376–377.

6. Agencies enforcing laws designed to protect the environment and public health from corporate products.

The business system fulfills and contradicts different basic values of American society. It is in the contradictions that we find the causes for continued government growth. Without an alternative system, the high rate of government expenditures and the growing control over the economy can be expected to continue.

The contradictions are most evident in those instances when business pollutes the environment, lays off large numbers of workers, engages in political bribes, exploits workers, practices overpricing, and destroys effective operations of small farmers or business people through monopolistic advantage. It is clear in many respects that the business system is not organized adequately to advance or protect the interests of people who are affected by it: consumers, minorities, aged, laborers, the unemployed, and many other categories of people. Such people have been forced to organize to protect their own interests through the government.

When people are unable to fight back within the private economy, the only alternative is to fight back through the government. This means creating welfare systems, labor departments, small business administrations, agriculture departments, conservation agencies, consumer affairs offices, and many more government agencies. The corporate system continues to create public problems, and the government continues to create agencies to solve them.

Put another way, if private corporations fire workers without being responsible for their continued well-being, the government must assume the responsibility for them and create public aid. If corporations produce goods without being accountable to the consumer for their quality and safety, the government must then assume the responsibility by creating health departments and consumer agencies. The private economy is thus slowly destroying its own viability as an independent social institution for lack of an internal system of responsibility and accountability to its constituencies.

Herein lies a major reason for publicly oriented self-studies. People lack the knowledge for creating viable alternatives outside the government system. Without too much simplification, we can say the contradictions are many and various. Farmers do not refuse to sell their goods to the government even though they are generally opposed to big government and are aware of the excessive costs of storing surplus foods. (Meanwhile many people are undernourished because the food is not made available to them.) Commercial banks do not refuse to invest 80 percent of their investment dollars in government bonds even though business has opposed big government. (Meanwhile jobs go unfilled for lack of capital for new private enterprises.) Congress does not refuse to increase the budget for foreign aid to protect business investments overseas even though Senators rail against the big federal expenditures. (Meanwhile, government money goes to military dictatorships, which then nationalize U. S.-owned subsidiaries.) Clearly there are reasons for national studies of social solutions to problems in the corporate economy.

The aim is to shape the economy to enable it to be more self-governing. The method is through self-study and self-help programs.

With this in mind, let us select specific problem areas in corporate organization that have been responsible for the continued increase in government controls. We will focus first on problems in the corporate system requiring professional studies and then look at the kind of social alternatives that will require corporate self-studies. These publicly oriented studies then point in detail to practical steps for developing a self-governing economy.

Problem I:
The System of Labor-Management Relations

The rise of the labor union as a legal force at the national level in the 1930s was a major breakthrough for the self-governing economy. It introduced a pattern of problem-solving within the private sector that may have avoided a government takeover of industry. But the unions stopped short of seeking broader solutions. Consequently, we are faced with a situation today that Carl Gerstacker of Dow

Chemical Company describes as destructive and counterproductive. The "adversary system" causes far more injury to third parties such as the consumer and the supplier than it does to its participants. The system continues to require government controls because it cannot be accountable to the people it affects. What are its major contradictions?

First, many government agencies, such as the Labor Department and the National Labor Relations Board, have been created because this system of industrial organization is not self-governing. Extended strikes in major sectors of the economy, for example, still pose a threat to the nation. They can cause severe shortages of goods to many industries outside the strike area and ultimately adversely affect the consumers. Government agencies are required to protect the nation from the economic repercussions. But there are economic alternatives to this "adversary system" that show greater self-governance, as we shall see.

Second, union oligarchy continually requires federal intervention. Union oligarchy and labor dictatorships are opposed to public norms of decency in the labor movement. But oligarchy in labor is interdependent with the command system of the corporation itself. The corporation is based on a system of command authority that places it in a superior position strategically to the labor movement formally based on a system of democracy. It follows that labor must organize a "command system" to bargain effectively with corporations. Public opposition to a command system in unions leads to legislation and government controls. The National Labor Reporting and Disclosure Act, for example, requires that unions follow democratic norms. In the meantime, the corporation remains free to administer its operations without major disclosures and reporting and without the requirement of democratic practices. The "command system" is maintained even though viable democratic alternatives for the corporation exist.

Third, the labor-management system produces the wage-price spiral. Labor's annual effort to raise wages and management's annual response in higher prices is an economic trap of the industrial system. The private system is not self-governable in this respect. It cannot handle the problem of inflation without government intervention. Without accountability to the larger public interest, the labor-management system again produces more government agencies and controls. Federal wage-price controls are in some measure a predictable part of the future in the continued spiral of income and costs in the corporate system.

Studies of Economic Alternatives

Economic alternatives to the labor-management system can be seen clearly in experiments conducted in other nations. Western Europe especially shows signs of solving these problems within the private sector without necessarily incurring additional government agencies.

The first basic modification in labor relations in Western Europe was introduced in Germany following World War II. In the coal and steel industries of West Germany, a system of "codetermination" was introduced in which union and management organized to codetermine major policies of economic enterprise. The top supervisory boards in these industries had representatives from both labor and management. Here the major conflicts within the industry became resolved by vote. Labor and management came to have equal access to corporate information and equal responsibility for making policies.[6]

The professional studies of codetermination show findings that are complex, but in general they point toward the success of the experiment in finding a new approach for resolution of conflicts within the private sector. Codetermination points the way toward establishing *a strike-free pattern of industrial organization that eliminates the necessity for state intervention.* Strikes have been eliminated for all practical purposes in the coal and steel industries largely because the issues can be fought coequally and coresponsibly. Codetermination introduces equal dignity for labor and management along with new responsibilities for both groups in the system. It broadens the "rationality" of the corporation to include all employees, who in effect become "citizens" of the organization. It is a step toward the elimination of the labor-management distinction itself in a still more decentralized system.

The codetermination law has recently been extended to include West Germany's 650 biggest companies and about 50 subsidiaries of U. S. concerns. Employees and shareholders now have an equal number of seats on the supervisory boards of these companies. The chair of the supervisory board is given the key vote in deadlocks. The chair is elected by both shareholder and employee representatives and officially may be drawn from either side, with the vice-chair coming from the opposite faction. The law also states that employees must include one white collar employee with junior executive status in addition to blue collar and plant-level trade union representatives.

Other experimental methods of conflict resolution are evident in Denmark and Sweden, where tribunal systems have been organized privately with representatives from both management and labor organizations. These "private courts" are given the final authority to settle major disputes at the national level. In Denmark, for example, the Labor Court consists of seven members, three chosen by the Federation of Labor and three chosen by the Employers' Association. A seventh "chair" is chosen jointly by both national associations. A Contract Board is similarly organized privately to settle disputes over interpretations of the cost-of-living index.[7]

Some experimental steps in this direction have been taken in the United States. Employees and employers of the electrical contracting business, for example, created the Council on Industrial Relations, which has solved problems in the industry for nearly 50 years without ever having one of their decisions violated. Other national groups have settled disputes privately. The American Arbitration Association has worked effectively at the national level in place of state compulsory arbitration for many years. No national system of joint determination of policy or conflict resolution has ever come about in the United States, however, thus making government intervention highly probable in major crises.

A system of "worker determination" of policy in economic enterprises has developed in Yugoslavia, where the distinction between labor and management lessens or disappears and all employees formally gain an equal status in their joint venture. Worker Councils run the factories. Here a distinction is generally made between "state ownership" and "social ownership" of production. State ownership refers to the centralized government, which is controlled by the Communist Party, while social ownership refers to the Workers Councils, which exercise relatively independent economic control over factory policy. Councils maintain a large measure of self-governance in the social sector of the economy.[8]

Corporate Self-Studies

The concept of an economic alternative like codetermination or Worker Councils is of no value without a concept of how to bring it about. Efforts to coerce people into economic alternatives with new duties and responsibilities toward one another can often result in civil resistance and in ultimate failure of the experiment. The concept of economic alternatives is part of the process of jointly studying shared problems and determining the steps toward their solution. Professional studies of economic alternatives then become part of a self-study process.

In this case, corporate self-studies would include a review of the range of worker responsibilities in "experimental companies" along with the range of worker rights to decisions. The following compilation of types of worker rights, for example, would come under review in a corporate self-study involving labor and management, only with an assessment of the range of responsibilities.[9]

I   *Cooperation* (Workers generally influence decisions but are not responsible for decisions.)
  1. Workers have the right to receive information.
  2. Workers have the right to protest decisions.
  3. Workers have the right to make suggestions.
  4. Workers have the right to prior consultation.

II   *Codetermination* (Workers participate in decisions with responsibility.)
  1. Workers have the right of veto
    (a) Temporary, after which management

(1) may implement its decisions
(2) must negotiate with workers
  (b) Permanent and final authority
2. Workers have the right of co-decision with management

III *Common Management* (All employees have equal right in decision-making
     through elected representatives)

At the same time, the types of decisions over which workers may assume responsibility is also subject to self-study. This means a common assessment of worker "interests," "knowledgeability," and "skills" in handling specific areas of management. Josip Obradovic developed a typology of these areas on the basis of his study of Worker Council meetings:[10]

1. Economic problems relating to the market
2. Economic problems in cooperating with other companies
3. Internal economic activity issues (e.g., relations among enterprise subunits)
4. Questions of remuneration
5. Technico-productive activity (research and development, construction, inspection materials and processes)
6. Personnel problems (hiring, firing, qualifications, education)
7. Human relations at the group level (conflicts among categories of workers or social groups within the enterprise)
8. Human relations at the individual level (complaints, for example, regarding dismissals or job evaluations)
9. Questions of standard of living and social welfare (communal expenditures, recreation, vacation, remuneration, travel, apartments, child care, aid to the handicapped and to workers' families, company food)
10. Company organization (definition and scope of responsibility of the units in the enterprise system)
11. Work organization (time and motion studies, planning the work flow)
12. Sociopolitical themes (relation of the company to political organizations outside the enterprise or within it)
13. Legislative activity (questions relating to legal enactments affecting the enterprise)
14. Formal activity of self-management organs (nominations, questions of agenda)
15. Miscellaneous

Experiments in the United States have involved workers in many self-studies at "job levels" of responsibility. The studies have generally resulted in a pattern of increased participation and self-determination in the workplace. One of the first experiments along these lines was in the 1940s in a pajama factory. Researchers found that work teams who participated in studying and designing new jobs for themselves proved to have significantly higher rates of efficiency and morale than groups who were relocated by management through standard procedures. Such experiments in worker self-management have generally continued to show an increase in job satisfaction, efficiency, and productivity.[11] European experiments simply show that the scope of self-management for workers can be increased to include higher corporate responsibilities than those assumed in these American experiments. This step toward higher responsibilities for workers is at best preceded by corporate self-studies that indicate employee interest and readiness to assume them.

Jaroslav Vanek, a Cornell economist, has given five defining characteristics of an enterprise that has fully achieved a system of self-management.[12]

1. Participation of all employees in the enterprise on a one-person, one-vote basis.
2. All participants share in the income of the enterprise on an equitable basis.
3. Absence of ownership (i.e., no right to sell or disband the enterprise and distribute the proceeds).
4. Operation in economic order which does not permit state interference in the internal order of the enterprise.
5. Freedom of employment.

An enterprise is not necessarily fully self-governing, however, when it formally meets these criteria of self-management. It must also demonstrate that it can be economically viable in the larger system. For economic viability, employees must be capable of maintaining an effective and productive enterprise that offers satisfactory monetary returns. This economic aspect of the enterprise leads us to investigate other problem areas of the self-governing economy.

Problem II:
The System of Corporate Ownership—Income and Security

The system of ownership in large corporations has produced contradictions that the private economy seems unable to overcome without government help. Companies are owned officially by private shareholders whose votes are not counted in the way public government counts votes, one vote per person. Shareholders cast votes according to one vote per stock. The more stock a person can buy, the more votes. This voting system has contributed toward concentrations of wealth and power in large conglomerate corporations. Corporate concentration in turn leads to monopolistic activities that require government expanding regulatory agencies.

The system of concentrated stock ownership and corporate monopoly has led to "unfair labor practices," "unfair pricing," and "unfair competition." The worker, the consumer, and the small business person have been adversely affected by the system of corporate power. For protection, people must add government regulatory bureaus like the Antitrust Division, the Securities and Exchange Commission, and the Small Business Administration to correct the deficiencies. Lacking a system of justice in the economy, citizens create "departments of justice" in the state.

The system of "buying votes" with the purchase of stock has led to new forms of economic power through fiduciary institutions such as *pension funds, insurance companies,* and *mutual funds.* These institutions accumulate large financial reserves to purchase stock, giving them what Adolf Berle calls "power without property." Berle has suggested that the new powers of stock purchase will require new legislation to avoid the misuse of these funds.[13]

Studies have shown that the investments of pension funds have led to situations where workers own the industries in which they work. Peter Drucker claims that the large pension funds now have a controlling interest in every single strategic position of the economy, including the 1000 largest industrial corporations. This also includes the 50 largest companies of the nonindustrial groups: banking, insurance, retail, communications, and transport. He says that at least 25 percent of the equity capital of American business is in the hands of institutional investors buying stocks that then belong, in name, to the workers. The pension funds of school teachers, public employees, and the self-employed add another 10 percent. By 1985 the funds will have increased their holdings to at least 50 percent of the equity capital of American business. Adding the personal ownership of stock by American workers, this means that the orthodox definition of socialism will have officially arrived to define American industry. Workers will "own the means of production," although they will not have effective control over it under present institutions. Institutional investors retain control over the funds and are required to invest the money for fiduciary purposes.[14]

A few more facts are important to review here, since they show the need for the government to correct the problems developing in the system. First, pension funds are making available "welfare payments" to the elderly, who are becoming a significant percentage of the U. S. population. A relatively large dependent (unproductive) population is emerging side by side with a relatively small productive working force. The corporate system now supports one older person for every four of working age. In the future the number of elderly is expected to increase further while the working force approaches zero growth. Therefore, a large percentage of the profits ("surplus value") will be returning to workers as elderly citizens, but those workers will have no productive part in maintaining the economic system.

A related problem is the fact that the fiduciary institutions such as pension trusts have begun to freeze capital that would otherwise be utilized for new investments in the economy. The working capital of the corporate system is limited by the peculiar operation of the pension system. Drucker has calculated that 20 to 25 percent of pretax profits go into the company's own pension fund and another 30 percent of post-tax profits go to other companies' pension funds through payment of dividends to pension trust shareholders. In the meantime, the money is frozen in these institutions and kept out of badly needed areas of investment. Retained earnings of corporations are well below what is needed for replacement needs, to say nothing of additions to the stock of capital. Pensions now get as much of the company's gross profits as the tax collector.

In sum, the problem is that "ownership by wealth" leads toward monopoly and will continue to produce a need for government agencies unless alternatives are found within the system. At the same time, institutional investors have risen significantly in the ownership of stocks in ways that freeze the use of major capital. What alternatives may be found to lessen the likelihood of new government controls and help establish a firmer ground for the self-governance of the economy?

Studies of Economic Alternatives

The publication of *The Modern Corporation and Private Property* by Adolf Berle and Gardner Means in 1932 was the first significant effort to show that shareholders own only a negotiable piece of paper. The actual control of the large corporation had already passed effectively in the main to corporate managers. We now see that the "negotiable paper" is becoming a type of insurance program for many older workers. It provides economic returns to fiduciary trustees, who in effect redistribute the funds to "welfare recipients." The trustees thus become like social welfare administrators working in a system similar in function to the federal system of social security.

With this in mind, public studies could focus on how greater equity can be developed in the nation's insurance system, looking toward local and regional organizations as a means for developing uniformity in the dispensation of funds. No one knows how many people are covered by pension plans and how much is paid to retired persons through these plans. Public studies could then be directed to questions of how to free pension funds to operate in the public interest in conjunction with other pension funds and government programs of income security. New approaches to local and regional organizations as "public trusts" of these funds can then be made. In this way we can begin to deal realistically with the separation of ownership, as a means of income security, from management, as a means of controlling the enterprise.

Jaroslav Vanek has studied employee-owned enterprises and has offered a unique answer to a unique problem of pension funds. He has found that workers who come to control their own company by purchasing shares are sometimes without pension support if the enterprise has not inaugurated a pension plan. Plywood companies in the United States, for example, have become owned and controlled by workers, but some of them have not operated long enough to supply adequate pensions for workers. To obtain pension money, workers in some cases have sold their stock to outsiders. But in doing so they of course dilute the effectiveness of worker self-management. To compensate for this tendency, Vanek's solution is to establish local and regional "supporting organizations" that maintain control over the stocks while at the same time they develop pension funds for workers in each enterprise. These supporting organizations are in effect holding companies. They maintain stock ownership of the enterprise like a public trust. The holding company has no authority over the internal operations of each member firm; it simply holds and distributes the pension funds as the administering agency of a regional federation of worker-owned companies.

The fact that large private companies in the United States already contribute so much pretax and post-tax profits to pension funds really puts them all in the same ball game. A federated group of holding companies for pension funds in the sense that Vanek describes is feasible by regions and by industries. Some steps in the development of a new insurance system follow.

First, whole industries could begin coordinating funds in the same manner that teachers already do it through the Teachers Insurance Annuity Association (TIAA). Teachers today can change jobs in any part of the country and continue their pension fund—in contrast to workers in certain companies who lose their pension when they change jobs. The pension funds could be extended equitably to everyone in the same industry through regional associations. Second, the pension funds could be collected and distributed later between all "industries." All teachers and auto workers should be entitled to a relatively uniform pension plan operated by regional holding companies.

The problem of unfreezing large capital reserves in these pension funds remains. Nine million people today are unemployed for lack of investment in enterprises that would create jobs for them. In addition, one and a half million new jobs are needed every year for young people entering the job market. The problem is how to "free up" capital in supporting institutions to aid in making investments for both the jobless young and the elderly. Here imaginative studies would demonstrate how material and human resources could be developed in local communities. Pension "reserves," in other words, are one source of investment for new self-governing enterprises in localities.

The regional holding companies administering pensions could be given the authority to invest in new enterprises that demonstrate their ability to be self-governing. The holding companies may then begin to help treat any problems resulting from a large "unproductive working force" of both the elderly and unemployed young people. Old and young who want to work may apply to these holding companies for investment capital. New enterprises for the retired, for example, could involve them in management consulting services where their skills can be utilized. Young people, on the other hand, may want to begin new

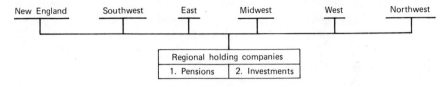

Figure 3.

recreation programs that show signs of profitability. New enterprises would need to meet standards for cooperative self-management. The stock in the new enterprises is issued in this case on a one person, one vote basis and held in trust by regional holding companies. The new companies are then offered opportunities to federate for the purposes of stimulating new investments and a uniform distribution of funds. In this way a program is built for people to help eliminate poverty and the debilitating effects of unemployment.

Problem III:
The System of Corporate Competition—Private and Public Interests

The problems of corporate price fixing, depletion of natural resources, marketing of injurious products, exploitation of labor, and many similar malpractices in the corporate system can be attributed in part at least to the "competitive environment." The competitive structure of business relations then leads toward government growth. The growth of the Federal Communications Commission and many other regulatory agencies are examples of what happens. These agencies are essential to protect the public from the excesses of business competition.

The intense competitive system in the nineteenth century led business itself to call on Congress for help. Business people lobbied for protection from themselves in the formation of early antitrust legislation.[15] The later Fair Trade Laws are similar creations of business people who sought protection from the competition of fellow businesses.

The criminal tendency stimulated by the competitive system of business was first studied by Edwin Sutherland, the Indiana criminologist. Sutherland studied 907 corporate cases involving commercial bribery, misrepresentation in advertising, misgrading of commodities, bribery of public officials, and many other criminal violations. He concluded that the evidence in the courts was only the tip of the iceberg of business criminality. Donald Taft, the Illinois criminologist, went further to state that "white collar crime had different causes than no-collar crime but both types are rooted in the competitive system of business organization."[16]

If intense competition results in violations of public norms and finally in more government agencies to control business, what are the alternatives? How can business be organized to govern itself socially in society?

Studies of Economic Alternatives

Proposals have been made to charter large corporations in the "public interest" as well as in their own self-interest to achieve a proper level of competition and partly to introduce a new measure of social accountability. Proposals call for federal chartering of big business with certain requirements that public standards of accountability be met.

Ralph Nader, Mark Green, and Joel Seligman have devised a method for federal chartering that recommends a full-time board of elected public directors, with a full-time staff available to monitor corporate performance. The "public board" would set the salary of the top executives, establish procedures to assure the law was followed, obtain a "community impact statement" when a plant is relocated, and approve or veto major management decisions. The board itself would be comprised of nine "constituency directors," each having the duty of acting both as a general director and specializing on behalf of a particular constituency affected by the firm. A separate director would be in charge of the following areas:

1. Employee welfare
2. Consumer protection
3. Purchasing and marketing
4. Environmental pollution and community relations
5. Shareholder rights
6. Profits and financial integrity
7. Management efficiency
8. Planning efficiency
9. Compliance with the law

Shareholders owning more than 0.1 percent of the stock could nominate three persons to serve as directors. All campaign costs for the election would be limited and assumed by the corporation. If three directors or people owning 3 percent of the voting shares were to find that a corporation facility were causing a public health hazard, the affected community could vote on a corporate referendum to decide what to do about the hazard.

Nader's proposal gives stock beneficiaries the right to vote their stock. This means that people and institutions who are represented by pension funds, mutual funds, and insurance companies would be given the option of voting. They could vote through representatives elected by them to regional boards. The beneficiaries, of course, include the major unions.

Federally chartered corporations would be required to disclose (1) each instance in which an applicable air pollution limitation was exceeded, the duration of pollution, the type of pollutant, and steps taken to prevent a recurrence; (2) each toxic substance present in each corporate workplace in any detectable quantity; (3) plant-by-plant minority hiring; (4) substantiation for advertising claims; (5) expenditures for legislative or executive lobbying. In the area of financial information, each federally chartered firm would regularly disclose its investment interest in all other companies, its annual tax return and major sales contracts with federal agencies, and the 100 largest shareholders in each class of stock.

Federally chartered corporations would be required to observe First Amendment requirements of free speech and assembly. They would not be permitted to retaliate against employees who in good faith communicate apparent corporate violations of law to directors or law enforcement agencies. These large companies would also be required to respect the privacy of their employees. They could not use hidden microphones or television cameras that violate worker privacy. Finally, employees would be able to examine their corporate personnel files in the manner now permitted by IBM.

These recommendations for accountability are consistent with the concept of the firm as a self-governing enterprise. The concept of federal charterment encourages only that degree of competition which is in the public interest. Toward this end, the Nader proposal recommends that no federally chartered corporation could acquire any firm among the eight largest in any industry where four or fewer firms control 50 percent of the market.

The Federal Chartering Act proposal would cover all industrial, retail, and transportation corporations that (1) sold over $250,000 in goods or services in the United States in any of the previous three years, (2) employed more than 10,000 persons, or (3) were listed on a national securities exchange with a record of 2000 or more American shareholders. Of the 1.8 million corporations in the United States, about 700 would be required by these criteria to obtain federal charters in addition to their state charters.

The Nader proposal suggests that the Securities Exchange Commission would enforce most of the Act's provisions, the FTC would handle disclosure sections, and the Antitrust Division would oversee the antimonopoly provisions.

While it is possible to strengthen existing government agencies to enforce the requirements for the federally chartered companies, it is also possible to conceive of social (nonstatist) systems of "enforcement" outside the government. The development of such systems then contributes to the social development of the economy as a self-regulating system. A system of social constitutions, tribunals, and review boards, for example, could enable the corporation to operate in the public interest without federal supervision. Let us look briefly at these concepts.

Corporate Constitutions. The corporation is the only major type of formal organization operating nationally without a constitution and by-laws guiding its conduct. A constitution of fundamental principles defining areas of authority and power for national organizations is common to churches, fraternal orders, women's clubs, welfare councils, YMCAs, and a host of other voluntary associations. A constitution requires that an association be socially accountable to its constituency according to democratic principles of organization.

A federal charter can outline the basic requirements for a large corporation to function in the public interest, but a private constitution outlines basic principles of self-management by which the corporation operates in its daily activities. Fully self-managed companies in the United States and overseas can develop constitutions as the basis for normal operations.

Bewley's Cafes Ltd. in Southern Ireland, for example, is a self-managed retail business that maintains five shops selling tea, coffee, confectionery, bread, and chocolates. It also maintains a bakery and a farm with a herd of Jersey cattle. There are about 420 people on the staff, and 50 retired members receive a pension. In 1972 it was decided that the private capital should be transferred in trust for everyone working in the firm. A constitution was written which states the principles under which the Company operated. In the following Article of the Constitution, for example, the employees express how they feel about the purposes of the company:

2. The organs of the Company shall have regard at all times to the fact that the basic purpose of the Company is to render the best possible service as a body corporate to the Community and to encourage thinking in terms of the welfare of the Community in which we live, rather than a desire for personal gain at the cost of others. Toward this end, capital should be used to serve the needs of human beings, not the reverse, and the operations of the Company will be directed to:

  (i) producing goods and services not only beneficial to the customers of the Company at fair prices and of as high a quality as possible, but also for the general good of mankind.
  (ii) Providing economic security for employees of the Company.
  (iii) developing the strength of the Company, its efficiency and organization and
  (iv) contributing toward the general welfare of society.[18]

A federal charter cannot "mandate" good will or a particular form of self-management. Only the employees of a private company can do this.

In Bewley's Cafes Ltd., it is deemed desirable that on all occasions members of the Company "endeavor to reach decisions without the need for a formal vote." Decisions are made reportedly on the basis of consensus arrived at "through debate and reconciliation of differences."

It is feasible to consider extending these principles of self-management to those large corporations where a high quality of leadership exists among its employees. This means broadening the scope of authority and responsibility of working people in the general management of economic enterprise. The successful operation of thousands of democratically run production, wholesale, and retail cooperatives in England and the United States demonstrate the viability of this concept of development. To implement this form of development, however, requires the involvement of employees in corporate self-studies.

The largest company in England operating on principles of democratic self-management is the John Lewis Partnership, with some 23,000 "working partners." The largest company in the United States is the American Cast Iron Pipe Co., with about 3000 employees. Experiments at this level of a working population can begin in the subsidiaries of large corporations.[19]

No large business corporations are known to have constitutions in the United States, but the efforts of small self-managed firms offer direction in the way they may be written. In Article 3(i) of Bewley's Cafes Ltd., for example, the principle of employee participation is noted without laying down in detail how it should be put into practice. In practice, a "council" of employees is in charge. The council consists of the head of every department, plus an elected representative from each department. The larger departments have two elected representatives. This gives a body of 45 people who meet monthly to discuss any matters relevant to the running of the business. But the original owner, Victor Bewley, states that the Articles do not explain in detail the nature of the operation because the Company wants to be free to experiment, "to try something and to scrap it if it is unsuitable, and to try something else instead." The writing of a constitution for a large corporation, therefore, requires a similar flexibility. Principles of organization can be formulated to guide the development of a democratic organization that is practical for each business situation.

A constitution generally provides for a discriminate hearing from all constituents of the organization and a method for acting on their behalf. Corporate constitutions then become the basis for making changes that are both far-reaching and "rational." A social constitution thus differs from state laws of incorporation because judgments of behavior are generally based more on "principle" than on "prescription." A constitution allows for greater flexibility in making alterations than is possible under certain restrictive and fixed forms of statutory and charter law.

Corporate Tribunals. Tribunal systems already exist to some extent in private corporations. The most well-known corporate tribunal is that within General Motors. It was organized in 1938 to protect local automobile dealers against unjust cancellations of contracts by middle management. The top executive officers of General Motors in this case serve on the corporate tribunal. They hear cases brought to them from dealers who feel that their contract or business interests have been violated by middle management. It has operated for over these decades with evidence of fairness in its decisions.[20]

The organization of the corporate court of GM with top management presiding, however, does not reflect modern principles of polity. It does not separate management as the "executive branch" from its "judicial branch." It does not permit peers to be members of the jury. Put another way, the judicial branch of GM's "corporate government" should at best include representatives of the National Dealers Association and perhaps customers themselves in the judicial hearing. The best type of corporate tribunal is one that is formed jointly by the parties who may offend one another. To know the proper judicial organization in a large corporation, therefore, requires corporate self-studies involving the people affected by corporate activities.

Public Review Boards. The Nader proposal for federal chartering provides funds for a staff of professional researchers who aid the elected public directors for each corporation. They review how well the corporation is doing in the corporate and public interest. Some key questions of organization remain, however, in the light of the proposal.

One question is whether the new directors and their staff can remain sufficiently independent of traditional management, who may seek "executive privileges" for themselves and unfair competitive advantages for the corporation over less powerful enterprises in the field. Another question is whether public directors who are not elected directly by the employees or by the customers of the corporation can fairly represent them without being directly accountable to them. Still another question is how a competitive industry or trade area as a whole can be monitored in the public interest without government controls.

These issues may be studied by nationwide review boards organized within specific industries or trade areas of the economy. The staff of Public Review Boards (PRB) would be funded jointly by business associations and trade unions in each trade area. Trade associations and unions in this case would be required by law to fund the work of the PRB, which would act independently in the public interest. The Board would keep an eye on the competition in the industry as a whole; it would also determine whether new methods of introducing accountability into the election of public directors becomes feasible over time.

The staff of a public review board could be drawn from nominees submitted by professional associations. Professional associations at the national level include accountants, lawyers, chemists, biologists, psychologists, sociologists, economists, engineers, and many other professionals associated with the issues of organization and technology in trade areas. The objectives of their associations are all very broadly conceived so that they fit perfectly into the requirements of publicly oriented research. The appropriate professional associations could be invited to select a set of nominees. A joint committee of representatives from unions and business associations would then select a staff from them to serve for a period of three years as board members. They would be given their own research assistants and full access to the records of the corporation and trade unions involved in that trade area. They would be given no legal power themselves as an agency, but they would have access to mass communications for reporting their findings and their recommendations.

Review boards could begin experimentally in specific trade areas to determine how best to select the research staff. The copper industry, for example, would require a board of independent environmentally minded chemists and biologists as well as professional people in the field of public administration. A government agency would be authorized to initiate the program but with the requirement that it disengage from the program once it becomes organized.

Problem IV:
The Corporation and the Consumer—Research and Representation

The production of "goods" in the United States has resulted in what some writers have called a consumption sickness. The sickness is evident in the consumer statistics on the staggering numbers of dangerously overweight citizens, alcoholics, drug addicts, therapeutic pill users, and cigarette smokers. When consumers cannot act back through private organizations, they exploit themselves with products supplied by corporations seeking primarily to make their own profit.

Many years ago the sociologist Robert Bierstedt noted that power is a function of social organization and not of the numbers of people. In this case the great number of consumers in the United States does not in itself give them much power. Consumers lack power because they are poorly organized. They select goods individually in the marketplace, but they are not organized to make decisions in the institutional economy in the way laborers and managers are organized.

Corporations *develop a product, assess its quality, judge its usefulness, determine its rate of production, decide on its areas of distribution, and plan massive advertising to increase its sales.* The consumer is not a part of this critical process.

When consumers feel they are ignored or exploited by the corporation, they must go to state and federal governments for protection. Today all fifty states and the federal government are involved in some minor form of consumer protection activity. This government activity can be expected to grow in the future partly on the basis of what Galbraith calls the "social imbalance."[21] As people compare the vast private expenditures of alcohol, drugs, and cigarettes with the relatively small expenditures on schools and hospitals, they become increasingly sensitive to the distortion of values. Given no alternatives in the private system, they go to the government for help. What are the alternatives?

Studies of Economic Alternatives

Public studies can explore at least two major social alternatives. First, the need is critical to offer opportunities in university settings to study consumer problems at the national level. This means organizing a profession arround "consumer studies" and constructing "consumer research stations." To do this, federal funds could be provided to private colleges and universities on a matching basis to organize departments dealing with the subject of consumership. A similar effort was made on behalf of unorganized farmers in the last century. Farmers were greatly aided in their organization through the Hatch Act and the Morrill Act. These acts provided the basis for building agricultural colleges to help farmers treat the problems they were facing. Agricultural research stations were constructed throughout the country to stimulate better farming. They were constructed even though many people thought there was no scientific base for doing so.

A curriculum for consumer colleges is easily developed from an integration of existing academic traditions including home economics, consumer economics, business administration, and consumer law. A job market can be created for students majoring in consumer studies by looking to consumer co-ops, federations, leagues, trade associations, Better Business Bureaus, departments of health and welfare, and corporations themselves creating consumer departments. New professional fields in consumer studies would likely be created. This follows the pattern of agricultural engineering and agronomy, which were developed with the creation of agricultural colleges.

The field of consumer studies should of course be distinguished from such fields as advertising and marketing.[22] Consumer studies deal with the whole network of consumer relations in society. Incorporating aspects of biochemistry, psychology, economics, as well as philosophy, consumer studies can distinguish more clearly between the types of goods that contribute to human development in society.

Second, private consumer cooperatives and consumer research groups can be encouraged at local levels in the private sector through tax incentives and low-interest loans. Consumer retail cooperatives already function effectively in some localities, with consumers controlling the boards of directors. Consumers decide on the kinds of products they want to buy locally. The effort to develop "consumer power" at the local level then leads us to examine the related problem of corporate subsidiaries.

Problem V:
The Corporation and the Locality—Local Councils and CDCs

The centralization of corporate power in metropolitan areas has led to a loss of economic self-governance in local communities. Whole communities have been both created and destroyed by decisions of metropolitan executives who decide to expand or terminate the operations of local plants. Executives can terminate major plant operations without consultation with local authorities. They can seriously weaken or even destroy whole communities without local consent.

Decisions by absentee managers to relocate plants or cut back employment in localities have cost the taxpayers billions of dollars in welfare, manpower, and public assistance programs. Executives in New York who lay off workers in Carbondale, Illinois have no official responsibility to pay for the consequences of local unemployment. They have freedom to act in their own interest without responsibility for the well-being of the community. The government then assumes the responsibility by paying welfare and public aid.

As a rule, the business corporation lays off workers in order to save money or make money. This happens every day through plant relocations and automation. When Studebaker decided to move all its auto-making facilities from South Bend, Indiana to Canada, it left behind some 6000 workers. In Washington, D.C., as a consequence, the President was forced to order the Departments of Agriculture, Commerce, Labor, and Defense to do something about the shattering effects on South Bend. Surplus foods and new industry were moved into the community. Eight months later, 1700 workers were still unemployed. One year later, of 3900 older workers who had passed through Project ABLE (Ability, Based on Long Experience), 900 were still on welfare looking for work.

The corporation stays in the black or "profits" while the community loses and all taxpayers pay for it. From 1956 to 1963, 38,000 jobs were lost in the meat-packing industry. Meanwhile, output per person-hour increased by 53 percent and production labor costs for the companies declined from 3.27 cents per pound to 2.94 cents, or 11 percent. Armour, Swift, and Cudahy closed their larger plants in the big cities and built smaller, specialized meat factories in smaller cities. The new machinery cut jobs from 200,000 in 1955 to under 160,000 in 1962. The government assumed responsibility for many of the consequences.

What are the alternatives to government-sponsored welfare, manpower training programs, and county public aid?

Studies of Economic Alternatives

First, welfare systems begin to be eliminated through the creation of community development corporations (CDCs) and local planning councils in all major poverty areas of the nation.

The CDC is a local community-oriented business based on cooperative self-management.[23] It is organized with some degree of worker or citizen participation in the enterprise, which guarantees its accountability to the locality. It can design economic enterprises suited to the needs of welfare recipients. The CDC can create: day care centers operated by welfare recipients for mothers with dependent children; contracts for home telephone services operated by the bed-ridden; professional services offered by elderly doctors, lawyers, dentists, business people, and others receiving Aid to the Aged; crafts shops organized by the handicapped, etc. Welfare money is then directed into productive use for individual fulfillment and community development. Such special "enterprises" have been highly profitable in the past, but any economic returns are an improvement over the unproductive welfare system.

At the same time, local planning councils can be organized to make the connection between CDCs and the diversion of welfare money into developmental channels.[24] Local planning principles can be formulated to create the right constructive activity for everyone in the community. Such principles might include:

1. Every person needing an income will be guaranteed a job.
2. A local effort will be made to find the right job or "activity" for each person in need of an income.
3. All people should have an opportunity for creative work.
4. Any person needing an income who refuses to work will have the right to local counseling services to determine how they may best contribute to community development and their own needs at the same time.

At the national level, legislation may be passed requiring that any profitable corporation that lays off workers must contribute financially to the retraining of those workers through local councils. Since some corporations have already established a procedure of retraining for discharged employees, the requirement would not apply to these instances. The packing-house industry, for example, retrains workers who are fired because of automation. Following a labor dispute over the layoffs due to automation, the corporations of Armour, Swift, and Cudahy agreed to retrain discharged employees.

According to the Nader proposal, a federally chartered corporation would be required to submit a "community impact statement" on any major change it makes in its local operations. A significant number of layoffs could therefore precipitate a local referendum. The basic principle underlying this plan is that no big corporation should be permitted to exert a high negative impact on a locality without correcting the problems it creates.

The welfare system continues to drain government money from productive opportunities for people to work creatively. It offers instead a stigma to people on welfare and contributes to the stagnation of economic life in localities. The alternative is to offer opportunities for community development. A nationally based system of CDCs and local planning councils in major poverty areas could provide the initiative for eliminating welfare and for building new grounds for a social economy.

Problem VI:
The Farm System—Land Trusts and Self-Sufficiency

In the field of agriculture, social economists are concerned with the way people organize to maintain proper nourishment and to develop self-sufficiency in the production of food in the regions of the nation.

The farm system in the United States has faced problems of "self-governance." It has been riddled with contradictions, which have caused an enormous growth of state and federal agencies to help manage the system. The government has assumed major controls over production through soil bank programs, loans, price supports, and food storage. The farm system in every region has become deeply involved in government supervision and control. There are 4 million farms in the United States; federal expenditures to maintain the system are in the billions of dollars. Federal government costs alone amounted close to $6 billion in 1969 and over $5 billion in 1972.[24] Recent administrations have sought to cut back on expenditures for farm income stabilization. In 1973 Congress approved legislation that permitted large reductions in subsidies while pressures continued to restore old "support programs." The 1975 Congress passed the Emergency Agricultural Act, which would have added $1.4 billion in wheat subsidies, $4.6 billion for feed grains, $1.1 billion for cotton, and millions for soybeans, dairy products, and tobacco.

Two reasons stand out for the high cost of government programs. First, members of Congress themselves receive federal payments through their own farm businesses, and this may cause them to maintain the subsidies. Senator Henry Bellmon, for example, was a key figure in the effort to reinstate federal payments. His family's wheat and feed-grain farm received more than $10,000 yearly during the last two decades until the subsidy program was abolished. Senator James Eastland's family farm received cotton price-support payments of $162,000 to $204,000 in the early 1970s. Second, the farm system itself is not organized to meet directly the food needs of the nation. Farm businesses operate in their own self-interest to increase profits, and the result has been unbalanced levels of production from year to year. Without overall planning for production to meet the needs of the nation, farmers overproduce and underproduce and thus cause instabilities in prices. To avoid shortages and maintain some stability in the system, government soil bank programs (paying farmers to refrain from production) and price supports (paying farmers for prices they cannot get on the market), are government alternatives. What social alternatives are possible?

Studies of Economic Alternatives

The basic problem in farm organization is how to plan for production in the interests of the nation without incurring major government controls. The organization of industrial production contrasts with farm production on this point. Private automobile companies can study "consumer needs" and "consumer buying power" and thus plan for the production of cars in light of their knowledge of the market. They are organized at the national level to do so. The government does not have to pay General Motors to stop producing too many cars. Nor does the government have to provide automobile companies with price supports. The companies plan production and administer pricing in the private sector. The challenge this presents to the farm system is in whether similar nationwide planning can take place on a decentralized basis of organization.

Public studies of the farm system can today be directed toward new methods of farm organization and planning. First, studies can be directed toward the development of a land trust system whereby farms and ranches that are involved in essential food production can be brought gradually into social (nonstatist) trusteeship. *Trusteeship* in this case means simply that the land is maintained outside state control; it cannot be sold on the market for profit and must be used in the public interest. Second, studies can be directed toward the development of a system of farm cooperatives in which farmers manage the system by themselves. Let us examine the meaning of these two principles in detail.

Land Trusts (Nonspeculation and Self-sufficiency). The land trust is a quasi-public body chartered to hold land in stewardship in the public interest while protecting the legitimate use rights of its residents. The land cannot be sold for private profit but it can be used for private advantage. The concept of a land trust is concerned not so much with common ownership as with ownership for the common good.[26]

The land trust can be seen in principle in the land reform programs of the Mexican *ejido* and the Indian *Gramdan* movement. In these cases the farm land surrounding local communities is held in trust by the village council while residents lease it for public use. The same basic principle exists in the organization of the Jewish National Fund. The Fund is a nongovernmental group of Trustees who hold title to Israeli land in the national interest. Land is leased to citizens who use it in the public interest.

A distinction is generally made in this type of organization between land ownership and land control. Land lessees (users) can determine how they use the land as long as they do not violate the public norms set by the Trustees. Land users may specialize within a range of public interest.

Land trusts already exist in the United States but not on a national scale. With this in mind, let us look at the way regional land trusts could be organized in the United States.

Agriculture departments in the fifty states may develop a tax incentive program to transfer land gradually into regional trusteeships organized first within each state and then by regions between states.[27] One method of organization is to permit the users of the land to vote for representatives on regional boards that hold the land in trust and lease it for general use. Regional boards would also be composed of appointees from state agriculture departments. These appointees then help anticipate food needs and profitable markets.

The first aim of the regional board is to keep the land from being sold for mere speculation or profit. The second aim is to assess the food needs of people in the region through agricultural statistics and determine where new lands could be placed productively into use to meet these needs. Still other aims then follow:

1. To respect the economic interests of lessees in their choice of land use.
2. To encourage production that helps meet the needs of the regions where climate and soil prevent self-sufficient food production.
3. To optimize the self-sufficiency of farm land in meeting the food needs in the Board's own region.

These purposes are stated formally in the charter of the regional land trusts. The proper balance of these aims is up to the voting members of the trust.

Regional boards must maintain a just balance of control between lessee (user) representatives. In some places, nongovernmental public interest representatives are added. Public interest representatives can be selected through joint agreements between lessee representatives and state agricultural appointees on the boards.

Let us say, for example, that the New England Regional Land Trust Board has five farm-lessee representatives, five state appointees, and five public interest appointees. Public interest appointees include professional agronomists, nutritionists, and soil experts. The purpose of the New England Trust then would be to set the public norms for land use and thus to guide farm development toward self-sufficiency in the region.

In the last twenty years, New England's decline in farmland has amounted to over 60 million acres.[28] According to Governor Salmon's Food Commission Report of January 1976, Vermont is almost totally dependent on external sources for food as well as for the feed grains, fertilizers, and petroleum that are essential to agriculture in that state. In light of this fact, a regional Land Trust of Vermont would seek to rectify the insufficiency following the norms of its charter. If it could not do it alone, it would then turn to the New England Land Trust, whose purpose is to guide the development of farmland toward greater self-sufficiency in the New England region.

Production and Retail Cooperatives (Prices and Income). The organization of agriculture in each region is then based upon principles of optimizing regional self-sufficiency and self-management. The aim is to increase the capacity of each region to raise the food needed for sustenance and at the same time to organize food production in a manner that broadens the authority of farmers to manage their own affairs without state interference. The process of accomplishing these ends involves a series of tax incentives and other public initiatives, including conferences between farm organizations and state agricultural departments. It also involves community self-studies that encourage farmers to offer their own solutions. In all of this, the cooperative movement among farmers is a most important and logical base for organizational development.

The relation between farm-producer cooperatives and marketing, wholesale, processing, and retail cooperatives becomes of central interest to public studies of this process of development. This is because a balance must be struck between the income needs of people working at each stage of the production and distribution of food and the prices finally charged to the consumer.

Resolving this tension between income and price involves organizing at the endpoints of both production and consumption. This means that the emphasis that is given through public initiatives to strengthen the democratic self-sufficiency and self-management of farming requires an equal emphasis on the development of retail food cooperatives. Here consumers develop some power to decide on pricing and the selection of food for their communities.* In this case, retail co-ops and farm co-ops may jointly organize wholesale cooperatives where these problems can be resolved. At this juncture of the wholesale cooperative, joint management is possible. Here agreements on food supplies and prices can be made through negotiation without resorting to government subsidies for storage, price supports, and "soil bank" programs.

Professional studies and public initiatives through conferences and tax incentive programs then together lead toward a balance in the organization for production and consumption. With the development of a network of producer and consumer organizations, the farm system takes major steps toward self-government.

AN OVERALL PERSPECTIVE

A philosophy of social development is implicit in these economic alternatives. It is based on a concept of self-governance that suggests that the proper course of development is to increase human resources as well as material resources within the smallest circle of people working in the economy. The purpose of a self-governing economy is to stimulate the self-generating resources of organized industry. The purpose of organized industry in turn is to increase the autonomy and resources of economic enterprises operating within it. The purpose of the

---

*A model program in this respect is the British retail cooperative system; see Chapter 5.

economic enterprise is to increase the resources and self-directing powers of all workers within it. The purpose of the larger community in this framework is to enhance the autonomy and the resources of the individual within it. This means organizing economic life in a manner that finally releases human imagination, deepens human sensitivity, and increases the skills of working people.

The solutions to national problems generated by the corporate economy lay partly in the development of regional organizations whose purpose is to enhance economic life at the local level. We noted the possibility of economic alternatives in regional boards holding the corporate shares of institutional investors voting for public directors. These same boards could be given the responsibility for investing in community enterprises that engage the unemployed in constructive work. They could also be the basis for creating a more uniform system of income security in local communities. Finally, regional boards for rural land trusts could be organized to stimulate self-sufficiency in food production. It may be added that regional urban land trusts can also be organized for the development of metropolitan land in the public interest. The regional urban land trust can be the basis for the decentralized economic development of cities.

These various economic alternatives are submitted here only as ideas for more detailed professional studies that may lead to the social development of the institutional economy. Each alternative requires careful study for its application to corporate economy in the United States. Changing the structure of the corporate economy is complicated within the philosophy of development outlined here. It requires emphasis on self-studies and on self-help programs at every level of economic organization.

Let us now look in more detail at one economic alternative for changing the structure of the large corporation. We want to examine the background and the rationale for chartering the large corporation at the federal level. We also want to see how corporations can decentralize their administration and thus develop local resources through the authority of federal charters.

NOTES

1. T. R. Batten, *Communities and their Development* (N. J.: Oxford Univ. Press, 1957; S. T. Bruyn, *Communities in Action* (New Haven: College and University Press, 1962); Phillips Ruopp, (ed), *Approaches to Community Development* (The Hague: W. Van Hoeve, 1953) Roland Warren, *Studying Your Community* (New York: Russell Sage Foundation, 1955).

2. K. W. Kapp, *The Social Costs of Private Enterprise* (New York: Schocken Books [1950], 1971); E. J. Mishau, *The Cost of Economic Growth* (London: Staples, 1967).

3. L. E. Preston and J. E. Post, *Private Management and Public Policy* (Englewood Cliffs, N. J.: Prentice-Hall, 1975).

4. The concept of "economy" is like "community" in the sense that neither is a formal association which sets goals, even though each has goal setting associations. Cf. Roland Warren, *The Community in America* (Chicago: Rand McNally, 1963).

5. These figures were calculated by Joseph Turiano, staff researcher, Department of Sociology, Boston College. While it is true that much federal outlay goes to private corporations, the point is that the source of growth and control is the government. Cf. William Baldwin, *The Structure of the Defense Market* (New York: Macmillan, 1968). Another index of government growth is the relative increase in the number of government employees over the years. The number of Federal employees has remained relatively constant since 1947 at about 14 per thousand population. But the number of state and local government employees has expanded greatly. In 1947, the percent of total government employees represented by state and local employees was 64 percent, while in 1977 it is projected as 82 percent. *Special Analysis of the U. S. Government Fiscal Year, 1977*, U. S. Govt. Printing Office, 1976. Similar types of government growth can be seen in other countries. In England, the proportion of government expenditures of the GNP was 31 percent in 1938. It rose steadily to 43 percent in 1970. See Michael Brown, "The Controllers of British Industry," in Ken Coates (ed), *Can the Workers Run Industry?* (Nottingham, England: The Bertrand Russell Peace Foundation, 1968), p. 40. If we combine government spending at federal, state, and local levels, we find expenditures on education, welfare, resource development, etc., growing more rapidly than defense expenditures.

6. W. Michael Blumenthal, *Co-determination in the German Steel Industry* (Princeton, Industrial Relations Section, Department of Economics and Sociology, Princeton University, 1956); Abraham Schuchman, *Co-determination: Labor's Middle Way in Germany* (Washington, D. C.: Public Affairs Press, 1957).

7. Cf. Walter Galenson, *Trade Union Democracy in Western Europe* (Berkeley: Univ. California Press, 1961), p. 231; T. L. Johnston, *Collective Bargaining in Sweden* (Cambridge: Harvard Univ. Press, 1962), p. 154ff.

8. The empirical work on "degrees of participation," worker attitudes, differential wage scale, etc., is becoming quite extensive. Cf. *First International Sociological Conference on Participation and Self-Management*, Vols. 1–6, (Zagreb: Institute for Social Research, 1973).

9. Adapted from Paul Blumberg, *Industrial Democracy: The Sociology of Participation* (New York: Schocken, 1969 [1968]), p. 71.

10. Josip Obradovic, "Distribution of Participation in the Process of Decision-Making," in *First International Sociological Conference on Participation and Self-Management* (Zagreb: Institute for Social Research, 1973), Vol. 2, pp. 137–162.

11. N. Babchuk and W. J. Goode, "Work Incentives in a Self-Determined Group," *American Sociological Review* 16, 1951; L. Coch and J. R. P. French, "Overcoming Resistance to Change," In Cartwright and Zander, *Group Dynamics* (Evanston, Ill.: Row, Peterson, 1953); L. C. Lawrence and P. C. Smith, Group Decision and Employee Participation," *Journal of Applied Psychology,* 39 (1955); Frederick Lesieur, *The Scanlon Plan* (Cambridge: MIT Press, 1958).

12. Jaroslav Vanek, *The Participatory Economy* (Ithaca, N. Y.: Cornell Univ. Press, 1971), pp. 8–12.

13. Adolf Berle, *Power Without Property* (New York: Harcourt Brace Jovanovich, 1959).

14. Peter Drucker, "Pension Fund 'Socialism'," in *The Public Interest,* No. 42, Winter, 1976.

15. Gabriel Kolko, *The Triumph of Conservatism* (Glencoe Ill.: The Free Press, 1963).

16. E. H. Sutherland, *White Collar Crime* (New York: Dryden, 1949); D. Taft, *Criminology* (New York: Macmillan, 1956).

17. Ralph Nader, Mark Green, and Joel Seligman, *Taming the Giant Corporation* (New York: W. W. Norton & Co., 1976).

18. From a company document obtained in personal communication with Victor Bewley (Oct. 24, 1975).

19. In France, 522 democratically run productive companies belong to the General Confederation of Workers Productive Societies. The largest firm manufactures telephone equipment and employs nearly 3000 people. Cf. Roger Hadley, *Workers' Self-Management in France* (I. C. O. M., 8 Sussex St., London, Pamphlet No. 3, 1973).

20. This type of court system incidentally offers top management an opportunity to keep an eye on the effectiveness of work of middle managers who are in touch with dealers. Peter Drucker, *The Concept of the Corporation* (New York: John May, 1940). Cf. William G. Scott, *The Management of Conflict* (Homewood, Ill.: Irwin, 1965); H. Vollmer, *Employee Rights and the Employee Relationship* (Berkeley: Univ. of California Press, 1960).

21. John Kenneth Galbraith, *The New Industrial State* (Boston: Houghton Mifflin, 1967).

22. Consumer services have been organized through university services on a small scale. The Survey Research Center of the University of Michigan, for example, was organized in 1946. Contract research with business and government agencies has been restricted to problems of public interest, and the results of all studies are published so that they are not designed to serve the competitive advantage of the sponsor. Cf. George Katona, *The Powerful Consumer* (New York: McGraw-Hill, 1960).

23. An evaluation study of CDCs has been conducted by Abt Associates for OEO. *An Evaluation of the Special Impact Program,* Vols. I–IV (Boston: Abt Associates, Dec. 1973). Cf. Jose A. Rivera, *Community Control of Economic Development* (Ph.D. dissertation, Brandeis Univ. 1972).

24. A similar concept is found in the Full Employment and Balanced Growth Act of 1976, also known as the Hawkins-Humphrey Bill; H.R. 50 and S. 50.

25. *The United States Budget in Brief, Fiscal Year 1977,* Executive Office of the President of the United States, p. 30.

26. Robert Swann et al., *The Community Land Trust* (Cambridge, Mass.: Center for Community Economic Development, 1972).

27. State agriculture departments have begun to take some steps in this direction because of the great loss of farmland to more "intensive developments." From 1954 to 1974, the amount of land devoted to farming in the United States decreased by 119 million acres, an area nearly three times the size of New England. See John McClaughry, "A Model State Land Trust Act," *Harvard Journal on Legislation,* 12 (1975): 563.

28. *U. S. Bureau of Census, Statistical Abstract of the United States,* 597 (95th ed., 1974).

FOUR

DECENTRALIZING THE LARGE CORPORATION:

A Proposal for Federal Chartering

A new concept of the business corporation as a social entity is developing with all the paradox and irony of a major national drama. It is developing out of a new consciousness of the public problems created by large corporations. National concern over corporate concentration, monopolistic practices, product safety, deception in advertising, corporate secrecy, white collar crime, environmental pollution, unemployment, welfare costs, and a host of other problems has led to a realization that the causes of these problems are to be found in the organization of the corporate system itself. Whether the large corporations with national and international operations should be chartered at the federal level has become a matter of serious debate.

The debate focuses on the question of how corporations should be chartered so that they do not create such public problems.[1] The business corporation is not chartered to be accountable to employees, customers, small businesses, localities, and the environment. It has not been designed to resolve the problems it creates. Increasingly, therefore, state and federal governments have been forced to assume the responsibility for resolving these problems. Hence, we witness the continued growth of government welfare programs, environmental protection agencies, conservation bureaus, regulatory commissions, agriculture and labor departments, consumer protection agencies, and so on. Governments have grown so large in the attempt to make corporations accountable and at the same time to solve the public problems they create that many people see the need to build this "regulatory system" into the private structure of the corporation itself. Federal chartering can be conceived as a method of building a private system of corporate responsibility and accountability.

The basic argument is that chartering large corporations at the federal level is a way of making business enterprises more responsive to social needs, more publicly accountable, and more decentralized in their operations. The corollary to this basic argument is that chartering encourages change to occur in the big corporation in ways that reduce the need for government controls.

With federal chartering the large corporation would be reconstituted within the private economy to function in the public interest as well as in its own private interest. Chartering would bring about a shift toward public accountability for the major economic enterprise without involving state management. Chartering would cause a significant change toward a social orientation in the life and behavior of the big corporation. And the size of the change implies a need for studies of how it affects smaller enterprises as well as how it alters business law at the national level.

We will look first at the history of federal charters in the United States and indicate how constitutional principles have been gradually introduced into the corporation through court actions. We then look at the efforts of both management and labor to decentralize authority in the corporation and how charters contribute toward this end in the interest of both parties. We then examine charter guidelines following the principle of decentralization and indicate the kind of consultation that allows chartering to run smoothly at the national level. Finally, we look at the overall picture and the need for periodic change in the corporate structure that is not brought about through government controls or supervision.

Federal chartering of the type described here encourages a search for new kinds of effective self-management in business. It encourages business executives and union leaders to experiment with corporate administration that offers new measures of social accountability. It helps overcome "public problems," because it authorizes a planning perspective within the private economic order; it calls for collaborative efforts among business people to introduce a social economy at all levels of organized life in American society.

CHARTERING, CONSTITUTIONALIZING, AND DECENTRALIZING THE CORPORATION

The idea of chartering corporations at the federal level was proposed originally by James Madison during the Constitutional Convention in 1787. Four years later, Jefferson and Hamilton were debating whether to incorporate a U. S. Bank. Hamilton lost the argument to Jefferson, who wanted to keep economic life decentralized. Jefferson's cause, however, was lost in the latter part of the nineteenth century when states effectively came to permit the consolidation of corporations at the national level. In 1866 New Jersey became the first state to allow corporations to hold property outside its territory, removing the ceiling on corporation capital from its state charter in 1875 and allowing corporations to hold and dispose of the stock of other corporations during the 1880s. I noted in the first chapter how subsequently the big corporations flocked to incorporate in New Jersey and other states were forced to adjust their laws to follow suit in the competition for corporate charters. The competition for charters permitted corporations to operate with considerable power at the national level.

This situation has led to repeated campaigns for federal chartering or licensing. William Jennings Bryan wanted a federal license for all corporations conducting interstate business. Presidents Theodore Roosevelt, William Taft, Woodrow Wilson, and Franklin Roosevelt all voiced support for a scheme of federal licensing or incorporation. However, campaigns for federal chartering or its equivalent were deferred repeatedly by major legislative compromises in Congress. Such compromises include the Sherman Antitrust Act in the 1890s, the independent regulatory agencies in the early 1900s, and the security laws in the 1930s.[2] Although compromises deferred large-scale chartering, they did not defer the process of preparing the corporation to function accountably in the context of society. By helping to shape the structure of the large corporation, they initiated a process that may be described, in part, as "constitutionalizing" the corporation.

Constitutionalizing the corporation in the broad sense refers simply to the introduction of constitutional principles of government into the private operations of business enterprise. This has been happening through federal laws, bureaus, and regulatory commissions, which have been forcing the corporation to become more accountable to its constituencies and to the public by introducing constitutional principles into the structure of business. An article in *Business Week* noted this process in which the First and 14th Amendments have been shaping corporate life. The article pointed to the Supreme Court rulings that "Gulf Shipbuilding Corp. could not ban distribution of Jehova's Witness literature in the streets of the company-owned town of Chickasaw, Ala., that a restaurant in a building owned by the Wilmington (Del.) Parking Authority could not refuse to serve blacks, and that Washington (D.C.) mass transit, when it was owned by financier Louis Wolfson, was obligated to protect passengers privacy."[3] *Business Week* noted further how a senior federal judge found Avco Corporation liable for damages for firing a worker at its Stratford Connecticut defense plant who had criticized the company in a newsletter. Although the criticism was in violation of an Avco rule against "vicious or malicious statements which affect the employee's relationship to his job," the federal judge found that Avco was not really a private employer since 80 percent of its work is for the military. He therefore called the company's actions a violation of the First Amendment of free speech. As a result, the right of free speech is now a constitutional principle contestable in large corporations that are significantly involved in defense contracts.

The introduction of constitutional principles into corporate organization changes the traditional model of command management. The process adds democratic values within the corporate system and implies a trend toward a decentralized system of organization based upon the federal model. It suggests a policy of decentralizing the responsibility of people within the corporate domain. A policy of decentralization then means increasing the opportunity for employees at the bottom and the middle of the corporate hierarchy— including people working in small localities who are affected by corporate decisions made by executives in metropolitan offices—to assume more responsibility over affairs that directly affect their lives.

The principle of decentralizing authority is the essence of what Thomas Jefferson was seeking in his fight to restrict corporate power to the jurisdiction of localities and states. Envisioning this kind of democracy, he emphasized the idea of people participating responsibly at the level of the ward. The problem today, however, is that the command model of nationwide corporations lends itself easily to the formation of the totalitarian state. In light of the complicity of large corporations in the rise of Nazi and Fascist governments in Europe, decentralization provides a major means of resisting such movements. Increasing the opportunity for people to participate with greater authority at lower levels of corporate organization decreases the prospects for the authoritarian state, and we move closer to a government "of, by and for the people." At the same time, leaders are more able to initiate ideas for planning and self-direction at the national level when a greater degree of responsibility and initiative exists at state and local levels. Nationwide planning can be coordinated without fear of dominance from the federal government when there is a greater degree of self-direction and more constitutional rights at local and state levels of economic organization.

The idea of social planning is based on the premise that decentralization of authority and responsibility in the political economy can continue in a direction that has already been initiated in both the United States and Europe. Corporate executives in this century have been seeking to decentralize corporate operations from the top down, while at the same time workers have been seeking to gain authority from the bottom up. This dual process of decentralization from the top and the bottom of the corporate hierarchy is important to review here to give proper background to the idea of federal charterment for business enterprise.

THE HISTORY OF CORPORATE DECENTRALIZATION

In the United States

The first signs of a federal structure appeared among independent corporations during the economic depression of the 1870s. As a consequence of rising production and falling prices, manufacturers wanted to control competition by setting prices and production schedules. Small producers of leather, salt, sugar, and other products joined in horizontal federations to protect their own interests. Since mergers were prohibited because the states did not permit corporations to own stock in other corporations, a federation offered a practical way of organizing in the interest of each separate corporation.

After the 1890s, however, the former "federation" of manufacturers became an "administrative consolidation" through the method of the holding company and trust. Instead of decisions beginning from within the former autonomous enterprises, central offices began to make the decisions on how to produce (or market) products and how to allocate resources for the future. The new consolidation then led to centralization of the corporation and vertical integration. National Biscuit, for example, transformed itself in this period from a "combination-federation" to a consolidated firm and then to an integrated, multidepartmental enterprise. The same development occurred with Swift, Singer Sewing Machine, General Electric, and other major corporations developing at the turn of the century. New lines of authority developed as well. The Pennsylvania Railroad was the first business to work out the line-and-staff concept of departmental organization. Territorial expansion and product diversification brought forth the multidivisional form of organization in the twentieth century.

From the Top Down by Management

Alfred Chandler, corporate historian, describes how Du Pont, General Motors, Jersey Standard, and Sears, Roebuck devised a new type of decentralized organization beginning in the 1920s.[4] He begins by describing the process within Du Pont "in transforming the highly centralized, functionally departmentalized structure into a 'decentralized,' multidivisional one." Chandler observes a similar process taking place within General Motors. In 1918, Chevrolet, United Motors, and General Motors of Canada were brought into General Motors to become operating divisions. The new organization remained "a loosely knit federation" until Alfred Sloan took over the company. Under Sloan, further centralization took place through an executive committee responsible for setting long-range policies for the divisions. Then decentralization was instituted strategically so that "autonomous divisions were given responsibility for making and selling automobiles with 'decentralized administrative control'." This system of decentralized authority was seen to work more effectively and had an influence on the reorganization of other major corporations. It continues to operate today at General Motors even as many business and Congressional leaders have spoken of a further need to decentralize ("deconcentrate") corporate operations within the industry.

Administrative changes in Standard Oil and Sears, Roebuck followed along the same lines socially engineered at General Motors. Autonomous, self-contained operating divisions became organized on a territorial basis. Sears, Roebuck was last to begin its reorganization. In the 1930s, when the new company president, Robert E. Wood, first decided to turn store management over to individual managers, his plan was opposed by top executives. "For efficiency," one executive said, these stores "must be organized in groups with centralized administrative management and a few low-priced men in charge of each individual store." Nevertheless, under Wood's direction, the territorial units eventually became "full-fledged multidepartmental divisions" and thus decentralized. The territorial officers were given complete charge of operations in their area.

The decentralizing model reverberated through many industries, receiving wide acclaim as an administrative success.

Recent efforts of management to decentralize authority have involved reorganizing small factories with the full participation of workers. The General Foods plant in Topeka, Kansas, has undergone a total reorganization based on principles of self-management. In this case, management has taken major steps to eliminate administrative hierarchy by having teams of workers circulate throughout the continuous flow process with complete authority over their work schedules.[5] Other plants have been redesigned with even more far-reaching objectives. The Proctor & Gamble program at a plant in Lima, Ohio, was designed by management to bring "industrial democracy" into organizational development. William McWhinney, a UCLA psychologist who has worked as a consultant with P&G, notes that workers take on more activities outside the workplace. Blue collar workers have been winning elections to the school board. Nearly 10 percent of the work force at one plant hold elective offices; and more workers are joining political organizations and social clubs.[6]

The movement to decentralize authority from the top down by management has not stopped since it began in the 1920s.[7] Other strategies have been in the making including total employee ownership and control over the company.[8]

The American Cast Iron Pipe Company (ACIPCO) was founded in 1905 and given over to its workers by its owner in 1922. A producer of valves, tubes, large-scale pipe and pipe fittings, and industrial coke, ACIPCO also manages industries involving glassware, food processing, nuclear energy, and aeronautics. Every year the employees of ACIPCO elect six of their number as new representatives to a Board of Operatives (work council) on which sit six employee representatives elected the previous year. In its nearly 50 years of worker-ownership and self-management, ACIPCO has grown from a few hundred to almost 3,000 employees and is recognized for creating major advances in iron and steel pipe manufacture.

International Group Plans (IGP), of Washington, D. C. is another type of business enterprise turned over to the workers by its owner. IGP, an insurance firm that employs 325 people who own 50 percent of the stock and elect half of the directors, is completely self-managed. The Company's clients will soon be offered the other 50 percent of the stock; they will then organize to elect the rest of the board. The company has grown rapidly since this present organizational scheme was launched about six years ago. This plan originated with the owner, Jim Gibbons, who is now president of the board.

Such cases suggest that chartering to decentralize authority from the top down is possible even though it is not the only route to achieve these social objectives.

From the Bottom Up by Workers

A history of worker authority developing from the bottom up begins with the union movement in the nineteenth century. Efforts by union leaders to acquire authority from the bottom up ranged from seeking rights to collective bargaining and job security to seeking control over all of industry. The right to bargain collectively, a major achievement of the 1930s, was only a part of a more complicated effort of labor to share in the authority of corporate organization. Labor's efforts to obtain job improvements, a guaranteed annual wage, health benefits, and profit sharing are also part of the movement to gain authority in the corporation from the bottom up.

In some cases workers have come to own and control their own companies.[9]

Some of the earliest business experiments with employee-ownership in the United States are the plywood companies in the Northwest. In 1921 a group of lumbermen, carpenters, and mechanics pooled their resources and built a plywood plant by their own labor in Olympia, Washington. About 125 laborers contributed $1,000 each by borrowing from friends, cashing in on savings, and mortgaging their homes. Workers in the company then each received a share of the company entitling them to employment, an equal return on profits, and an equal vote in directing company affairs. The original company, Olympia Veneer, soon developed a reputation for high quality production. Its example inspired the formation of other worker-owned companies in plywood manufacture. When a comprehensive study was made in 1964 there were 23 such companies. The companies, ranging in sales from $3 million to $15 million annually, were all independent and each employed between 60 and 450 worker-shareholders.

The older pattern of worker-ownership is being matched by a new pattern, developing within the last decade. The workers in subsidiaries of national corporations today are finding it possible to own and manage their own operation through collaborative efforts with the parent company. In Lowell, Vermont, 180 asbestos mineworkers bought the local quarry business of the parent company, GAF, Inc., of New York. GAF was ready to shut down the large quarry unit in Vermont because they were under pressure to solve costly environmental problems. The mineworkers then bargained to buy the local company for $400,000.

They sold $50 stock shares to themselves and friends and elected a 15 member board of directors from among their union ranks.

Other cases show similar patterns of change. Cluett, Peabody & Company allowed employees to put up 85 percent of the capital needed to purchase a knitting factory in Saratoga, New York. The employees range from switchboard operators to a vice president.

Such cases show a basic change in work organization, involving concepts of self-management that are compatible with the concept of federal charterment.

Labor unions have shown an interest in gaining stock and managerial control over U. S. companies.[10] Under the leadership of Walter Reuther, the United Auto Workers sought to make the receipt of stock in American Motors a part of the bargaining process. Although plans to obtain the stock were never completed for many reasons, including the resistance of rank-and-file union members as well as Reuther's untimely death, other unions have moved in the same direction. The International Association of Machinists has purchased significant percentages of stock in companies where they work. One reason for taking such action is to stem the tendency for management to shut down U. S. plants in order to reopen them overseas at lower wage scales. The motivation of union leaders for buying stock in these companies has been to gain some leverage at the bargaining table to stop runaway plants. At the same time, the entry of the union into the role of major stockholder-owner of the company clearly changes the former structure of labor-management relations.

Legislative efforts to create "worker ownership" are also evident. Legislation signed by President Nixon in 1973, for example, called for eventual employee ownership of the Northeast railroad industry as one part of its reorganization. The 1974 Pension Reform Act sanctions capital ownership by employees through effective tax arrangements, and the tax cut supports by President Ford in 1975 gives companies an extra 1 percent tax credit on top of a 10 percent investment credit if the 1 percent is used to set up new employee-owned stock.

In Europe

Collective efforts to decentralize authority in large European corporations are similar to efforts in the United States, but their effects have been more widespread. Several events in the last decade can serve to illustrate the changing mood among workers in Europe.

One critical event was the student-worker revolt of May 1968 in France. Here the issue of "workers' management" was consciously raised. The major French unions are today still arguing for "workers' management." The famous "Lip incident" testifies to the extent to which this idea captured the imagination of the French workers.

In 1973 the Lip watch company in Besançon announced that all operations were to be shut down. The employees immediately took over the company and operated it themselves for a number of months, without government intervention. Confiscating finished goods at the plant as a kind of hostage, the employees demanded that company operations continue with no layoffs and promoted the idea of *autogestion* (self-management). In 1974 the employees accepted a compromise with employment guaranteed to a portion of the work force and certain promises from management on retraining and reemployment for other workers. By late 1974 the company was back in operation, making some gains from the takeover by advertising that it was the "love of men and women for their professions" that had salvaged the company.

A different case in Sweden can illustrate the complexity of the process of change. In 1975 workers in Sweden's major flat-glass manufacturer, Emmaboda, protested against a management decision that a majority of its stock could be taken over by a French firm. The workers feared they would lose some of their independence and democratic management by the change in ownership. When the Swedish government intervened and took advantage of a law requiring government approval for acquisitions of over 40 percent equity in a company, they extracted promises from the French company that the workers' democratic concerns would be completely respected.

These cases are not isolated; rather, they are illustrative of a basic change in the structure of management in European countries that involves a new level of worker participation in managerial functions. Workers are now represented on the top board of directors of major companies; workers are also in the middle-management levels (work councils); and they are participating at the bottom level of the corporate workplace, making decisions about how to design their own jobs. These changes affect the charters of big corporations. Federal chartering must take account of them since the need for making such changes may be felt jointly by U.S. labor and management in the future.

Board of Directors

In Sweden, Norway, Denmark, and Luxembourg, workers must be given minority representation on top corporate boards. Other countries show signs of moving in this same direction.[11]

Since April, 1973 all companies in Sweden with more than 100 employees have been required to accept two worker representatives on their board of directors. No company action is legally required in this respect, however, unless the employees themselves specifically take the initiative to request it. Not only has there been little resistance to the law and its implementation, but also many Swedish employees welcome it as a step toward better labor-management communications. In fact, some national companies in Sweden conduct training programs for workers who will serve on the board. The heavy electrical equipment company of Asea, for example, trained some 75 worker representatives in 40 to 50-hour programs on how to be a company board member, presenting actual case histories of decisions the board members generally must face. The workers thus had an opportunity to practice being board members before actually serving on the board.

Other companies have gone even further to decentralize subsidiary operations. A specialty steel maker, Fagersta AB, recently decentralized its operations into a number of independent profit centers. *Each center now has its own board of directors including employee representatives. In the process of decentralization some 80 employees were given training to assist them in performing the new responsibilities.* Proposals have been made to decentralize in this direction within the European Economic Community (EEC). An EEC Commission has had a "Eurocompany statute" pending since 1970 that would provide a legal structure for companies wishing to carry out cross-border operations or joint ventures, specifying a model of "codetermination" for each venture. One-third of the board members would be employees' representatives, unless two-thirds of the employees vote to reject the representation. The proposal also provides for work councils with certain rights of veto and consultation in various areas of decision-making.

In 1972 the EEC Commission issued a draft called the "Fifth Directive" that would establish uniform legislation on company structure in member countries. Including the two-thirds board system common to Holland and Germany, it would give one-third of the places on the top supervisory board to workers according to the German model and veto power on the board nominations to both workers and shareholders according to the Dutch model.

The movement toward increasing labor participation on the boards of directors of national corporations partakes of the same pattern of change occurring at other levels of operation. At middle and bottom levels of management, other types of participation are developing, as we shall see.

Shop Floor Committees and Work Councils

European workers on the shop floor increasingly are encouraged to institute changes in the system of work that make it more interesting and enjoyable. Workers often participate with management and professional people in efforts to redesign jobs. Job redesign generally means one of three things: *job rotation* (people alternately engaging in certain tasks to share the load), *job enlargement* (expanding the number of tasks to add variety to work), and *job enrichment* (increasing the discretion and independent judgment of workers in performing their tasks). This practice of giving more authority to workers to design their own jobs respects individual intelligence, imagination, and native capacities. By developing the social domain within the national corporation, a secondary reward of reducing the costs of supervision can result along with a rise in productivity.[12] These experiments in worker participation become important to consider in the decentralized development of big corporations through federal charterment.

Decision-Making Areas (Examples). The areas of worker participation in decision-making can now be said to have covered every facet of corporation governance. These areas include the following:

Top Management
1. Capital investments, stock options, mergers, changes in charter
2. Government relations, lobbying, taxation
3. Trade association activities, trade fairs, industrywide conferences
4. Allocation of corporate profits, stock dividends, new product lines
5. Research and development
6. Major construction, new buildings
7. Intracompany relations, accounting practices, credits, subsidiary sales
8. Price determination, choice of markets, quality control
9. Promotion and dismissal of top executives
10. Wage and salary levels

Middle Management
11. Vacation scheduling, new payment programs
12. Supervisory methods
13. Safety rules, health insurance, personnel disputes
14. Hiring and firing, guidelines for personnel selection
15. Job evaluation procedures
16. Control over company newspapers

Lower Management
17. Accident prevention programs
18. Handling employee grievances at shop level, interpretation of company rules
19. Job control (job rotation, enlargement, enrichment)

These areas of decision-making become significant to review through corporate self-studies if unions and management seek to decentralize authority in the corporation under federal charterment. The decentralizing process leads toward the increased participation of employees in the so-called higher decision-making areas of corporate life.

The Benefits of Decentralization

While administrative centralization of business is associated with rapid industrial growth, it is also associated with major social and environmental costs and with an increase in government regulatory agencies. The singular emphasis upon centralization through mergers and the creation of new conglomerates clearly has led to new corporate problems requiring new government controls. Therefore, many economists and social scientists give reasons for decentralizing the large conglomerate corporation.

First, decentralization is *economizing.* Research indicates the need to create "economies of scale" for operational efficiency and for technological progress. The special technology required in many industries leads to their optimal efficiency being realized in smaller plants. Many multiplant industrial giants have gone beyond their optimal size. United States Steel, for example, is said to be no more than several Inland Steels scattered across the country as far as technical efficiency is concerned. The consolidation of these plants adds nothing to operating efficiency. Furthermore, in a study of the 60 most important inventions of recent years, it was found that more than half came from independent inventors, whereas less than half came from corporate research, and still less from the research done by large corporations. In other words, large size does not necessarily lead either to technical progress or to efficiency.[13]

Second, decentralization is *humanizing.* Steps toward decentralization already have been shown to be a social innovation of considerable significance. Decentralizing adds value to the corporation in its social domain by increasing the ability of employees to handle corporate problems themselves and enhancing individual responsibility and authority in company operations. It is reasonable to assume that further decentralization, which allows for regional and local autonomy, should add still more democratic and human values to the life of the corporate system. It should help to balance the current emphasis on economic growth and encourage the development of the larger values by which people live. Economic growth by itself has its limits.[14]

Third, decentralization contributes to *community development.* National programs that have encouraged decentralization have resulted in more jobs and lower welfare costs in local areas. Moreover, the principles of federal chartering coincide with the kind of legislation originally introduced in the 90th Congress to stimulate the formation of community development corporations (CDCs) in poverty areas. Although the legislation was not passed with large funding, CDCs were given financial assistance on a small scale, and many of them have accepted contracts with large corporations to facilitate the production and distribution of goods. These community corporations have then sought both social and economic objectives in their localities; creating jobs for workers; training the unemployed, the aged, the handicapped, ex-convicts, and other low-income groups who would normally end up on the welfare rolls; investing in local housing, street improvements, schools, and hospital construction; and contributing significantly to the social and economic development of the community. Thus, federal chartering that decentralizes corporate operations encourages this kind of programmatic change in economic organization.[15]

DECENTRALIZATION THROUGH FEDERAL CHARTERING

Decentralization of corporate power and responsibility can be aided in the United States by means of new chartering legislation, which reduces the necessity for states to compete with one another to win corporate charters and at the same time offers an opportunity to shape corporate growth and development without government management.

Chartering is Not Nationalizing

Federal chartering does not mean "nationalizing" the big corporations, nor does it entail placing them under the control of the federal government. The experience of Great Britain with certain key industries has shown the fallacy of creating standard government controls, since the problems of the big corporation with its great size and bureaucracy is only compounded with government bureaucracy. Also, worker discontent continues under state authority. The European experience with nationalization has shown further that "legislating changes" at the top is simply not sufficient to eliminate the problems of corporate bureaucracy and worker alienation on the job.

U. S. legislators may take a new route, however, through federal chartering without state management. The process requires the interest and support of national federations of unions and management to initiate key changes in the national system of production and distribution. In light of what we know of the national corporation, what are the major steps of federal chartering that lead toward decentralization?

A Proposal for Federal Chartering

Three steps appear most likely to reach successful conclusions: (1) the initiation of feasibility studies, (2) the creation of a chartering law and chartering agency, and (3) the authorization of financial support for organizational self-studies by corporations.

Step One: Feasibility Studies

Feasibility studies are important because of the complication of making major social changes in the corporate order. The purpose of these studies is to clarify the problems that would be encountered in the chartering process. Once they are clarified, legislation for chartering can anticipate them. The chartering agency, then, can proceed with greater certainty of success.

One problem to be settled through feasibility studies involves the *definition of a target area* for chartering. Specific criteria are needed to determine what size of national corporation should require a federal charter. If federal charters applied only to corporations with assets exceeding $1 billion, only 100 industrial corporations would be covered and perhaps another 150 in all other fields. Donald Schwartz of the Law Center at Georgetown University has recommended that all corporations in interstate commerce with over $10 million in assets and 300 shareholders be targeted for federal charters. This would include all companies on the Fortune 1000 list with at least 300 stockholders.

A second problem has to do with the *schedule of chartering.* All major corporations of a certain size could be chartered simultaneously. On the other hand, the top ten or twenty corporations could be chartered on an experimental basis to determine the social and economic consequence of the action at the national level. Given the information gathered experimentally, the chartering could then proceed with the next largest corporations and so on until a certain corporate size had been reached.

A third problem is how to move with *maximum support from both management and labor.* The hope would be that productivity would not be impaired and that working conditions might be improved, with new measures of equity introduced into the system. Part of the purpose of feasibility studies would be to determine the various ways in which the chartering process would benefit all major constituencies of the corporation.

Step Two: The Chartering Agency

The process of decentralizing the national corporation then can be proposed somewhat as follows. A federal chartering agency is established by law with the task of initiating the chartering process. Next, the agency notifies the executives of the target corporations of their official involvement. At the same time, notification is given to union leaders, and conferences are arranged to discuss the implications of chartering. Then, other constituencies of the corporation are included in conferences as they become known to be significant to the process. In addition, guidelines for chartering are brought forward by the chartering agency for discussion. These guidelines then are utilized by each corporation to write a constitution for itself. The key change in operating principles lies in the fact that the corporation is now defined as existing in the public interest as well as its own self-interest. Consequently, the main issues in writing a corporate constitution lie in how the corporation becomes formally accountable to its constituencies.

The chartering agency, on the one hand, provides models and principles for corporations to follow on such matters as a bill of rights for constituencies, a tribunal system, a public review board, public disclosure requirements, legal expectations for decentralizing authority to the regions and localities in which the corporation operates, areas of accountability to the public, constitutional forms, etc. The corporations, on the other hand, utilize these models and principles to review their own situation and submit proposals for approval of a constitution and a detailed plan for implementing the changes to meet the requirements of the chartering agency. The chartering agency in turn reviews the proposals of the corporations to determine the degree to which they have followed the guidelines put forth in previous consultations. At the same time, the agency reviews all the corporate plans together for their degree of uniformity and consistency.

The federal charter itself lists the basic principles and general guidelines of organization for corporations in different classes of industry and commerce to follow in writing private constitutions. The charter requirements for corporations in banking, for example, differ from those for corporations in the petroleum industry. Since different constituencies are involved in different industries, different forms of accountability are indicated. A federal charter then sets the guidelines for a private constitution for each large corporation based upon charter principles and guidelines.

The type of federal charter I am suggesting in this case has a different emphasis than the one proposed by Ralph Nader. The emphasis here is on experimentation with civil development. This type of charter emphasizes the development of corporate democracy and the decentralization of authority toward community levels of enterprise. The chartering agency in this case determines only the basic principles of public organization important to different types of businesses such as banking, manufacturing, and retailing. It helps determine who are the major "constituencies" of the corporation affected by the corporation's activities and who may organize to advance their own interests in relation to it. A federal charter then sets the guidelines for each designated corporation to write a private constitution, adapting those guidelines to its own situation.

A federal charter, for example, specifies principles of social decentralization, autonomy for member units, and democratic rights for major constituencies. Some of these principles were included in state charters during the nineteenth century; many others, however, are part of the constitutionalizing process. An example of charter principles for a large corporation follows:

Constitutional Guidelines (Examples)

1. The board of directors of the corporation must be composed of representatives from its major constituencies with designated voting rights in each case. Representation of employees must be included *if requested by them* as a body within the corporation. Proportionate representation of other constituencies is defined by the nature of the industry and approved by the chartering agency.
2. The corporation must function according to the laws of the state in which it operates. This reverses the present principle in which each state accepts the

rules of the corporation's home charter in another state. The guidelines set by the *chartering agency* have precedent over all state charters, but state charters may vary within those guidelines.

3. Community charters must be established for large local units:
   (a) Local subsidiaries, retail outlets, manufacturing plants, stores of corporations must be chartered within local governmental units such as a city.
   (b) Local units of the corporation are required to have their own boards of directors and by-laws *if requested by the locality*. The local board then involves the participation of local constituencies. Local constituencies include workers, consumers, community representatives. The proportion of constituent representation is indicated in the constitution and filled at the formal request of each constituency. The proportion is reviewed periodically. A request for a change in the proportion can be submitted to the corporate tribune for determining the degree of equity and efficiency in operations involved in changing the proportion of representation. A constitutional plan provides for increasing local authority in stages, that is, according to criteria specifying what constitutes "responsible enterprise" developing through a local board.

4. The corporation must formulate a *bill of human rights* to be accorded to its constituencies (e.g., stockholders, employees, and customers). It must also state its method of handling breeches of those rights.
   (a) Employee rights (examples)
      (1) The right to secret balloting where voting is indicated.
      (2) The right to assembly under specified conditions.
      (3) The right to free speech about corporate organization.
      (4) The right to be heard by a jury of peers when fired from a job.
      (5) The right to retraining with pay when "laid off" from a job.
   (b) Tribunal principles (examples)
      (1) Constituencies have a right to be heard fairly and speedily.
      (2) Constituencies have a right to legal assistance in serious disputes with the corporation.
      (3) Constituencies are presumed innocent until proven guilty of major offenses in the corporation.

5. The corporation must indicate the form of *public review* wherein its administration is made socially accountable to constituencies and the general public.
   (a) A *public review board* can be selected independently of the corporation and the government through elections by constituencies and appropriate professional associations at the national level. (Corporate funds may be set aside for paid professional staff who are under mandate to respond to needs of constituents as well as their own standards for evaluating corporate performance.)
   (b) The board is given complete access to all corporate information deemed in the public interest.
   (c) The board has legal access to mass media (e.g., national television) to report on performance in industries.

(d) The board submits an annual *social audit* of corporate operations to corporate constituencies. (This includes a report on employment of minority groups, steps toward equalizing opportunity, data on pollution, workers' safety and injuries, etc.)

6. The corporation must state its form of (a) periodic meetings with its constituencies to report on its progress and (b) representation accorded to each constituency at appropriate levels of administration.

7. The corporation must state its *asset limits* consistent with other corporations in its industry. (A national corporation, for example, may not acquire over $2 billion in assets.) This changes the asset structure of large corporations so that major divisions and subsidiaries may assume a greater capital base. The main unit may develop an administrative and coordinative role in the development of the industry.

8. The corporation must guarantee continuity of employment throughout the year either through its own operations or by contract with other firms during seasonal layoffs.

9. The permissible salary range (e.g., 8 to 1) for all employees must be stated. It must show some measures of consistency with other corporations in the same industry.

10. The corporation must disclose:
    (a) the names of major stockholders (e.g., all interests over 1 percent for very large companies and over 5 percent for medium-sized companies)
    (b) Its annual corporation expenditures toward:
        (1) political activities (lobbying, gifts).
        (2) acquisition of new companies (e.g., subsidiaries, franchises)

11. The corporation must state how it is organized to provide continuing attention to technical progress and development in the public interest.

The targeted corporations must be given a specified period of time to return their constitutional statements to the federal chartering agency. The third stage of corporate decentralization, then, begins as corporations implement the changes intended in the constitutional statements.

Step Three: Agency for Organizational Self-Studies

A federal agency for Organizational self-studies can be established to enable associations affected by the change to examine the implications for themselves and act back on the process. In order to help the trade associations, trade unions, small businesses, trade cooperatives, and consumer research groups make such studies, national financial aid can be supplied.

Such changes can seriously change the ecology of business. As the big corporations begin to decentralize their functions in the public interest, the process can affect whole regions and localities. Under the new system of authority top management cannot make certain important decisions unilaterally—for example, it cannot decide arbitrarily to relocate plants and stores without receiving some measure of local consent. Since large numbers of employees cannot be discharged unilaterally without agreements to retrain and relocate employees, the massive firings and discharges of the past that led to public welfare, public assistance, and unemployment compensation can now be avoided because of the new order of responsibility within the corporation. Federal support can be supplied in cases of unavoidable financial reverses in the corporation that make it impossible for it to maintain its employment responsibilities without incurring bankruptcy.

To be successful, decentralization must be accompanied by benefits for all concerned parties. Hence a process of reciprocal action and planning between central offices and branch units becomes important. To initiate the process, the executives of the central offices, for example, may submit a decentralizing plan to employees in a branch unit and ask for their suggestions for broadening their local responsibilities. Covering a ten-year period, the plan may anticipate assistance from the Agency for Organizational Self-studies during the decentralizing process and might run as follows, according to the discretion of employees of the local branch:

First year: Establish a local charter with some participation of local employees in the process.

Second year: Encourage a more active participation of local employees and the reorganization of the local unit on a self-management basis.

Third year: Include local citizens (or consumers) as members of the local board of directors. (A local assembly plant of General Motors may need representation from interested *citizens* on the local board because of a concern about excessive noise or waste in the neighborhood, while a branch unit of Sears, Roebuck may need representation from *consumers* who have a concern about the kind of goods sold in the neighborhood.)

Fourth year: Issue branch stock for purchase by local constituencies and the official disengagement from the command authority of the parent corporations.

Fifth year: Negotiate contracts (rather than filling orders) with the parent corporation devising plans for higher sales or productivity on the part of the local unit.

Sixth year: Continue contracts with the parent corporation, but negotiate new contracts with other corporations that complement the work done locally.

Seventh year: Start independent local enterprises with the economic returns gained from the work completed under contract with outside corporations.

Eighth year: Develop a local housing program or an educational program for local residents who are in need of human services.

Ninth year: Send local consultants to the parent corporation to train people in other branches to decentralize authority in a manner that is mutually advantageous to both parties.

Tenth year: Make new capital investments in technology. Also, assist in reorganizing the larger corporate complex so that executives in the central offices of the parent organization help develop a federation based on mutual services.

The national corporation that decentralizes its administration loses its former pattern of authority based on a bureaucratic command system. Therefore, unless a corporation creates a new mode of authority based on mutual interest, mutual advantage, and consensus, it stands to lose on other counts including its economic returns. Central offices must grow in their own capacity to provide social and economic advantages to local branches. Such provisions can be provided through their ability to coordinate technical services, interstate information on markets, training programs, and insurance plans on a national basis—advantages stemming from a national base of operations.

These changes in authority structure, however, require assistance from an Agency for Organizational Self-studies. Such an agency can guide the process of change by its capacity to offer financial support for professional consultation and technical studies and by its own dedication to serving the common interests of all the involved parties.

Effects of Federal Chartering

The process of decentralization affects not only the vertical and horizontal relationships of the corporation at the national level, but also the functions of these relationships. Let us now look hypothetically at these aspects of change as an Agency of Organizational Self-Studies might observe them.

Change in the Nature of Authority in Organizations (Problems)

The national corporations, the trade unions, and the trade associations are organized vertically at the levels of the city, the state, and the nation. The change in the authority structure of the corporation implies a realignment of authority within all three corporate bodies at each level. It calls for a new statement of purpose and new functions for each federation at each level. Increased participation of workers in the corporation can threaten the existence of the union or it can strengthen it, depending upon how the decentralization takes place. The change requires joint studies of labor and management in each industry.

The shift in authority structure could lead some unions to purchase whole corporations. In doing so, they run the risk of antitrust suits. The purchase of American Motors by the UAW may suggest to the Justice Department the potential for monopoly, since laborers in the same union of American Motors are also working for Ford and General Motors. Of course, the purchase of corporations by unions does not necessarily spell a major difference in the type of management. Union management may still be just as hierarchical and competitive on the larger scene as corporate management. Workers may still have no direct control over the immediate problems they face on the job. Local assembly plants may continue to be dominated by the national union. Union headquarters may be as distant from a plant as that of the former management. A command authority within the union may simply replace the command authority within the traditional business system.

An Agency for Organizational Self-Studies, therefore, is interested in helping within three areas of change in business administration: (1) intraorganizational problems, (2) employee rights, and (3) interorganizational problems. The academic field of organizational studies finds direct application through such an agency designed for consultation with private enterprise in the aftermath of chartering.[16]

The first area is concerned with the *kind of decision-making power that employees maintain over key problems within a corporation.* This power may range from a low to a high participatory authority as follows:

(Low) (a) obedience to *orders* from superiors without being able to raise questions, (b) following managerial advice according to tradition, (c) always following managerial *suggestions* and *information,* (d) initiating new ideas and beginning to *negotiate* differences, (e) joint consultation between labor and management, (f) equal participation of all employees in final authority of decisions at equal levels of work, (g) *choosing representatives* to act at higher levels of administration on decision-making. (High)[17]

The second area of interest in providing consultation when requested is related to the *kind of problems which employees have the right to resolve.* These problems can arise in corporate administration, education, welfare, personnel relations, and economic performance. The rights of employees to participate in decisions are specified by the new constitution, but changes are still appropriate from time to time. The consulting agency may offer suggestions on how to increase participation without the loss of effectiveness in the administration of the enterprise.

The third area for providing consultation is focused upon *interorganizational relationships.* Roland Warren, Brandeis University sociologist, describes four interorganizational contexts for decision-making that become significant in the new alignments of economic associations. They are (1) unitary; (2) federative; (3) coalitional; (4) social choice. The *unitary context* is exemplified by the business corporation that ultimately locates policy at the top of the structure. With this model, all units are expected to orient their behavior toward the well-being of the corporation rather than toward their own subgoals. The *federative context* is exemplified by the trade association that has a formal organization for the accomplishment of common goals and a staff to implement them but centers authority principally at the unit (member) level. While certain administrative prerogatives are delegated by the member units to a formal staff, units are structured autonomously. The *coalitional context* is exemplified by a group or organization cooperating to attain some desired objective such as persuading a new industry to locate in the community. In this model, no formal organization is necessary because decision-making takes place at the level of the units themselves as they interact with each other on an ad hoc basis. The *social choice context* is exemplified by the autonomous behavior of a number of organizations and individuals as they relate to issues that concern them. The issue may be medical care, housing, or whatever. With no commitment to a leadership system, there is only a common consciousness of an issue in which different units act separately.[18] The consulting agency then studies the problems that arise between corporations in the aftermath of chartering and offers solutions in the public interest. The agency acts "out of court," so to speak, through joint consultation with opposing interests.

Let us look further at the kind of organizational problems to which an Agency would respond.

Change in Organizational Relationships (Problems)

The realignment of authority of corporate units at different geographical levels implies a new relationship to production and distribution of goods and services in the public interest.

Trade associations have maintained a careful accounting of trade activities in major industries. This trade accounting system then becomes a basis for computing the distribution of goods and services in regions of the nation. The Agency for Organizational Self-Studies now seeks to enable economic associations to judge the best manner of adjusting trade in the national interest as well as the market and corporate interests. It offers funds for organizations to study the way in which this can be done effectively.

Federations of consumer research groups and consumer cooperatives are funded where appropriate. They become part of a public review of the operations of specific industries. One purpose of these federations then becomes the "reporting and monitoring" of the fair distribution of goods and services according to geographic regions in the public interest. The agency has the power to fund programs of study that lead in this direction. It maintains no power to coerce redistribution and retains only the power of public reporting of findings of organizational studies made in the national interest.

National corporations begin to operate more closely with trade associations, unions, and consumer federations, which change their administrative functions.

Executive offices of some associations become central planning and coordinating agencies for the distribution of goods and the administration of services in major trade areas of society.

(a) As new alignments are made among economic associations, it becomes feasible to coordinate insurance and pension plans on a national level without their restriction to a single corporation, union, or trade association. Planning in the private sector then introduces standards of equity in insurance and social security regardless of the economic status of people in the society. Intercorporate coordination and planning on insurance, for example, frees those employees who fear losing their insurance plan by joining another company.

(b) As new alignments are made, it becomes possible to guarantee employment nationally under specified conditions.[19] This becomes possible with the following developments: (1) Computerized methods for locating jobs needing to be filled and unemployed who desire jobs. (2) Centralized information on plant developments. (3) National coordination of information to regions and cities to bring people jobs and jobs to people.[20]

Areas of Administrative Change:
New Measures of Corporate Performance

As public attention is directed toward the social organization of production and distribution of goods and services, new measures of corporate performance become devised. As business operations become increasingly judged on social standards, and national associations develop professional criteria for judging corporate behavior, a new climate for economic transaction is produced. Thus, corporate law changes substantively as national corporations become structured in the public interest. The concept of "workable competition" is changed to "workable cooperation" in the public interest, making it possible for corporations in the same field to cooperate under specified conditions. If they have constitutionalized their operations and are organized with significant representation from their major constituencies (especially business customers and consumers), they can be allowed to cooperate without being held in restraint of trade.

At the present time, courts take indices of market competition as the basis for determining corporate performance in the public interest. If national corporations are constitutionalized, courts can develop indices of social accountability; that is, they can develop criteria to assess corporate performance on the adequacy (or workability) of its accountability system. The court would examine the structures of public accountability adopted by the corporation to ensure that it continues to function in the public interest. If these structures are deemed adequate, then measures of competition are less significant than measures of cooperation in judging performance. Measures of economic accountability in the public interest are already being developed in the field of public utilities. For some time, economists and legal scholars have studied the problem of marginal cost pricing in relation to the general welfare.[21]

Gardiner Means believes that a legal category should exist for the "collective enterprise" that stands midway between the public utility and the large private corporation. In order for the large enterprise to achieve the ends set for it by the classical theorists, it must be measured by the following norms:

1. Prices are in reasonable relation to costs.
2. The benefits to labor and to capital arising from production are reasonably related to their respective contributions to production.
3. As nearly as possible, optimum use of resources is made so that no more of a given resource is used than is necessary for the end product and that combination of resources is used which involves the least cost.
4. There is technical progress to reduce costs, improve product and introduce new products.[22]

The potential now exists for computerizing information on the performance of national corporations on the basis of norms if certain barriers are overcome. First, some legal problems exist in obtaining access to corporate information since the present law is based upon the theory of competition. If public review boards are provided and given legal access to corporate information to judge their performance, then suitable norms can be devised. In fact, separate review boards could collaborate nationally to develop such norms and offer them for public debate.

Second, some professional problems exist in present accounting systems. Many accountants feel a higher responsibility to management than to investors, creditors, labor, consumers, or the government. This fact leads to problems in standardization and public review. In this regard, the American Institute of Certified Public Accountants has been seeking to develop a statement of basic goals and to develop a national constitution for the profession. The aim is to broaden their professional responsibilities to the larger society.

Once the legal rights to corporate data are cleared, target rates for return on investments and general evaluation of corporate performance can be made. A file of information on the following types of corporate information would then be required.[23]

1. An estimate of the cost of capital to the enterprise, which would be used as the target rate of return.
2. An estimate of the average rate of operation to be expected over a period of years which would be used as the standard rate of operation in target pricing.

3. An estimated schedule of the effect on earnings to be expected from operations at rates above or below the expected average.
4. An estimate of the total capital to be employed by the enterprise.

The performance of the corporation can be judged in part with this kind of information. Even though the measurement of economic performance is just as crucial to socially oriented corporations as it is to the profit-oriented corporation, the measurement of social performance is just as solvable as a professional problem in accounting criteria as is the current measurement of profit.

Certain national programs follow the federal chartering of private corporations. Wages and prices can be reviewed by a public board independent of the federal government.[24] A public board in the private sector becomes feasible after the realignment of corporate structure. In other words, in the realignment process it becomes possible to develop legal, normative, and federated controls through public access to corporate data. This process requires defederating regulatory commissions, special bureaus, departments, and divisions of the central government while federating new sectors of the social economy. Professional standards of performance can thus be developed that take serious account of the economic factor without being wholly dominated by it throughout the system.

THE DRAMA OF TRANSITION

The corporation has already changed its organization remarkably in the last century for many reasons. It has changed partly because of the impact of social research and the applications of scientific findings in corporate policy; partly because of the introduction of new administrative techniques; partly because of the outlook of scientists and professional people who have become an important part of corporate life; partly because of federal laws and agencies that have been created to monitor, limit, and regulate corporate behavior; and partly from the necessity to adjust to its own large-scale growth. Now federal charterment enters to help the corporation decentralize its powers and increase its accountability without "nationalization." The large corporation's separate units (subsidiaries, franchises, local plants, retail outlets) have been developing new types of administrative autonomy within the old context of a formally vertical bureaucracy. The signs of a new federal structure are evident in the national and multinational corporation. They suggest that a decentralizing trend is taking place within the more obvious shifts toward corporate concentration. Thus, a corporate structure based on a federal model has been emerging to compete with the older forms of bureaucracy and command. Corporate subsidiaries and other units are developing an autonomy partly out of the need to maintain administrative efficiency.

The corporate system shows signs of a transition from a feudal structure to a federal structure.

Federal chartering is a method for advancing this model of economic life without state management. It can become a basis for decentralizing corporate authority so that it becomes more efficient and at the same time more human in its organization. In this process, then, business begins to contribute to the development of community life. The paradox and irony of this great change on the national scene is in its contradictory character, which is at once revolutionary and gradual, liberal and conservative.

The change through chartering is revolutionary because it anticipates basic contradictions in business law and conflicts with fundamental traditions; it is gradual because analysis shows its social development over a long period of time. Federal chartering is liberal because it humanizes the corporation and requires it to become socially accountable; it is conservative because its intent is to preserve the separation of the private sector from state control. Thus, the older ideologies yield to a new ideology and at the same time they go beyond ideology. Human values become part of the basis for judging the great change. The study of values in economic organization becomes increasingly important, and social development moves beyond the classic ideologies explaining the business system.

The Great Changes in Society: Interorganizational Research

Research on the social and cultural structure of corporate life is not unlike the geologists' study of the major rock formations in the earth structure. The rocks that make up the outer layers of the earth are continually being squeezed and stretched by forces from within the earth. Geologists say that the forces probably come from the enormous heat of the earth's interior at a depth of 100 miles. When the strain becomes greater than the rocks can stand, the rocks rupture and cause an earthquake. The ruptures are properly called *faults* and generally lie well beneath the surface of the earth, but some are visible; for example, the San Andreas fault, which can be seen in California, is 600 miles long.[25]

Geologists recently discovered that tremors had been caused by the actions of certain oil drillings made near the San Andreas fault line. Upon investigation, they learned that injecting water in a drilled hole and then drawing the water out again caused the tremors to begin and alternately to subside. Further investigation led the geologists to conclude that the "inevitability" of a major earthquake could be avoided by "engineering" small quakes within limited geographical areas in sections along the fault line, thus allowing the shift in the interface to take place gradually. A hole drilled every 50 to 100 miles along the fault line and treated periodically would provide the opportunity for the rock to relocate itself in sections and then "quake" under control. Geologists believe the experimental shifts are absolutely necessary to avoid another catastrophe.

In the treatment of the deep fault in the social and cultural structure of American society, it is equally possible to avoid the destructive aspects of future revolutionary quakes. Evidences of a major fault are visible in the cracks of social institutions. They indicate that a fault lies deep within its corporate substructure.[26]

Major social quakes have occurred every 100 years in American history: the American Revolution in the eighteenth century, the Civil War in the nineteenth century, the Great Depression of the twentieth century. The centralization of the federal government averted a major catastrophe in the depression of this century, but it did not treat the fault. Instead, it added to the problem of the transition by instituting a political bureaucracy that is growing out of proportion with fundamental beliefs. Overloading the system of central government has set the stage for another quake.

Some analysts claim with scientific certainty that another quake will occur before the end of the century. The entire social system is moving out of line with its cultural beliefs. In the liberal tradition one can argue that the way out is to engineer small political quakes that allow institutions to reconstruct themselves and gain a new authority in society. The aim would be to reverse the trend toward centralized government by increasing social accountability within the economy. This effort requires decreasing political controls while increasing the public responsibilities of major corporations and decentralizing their authority. Another requirement entails creating conditions in which the "private governments" of the corporate system become accountable to their constituencies, including workers and the communities in which they operate. In the Marxist tradition, on the other hand, one can argue that the revolutionary process does not arise from within the politics of business but rather from the oppressed classes of the society. A revolution is not initiated from the top down but from the bottom up under capitalism. No social engineering by politicians or intellectuals can remove the necessity of social struggle by oppressed classes. Only through the struggle of people who are oppressed can a new authority and purpose be achieved in a capitalist society.

Social transformation of the corporate system in the United States will probably come both from the top down and from the bottom up. The joint movement stimulates further activity, especially among those at the bottom who are not part of the formal organizations of the economic order. At present, the formal organizations of the U. S. economy do not fully represent many groups who are significant to the process of change. The labor unions do not fully represent the poor and economically disenfranchised in the United States. The welfare recipient in the city and the rural poor remain outside the formally organized economy. The consumer is relatively unorganized and underrepresented. Many minorities—women, blacks, students, Indians, Puerto Ricans, Mexicans, Chinese, and others—have not been incorporated into the upper echelons of the trade union, the corporation, and the trade association. Nevertheless, they are a fundamental part of the change process that will overturn the centralized systems.

Conclusion: Planning for the Social Economy

An important goal of decentralization through federal charterment is to increase the opportunity for local communities and corporate employees to resolve key problems that affect their lives, to achieve a measure of self-direction without state management. As big corporations become decentralized, people are given the opportunity and initiative to gain greater control over local enterprise. Thus, a community consciousness is encouraged that in turn leads to the development of community-oriented enterprises. These enterprises then offer an opportunity for people to experience the full round of work life, including decisions on capital investments for both social and economic purposes. Federal chartering in this sense promotes self-reliance and self-determination in the social organization of the economy.

Federal chartering encourages decentralization as an experiment in developing local authority without encouraging local prejudices, elitism, and provinciality. Chartering is a "reciprocal action" between the federal government, big enterprise, and local interest leading toward social control over private enterprise. Federal chartering then initiates an experiment in *providing local citizens with a higher order of responsibility and a greater role of decision-making in matters that affect their daily lives.* At other levels of economic organization, people learn how to adjust market mechanisms with "social management" of distribution and production. Thus, federal chartering offers a method of advancing the economic interest of business enterprise by encouraging a *new model of cooperation in the public interest.* New experiments with democratic relationships are made possible by way of a federal model without loss of economic returns. Finally, by creating an atmosphere for social growth at the top, middle, and bottom of the corporate system, federal chartering provides a way in which local people can build community life and thereby establish a new relationship to the larger society. Thus, a major step is taken toward a consciously created social economy.

NOTES

1. In October, 1971 Ralph Nader sponsored a Conference on Corporate Law in Washington, D. C. devoted entirely to the subject of federal chartering of corporations. For a recent

outline of the idea, see Donald E. Schwartz, "The Federal Chartering of Corporations: A Modest Proposal," in S. Prakash Sethi (ed), *The Unstable Ground* (Los Angeles: Melville, 1974). These recent proposals have not emphasized decentralizing responsibilities and developing corporate democracy in the way I am suggesting here.

2. Congress has the constitutional power to prohibit a firm from doing interstate business unless it first obtains a federal charter. The question of whether the federal government can incorporate was answered affirmatively in the opinion of Chief Justice Marshall in *McCulloch v Maryland*, upholding the constitutionality of the first U. S. Bank. Ralph Nader, "The Case for Federal Chartering," in Ralph Nader and Mark J. Green, *Corporate Power in America* (New York: Grossman, 1973); Ralph Nader, Mark Green, and Joel Seligman, *Taming the Corporation* (New York: W. W. Norton & Co., 1976).

3. Daniel B. Moskowitz, "Constitutionalizing the Corporation," *Business Week,* October 26, 1974, p. 109.

4. The discussion that follows draws upon the work of Alfred D. Chandler, *Strategy and Structure: Chapters in the History of Industrial Enterprise* (Cambridge: M.I.T. Press, 1962), pp. 44, 125, 277.

5. Richard Walton, "How to Conquer Alienation in the Plant," November–December, 1972, *Harvard Business Review,* pp. 70–81.

6. David Jenkins, "Democracy in the Factory," *Atlantic,* April, 1973, p. 83.

7. For stories of managerial efforts to transform the Welch Grape Juice Company and other firms into producer and consumer cooperatives, see Murray Lincoln, *Vice-President in Charge of Revolution* (New York: McGraw-Hill, 1960).

8. This is my summary drawn from various reports. For a critique of ACIPCO, see Daniel Zwerdling, "Managing Workers," in *Working Papers,* Vol. II, No. 3 (Fall, 1974); Paul Bernstein, "Three Existing Democratized Enterprises in the U. S. and Britain" (American Friends Service Committee, 48 Inman St., Cambridge, Mass.); "The Corporation of the Future," in *Engage* (100 Maryland Ave., N.E., Washington, D. C.)

9. This is my summary drawn from: Paul Bernstein, "Run Your Own Business," *Working Papers for a New Society* (Cambridge, Mass.: The Cambridge Policy Studies Institute, Inc.), Vol. II, No. 2, Summer, 1974, p. 24ff; Katrina V. Berman, *Worker-Owned Plywood Companies* (Pullman, Wash.: Washington State Univ. Press, 1967); Cf. George Benello et al., *Self-management in North America: Thought, Research, and Practice* (Ithaca, N. Y.: Cornell University, 1975) No. 11 Program in Participation and Labor-Managed Systems.

10. A historical review of labor's interest in this matter is provided in Jim Wilson, "Self-Management, Participation, and Organized Labor in American History," paper presented to the Second Conference on Self-Management, Cornell University, June 6–8, 1975.

11. The report on cases in this section draws upon David Jenkins, *Industrial Democracy in Europe* (Geneva, Switzerland: Business International, 1974); Michael Z. Brooke and H. Lee Remmers (eds), *The Multinational Company in Europe* (Ann Arbor: The University of Michigan Press, 1972); Innis Macbeath, *The European Approach to Worker-Management Relationships,* British-North American Committee (U.S.A.: National Planning Association, 1973).

12. Rolf Lindholm et al., *Job Reform in Sweden* (Stockholm: Swedish Employers' Confederation, 1975).

13. Walter Adams, *Planning, Regulations, and Competition in Hearing Before Sub-Committees of the Select Committee on Small Business:* U. S. Senate 90th Congress, 1st Session (Washington, D. C.: U. S. Government Printing Office, June 29, 1967). See U. S. Antitrust and Monopoly Subcommittee, *Economic Concentration,* pp. 1541–1551. Jawkes, Sawers, and Stilberman, "The Sources of Invention," Chapter IV, quoted in Adams, *ibid.* Barry Stein, *Size, Efficiency and Community Enterprise* (Cambridge, Mass.: Center for Community Economic Development, 1974).

14. Donella Meadows, Dennis Meadows, Jorgen Randers, and William Behrens, III, *Limits to Growth* (New York: Universe Books, 1972).

15. Stewart E. Perry, "Federal Support for CDCs: Some of the Committee for Community Economic Development History and Issues of Community Control," (1878 Mass. Ave., Cambridge, Mass.): Abt Associates Inc.; *An Evaluation of the Special Impact Program*, Vols. I–IV (Cambridge, Mass.: Abt Associates, Inc., 55 Wheeler St., 1973).

16. Paul M. Hirsch, "Organizational Analysis and Industrial Sociology," *The American Sociologist*, Vol. 10 (February, 1975).

17. Delbert Miller and William Form, *Industrial Sociology*, 1964. See Chapter Two.

18. Roland Warren, "The Interorganizational Field as a Focus for Investigation," *Truth, Love, and Social Change* (Chicago: Rand McNally, 1971).

19. In the Netherlands employees cannot quit their jobs without express government permission if their employers insist on keeping them. *Nor can employers discharge employees without government permission if the employees want to stay.* Acceptable proof of urgency must be given to the proper government agency. Most of the time terminations come about through mutual consent, so that the law does not come into play. Employers do not generally try to hold employees who want to quit for their motivation to work is usually low. Employees do not generally try to block a discharge because they believe an employer who really wants to get rid of them will eventually find a way to do so. For a critical review of this practice, see John P. Windmoller, "Legal Restriction on Employment Termination in the Netherlands," *Labor Law Journal*, 1967.

20. A bill was introduced in the 1st session of the 94th Congress to "establish a national policy and nationwide machinery for guaranteeing to all adult Americans able and willing to work the availability of equal opportunities for useful and rewarding employment." The bill calls for local planning councils, community job boards, standby job corps, a congressional joint economic committee, and a National Institute for Full Employment. See HR 1609, HR 50 in the Committee on Education and Labor.

21. Cf. Harold Hotelling, "The General Welfare in Relation to Problems of Taxation and of Railway Rates," *Econometrica*, 6 (1938): 242–269; Nancy Ruggles, "Recent Developments in the Theory of Marginal Cost Pricing," *Review of Economic Studies*, 17 (1949–50): 107–126.

22. Gardiner Means, *Pricing Power and the Public Interest* (New York: Harper & Bros., 1962), p. 287.

23. Gardiner Means, *op. cit.*, p. 305.

24. Price controls in the United States during the two world wars provide considerable background for the kind of problems that must be resolved in the "transition." For an introduction to the climate of opinion during the Second World War, see Julia E. Johnsen, *Federal Price Control and Permanent Price Control Policy* (New York: H. W. Wilson, 1942). See especially Max Lerner's discussion of six problems: horizontal, vertical, political, geographical, chronological, and tactical; also, Thurman Arnold's stress on consumer participation.

25. Treating the strain in the shifting interface of the social and cultural structures in corporate life is a little like treating the San Andreas fault in California, and so the analogy is worth following. San Andreas is the most active fault in California. In 1906 the horizontal movement of its two blocks of rock caused the great San Francisco earthquake. Geologists now say that the seismic region of California may expect a catastrophic earthquake every 50 to 100 years. Another major quake is inevitable unless the fault can be treated by human engineering.

26. Top management specialists like Peter Drucker have begun to see the importance of "federal decentralization" for large corporations. This has been a breakthrough in management policy leading toward an expertise among top managers that allows for treating the strain in the structure of big corporations. See Peter Drucker, *Management: Tasks, Responsibilities, Practices* (New York: Harper & Row, 1973) pp. 572 ff.

The long-range problem of which we speak here, however, goes still deeper into the substructure of society. The pattern of earthquakes in the historical study of geological formations is analogous for our purposes to the pattern of revolutions in the historical study of societies. Major fault lines with differences in the lines of force are visible in modern society. We know that a continued shift in the social and cultural interface of modern society is inevitable, that the eventuality of quakes with various magnitudes is scientifically certain. We also know that the treatment of the fault is to be found through the creative application of federal principles. This is why we devote Part II to the concept of federalism and what it means generally for the political economy in the United States.

PART II

The Federal Economy

KARL MARX. [People] do not build themselves a new world out of the fruits of the earth, as vulgar superstition believes, but out of the historical accomplishments of their declining civilization. They must, in the course of their development, begin by themselves producing the material conditions of a new society, and no effort of mind or will can free them from this destiny.

EMILE DURKHEIM. [By] an endless series of oscillations we alternately pass from authoritarian regulation made impotent by its excessive rigidity to systematic abstention which cannot last because it breeds anarchy. . . . The only way to resolve this antinomy is to set up a cluster of collective forces outside the State, though subject to its action, whose regulative influence can be exerted with greater variety. Not only will our reconstituted corporations satisfy this condition, but it is hard to see what other groups could do so. For they are close enough to the facts, directly and constantly enough in contact with them, to detect all their nuances, and they should be sufficiently autonomous to be able to respect their diversity.

MAX WEBER. To all of these, the village chief, the judge, the banker, the craftsman, we shall ascribe domination, wherever they claim, and to a socially relevant degree find obedience to, commands given and received as such. No usable concept of domination can be defined in any way other than by reference to power of command; but we must never forget that here, as everywhere else in life, everything is "in transition."

FIVE

SOCIAL FEDERALISM:

Toward an Economic Republic

To comprehend fully what is happening in the private economy we must understand the concept of social federalism. This concept becomes especially important if we want to grasp how large corporations can decentralize authority and simultaneously contribute to the development of economic responsibility at local levels of business administration. It helps explain why it is possible through national policy to decentralize the administration of business without incurring a loss of control or requiring rigorous state intervention.

The decentralization of corporate authority in a federated economy means more than the "deconcentration" of corporate monopoly in a laissez-faire economy. It means more even than the elimination of unemployment and welfare, although these conditions remain an important part of any decentralized economic development. It means essentially the transition from a command system of authority to a federal system of authority outside the state. It means an increase in nonstatist local and regional authority in the economy.

This shift in social control from a command system to a federated system implies a development in the personal authority of more people at local levels in managing their own affairs. They can assume a greater responsibility for local management with fewer rules decided by people above them and consequently fewer commands from the top offices of the corporation requiring their obedience. Decentralization means less outside supervision from absentee managers and less interference from government agencies.

Social development along these lines suggests that new types of contractual relations may encourage accountability at regional and local levels. It implies at the same time an increase in social consciousness and responsibility of local people to the larger corporate industry of which they are a part.

This kind of social governance involves a concept of democratic federalism in the economy. Social development in this direction means encouraging what is already beginning to happen: the democratic organization of economic enterprises at local, regional, and national levels based on fair representation of economic and social interests.

The "federalization" of the economy is well under way. It began with the efforts of labor leaders to organize union federations, of business executives to organize trade federations, and of consumers to organize cooperative federations.

To see the significance of democratic federalism in the economy we must see its place in history. We begin in the first section of this chapter with the history of federalism as a political idea for organizing governments. We look at the Western origins of federalism in European philosophy and thus at the background for the revolutionary formation of the United States. We also look at the crises of the government system in U. S. history and the gradual emergence of private federations to solve problems that the government alone could not solve. Here we see the need to study the private federation as a method for organizing the corporate economy to solve its own problems.

In the second section we note the importance of taking the federation as a scientific concept or model for purposes of research. We are then able to look objectively at the varied formations of private federations in the U. S. economy.

In the third section we examine the varied formations of union federations, business federations, and cooperative federations. We see them as private governments forming a vital and essential part of the political economy. The study of these private governments then allows us to critically evaluate their operations. We can see not only how they have functioned as systems of dominance but also how they have enabled human values to develop in the organization of the economy. We see how social development occurs within the business society without the need for state regulation.

In the fourth section we suggest the basis for a theory of decentralized federal development outside the state. Our hope is to initiate the kind of theory that can guide scientific studies of the emergent social economy.

HISTORICAL PERSPECTIVE

Origins of Federalism

Plato and Aristotle never developed a concept of federalism even though two federative alliances existed in their day—the Achaean League and the Amphictyonic Council. Polybius described the Achaean League with its unitary laws, weights and measures, coinage, councils, and judges, but he did not describe it as an independent state. It existed really as a loosely formed alliance, an antecedent to the federation. Likewise, the Amphictyonic Council was a voluntary association of city states in which deputies were appointed by citizens, but its authority was weak and it was limited to matters of common welfare. Each city-state retained its supreme sovereignty.[1]

The important concept in Greek thought was the *polis,* the political community of the city-state. The *polis* concept never extended to interstate relations in the sense of a higher community. The concept of federalism, therefore, did not fully appear until the nation-state came into existence.

The first advocate of the sovereign state was Jean Bodin, who also reportedly made the first reference to a federal concept. In 1577 he emphasized the federal character of cooperative relations between states. His concept, however, was limited to that of a confederation. It retained the Greek notion of sovereign states joined in loose union for mutual protection. The cantons of Switzerland, he said, were such a confederation, but in no sense were they yet an independent nation.

It was left to Johannes Althusius to explain the federal principle on the basis of its wider range of authority. In 1603 he described two types of confederation, the "complete" and the "incomplete." They were extreme models on a continuum of cases. The complete confederation existed when all component bodies were dissolved into a single state. The incomplete confederation consisted of states that maintained their full sovereignty but pledged themselves to mutual assistance for their common good.

There were many examples of incomplete confederations developing in medieval Italian cities. Max Weber described the early civic confederations (*conjuratio*), the movements toward religious unification, the creation of *confraternitates* and merchant guilds, which were in a sense experiments with the federation concept. Guilds were governed by a single authority in accordance with a common pact between the members of the association.[2]

Other early political philosophers followed Althusius' beginnings. Hugo Grotius, founder of the concept of international law in the modern period, developed a "natural rights" theory of political union. A federal society, he said, was composed of a number of provinces or states whose main purpose was the continuation of the union but with independent security of the separate states. He stressed the fact that a separation of powers existed between the central government and its independent states.

Other European philosophers touched significantly on the concept of federalism. Jean Jacques Rousseau wrote at some length on the subject, although some of his work was destroyed in the early months of the French Revolution. He believed in the *polis* in which every citizen would participate directly in political life. His doctrine was one of "federated self-governing communes, small enough to allow each member an active share in the legislation of the comunes."[3] His concept of decentralized federalism was antecedent to that of Thomas Jefferson's notion of federal polity, as we shall see.

The American Concept of Federalism

American history is the record of a political struggle to organize modern society on federal principles. Each century of U. S. history has seen a major crisis in the development of federalism at local, state, and national levels.

The first crisis was at the end of the eighteenth century in the American Revolution. The revolt of the American colonies harbored the beginning of a federal republic. The issue was the right to secede from England. In a series of 85 letters written to newspapers in the American colonies, Alexander Hamilton, James Madison, and John Jay urged the ratification of the U. S. Constitution, which would strengthen The Articles of Confederation. The Articles had begun to unite them in their struggle for independence. These men were against maintaining a "confederation" and argued for uniting into a strong centralized body of federated states. They emphasized the need for protection against British and Spanish sea power and pointed to the threat of anarchy under The Articles of Confederation. Their letters, later published as *The Federalist Papers,* proved to be powerful arguments for creating a new federal union.[4]

The type of federal union that was finally created in 1787 had never existed before in world history. The American federation of states developed in an unprecedented form. For this reason, federalism is often spoken of as an American invention. Never in history had so close a union been combined with so much freedom and independence of the component parts. All previous attempts could now be readily classified as alliances, leagues, and confederations, in that order of central authority.

Each U. S. citizen was now identified with different political levels of a federated community: the city, the county, the state, the nation. The federal government was designed to exercise only those powers specifically assigned to it, while the states were to retain "residual powers."

The dispute about the degree of centralized versus decentralized authority was sharp. Thomas Jefferson sought decentralization and a strict interpretation of the Constitution. The concept of individual rights was closely linked to the concept of states rights in a vertical system of political authority. Jefferson described the composite levels of the federal "whole" with power to be given to:

1. The general federal republic for all concerns, foreign and federal
2. That of the state for what relates to its own citizens exclusively
3. The county republics for the duties and concerns of the country
4. The ward republics, for the small and yet numerous interesting concerns of the neighborhood

Jefferson thought of the wards as "pure and elementary republics," each autonomous within its proper sphere. It was in the local neighborhood that people could participate directly in government.

Jefferson envisioned "coordinate governments," each sovereign in its own sphere. He believed in the right of secession and "nullification." The Kentucky Resolution, drafted by Jefferson, proclaimed that "the United States of America are not united on the principle of unlimited submission to their general government" but rather each state contracted with other states and that "as in all other cases of compact among parties having no common judge, each party has an equal right to judge for itself."

John Calhoun's *Disquisition on Government* (1851) developed this idea of federalism, which involved "concurrent majorities." This meant that each community's will could be ascertained only by taking account of the majorities in each of its primary constituent groups. The United States was a "community of states," not the government of a single state or nation. Calhoun claimed sovereignty for the states to be indivisible. *Nullification* of federal acts not acceptable to the people of a particular state—the complementary concept of *secession*—was included in the American concept of federalism according to Calhoun.

In Europe a parallel form of federalism was being developed by Pierre Proudhon. Proudhon believed that a properly designed federal contract among the various organizational levels—heads of families, communes, cantons, provinces, and states—would mutually benefit people at each level. Federalism was a continuous form of mutual exchange between the so-called lower order and higher order communities. The function of the higher order community, however, was to be of service to the lower order. The relation between communities had the character of a confederation where authority was located primarily in the member units rather than a federation where the greatest authority is given to the administrative center. It was a federalism more compatible with that of Jefferson and Calhoun than with the Hamiltonian federalism that actually developed on the American continent.

The second crisis of American federalism was in the Civil War of the nineteenth century. The Civil War was a regional breakdown in political economy exacerbated by racial strife and the slavery issue. The North defined the Civil War in part as an issue of racial justice and equality. But it also meant the preservation of the federation or "Union." The South defined it as an issue of freedom and independence of the states. But it also meant the creation of a "Confederacy." The confederacy offered the right to secede from the union when the majority of people in the states wanted to do so.

The issues of racial justice and federation won in this Civil War, while the right to secession and political independence was lost to the states. The need to preserve the union was seen to be critical in a world of competing nations. The decades of the succeeding century then involved gradual increases in the powers in the federal government.

The third crisis occurred in the Great Depression. The central government took action before total chaos and perhaps revolution could begin. The National Recovery Act (NRA) strengthened the central powers of the federal government in an effort to solve the cirsis in the economy. The NRA enabled top business leaders to begin setting codes of conduct through trade associations in cooperation with labor leaders in trade unions. They were also jointly to establish guidelines for pricing and distribution of goods. The NRA, however, failed to resolve the problems of the Great Depression. It was declared unconstitutional by the Supreme Court partly because it was not organized fairly and democratically in the public interest. Collusive practices of price-fixing developed in spite of the expressed ideas of NRA programs.

Ellis Hawley describes the paradox latent in the Great Depression. He says that if the philosophy of the Supreme Court under the influence of Justices Brandeis and Frankfurter could be summed up in one word, it would be "decentralization." When one considers the legislation of the post-NRA period, however, "he is forced to conclude that most New Deal planning was in the nature of government-sponsored cartelization" and centralized planning:

It came at the behest of organized economic groups intent upon strengthening their market positions through legal sanctions or government supports. It came, moreover, in a disjointed, almost haphazard manner, in response to specific pressures, problems, and needs, and without benefit of any preconceived plan or integrated theory. And its purpose, although this was often disguised as something else, was to help individual industries or particularistic pressure groups to promote scarcity and thus balance their output with demand, regardless of the dislocations that such action might bring in other areas of the economy.[5]

From a political, ideological, and practical standpoint, Hawley concludes, "cartelization" and "centralized planning" were not realistic alternatives in the context of American life. The efforts to use the government to foster consumer organization and enhance the market power of consumers were probably doomed to failure. Consumers had neither the desire nor the political organization "nor the well developed consumer ideology that would have been necessary to establish anything more than a token program."

The solution to the economic crisis then began to fall more heavily upon the federal government through the new fiscal and monetary policies based upon the theories of the English economist John Maynard Keynes. The "Keynsian revolution" in economics led more slowly toward centralized controls within the federal government. The critical problems within the federated economy, exposed in the Great Depression, thus remained unsolved in the transfer of fiscal and monetary control to the federal government.

The Great Depression was a major turning point in American history. The major problems of the economy began to be diagnosed and acted upon through federal agencies and commissions. The government began broad-scale efforts to solve the problems of poverty, depressed cities, corporate monopoly and exploitation, generated by the business sector.

But the government grew increasingly centralized and bureaucratic. Indeed, the government became a problem to itself following World War II with the growth of the welfare state. The government's War on Poverty bogged down in bureaucratic red tape and the welfare system expanded, out of control with prohibitive costs to the taxpayer. The federal program in Model Cities suffered major set-backs through multitiered levels of decision-making. Federal policies on revenue sharing began to cost more than they were worth. Gradually, it became apparent that the government could not solve all the problems generated by the business economy at the national level. The business economy itself must do it.

This is where our scientific problem begins. We want to examine the extent to which the economic order is socially organized on a federal basis so that people manage their own affairs without state controls. We then want to examine the possibility of a system of social federalism that could monitor and develop free enterprise in the public interest with a minimum of oversight from federal and state governments.

The Scientific Study of Federalism

The scientific study of federalism in contemporary economic affairs is guided by a research model called the "ideal type." The ideal type was originally formulated by Max Weber, who described it as a "historical configuration" of traits. For research purposes, the sociologist would "select" and "abstract" a pattern of traits from events in history. This pattern could then serve as a model for the examination of social reality. The model could be applied to concrete instances for comparison and finally for analysis of the way the pattern was repeated or changed over time under different circumstances.

Weber himself selected the historic traits of "bureaucracy" as a research guide into the nature of modern society. He considered bureaucracy to be the most important social structure of this modern period and "rationality" the most significant value. Bureaucracy was the accepted mode of "legal rationality." It had serious flaws, but it was the most rational method available for organizing human resources.

This pattern of social scientific modeling introduced by Weber in his concept of bureaucracy applies to the concept of a federation. A federation is a more complicated organization than a bureaucracy and probably more critical to modern development. The problems of federalism are intercorporate, intercultural, and interinstitutional. The federation itself may express some traits of bureaucracy, but it is a totally different type of organization. Its central value is "democracy." It has its own rationality. The federation lies partly beyond bureaucracy as a major historical configuration of the modern period; it could help solve many of the problems of modern bureaucracy. In the long run its development may be of the greatest consequence to the well-being of society and, indeed, the world.

Federations are organized locally, statewide, regionally, nationally, and internationally. A local community council, for example, is a type of federation. It may include the Boy Scouts, Girl Scouts, YMCA, welfare agencies, and business groups. Here we see different institutions as well as different types of corporations involved in a federation. At the world level, the United Nations is a federation of 135 countries that must adjust to one another democratically. They must solve the toughest problems with the widest differences in social, cultural, political, and economic life represented in the membership.

The growth of federations in the modern period, therefore, is not simply characteristic of the political order. It is characteristic of all major social institutions and associations. The federation has developed within the sciences, the professions, organized religion, social services, and among fraternal groups. Major national associations in the United States are organized around the concept of the federation. The federation is a pattern of organization whose significance extends beyond bureaucracy.

The historic model of bureaucracy has no horizon extending outside a corporation's own self-interest. It cannot treat intercorporate or international problems. It cannot answer some of the most critical problems of conflicting interests in the modern period. Nor can it answer the problem of ideology; it cannot deal with the singular devotion of members to a corporate set of duties. One person may become a patriot of the bureaucratic state, another a zealot of the bureaucratic church, and another an "organization man" of the bureaucratic business. The model of bureaucracy by itself does not deal with the broader purposes and methods of living together in society. It does not treat the problem of "value" and the cultural factor in society.

For our purposes, a theory of bureaucracy by itself does not lead researchers to see the resolution of intercorporate problems in the economic order. It does not treat the problems of corporate competition and conflict that are endemic to the capitalist economy. It cannot help resolve the problem of monopoly in the business community. It cannot tell us how to retain corporate autonomy and integrity in the battle of business firms for economic supremacy.

Our key hypothesis is that the social development of the economic order involves the formation of decentralized federations in the production, distribution, and consumption of goods and services. We note here that these decentralized federations have already begun to develop on a significant scale. But our theory of development carries this further into the realm of social planning. We contend later that social planning from within these federations can reduce the pace of growth in government bureaucracy; that the elimination of corporate monopoly, dominance, and exploitation is not the primary responsibility of government but rather of organized business and labor acting in the public interest.

The concept of federalism in the order of economic life has the potential for helping to resolve the most critical problem of the capitalist society in *the growth of the state.* It may even provide the basis for eliminating the "unresolvable" problems of corporate bureaucracy itself: excessive centralism, administrative inefficiency, resistance to change, red tape, complex office hierarchies, dependency on "expertise," and the injustices resulting from "command authority."

The meaning of Federation in the Economic System

Webster's Dictionary defines a federation as "a state consolidated from several states which retain limited powers . . . ." This definition assumes that a federation is a political body of independent "states." The concept of *federation*, however, has emerged importantly beyond the concept of the formal state. It has developed in great variety in every major institution of society.

Here we define a federation as a group of people belonging to relatively independent associations who join together in a larger body to further goals common to all members. A federation is a form of democratic governance in which organizations agree to grant formal control over certain common affairs to a central authority while retaining control over their own affairs. In the broad sense, then, the federation is a combination of autonomous groups that have joined forces to enhance their individual purposes.

Our general hypothesis is that the capitalist economy has been moving gradually from a type of economic feudalism, where corporate monarchies battle for supremacy, toward a type of economic federalism, where autonomous organizations seek a common ground to regulate their economic affairs together. The growth of trade union federations among laborers, trade association federations among executives, and cooperative federations among consumers constitutes a major form of social development in the economic order. It bears no resemblance to the mythic images of laissez-faire where small firms compete with one another in the marketplace. These federations are now defining major policies in the economic system of the United States.

In light of this development, our first task is to examine these federations to determine how they function in the economy. We can then indicate the kind of scientific studies that will lead us toward a policy encouraging the social development of federations in the economic order.

The Federated Economy

A study of federalism relative to the economic order begins with an examination of actual federations already existing among workers, managers, and consumers. We are interested first in how these federations express the values of social democracy and justice and second in how they express bureaucratic dominance. These perspectives then become important in conducting self-studies.

Federations of Trade Unions

In 1955 the American Federation of Labor and the Congress of Industrial Organizations joined to form the AFL-CIO. In 1960, the AFL-CIO represented 184 unions with U. S. membership of more than 18 million workers. It accounted for about 97 percent of all union members. The UAW later withdrew from the federation, and other unions such as the Confederated Union of America remained outside the AFL-CIO.

The old and the new federal structures can be described as follows:[6]

The old American Federation of Labor was an organization of 103 unions that were almost completely independent. The only power granted to the Federation was the right to expel a constituent union. The Federation had no power to dissolve a union or discipline its members. The AFL included some 50 state federations, 800 city and country organizations, and over 1200 locals not affiliated with a national union but directly affiliated with the central body of the AFL.

The supreme law-making body of the AFL was the annual convention. Delegates from the national unions were allotted on the basis of membership, which guaranteed control to the larger unions. These delegates attended an annual convention to choose a president and 13 vice presidents, who composed the Executive Council. The Executive Council carried out the decisions of the convention, kept an eye on government legislation, conducted research, and supervised organized drives.

Financial support for the AFL activities was obtained mainly from a tax of 4 cents each month collected from each member of the national unions. The central body also received money from its directly affiliated locals, from state federations and city centrals.

Although the AFL was organized on craft lines, it authorized the creation of "departments" with similar interests: the Building and Construction Trades Department, the Metal Trades Department, the Railway Employees Department, etc. The functions of these departments included "union organization," settling jurisdictional disputes, assisting in collective bargaining.

The CIO was organized along similar lines before the merger. The supreme law-making body of the CIO was the national convention to which delegates were sent from regional groups. Similarly, the CIO was a confederation of independent national unions with large unions in control. Its Executive Council functioned very much like that of the AFL. The Council exercised much more control, however, largely because of a different organizational history. Most of the national unions were originally created by the CIO, and therefore the central body exercised more influence over them than the AFL had over its national unions.

The new "combined" federal structure of the AFL-CIO differs slightly from that of the older unions. The supreme governing body is still in the convention, but

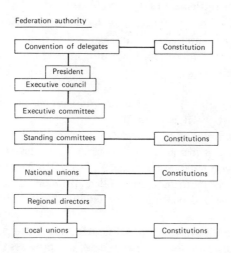

Figure 4.

it meets every two years rather than every year. Delegates are assigned according to the membership of unions, which assures more than twice as many votes for the old AFL unions as for former CIO unions. State and local bodies affiliated directly with the confederation are assigned one vote each. An Executive Council consisting of 27 vice presidents meets at least three times a year at the call of the president. The Executive Council is empowered to carry out the wishes of the convention and to take appropriate action to safeguard the interests of the federation. The Executive Council chooses an executive committee composed of six vice presidents, which meets bimonthly. Its duties are to "advise and consult with the executive officers on policy matters."

Various standing committees, responsible to the Executive Council and the convention, deal with matters of interest to labor. There are standing Committees on legislation, civil rights, political education, ethical practices, international affairs, education, social security, economic policy, community services, housing, research, public relations, safety and occupational health, and veterans' affairs.

Unions in the AFL-CIO subscribe to four constitutions. First, the AFL-CIO has a general constitution, which is compatible with all others. Second, each department, such as the Building and Construction Trades Department and the Food and Beverage Trades Department, has its own constitution. Third, each international or national union has a constitution. Fourth, each local has a constitution. (See Figure 4.)

National constitutions state "union purposes" such as aiding workers in securing improved wages, hours, and working conditions. The constitution of the Tobacco Workers, for example, states that the union is formed in part "to promote the acceptance of mutual working agreements between the employer and the employees and the settlement of disputes by arbitration."

The constitution of the AFL-CIO provides that membership shall be open not only to national and international unions but also to state and local bodies. The federation is oriented to certain basic principles as guides to policy and social action:

1. The autonomy of each national or international union is constitutionally recognized. (Article III, Section 7)
2. Each affiliated union is to respect the jurisdiction of other unions and agree to cease raiding of membership. (In cases of disputes, the matter is settled in consultation with federation officials.) (Article III, Section 10)
3. The principles of both industrial and craft unionism are recognized as "appropriate, equal and necessary" for union organization. (Article VIII, Section 9)
4. The union specifically condemns discrimination in trade unions on the basis of "race, creed, color, or national origins" and provides the machinery to end such discrimination.

National unions remain relatively autonomous. They are dependent upon the AFL-CIO central body for aid in crisis, for organizational drives, and for specialized tasks. But they are independent in regard to internal administration and union policy, as long as that policy does not violate the principles of the central body. The national unions vary in size from less than 100 members to hundreds of thousands. They vary in internal organization from almost pure democracies to pure autocracies.

In most national unions the president is reelected year after year for as long as he or she wishes to be president. The power of the president and the executive board varies from union to union. John L. Lewis in the United Mine Workers and James Caesar Petrillo in the American Federation of Musicians ruled by command. In other unions the power of the president and executive board is under more democratic control. But even in the more democratically structured unions the power of union officers is similar to that of executives in the business corporation. The union's executive board has the power *to issue charters to locals and to withdraw them, to repeal locals' rules that violate the union constitution, to oversee the union press, and to prepare the report for the convention.*

The local unions vary considerably in their organization and membership. Some locals include all workers of one employer; others, all workers in a given plant or series of plants and employers. Some craft union locals are formed on an industrial basis when the national union is industrial in nature. Most locals have one or two hundred members, but some have fewer than a dozen members, and two or three have more than the smaller national unions.

The constitutional functions in the local of a national union can be summarized as follows:

1. The governing of the local, including election of its officials and the collection and allocation of dues.
2. Participation in collective bargaining and grievance procedures.
3. Discussions and decisions concerning strikes.
4. Limited employment service.
5. Communication between the members of the local on the one hand and the international and other union bodies on the other.
6. Social services for members, such as credit unions, housing cooperatives, scholarships for members' children, and medical clinics.
7. Educational and recreational programs for members.
8. Community activities, including participation in the United Way Drive.
9. Promotion of legislation.

The national union usually has the right to approve or reject the constitution of the local. The national also has the right to determine the jurisdiction of the union and qualifications for local membership, and the power to suspend or expel locals from the union. At the same time, the local union has the right to send its own delegates to the national convention in proportion to the size of its membership.[7]

National unions divide the United States into sections with *regional headquarters*. The UAW, for example, is organized in regions with some eighteen directors, depending upon the number of members. The regional director in charge of each region is elected during the biennial national convention by delegates from locals within the region at a meeting of their own. The regional director is in a special position because of the dual nature of the office. The regional director represents his region on the International Executive Board; he is also an official representative of the International within his region, implementing the policies of the International and carrying out the policies of the Board in the region.

Union Federations and Values

The union structure reflects a mixture of bureaucratic and managerial models of operation combined within the federal model. The union is also an expression of basic values of democracy and justice as conceived within the larger society. It is interlaced with many different interests and values, which require attention in the process of studying the federal dimension.

Structures of Social Democracy. The democratic dimension of union structures was studied by Lipset and Trow in a model case. Taking the typographical union for their research base, they showed how *tendencies toward oligarchy were reduced by creating democratic structures.*

In the typical union, the salaries of the top leadership are sizable compared with the wages of lower echelon workers. They do not compare equitably with the rank and file nor with middle-range leadership in the union. This means that top officers will have added incentive to hold on to their positions at the time of reelection. There is a special material incentive built into the salary structure that creates a desire to maintain leadership beyond the purer purposes of furthering the larger interests of the union. The salaries of the top officers in the typographical union, however, are not much higher than the top paid positions of the typographers themselves on the job. That means that if a union officer were not reelected, and he were again to become a worker, his salary would not change appreciably. His interest in keeping his official position is more likely to be focused on the interest of the union.

The popular conception of unions has been that there is often little room for debate of issues since the top officers of the union control the information and the ideas for change. In the typographical union, however, there is a competitive party system similar to the political order. Issues can be debated, with support provided for minority opinion. Furthermore, the union newspapers print these differences so that the rank and file can be aware of the issues among leaders contending for office at the national level.

It is important to note that the "oligarchy" that is described as prejudicing federal organization is a concept drawn from a democratic model of performance. It is not conceived to be the central problem from a managerial model. The managerial model is judged from values of efficiency, productivity, effectiveness, and growth, while the democratic model is judged from values of rank-and-file participation in decision-making, equal opportunity for leadership, and fair representation of the issues. If corporate management were judged on the latter values, their performance would be poorly recorded, but the union is responsible for reconciling both sets of values as an expression of its federal structure.

If democratic practices are not observed within the national and local unions, the federal government enforces them. The 1959 passage of the Labor-Management Reporting and Disclosure Act is an example of this fact. According to Title I of this act, the *union must engage in democratic voting procedures, must use the secret ballot,* and must see that every member receives a copy of the current contract with management. Title II requires that *each labor union have a constitution and by-laws and be given specific information concerning the amount and use of union funds.* Title III provides for trusteeships in which the national or international union may take over a local and administer its affairs only *under specific conditions so that it does not interrupt democratic processes in the local.* Title IV states the procedures required for honest elections and empowers the Secretary of Labor *to investigate departures from these procedures upon complaints from union members.* Title V requires bonding of financial officers of the union and prohibits any union from lending its officials more than $2000.

One effect of the act was to relate the union federation more closely with the government. Another effect was to enforce a transfer of democratic practices from the political to the economic sphere.[8]

Structures of Social Justice. In the interest of maintaining standards of fairness and equity in administrative practices, a Public Review Board was established in the United Auto Workers under the leadership of Walter Reuther. Its purpose was to strengthen the appeal procedures within the union as they affect the rights and privileges of individual members and affiliated union groups. The conditions of operation of the review board were written into the constitution of the union.

The members of the review board are appointed by the president subject to approval of the executive board. The board members are selected for their personal integrity and independence of UAW influence. The board has authority to make final binding decisions on all cases appealed to it on matters related to ethical practices adopted by the union. Any person can issue a complaint. If it arises within a "subordinate body," individuals must seek redress first through appeal to the local union. Failing there, they submit their complaint to the executive board, which forwards a copy of the complaint to the chairman of the Public Review Board. The executive board has the initial responsibility for investigating the complaint, while the review board chair is kept advised of the case. If the complaining member is dissatisfied with the investigation or disposition of the case at this point, he or she may appeal directly to the review board. If the review board is dissatisfied with the investigation, it may also act independently of the executive council to take the case.

The Public Review Board is constitutionally required to submit an annual report of its activities in which it draws the attention of the membership to any situation it has found to be improper and comments upon the steps that have been taken to correct the situation. The board is required to include a summary of all appeals it has handled during the year. Copies of the board's annual report must then be mailed to all local unions, and notice of this fact published in the next edition of the union newspaper, *Solidarity.* Copies must be available to members upon request and distributed to all delegates at the annual convention. They must also be made available to the public.

The review board must establish an office separate and apart from any union building. The operating costs are maintained by the union, but the staff and personnel are independently selected by the board. The union is bound by its constitution to accept the decisions of the board as final.[9]

Social Criticism of Union Federations

Democratic practices within the union have begun to develop in these important ways, but they are not yet well established. Certain aspects of union structure have been strongly attacked by many union leaders. The following outline summarizes basic problems concerning union democarcy in the national unions:

Problem I. The union convention is the supreme law-making authority according to the constitution, but in reality it does not serve in that capacity.

1. A few unions hold a convention every year, some every other year, others every third and fourth year, still others at irregular intervals. (The prohibitive cost of travel time and expenses is part of the reason for few conventions at intervals exceeding two years.)

2. While some conventions are merely audiences registering approval of programs presented by the officers, others are deliberative bodies. Yet, in the latter case, the work is done in committees whose membership is often selected or influenced by the union president.

3. Conventions frequently do not exhibit fair representation among small locals. For example, the Typographical Union convention in 1950 had 368 local delegates out of a total of 900 locals.

4. Conventions are sometimes too large to operate effectively or democratically in the time alloted to them. At the Steelworkers convention in 1958, there were about 3500 delegates.

5. Special conventions can be requested by the union membership but only with great difficulty. The majority of unions demand a petition of 15 to 20 percent of the membership and require that petitioners come from a specified number of different localities.

6. In some unions the reports of committees to the convention may not be amended. While some unions may bar amendments, others do consider motions from the convention floor to "recommit" committee reports.

Problem II. Union authority is highly centralized, first in the office of the president and second in the executive board and standing committees.

1. Between conventions, the supreme powers are vested in the president and executive board. In over two thirds of the unions, the convention elects the national officers and then confers executive and legislative powers on them between meetings.

2. Committees are generally appointed by the president or executive board subject to approval by the convention. If committees are to be kept of workable size, the majority of local unions must have no representation on any of them.

3. In a 1968 survey among unions, of presidents in office, those with the longest tenure were President J. P. Tahney of the American Railway and Airline Supervisors Association and President Eric Lindberg of the Machine Printers and Engravers Associations of the United States, both of whom assumed office in 1934. At the same time, changes had been made. Almost 67 percent of the union had presidents elected since 1960.

4. The members of the executive board usually run on the same slate as the president. The executive board member, therefore, is often handpicked by the president and must make his decisions with the knowledge that he will need support in future elections.

Problem III.   The judicial system of unions is not based on the principle of separation of powers and in many cases is patently discriminatory.

1. Local members who have committed offenses are usually tried by the local executive board, which may contain members against whom offenses have been committed.
2. Breeches of discipline carrying penalties (e.g., fines or suspension of membership) are often vaguely defined. They include such phrases as "conduct unbecoming a union member," "creating dissension," "slandering officers." At the same time, it should be noted that enforcement powers are highly limited.
3. The national union has the right to suspend or expel locals, and to approve or reject local constitutions, with no judicial recourse for local members.
4. Among the duties of the Executive Council of the AFL-CIO are keeping the federation free from corrupt "communist influences." To achieve the latter, the Council has the right to investigate or make recommendations to, the affiliate involved. The Council may suspend a union found guilty on charges of corruption or subversion. The Council has the right to remove from office any executive officer or council member found to be a follower of a subversive organization.
5. Racial discrimination has been an open practice in certain unions and in the past has included discriminatory provisions as part of the constitution.

Problem IV.   Union publications such as bulletins and newspapers are centralized administratively within the jurisdiction of top elective officers without opportunity for the opposition to be heard.

1. In a survey of 189 national and international unions, 164 issued a total of 193 publications. Of the 25 unions reporting no publications, all had fewer than 65,000 members; 14 had 2000 or less. The union president was reported as editor by 51 national and international unions; other union elective officials were reported by 23; in 35 unions, a "specifically designated person" was editor.
2. The provision of the Laundry Workers' constitution requiring that its journal or bulletin print such "matter as the General President may direct" describes the prevailing constitutional fact.

Professional research and union self-studies must take these critical features of federal organization into account. The study of trade unions in the decentralized federal economy is clearly one of the most complicated and challenging areas of social research today.

Federations of Business and the Professions

The trade association is a nonprofit organization consisting of business competitors who join together to advance mutual business interests. It can best be understood in its historical context.

Its historical origin can be traced back to ancient times in China, Egypt, the Middle East, Greece, and Rome. Artisans and merchants in those times found it in their mutual interests to organize. The medieval phase of trade grouping is found in the guild system from the thirteenth to the seventeenth centuries. The main objectives of the Guilds were the production of high-quality items and the establishment of a fair price for the goods produced.[10]

When the guilds collapsed at the end of the medieval period, trade associations did not immediately assume their place. It was only after a century and a half, from 1700 to 1850, after relatively unrestrained and unregulated rivalry in trade, that the new associations were created. Competitive conditions and widening markets following the Civil War forced entrepreneurs into combinations of one kind or another. Their motives seem fairly clear. They wanted to gain economic advantages through cooperative trade expansion, to protect themselves from their own excesses in trade conflict, and, finally, to protect themselves from the rising demands of labor unions. It was a step toward self-governance beyond the framework of the independent business enterprise.

From the beginning of the twentieth century to the present time their growth has been irregular but with a steady increase observable over the long run. In 1910 there were a total of 800 associations (local, state, and national); in 1920 there were 2000; in 1930 there were 4000; in 1940 there were 8000; in 1950 there were 12,000.[11]

In 1966 W. Lloyd Warner and associates sent an eight-page questionnaire to more than a thousand large-scale associations in transportation, communications, utilities, finance, insurance, real estate, agriculture, manufacturing, and other national businesses. Their answers (on a questionnaire return of 72.5 percent) revealed the following facts:

Over a third of these associations had annual incomes over $500,000. Some incomes ran into the millions. Most of them obtained their money from their membership. About a third had staffs of more than thirty employees; 10 percent had more than a hundred employees. Three cities—Washington, D. C., New York, and Chicago—contained the overwhelming majority (69%) of the headquarters of all trade associations. Affiliation with other trade associations was popular among all varieties of trade and business associations. Fifty-eight percent of all trade associations took public stands on social, political, and economic issues.[12]

Federated Structures

Trade associations are organized either vertically or horizontally and through either direct or federated memberships. A direct membership consists of *persons* or *businesses* directly affiliated with the trade association. A federated membership consists of *associations* affiliated with a parent body, which may in-

Table 7. Functional and Geographic Groupings of Trade and Professional
Associations

Manufacturing	Distributive	Service	Professional
		National	
Automobile Manufacturers Association	Association of Food Chains	Linen Supply Association of America	American Institute of Architects
		Regional	
Southern Brick and Tile Manufacturers Association, Inc.	Southern Industrial Distributors Association	Southwest Warehouse and Transfermen's Association	Western Society of Engineers
		State	
Pensylvania Bakers Association	Texas Butane Dealers Association	Oklahoma Restaurant Association	California Osteopathic Association
		Local	
St. Louis Association of Ice Industries	Chicago Association of Tobacco Distributors	Laundryowner's Bureau of Boston	Los Angeles County Medical Association

clude some direct memberships of firms or individuals, depending upon the constitution.

A horizontally organized association consists of members who are in the same or similar fields of endeavor. The Rubber Manufacturers Association is a horizontal group of manufacturers of rubber products in which members are directly affiliated. Another example is the National Association of Retail Grocers, who are interested in retail food sales.

Vertical associations are fewer in number. They generally cover a product in a trade area from producer to the untimate consumer. Members may consist of manufacturers, wholesalers, retailers, and related groups having a common interest in a product. An example would be the Better Vision Institute, which includes manufacturers, distributors, and service people in the optical products field. Another example is the American Dental Association.

Trade associations can be classified functionally and geographically.[13] (See Table 7.) National associations contain the largest corporations in American society with their own elaborate, complex hierarchies.

While trade associations are nonprofit corporations, their purpose is to advance the profit-making of each member and generally to benefit business.[14] They are voluntary organizations with formal rules. Members maintain separate legal independence and are usually in active competition with each other. They are free to enter or withdraw from membership at will. In most cases, eligibility for voting members requires that the candidate be engaged in the business or industry covered by the association. The by-laws of the association govern corporate affairs and provide a documented guide to the association's structure and operation.

Top authority in the association rests with the board of directors, who decide the governing policy. The administration is in the hands of a salaried executive and paid staff. As a rule, the paid executive provides continuity, while nonsalaried officers and directors alternate in brief terms of office. The executive has complete authority and responsibility over the staff, makes his or her own selections as to personnel, and determines personnel policies. It is not unusual today for an association executive to be paid a salary in excess of the amount paid to most chief executives of the association's member companies.

The income of most associations is based upon dues. A basic question is how to assess membership dues given the various assets of member business firms. In a survey conducted by the American Society of Association Executives, it was found that *sales* is the single most popular dues structure.[15]

Federated Activities

The activities of trade associations are important to examine because they tell us the key areas of common governance among firms. They tell us where social development is possible given existing federated arrangements.

Trade association activities can be categorized in the following ways:

1. *Clearinghouse and Communications.* Member firms are kept aware of activities through publications (newspapers, journals, annual reports, bulletins), which provide information about government legislation, trade conferences, staff projects, news about firm members, etc.

2. *Government Relations.* Staff members conduct studies on laws affecting their industry, make congressional appearances, and exert political pressure on legislators.

3. *Trade Relations.* Associations search for new markets, coordinate advertising, contact related trade industries. For example, a specialty group in medicine might meet with manufacturers of surgical equipment to discuss new techniques and encourage development of special instruments for newly devised procedures.

4. *Trade Practices.* Staff studies unfair competition and business ethics (e.g., defamation of competitors, style piracy, breaches of contract, blacklists, rebates, fake fire sales, bankruptcy, frauds). Enforcement of trade practice rules adopted by an industry, however, must be carried out by the Federal Trade Commission in supplemental legal proceedings.

5. *Public Relations.* Staff deals with adverse publicity and suggests courses of action for the industry to take remedial steps. It may distribute public relations packets or bulletins to member firms.

6. *Trade Conferences and Sales Promotion.* Staff helps member firms develop management skills, know-how about financial controls, sales techniques. Sales promotion programs are effective with these industries composed of many small manufacturers in local business.

7. *Labor Relations.* Some associations enter labor relations. The association executive can be a labor negotiator.

8. *Statistics.* Some associations report on productivity in sales, engage in sales planning, and provide information on inventories and raw material supplies.

9. *Market Research.* Some associations conduct market surveys and employ market analysts, who interpret results for a course of action for the industry.

10. *Technical Research.* Some associations maintain laboratories of their own, and also contract with colleges and technical schools for industrial research.

11. *Other Activities.* Uniform cost accounting; standardization; simplification of products; inspection; grading; certification; commercial arbitration; foreign trade promotion; legal advice to members; credit reporting; insurance studies; packaging and warehousing; patents, copyrights, trade marks and design protection; machinery and equipment exchanges; employment placement bureaus; engineering services; library, visual aid services.

Trade Federations and Values

Trade associations operate to control economic activities in the larger society as *alternatives* to government control over these same activities. Many of the functions and activities just listed serve as "federal equivalents" or functional alternatives to state and national government agencies.

Put another way, these federations function like trade unions to fulfill certain basic values of the society. The societal values fulfilled in these alternatives are related to the values of social democracy and justice. We can see the key issues resolved by federations center around the norms of "fair representation" and "equity." Such norms are considered important to the constituencies of trade associations.

Structures of Social Democracy: Alternatives to State Regulatory Commissions. Trade associations have long sought to control bribery, rebates, misrepresentation in advertising, adulteration of products, and many other practices of business that are not in the public interest. Their history is written with failure as well as with success. But most significant is the close parallel in regulatory action taken by both private and governmental agencies. The private alternative clearly serves as a "functional equivalent" of formal government.

The following series of cases illustrate the close functional relation between state governance and social governance.

Trade bureaus.   At the beginning of this century, paint manufacturers were privately studying how to deal with the problem of bribery that had crept into their business. Sharp competition had brought them to the point where manufacturers realized that if they continued to tolerate or support such practices they would soon destroy the industry. In 1917 two trade associations of paint and varnish manufacturers adopted an iron-clad Anti-Rebate Agreement as a condition of membership. They jointly agreed not to pay any gratuities, commissions, rebates, or loans to employees or business concerns to whom they sold their product and not to permit their salesmen expense money for other than legitimate expenses. The two associations set up their own Unfair Competition Bureau, which functioned to solve these problems by investigating complaints and settling issues through consultation with the parties involved.[16]

That very same year the Federal Trade Commission was established by the government to do the equivalent thing—to regulate business in the same categories, only on a broader scale.

Democratic governing boards.   The efforts of the FTC and the federal courts have been directed toward strengthening trade structures that function in the public interest. An early case in the lumber industry where trade associations ran afoul of the law illustrates how this is done.

Certain lumber associations sought to "guarantee" their products in the public interest by providing an official stamp marking the grade of lumber being sold. The lumber firms were interested in protecting the building trades and the average customer from cheap and unreliable products sold competitively by companies out to make a quick profit from the public.[17] However, as this practice developed, the association's grades came to serve as the basis for unfair competition with firms who were not members of the association but whose lumber was comparable in quality. Court decrees were issued against abuses in advertising, and the court required one trade association to organize a *democratic governing board* that would be representative of all lumber companies and would then minimize the likelihood of unfair practices in the future.

The case in point involved the Southern Pine Association, which was ordered by the court to set up a "separate and autonomous bureau" to conduct grade marking services, which were to be available "on equal terms to all manufacturers of southern pine lumber" regardless of their membership in the particular trade group. Charges were to be assessed against "subscribers" uniformly, and the Bureau's affairs were to be managed by a Board of Governors. The Bureau could promote the sale of Southern pine as distinguished from lumber of other species, but it could not promote the sale or use of lumber manufactured by any single firm. At the same time no attempts could be made to discredit the work of any other competent lumber-grading and inspecting agency.[18]

In such cases the court determines the conditions under which voluntary activities can operate, so there is no need for a government agency to supervise or monitor the activities.

Structures of Social Justice: Alternatives to State Statutes and Courts.

Intercorporate standardization. The grading practice of lumber industries is part of an exceedingly complex area called standardization. It is an area in which trade association activities serve as functional alternatives to federal bureaus and state courts. In this case trade associations work in tandem with the Bureau of Standards of the Commerce Department.[19]

The American Standards Association is foremost among all those concerned with this problem, serving as a clearinghouse for standards of activity in the private sector. It does not develop standards itself but it provides educational materials and recommends procedures for those who are interested in standardization. It serves as a federation of over 100 trade associations, technical societies, professional groups, and consumer organizations, in addition to a membership of 2300 firms. Its organization has developed almost 1600 standards dealing with almost every facet of the economy.[20] The result of private efforts to standardize in the public interest is summed up in a statement by the American Society of Association Executives:

Through cooperative efforts in research, development and dissemination of the Nation's goods and services, associations have made it possible to manufacture a light bulb in New York that will fit a socket in Los Angeles, for a size 5 shoe made in Boston to fit a wearer in New Orleans and for a doctor's prescription issued in Pittsburgh to be filled safely in Denver. Standardization has made America a consumer giant and only through the voluntary exchange of information combined with efforts toward uniformity—made possible through associations—has this been accomplished.[21]

Intercorporate code making. Trade rules and ethical codes have developed gradually through the leadership of trade association executives with government pressure and support. The Federal Trade Commission began working with trade groups as far back as 1919 to promote fair practices and introduce concepts of fairness and justice into the system.

Trade practice rules have developed in some 160 branches of industry through the aid of the FTC in conference with industrial groups. They are generally divided into two groups. One group consists of rules that are "mandatory" insofar as they simply clarify the existing law that applies to a particular industry. A second group consists of rules that are "voluntary" insofar as they are recommendations of ethical practices that may or may not be legal, depending upon special circumstances. Trade associations play an important part in the formation of these rules in FTC conferences.

For example, the Orthopedic Appliance and Limb Manufacturers Associations have established Group 1 mandatory rules covering such malpractice areas as deception, promises that the product will "fit," deceptive testimonials or demonstrations, misuse of the term "custom made," use of the word "free," false advertising and invoicing. The Association's Group II voluntary rules cover matters such as sharing improved techniques, the importance of a personal fitting, and cooperation with doctors.[22]

The norms of everyday industrial and commercial practices have helped to develop a business ethic. Ethical codes have developed among trade associations in a form comparable in many ways to those established in professional legal and medical associations. We need to know more empirically about the extent to which practices follow the norms, but we do know that official procedures and agencies exist to support these codes. Trade associations have created institutions of counsel, mediation, and arbitration where questions of ethics and justice are involved in business activities.

Intercorporate arbitration boards. The arbitration board was established as a way of handling trade conflict early in the history of the trade association movement. Over thirty years ago, Edgar Heermance described how private boards were formed in the public interest. Joint trade councils brought members into "closer alignment" for the purpose of removing the causes of warring competition, which impaired the efficiency of firms and adversely affected the consumer. Heermance's attitude regarding court delays and legal costs involved in arbitration would be shared by trade association executives today.

In the shoe and leather industries, for example, a Joint Council of Arbitration was formed in 1920 by the organizations of manufacturers, wholesalers, retailers and tanners. A considerable proportion of the disputes which arise are submitted to the Council. . . . [The rules of procedure state that the arbitrators "shall be guided by principles of equity and fairness. Technical or legal points should not prevail against the establishment of an equitable claim."] In the silk industry, where arbitration was established in 1898, this means of settlement is practically universal. It has come to be recognized that differences between seller and buyer cannot properly be settled by the courts, because of the expense and delay involved, the bad feeling engendered, and the ignorance of the courts and lawyers as to the technical points. Up to the close of 1930 a total of nearly 500 disputes had been settled in this way. The digest of cases, published annually by the Silk Association of America, makes interesting reading for the student of self regulation.[23]

In 1958 the Chamber of Commerce conducted a survey of 634 trade associations. It was found that 195 associations were engaged in some form of commercial arbitration. Some associations heard and settled problems among themselves; at least 133 associations reported cooperating with other associations in forms of arbitration.[24]

This functional alternative to government arbitration has been developing over the years to adjust trade conflict in the interest of all associations. The end result has been in the public interest and toward the development of the economy as a self-governing institution.[25]

Of course, a legal risk is taken by businessmen establishing judicial institutions. A trade association may find that by acting as a bureaucratic court of law and imposing penalties on offenders it may be violating the antitrust laws. Private "judicial" decisions cannot interfere with an alleged offender's right to do business. If they interfere, the decision is illegal.

Since competing members within an association tend to act prejudicially when in judgment of one another, most association executives find that it is important to locate professional arbiters outside the association itself. Trade association executives recommend the American Arbitration Association in most cases. The Association maintains an important function as a clearinghouse for commercial disputes of all kinds. Panel members of the Association who have specialized in various fields of industry are available as consultants and arbiters to firms in dispute.[26]

Social Criticism of Trade and Professional Federations

Trade and professional federations engage in activities to protect their own self-interests and advance their common cause. These activities, however, can act to the detriment of nonmembers such as customers and competing business. Social criticism of their organization is essential to the development of public policy and to federation self-studies.[27]

First, the lobbying power of federations in Congress is said to be very great as opposed to other groups. Even though it has been difficult to measure their power since expenditures have been kept secret, their influence on government and its agencies is generally accepted to be among the most powerful. Nicholas Johnson, a Commissioner of the FTC once described it as part of a "subgovernment" that "endures" and is "unaffected by the tide of opinion and efforts for reform."

The relationship between the members of regulatory commissions who are public officials and the executives of big corporations and their trade associations can be very close. Those commissioners who perform their government task without incurring too much antipathy of business people are said to be rewarded by key positions in the industries they have sought to regulate. In any case, the interchange between positions of public and private offices is clear. Clifford Hardin, for example, resigned as Secretary of Agriculture to accept a top position with Ralston-Purina, a major agri-business corporation benefiting from federal programs. Carl Bagge, former member of the Federal Power Commission, later became head of the National Coal Association.[28]

The federal agencies can develop a close interlocking relationship with the industries they are designed to regulate in ways that are not in the public interest. At present there are over 50 federal administrative bodies with either direct or indirect influence over consumer affairs. Numerous studies have shown that even though these agencies were designed to serve the public interest they are often not as powerful as the trade associations.

The agencies tend to become umpires not of consumer versus industry interests but of industry versus industry. Taken together, regulation tends to perpetuate the protection of industry and the disregard of consumer interests, including the consumer interest in industrial competition.[29]

Second, the power of trade federations is advanced still further by special tax advantages. The contributions of business firms to their trade associations for lobbying expenses are tax deductible. The tax reform act of 1962 allowed deductions to be made for lobbying costs from the corporate income tax. Since the corporate income tax is set at 48 percent of net earnings, the ability to include lobbying expenses as a business expense means that the taxpayers are, in effect, paying about half the cost of that lobbying.

Third, business scholars have noted that trade federations are a "society of unequals." Their aims are worthy of pursuit, but "their realization is often rendered difficult by distrust and jealousy among member companies and inability to find men of a caliber to carry out the job." Most important, the big corporations often dominate the association. When corporate members use their power wisely, the association can be effective; but when they use their power "for their own selfish ends, the organization will prove largely ineffective."[30]

Finally, there are signs that the system of adjudication in trade and professional federations does not always function well. Studies by the Consumer Affairs Office in Boston, Massachusetts, for example, suggest that these systems are delinquent in their duties especially when linked to state boards. Citizens who have a grievance against a business or a profession (an electrician or a veterinarian) can turn to 27 different official boards in Massachusetts charged with regulating their activities. These boards have been formed to investigate complaints and determine the validity of grievances. They can take punitive action against offenders. But the Consumer Affairs Office reports that the response has been poor. The Board of Registration of Hairdressers, for example, received 6250 complaints in 1969–1970 but held only one hearing. It revoked or suspended only one license. In the same period, the State Examiners of Electricians received 6025 complaints, held five hearings, and suspended or revoked only one license. The Board of Registration in Veterinary Medicine received 48 complaints held two hearings, but suspended or revoked no licenses at all.[31]

Not all the blame for such signs of inadequacy in this case can be cast purely on the self-interests of professional associations. The problem lies partly in the structure of the boards. Board members generally work part-time for minimal compensation.

In sum, the structures of justice and democracy generally associated with trade and professional federations are said to be far from adequate. Correcting their operations involves social planning based on both scientific research and corporate self-studies.

Federations of Cooperatives and Consumer Organizations

The cooperative in the United States is a business owned generally by its customers. Federations of cooperatives and consumer organizations exist in significant numbers in the United States even though their power and influence is not as great as large-scale trade associations. Many people believe, however, that the consumer movement in the United States is leading toward a new balance of power. Leaders in the cooperative movement now see a basis for strengthening cooperative federations at the national level. Jerry Voorhis, former executive director of the Cooperative League of America, made this point in his overall assessment of the work of cooperatives in the 1960s. He sees the development of cooperative federations as a balance wheel to the organization of unions and trade associations in the context of American society. He summarizes what he has observed about the "growing power" of cooperative federations at the national level.

But like the actions of the 1960 Congress of the Cooperative League, the Consultations were symbolic of the new spirit that had begun strongly to run through cooperatives in the United States as the decade of the 1960s began. The day of "playing store," the day of the indifferently conducted "farmer's cooperative" was past. In its place had come the modern cooperative enterprises which aimed at no lesser goal than to become an effective balance wheel in a just and truly free economy of tomorrow.[32]

Cooperatives are businesses with social purposes. They pay taxes comparable to their business competitors and are under the same tax laws, with minor exceptions.[33] In many rural communities, a cooperative business will be the largest taxpayer in town. Cooperatives pay school taxes, excise taxes, social security taxes, property taxes. Since their operations are public by virtue of annual membership meetings, they cannot hide their earnings to avoid taxes. The tax difference between the cooperative and the typical business lies in the distribution of revenue to the employees or the customers. Since the cooperative is owned by its customers or its employees, it is obligated to distribute its excess income to them. The customer or employee must then pay income taxes on that received revenue.

The manner in which the cooperative system is developing as a federated part

of the economy can be anticipated in a general way by examining the cooperative sector of England, which has concentrated its cooperatives in the retail
sector of communities. It is noted later how cooperative legislation in the United
States may result in a federated society of retail cooperatives similar to the
British model.[34]

Cooperative Federations: The British Model

In England over nine million British citizens are members of retail cooperative
societies that are distributed locally according to communal units suitable to the
population: the city, the town, or the sparsely populated region. All cooperatives are incorporated under British law, which sets certain requirements for
their operation. One of these requirements, for example, is that no member may
hold more than 200 pounds in shares. This restricts any concentration of power
in the hands of one individual. However, regardless of the amount of investment
made by anyone, the one-person, one-vote policy of cooperatives is a legal requirement.

Any citizen is free to join a local retail society by obtaining a membership
form and paying a minimum of one shilling toward the first one pound share
that eventually he or she must hold as a full-fledged member. As a customer the
member buys goods, his or her number is recorded with the amount of purchase,
and a check or receipt is given. In some localities a member has a wide range of
services in the retail unit: The member can generally buy groceries, get a haircut,
eat at a restaurant, buy clothes, shoes, coal, and have laundry done through
the society. The member does not have to patronize the stores but knows that
about 10 percent is usually saved by purchasing there. Members' savings are cred-
ited to accounts, and they can withdraw it at any time; but they also know that
if they keep the savings with the society they will accumulate interest on their
shareholding. Most purchasing follows the original Rochdale principle of trading
on a cash basis only; but some societies run credit co-ops and installment purchases are possible.

The members of the local retail organization elect a board of directors. This
means that such citizens as housewives, laborers, businessmen, and professional
people may serve together on the board to determine overall policy. It does not
mean that they make particular decisions regarding merchandising and distribution, which require professional training. It means, however, that they are responsible for hiring the key administrators who do make these decisions. Their
capability in meeting the demands of such a arrangement should be no more
questioned, say the cooperators, than the capability of people to choose responsible political leaders in a democratic society. They must objectively consider
the background and experience of proposed administrators before making the

decision to hire them. From this point on, the business is conducted in a manner similar to other private businesses in the community.

Retail societies are linked to wholesale societies and producer societies. Retail societies buy from wholesale societies and are given voting rights in the latter societies. These voting powers are generally based upon the extent of purchasing that a retail society does with the wholesale society. There is no absolute requirement that purchases must be made from any particular society, but the granting of this privilege encourages such action. Wholesale societies, in turn, have organized producer societies. The Cooperative Wholesale and Scottish Cooperative Wholesale societies operated together about 260 factories and workshops in the 1940s. Producer societies include in their organization the right of workers to share in management and to purchase shares.

Retail societies have also organized producer cooperatives. Most of them are on a small scale. Hundreds of local societies have small workrooms for dressmaking, tailoring, millinery, textile making, cabinet making, upholstery departments, and so on. Large numbers bake their own bread, process their own meat; some make jam, and some have entered the bookbinding business. In any case, the profits are ultimately returned to the consumer.

Thus, social power becomes decentralized and the profits return from the top of the corporate structure back down to the consumer. The social organization of the economy is linked democratically on a voluntary basis and allows complete freedom for individual initiative to develop private enterprise outside of the cooperative sector.

The federated pattern can be diagrammed vertically even though its vertical meaning has changed. (See Figure 5.) The power and the profits are distributed throughout the system. Yet the authority ultimately rests with the consumer. The voting rights follow the pattern of customer ownership but with varying practices. In some cases these practices include worker participation in the governance of the cooperative.

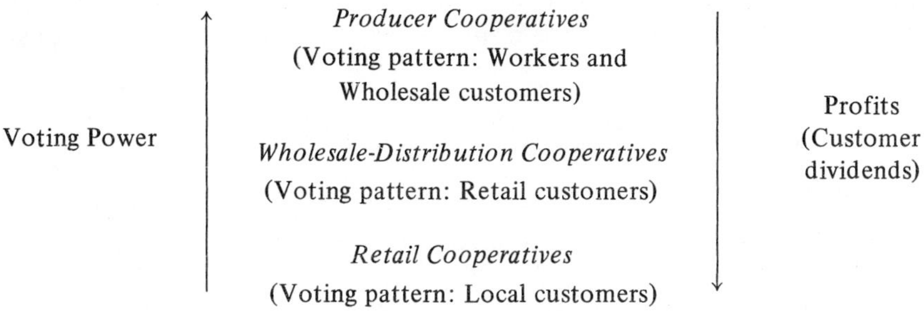

Producer Cooperatives
(Voting pattern: Workers and
Wholesale customers)

Voting Power

Profits
(Customer
dividends)

Wholesale-Distribution Cooperatives
(Voting pattern: Retail customers)

Retail Cooperatives
(Voting pattern: Local customers)

Figure 5.

Cooperatives in the United States

In the United States there are a dozen or more national federations of cooperatives. While they have grown in less orderly fashion than in England, they approximate this model to a degree. There are two national cooperative wholesale federations, for example, and two national federations of agricultural cooperatives. But the American mixture is difficult to describe relative to the English.

In England we find a great emphasis on local retail cooperatives. They are the foundation of the cooperative system. In the United States, we find that farmers are most heavily engaged in cooperatives. Here the National Council of Farmer Cooperatives has most of the agricultural marketing and regional cooperatives of farm supply. Some 26 "cooperative councils" are affiliated with the National Council. The National Federation of Grain Cooperatives is the agency for the grain marketing cooperatives. The National Milk Producers' Federation represents dairy farmers.

Cooperative federations in the United States are broadly based in many different economic activities. There are credit union leagues, for example, in almost every state. Their societywide federation is called the Credit Union National Association. Other types of nationwide federations include the National Association of Housing Cooperatives, National Telephone Cooperative Association, and the Cooperative Grange League Federation Exchange. The list of cooperative federations extends into insurance, food distribution, petroleum, communications, health, education, farming, and a variety of industries. The types of cooperatives in these fields include marketing, production, credit, and purchasing.

The Cooperative League of the United States was founded in 1916 for the purpose of promoting the cooperative movement. Its membership includes a number of the major regional cooperatives and offers a common meeting ground for cooperative federations, although it in no way contains all of them. Its interest is in customer cooperatives rather than producer cooperatives. The customer-cooperative system in England at this point appears to show a greater degree of coordination at the national level than in the United States. But the number and variety of federative cooperatives in the United States cannot be matched anywhere else in the world.

Social Criticism of the Cooperative Federation

The main criticism of the cooperative movement in the United States is generally similar to that applied to the labor movement. The argument is that it fails to live up to its ideals.

First, big cooperatives are criticized for their excessive power and for exploitation in particular cases. Big cooperatives act like big business at the national level. They can seek to maximize profits in their own interest to the detriment of others. Some critics say that the problem does not originate with the nature of the cooperative so much as with its size as an economic enterprise. It is said that big corporations of any type will lead to some exploitation regardless of ideals. Put another way, all large-scale organizations will begin to dominate people through their bureaucracy. Other critics have said that it is not size so much as the capitalist environment. The competitive requirements to survive in a business society lead well-intended cooperative leaders to protect their own interests. They therefore become involved in monopoly and "political payoffs" in the same manner as big business because the system requires it.

Second, the cooperative movement is criticized for being too weak. It has failed to develop the power to help transform society. It has not attained the power of either the labor movement or big business. It cannot challenge the capitalist organization of the economy. It has failed to organize consumers around the marketplace in any way comparable to the way the labor movement has succeeded in organizing laborers around the workplace. It has therefore failed to achieve in effect the hopes that Jerry Voorhis claimed would be forthcoming in the decades ahead.

Social Theory of the Federated Economy: Primitive Propositions

It is now possible to bring what we know about federations together with a theory of their place in the social economy. We begin with the concept of social governance, which refers to the nonstatist management of the economy. This will bring us in turn to a concept of how private federations govern themselves in the public interest.

First, a methodological note on this matter is important here. The concept of social governance is applied scientifically to different levels of management in the economy including the individual in the workplace, the business firm, and a whole industry. This concept guides us to formulate models that define self-governing norms under which people manage their own affairs at each unit level.

We may now introduce the primitive proposition that *self-governance at each level of economic management is enhanced or retarded by the way people are socially related in their corporate association.*[35] This proposition can be tested by defining the norms of self-governance in such a way that they can be measured. If one norm of self-governance is autonomy, for example, we can say that autonomy increases according to degrees of democratic governance in the corporation.[36] Specifically, the opportunity for people to optimize autonomy in their workplace depends on the way they are related together democratically in the governance of the corporation. In turn, the opportunity of business corporations to optimize autonomy in the marketplace depends in part on the way they govern themselves democratically in the trade association. Our underlying proposition, then, is that the way people are formally involved in democratic systems of governance affects the degree of self-governance that it is possible to attain at each unit level.

One other dimension of social governance of importance here is *mutual governance.* Mutual governance refers to a social arrangement in which people collaborate democratically to manage their own affairs. Examples of mutual governance in society would be federations, confederations, cooperatives, community councils, democratic clubs, and village associations. The federation is one system of mutual governance that offers people the opportunity to manage their own affairs and enhance their own self-interests.

We may now propose theoretically that the *norms of self-governance at each unit level are optimized as we move from bureaucratic systems of command authority to systems of mutual governance such as the federation.* We can propose that *autonomy is increased as we move from a command system to a democratic system of organization.*

We can propose that very little self-governance is permitted under a command system of authority in a business corporation. The same would be true of a socialist enterprise operating under the command authority of the Communist Party. The federation, in any case, encourages the autonomy of its members. This is because the central governing body exists by the consent of the membership. The degree to which the central body in reality serves the members' interests is of course a matter of study. But *some degree of autonomy and self-governance is advanced by the federation* compared with systems that lack democratic participation and consent of the membership. This concept then offers a sense of direction to the social development of the economy.

Now the underlying question in our theory of social governance can be stated: How can the economy be governed with the least amount of state management or regulation? Our proposition is that *self governance increases the more the major zones of management in the economy become organized through systems of mutual governance.* The more the economy becomes managed through such systems as the federation, the more the social (nonstatist) governance of the economy becomes possible.

The major zones of economic organization are conceived here as "production, distribution, and consumption." We can now say that mutual systems of governance have begun to develop within and around each zone. They can be seen in terms of trade union federations (production), trade association federations (distribution), and cooperative federations (consumption). These three types of federation are significant to the social economy because they stand outside the formal state. They exist at local, state, regional, and national levels as part of the voluntary order of economic life. Together the three types of federations contain a major reservoir of power, authority, and collective responsibility for guiding the economic life of the society. Furthermore, together they serve as a social foundation upon which the economic order could function in the public interest with much less state regulation that exists today.

This theory takes one more step. We propose that *if* the social roles of the consumer, the manager, and the laborer were equitably represented and finally integrated through these systems of mutual governance, the need for state supervision and control over economic affairs would be significantly reduced. We discuss this proposition later in more detail. At this point it simply serves as one of the primitive postulates underlying our specifications for research in the social economy.

These federations involving the production, distribution, and consumption of goods and services in the economy are in the throes of change and development in the United States. They have been generated in the capitalist environment to protect and advance the interests of people concerned with each major aspect of the economy. They are the social setting of autonomous organizations; they are the framework within which the social economy develops. The question now is: In what direction are they moving? And how can we best study them to anticipate their direction of development in society?

NOTES

1. Sobei Mogi, *The Problem of Federalism* (London: George Allen and Unwin, 1931), p. 21ff.

2. Max Weber, in D. Martindale and G. Neuwirth (eds), *The City* (New York: The Free Press, 1958).

3. Carl J. Friedrich, *Trends of Federalism in Theory and Practice* (New York: Frederick A. Praeger, 1968), p. 37ff.

4. Alexander Hamilton, James Madison, and John Jay, *The Federalist*, in Robert Maynard Hutchins (Editor in chief) *Great Books of the Western World* (Chicago: Encyclopedia Britannica, Inc., 1952).

5. Ellis W. Hawley, *The New Deal and the Problem of Monopoly* (Princeton, N. J.: Princeton University Press, 1966), p. 270.

6. The summary that follows is based on the following sources: W. Lloyd Warner (ed) *The Emergent Society* (New Haven: Yale University Press, 1967), pp. 349–407; Eugene V. Schneider, *Industrial Sociology* (New York: McGraw-Hill, 1957), pp. 245–269; AFL-CIO Constitution; UAW Constitution; correspondence with the Administrative Assistant to the Secretary-Treasurer of the UAW; Seymour Lipset, Martin Trow, and James Coleman, *Union Democracy* (Glencoe, Ill.: The Free Press, 1956); U. S. Bureau of Labor Statistics, "Directory of National and International Labor Unions in the United States, 1969, Bulletin 1665, 1970. The facts and figures contained in the discussion of "Issues of the Union Democracy" are drawn largely from this latter source. The outline of issues, however, is my own.

7. The external forces operating on the union are in many ways more important than its constitution in determining its structure. The relationship of the local to the national is likely to be determined by industrywide bargaining. Mass-production industries, for example, tend to strengthen the hand of the national union. Only the national union is really in a position to bargain with an entire industry. Only the national has the staff to give expert

advice on bargaining and to provide legal counsel and specialized economic data. Where bargaining takes place locally (e.g., in the building trades) the local power is strengthened. Also, locals that are spontaneously organized without having been organized by nationals have stronger powers.

8. Unions exist in a complicated social context that affects the structure of their federation. The union system is considered "private" and "voluntary" in the context of the larger society. The concept of "private" is opposed to the "public" (meaning "government"); and the concept of "voluntary" is opposed to "coercive." Yet the "private" actions of the union affect the "public" (meaning "general") level of wages and prices; the private actions of unions affect public access to jobs, the continuity and volume of production within society and many other matters of public concern and involvement. The extent to which membership is "voluntary" is equally as indistinct in particular cases. It is usually not possible for a union member to withdraw from the union in protest without great personal penalty, which may include losing his job. Even in the absence of a closed or union shop, the need to join a union may be more "coercive" (mandatory for keeping a job) than voluntary.

9. Recent members of the Review Board have included: Monsignor George G. Higgins. U. S. Catholic Conference; Dr. Robben W. Fleming, President, The University of Michigan; Dr. Jean T. McKelvey, New York School of Industrial and Labor Relations; Rabbi Jacob J. Weinstein, San Francisco, California; Professor Harry W. Arthurs, Osgoode Hall Law School, York University; Dr. James E. Jones, Jr., Professor of Law, The University of Wisconsin; Mr. David Y. Klein, Detroit, Michigan; Mr. Frank W. McCulloch, Washington, D. C.

10. The modern trade association differs from the guild in at least four ways. First, the medieval guild served as a monopoly in fixing prices and controlling output, whereas the modern trade association is restricted by law from regulating the market. Second, the medieval guild was composed of all employees in the industry, whereas the trade association is limited to entrepreneurs. Third, the guild had power to impose serious sanctions on members who violated its rules, whereas the trade association relies on voluntary cooperation and is limited in the amount and kind of enforcement permissible in its organization. Fourth, the guild restricted its membership, whereas the trade association in formal policy seeks new members among entrepreneurs in the industry.

11. United States Department of Commerce data.

12. This is my summary of selected facts. W. Lloyd Warner, op. cit., pp. 314–346.

13. "Your Answers About American Trade and Professional Associations," American Society of Association Executives, 1968 (Loan File). For general discussions of trade associations, see Joseph F. Bradley, *The Role of Trade Associations and Professional Business Societies of America* (University Park: Pennsylvania State University Press, 1965); George P. Lamb and Sumner S. Kettele, *Trade Association Law and Practice* (Boston: Little, Brown & Co., 1956); George D. Webster, *The Law of Associations* (Washington, D. C.: American Society of Association Executives, 1971).

14. Trade associations may be incorporated or unincorporated, but corporate status is the most prevalent structure. Approximately 87 percent of the associations are incorporated. The main advantage of incorporation is limited liability.

15. Webster, Op. cit, pp. 10, 15. There are no studies on the different degrees of influence that exist among members because of the dues structure or other variables related to the constituency of the association.

16. Edgar Heermance, *Can Business Govern Itself?* (New York: Harper & Bros., 1933), p. 204.

17. *Ibid.*, p. 94.

18. The Western Pine Association was also subjected to a legal decree of a similar sort except that its grade marking activities were not separated organizationally from the trade association itself. Cf. George P. Lamb, op. cit., pp. 92-93.

19. A "standard" is perhaps best described in the By-Laws of the National Electrical Manufacturers Association: "A standard of the NEMA defines a product, process or procedure with reference to one or more of the following: nomenclature, composition, construction, dimensions, tolerance, safety, operating characteristics, performance, quality, rating, testing and the service for which it was designed." While uniqueness and diversity are valued features of trade products, such features can lead to confusion among customers and unfair competition among businessmen. Standardization within the private sphere, therefore, has functioned to reduce the need for government action. Standardizing is an important activity of trade and professional groups like the American Society of Mechanical Engineers, the American Welding Society, the National Fire Protection Association, and the Society of Automotive Engineers.

20. Kenneth Hence, *Association Management* (Washington, D. C.: U. S. Chamber of Commerce, 1900), pp. 1-14, 44-45.

21. *Ibid.*, p. 317.

22. *Ibid.*, p. 331.

23. Edgar Heermance, op. cit., p. 93.

24. Chamber of Commerce of the United States *Association Activities* (revised: 1958), p. 8.

25. Many other trade groups have reduced the need for government controls by providing activities functionally similar to those of government agencies. In transportation, for example, the National Safety Council has a trained staff of more than 300 persons equipped to aid business on safety problems and also to help the government and the transportation industry to reduce the tremendous number of traffic injuries and deaths from auto accidents. The American Automobile Association also functions as a nonprofit organization to reduce traffic deaths through educational methods. Their safety programs (which local police would otherwise be pressed to undertake) are functionally equivalent to local government action. Still other kinds of trade activities that are functionally equivalent to government activities include programs for the conservation of natural resources, educational services to the schools, and staff consultation for the purpose of reducing prejudice and discrimination in industry and technical research.

26. Robert Coulson, *Labor Arbitration: What You Need to Know* (New York: The American Arbitration Association, 1973).

27. *Social criticism* refers to popular concern that an organization is not operating in the general interest of the people it affects. *Social critique* refers to a more penetrating analysis. It looks at the roots of a problem and points toward the ultimate resolution. It is in this latter sense that I am writing about federations and the social economy.

28. Fred R. Harris, "The Politics of Corporate Power," in Ralph Nader and Mark J. Green, *Corporate Power in America* (New York: Gross, 1973).

29. Louis M. Kohlmeier, *The Regulators* (New York: Harper and Row, 1969), p. 81. Cf. Marver H. Bernstein, *Regulating Business by Independent Commissions* (Princeton, N. J.: Princeton University Press, 1955).

30. Richard Eells and Clarence Walton, *Conceptual Foundations of Business* (Homewood, Ill.: Richard D. Irwin, 1951), p. 374.

31. *The Boston Globe,* December 26, 1973, p. 19.

32. Jerry Voorhis, *American Cooperatives* (New York: Harper & Bros., 1961), p. 207.

33. *Ibid.*, pp. 19–21.

34. The following summary is drawn principally from E. Topham and J. A. Hough, *The Cooperative Movement in Britain* (London: Longmans Green, 1948).

35. Self-governance at each level is always a function of social governance. Individual management is made possible only by social relations. Individual businesses can exist only because they are socially involved with others, as in trade associations. Individual laborers exist only as they are socially involved with others, as in unions.

36. Autonomy then becomes one sign or measure of self-governance. If we become fully operational in our model, however, we must add other norms and further divide the norm of autonomy. Autonomy can be understood by such subconcepts as "self-reliance" and "independent judgment," which in turn can be subclassified for more precision in research. Such a series of concepts then leads us to a "model" that allows us to measure how the economy governs itself at its various levels of operation. In Chapter 8, I examine a model of self-governance in more detail.

SIX

THE DEVELOPMENT OF SOCIAL FEDERATIONS:

Trends Within Developing Nations

In order to find a direction to this diverse and complex growth of social federations in the economy of the United States, we must look further into what is happening currently here and abroad. We keep in mind the key zones of production, distribution, and consumption as we look at social trends in the United States, Sweden, England, Peru, and Northern Spain. Our interest is directed especially to the way organizational activities among these three zones are becoming coordinated and integrated while at the same time advancing the autonomy and life interests of people within each zone. We are interested in how human resources are developed along with material resources in the organization of the economy. The issue is how social authority and responsible power are more widely produced within the lives of people in each zone of the economy.

These social trends in the United States and other nations can then tell us more about how to extend our theory of social governance to a theory of social development in the United States.

THE AMERICAN SCENE: RECENT SOCIAL TRENDS

Merle Fainsod, Professor of Government and Director of the Russian Research Center at Harvard University, speaks directly to the practical side of development:

Anyone who has traveled in underdeveloped countries and talked with those responsible for development programs soon runs into a familiar complaint. Over and over again he is told: "We know what needs doing; the real problem is how to get it done." At issue is more than the skeletal framework of organization for development.[1]

Blueprints and organizational charts are meaningless, Fainsod says, unless some political support, social legislation, and enlightened leadership are available for development. Following this practical concern, we want to look at areas of support, legislation, and leadership in the United States that offer a basis for development. We look at the United States as a developing country first before we turn to examine what is happening in other developing countries.

Trade Union Federations: Production Zone

American union leaders have been moving very cautiously in the direction of greater participation in corporate decision-making relative to what union leaders have been doing in many other countries. Union leaders within the United Auto Workers have probably been making more headway in the United States in this area than any other union federation. Leonard Woodcock, the UAW's president, said during a trip to Munich in 1976 that he planned to propose worker directors for the board of directors of the Chrysler Corporation. The decision was reportedly based on an offer Chrysler itself made a year previously to the 54 unions at its British subsidiary. As it turned out, the British union did not accept the two board seats offered to them, but they did establish joint committees made up of supervisors and workers in major command positions involving job assignment and work scheduling in the British plants. Chrysler's offer, however, set a precedent for collective bargaining.

Woodcock's move to place two unionists on Chrysler's board of directors was not successful. Nevertheless, it represented the first attempt at top-down decision-making for a major union federation in the United States.[2]

The UAW has been interested heretofore in the "down-up" process of worker participation. The Bolivar project in southwest Tennessee, for example, is an experiment of worker control and management of an automobile mirror factory. The project originated with officials of the UAW, notably Vice President Irving Bluestone, who has been interested in the "humanization of work." His business counterpart in this case was Sidney Harman, president of Harman International Industries, who has been interested in making a "progressive example" for business firms. The project began with the active involvement of the union as well as management. A staff of social scientists was invited to join as an independent third party. The project has included the entire Harman auto mirror factory at Bolivar, Tennessee, including industrial processes such as die casting; polishing, painting, plating, assembly packing, and data processing. The principles of "democracy, security, equity, and individuation" were selected as guidelines for the organization of the plant. Irving Bluestone said of Bolivar: "If this experiment is successful, it gives us a lever to present to other companies of what direction to take. We are not starting from scratch here as in other experiments with a fresh, clean plant and a new work force. If these efforts are going to spread, they've got to spread in the old plant."[3]

While U.S. experiments n worker *management* have begun at a "walking" pace from the bottom up, experiments in worker *ownership* have been "galloping" from the top down. The rapid acquisition of corporate stock through union pension funds that began in the 1950s has been accelerated by a new program of individual company planning. Thousands of U. S. workers are now being given, free, an ownership interest in the companies where they work, through Employee Stock Ownership Plans (ESOPs). Recent favorable tax legislation has encouraged over 300 corporations to adopt ESOP. ESOP is a complicated legal mechanism that must conform to detailed requirements of federal statutes. We cannot discuss the details here, but we can point to its significance for the trend toward employee ownership and self-management in American industry.

Companies use ESOPs as a way of easing the cost of obtaining capital at the expense of the federal government. The interest of business executives in ESOPs has been stimulated by four pieces of federal legislation. They are the 1974 Pension Reform Act, which gave Treasury-approved employee pension trusts greater power to buy employer-company stock with borrowed money; the 1975 Tax Reduction Act, which gave an additional tax benefit incentive for establishing ESOPs to corporations taking advantage of the tax credit for new investment; the Trade Act of 1974, which requires that 25 percent of *any* government-guaranteed loans authorized for companies in communities hit by import competition *must* be made through an ESOP; and the Regional Rail Reorganization Act of 1973, which directs the government corporation planning the Conrail reorganization of northeastern railroads to study the feasibility of using ESOPs in initial financing. Behind all this legislation has been a Congressional concern about the concentration of wealth in the United States.[4]

The ESOP plan can be used as a basis for capital financing without any cost to the company or to the employees. It generally follows these steps: (1) a corporation organizes an Employee Stock Ownership Trust (an employee pension trust); (2) the trust obtains a loan from a bank or other source; (3) the Trust uses the loan to buy stock newly issued by the company; (4) the company guarantees repayment of the Trust's debt, agreeing to contribute annually to the Trust to amortize the loan; (5) as the loan is paid, the stock held by the Trust is allocated on the Trust's books to the accounts of individual employees usually in proportion to their compensation in the company; (6) the stock shares become "vested" according to a formula often based on length of employment in the company; (7) the stock is allocated directly to the employees upon their retirement, disability, or death. Dividends paid on stock in the Trust are added to the individuals' trust accounts.

The advantage of this to the corporation lies in tax avoidance. A $100,000 loan requires only $100,000 of earnings to pay off in addition to interest with before-tax dollars, whereas the corporation would otherwise need over $192,000 of earnings with after-tax dollars. The government in effect pays nearly half the financing by forgoing a 48 percent tax.

The owner of Mulach Steel Co., J. F. Mulach, has organized an ESOP as part of his estate planning. When he retires in ten years, the company will be fully owned by the 150 employees. No loan is involved in this case. The ESOP trust is buying the owner-president's stock for cash, using an annual contribution from the company equal to the allowable tax deduction. Stock issued to the employees at his retirement will be bought back by the Employee Stock Ownership (ESO) trust. When he retires, Mulach intends to name key employees to the Board for management continuity.[5]

Companies and unions have not often sought arrangements under ESOP that would offer workers managerial control and equal voting rights, partly because the primary incentives of these acts has been to make financial returns more available for everyone. Nevertheless, worker self-management is possible with equal voting rights simply by providing in the ESO agreement that trust beneficiaries (the workers) exercise the voting rights of their allocated common stock directly in choosing directors. Equal voting rights can also be assured. Under the Trade Act, an arrangement can be made for shares allocated under the ESOP to be divided into one voting share per member, with the remainder as nonvoting shares. The remainder then divides the economic returns according to an individual's compensation in the firm.

We note later how this relatively fast pace toward company ownership on the one hand and slow pace toward participation in management on the other hand is reversed for unions in Europe. If the two trends continue, it will mean that *within another decade the organization of production in western society will be moving very clearly into the hands of the workers.* Given this real possibility, a question then remains about business federations and their role in the economic order.

The Trade Association Federation: Distribution Zone

While union federations and private corporations have been primarily involved with the organization of production, business federations have been primarily involved with distribution and commerce.

The major political and legislative trends of importance concerning trade associations has been toward sanctioning their operation in the public interest. On the one hand, Supreme Court decisions have been encouraging trade associations to function in the public interest; on the other hand, federal legislation has been curtailing their activities that are not in the public interest.

The Supreme Court's sanction of trade association activities is stated most clearly in the Maple Flooring and Appalachian cases.

In the Maple Flooring case, the Court stated that trade associations could *openly and fairly gather and disseminate information as to the cost of their product, the volume of production, the price the product brought in past transactions, stocks of merchandise on hand, and approximate cost of transportation from the point of shipment,* as long as members of the association did not attempt to reach any agreement with respect to prices or production that would restrain competition.[6]

In the Appalachian Coal case, the Court spoke directly to the importance of these activities contributing to the public interest:

Voluntary action to end abuses and to foster fair competitive opportunities in the public interest may be more effective than legal processes. And cooperative endeavor may appropriately have wiser objectives than merely the removal of evils which are infractions of positive law. Nor does the fact that the correction of abuses may tend to stabilize business, or to produce fairer price levels, require that abuses should go uncorrected or that an effort to correct them should for that reason alone be stamped as an unreasonable restraint of trade. Accordingly, we have held that a cooperative enterprise otherwise free from objection, which carries with it no monopolistic menace, is not to be condemned as an undue restraint merely because it may effect a change in market conditions where the change would be in mitigation of recognized evils and would not impair, but rather foster, fair competitive opportunities.[7]

In other cases the Court's opinion has been less lenient. Clearly, the Court does not sanction the gathering of trade information for the purpose of restraining competition. In the Hardwood[8] and Linseed Oil[9] cases, statistical reporting plans were held illegal because the Court found they represented a combined effort on the part of associations to regulate prices and production. In effect, any attempts to control prices, production, or the market, or to institute boycotts, are beyond the law. Trade association members may exchange information for business interests as long as members retain complete independence to act in accordance with their individual judgment.[10]

In spite of all their lobbying efforts, trade associations have been forced to respond to consumer legislation that curbs the malpractices of their members. The trend toward legislation protecting the consumer from unfair practices in trade areas includes the Wheeler-Lea Act of 1938, which authorized curbs on false advertising; the Wool Labeling Act of 1939 and the Fur Products Act of 1953, which authorized promulgation and enforcement of standards of flammation of clothing fabrics; and the Textile Fiber Products Identification Act of 1958, which added a requirement of informative advertising. The consumerism period of the 1960s added still more legislation. This has helped change the climate within which trade associations have operated and has led many of them to develop programs engaging in "social responsibility."

A survey in 1972 conducted by the American Society of Association Executives concluded that 73 percent of all the associations in the United States were currently involved to some degree "in helping to solve the nation's economic and social problems." Thirty-five percent of the associations responding to the survey claimed to have "programs to aid the disadvantaged." Over 50 percent of the respondents claimed that such programs were from local associations, suggesting a decentralized effort to participate in community development.[11]

At the national level other programs have been developing. In 1972 the four major life and health insurance associations established a committee on corporate responsibility to serve as an industrywide clearinghouse. The Institute of Life Insurance, the public relations arm of the industry, publishes a bimonthly newsletter, *Response,* to accomplish the purposes of the clearinghouse. On the matter of product liability, the board of directors of the U. S. Chamber of Commerce adopted a statement on warrantees setting forth "basic elements to be recognized in every warranty and guarantee and emphasizing the importance of clarity and nontechnical language in product warrantees and guarantees."[12]

A fundamental shift in the law from the traditional view of consumer purchases as private, contractual relationships with the immediate seller toward viewing the corporation as a responsible public agency is taking place in the United States. Trade federations are coming to recognize the shift toward corporate responsibility; the concept of *caveat emptor* is disappearing. Note the words of the Council on Trends and Perspective on Business and the Consumer of the U. S. Chamber of Commerce:

There has been a fundamental shift from the principle that all business is essentially private and accountable only to stockholders and the free marketplace to legal doctrines that make large enterprises, in particular, "quasi-public," and thus more and more accountable to the general public. This change is further reflected in the shift from laws which impose minimal liabilities on enterprising activities toward laws which impose *strict liabilities* on industry even for unintentional and non-negligent harm inflicted on consumers and other groups in society.[13]

The shift toward strict liability has been grounded on the judicial concept that a company assumes a responsibility to anyone who may be injured by it. The courts have begun to hold the proposition that the public has a right to expect that reputable sellers will stand behind their products. Furthermore, the burden of accidental injuries caused by a product should be borne by those who distribute it.[14]

The most important fact is that trade associations have access to all relevant information controlling commercial exchange: the volume of production, prices, stocks of merchandise, transportation costs, etc. This fact gives them a most critical role in the management of the economy. Their access to critical information was one reason why the federal government asked the trade associations to exercise control over the problems of commerce and distribution during the Great Depression.

During the Great Depression, business leaders spoke favorably of establishing some social control over prices and the fair distribution of goods and services. Under the National Recovery Act, 874 draft codes were drawn up to control sales, prices, markets, production capacity, and channels of distribution. The codes were administered by "authorities" whose membership was chosen principally by the trade associations. The codes were submitted to two advisory boards, one representing labor and industry, and the other the consumers. The codes were approved if labor and consumer representatives could agree with the decisions of business leaders in these associations.

But labor had little power relative to business during the Depression. Consumers had less power, and the government virtually delegated the control over commerce to the trade associations. Subsequently the Supreme Court declared the NRA to be an unconstitutional delegation of legislative power.

Our theory is that business federations will become increasingly legitimate as social regulators of distribution, the more that labor and consumer federations gain limited controls over production and consumption. In the United States the trade unions are beginning to develop those limited controls, as we have seen. Let us now look at the trend toward "consumer power" and its meaning for the social development of the third major zone of the economic system.

Cooperative Federations: Consumption Zone

The recent appearance of a consumer movement and the growing numbers of consumer groups in the United States is a social trend matched only by the growth of the labor movement in the last century. It is a movement closely associated with the cooperative movement and the recent interest in a type of cooperative called the Community Development Corporation (CDC).

Many people in the city ghettos and rural areas of poverty have begun to work together in economic enterprises that have the character of a local retail-producer cooperative. The CDC is a business corporation owned and controlled by residents of poor neighborhoods who are using business methods to generate revenue and social benefits for themselves. The CDC is a cooperative in which citizen consumers rule at the local level. It is also a place where the production of certain types of goods can begin to offer a measure of autonomy to localities against the power of the national market controlled by big corporations and trade associations.

In the 90th Congress both Republican and Democratic senators joined in sponsoring a bill called the Community Self-Determination Act. It was designed to initiate CDCs in poverty areas across the nation. The original bill was never funded, but a CDC program was begun through the Office of Economic Opportunity in 1967, based on the authority of the Special Impact Program, which supplied funds to many CDCs that had already shown their effectiveness as economic entities. Support was given to the Bedford-Stuyvesant Restoration Corporation, the Hough Area Development Corporation, United Durham, Inc., and forty other community-based economic development enterprises. The aim was to initiate local authority and responsibility for economic development in areas that had been neglected by the market economy.[15]

Experience has shown that CDCs can plan and implement a broad range of businesses, including housing construction, shopping plazas, electronics plants, sewing plants, supermarkets, restaurant franchises, and job-training programs. CDCs have proven that such diverse enterprises can be linked into a comprehensive local development program. They can create protective environments for marginal business and at the same time create jobs for seriously disadvantaged individuals.

The next step in the development of CDCs at the national level involves support on a broader basis through long-term planning, equity capital, debt financing, technical assistance, and new markets. Achieving these goals at the national level, however, will require new legislation and changes in the operations of federal agencies.[16]

The CDC is both a consumer-oriented and producer-oriented cooperative designed to represent people in a defined locality. It gives local individuals the opportunity to purchase shares that give them one vote each, according to basic cooperative principles. The Community Self-Determination Act therefore marks a change in the role and identity of the small corporation in American life. The corporation becomes "democratically representative" and an integral part of the social life of people in a locality.

The functions of the local CDC as envisioned in the bill then become part of the larger federation of locality-cooperatives. These functions are summarized as follows:[17]

First, providing neighborhood services and community development: e.g., basic education, child welfare, day care, preschool training, health, assisting in consumer education, home-ownership counseling, college placement assistance, job finding, recreation, legal aid, etc.

Second, owning and managing stock of business enterprises in the locality.

Third, sponsoring, owning, managing housing in the community.

Fourth, advocate planning for neighborhood renewal and redevelopment.

Fifth, representing community interests in other areas of public policy and concern.

Sixth, encouraging business, labor, religious, and other voluntary groups in the locality.

The financing of the CDC is summarized as follows:

First, earnings from affiliated business.

Second, contracts for services, with private sector and government agencies, on a cost-plus-fixed-fee basis.

Third, grants from the community development fund, earmarked for educational purposes which would not be subject to federal tax.

The fact that the CDC contains within it both a producer and a consumer orientation makes it a complex enterprise. Since legislative proposals require the enterprise to be community owned and managed, it is clearly beyond being only a producer or a consumer cooperative in its type of orientation but not beyond the strains contained within these separate interests. Local citizens in the neighborhood of the CDC are the ultimate authority for its operations, but workers in the enterprise may also be organized democratically to determine policies relative to their labor.

The actual balance of power between local citizens and workers varies in different CDCs. Here the conflict between producer and consumer must be resolved within a single organization rather than between federations. This presents a special challenge to its survival. Add the fact that the classic conflict between social and economic interests must also be resolved in this enterprise and we see why the CDC is a "front line" organization vulnerable in the context of the business society. Like the kibbutz in Israel, the CDC is subject to a great strain due to a conflict and unevenness in the laws and organizational demands of the larger capitalist society. It mirrors the problems of the society even while it holds the potential for partially resolving them in its local structure. For this reason we can guess that CDCs will be fragile institutions for some time and will tend to be drawn either toward a producer or a consumer orientation in the next years of their development.

The cooperative movement in the United States has drawn heavily upon British philosophy and emphasized *consumer interests*.[18] United States cooperatives in the fields of health, housing, credit, electricity, and retail stores tend to be owned and managed by their customers.

Producer cooperatives are similar to consumer cooperatives in their tendency to be decentralized and community oriented. The ESOP plan today, for example, may contribute directly to the organization of worker owned local enterprises or producer cooperatives. ESOP can be organized through cities to create worker-owned enterprises. Furthermore, they can establish revolving funds to create more of such enterprises. They are community oriented but they are not strictly community owned.[19]

The CDCs organized in the United States today have a producer emphasis but their community orientation links them logically to the burgeoning consumer movement. The consumer movement is developing strength at national and state levels of organization in ways that complement the local orientation of the CDC. The Office of Consumer Affairs reported in 1971, for example, that 43 states had developed some form of officially designated consumer offices. In 15 of the 43 states, there were two or more government consumer offices with divided or coordinated responsibilities.

More significantly for our purposes, there were almost 50 statewide and metropolitan areawide consumer federations organized on a voluntary basis. These include the Consumer Federation of Illinois, the Arizona Consumers Council, the Association of Pomona Valley consumers, the Minnesota Consumers League, the Mississippi Consumer Association, the Metropolitan New York Consumer Council, and the St. Louis Consumer Federation. These statewide alliances, councils, leagues, and federations, of course, have other affiliates and chapters associated with them. At the national level we find the Consumer Federation of America, National Consumers League, American Council on Consumer Interests, Consumers Union of U. S., Inc., and the National Student Consumer Protection Council.[20]

It should not be too surprising to find CDCs and consumer federations combining interests and both of them getting increasing aid from government legislation in the next quarter century. Such a trend follows logically in the wake of our two other historical movements in the American economy concerning the entrepreneur and the laborer. *The growth of business and the growth of unions as separate movements had to be aided by the government in order to survive and flourish.* Each movement was resisted at first by the government but was later encouraged and helped by new legislative action. After this twofold and sequential development of business federations and union federations, we may now anticipate at least the possibility of a third major development in the consumer movement organized federally at local, state, regional, and national levels.

In the light of these recent trends in the United States, we now want to turn our attention to what is happening in other developing countries. A focus on what is happening in the zones of production, distribution, and consumption can hopefully lead to propositions about the direction of social development in modern economies. We are interested especially in how coordination and integration of economic activities may enhance the autonomy and individuation of social groups. Our ultimate aim here is to formulate essential guidelines for research that build from the trends visible in the United States.

THE INTERNATIONAL SCENE

We look now at socioeconomic trends in nations overseas that show new directions of development. In Sweden we observe how the separation of ownership and management in the business system is being challenged by new initiatives from union federations. In England we look at a design for production in the steel industry that is intended to cultivate managerial authority within rank-and-file workers in the industry. In Peru, we look at the way a military government is starting to organize different industries through democratic regional federations. In Northern Spain we observe how a regional economy has developed democratically through the organization of both producer and consumer cooperatives, forming a federated network outside the state. Each case is, of course, only a rough sketch, inviting readers to explore them independently in more detail. They offer us the opportunity to develop a general theory about social federations in production, distribution, and consumption and to offer suggestions for social research in the United States.

Sweden: Overcoming the Separation of Ownership and Management in Production

We have discussed how trade unions in the United States are becoming the principal owners of corporations in major industries through their pension trusts, but that union leaders have not shown a strong interest in corporate management. We have also discussed how trade unions in Western Europe have taken strong steps toward corporate management at all levels but do not own the corporations. Increasing worker involvement constitutes a major trend within the production zones of Western countries.

The separate trends toward worker ownership in the United States and toward worker control in Europe, however, have within them the likelihood of convergence. Today in Sweden, for example, the largest trade union federation, the LO (for *Landsorganisationen*), has endorsed a plan which could lead toward majority ownership by labor of every important industry. Recent laws have led workers toward sharing management at virtually every level of corporate operations, but the management has not been based on ownership. Without ownership, the union claims it cannot proceed with plans for more equitable development of income and wealth in Sweden.

The LO is a union of blue collar workers with more than two million members. The Union's plan involves the transfer of 20 percent of a company's annual profit before taxation, in the form of a special issue of stock, into a "collective employee fund." This would be a system of funds controlled by the local union and the labor federations. The share would not be allocated to the company's own employees but would be held collectively in the fund system. As long as the fund's holdings did not exceed 20 percent of the company's capital stock, the union shareholders' right to appoint board members would stay on the local level. But when labor ownership passed the 20 percent mark, the central funds would assume an increasing share of the votes for the board members. The system would embrace all companies in Sweden with 50 or more employees.

The first goal of this "wage policy" is to support what the union calls "solidarity." Solidarity means a policy to equalize wages among all workers. But union leaders claim that under the present circumstances they cannot ask the best-paid workers to restrain their wage demands so that the lowest paid workers (e.g., women, textile and restaurant workers) can catch up, because they would simply be giving more money to the employers and stockholders. The union plan is to restrain the wages of the best-paid workers by having profits paid into the union fund and then share those gains among all workers. The union leaders claim other goals, which include equalizing the structure of wealth and diffusing the influence and power more equitably within the society.

The author of the plan, Dr. Rudolf Meidner, states that it cannot be advanced without taking account of two economic factors. First, it cannot hinder full employment. Sweden is heavily dependent on foreign trade and must stay competitive in world markets if full employment is to be maintained. Second, the system cannot hinder the achievement of a sufficiently high rate of capital formation. The advocates of the plan claim it can account for these factors. The plan should promote both investment and economic growth.

The Swedish plan is not entirely new. A similar plan was suggested by President Charles de Gaulle in France in the 1960s. The ESOP in the United States has comparable features. Such plans for worker ownership are part of a trend in public policy that is emerging in social democratic countries today.

Labor union federations in Western European countries have been steadily gaining power and responsibility for the organization of production in the European economy. Business federations have not completely rebelled. They have rather sought to "moderate" any rash moves on the part of organized labor to gain greater control over production. For example, the Swedish Federation of Industries led by Axel Iveroth believes that business people must take a positive line on the recent proposal by the LO rather than sink into an "unresponsive negativism."[21]

But the growing union interest in control over the organization of production leaves unanswered many questions about how competing corporations may function together in the same industry under union authority. In a state socialist or a capitalist society with nationalized industries, the corporation is administered by the authority that originates from the top of a political party rather than from the industry itself. In the fully self-managed industry, however, authority develops from the bottom up. The issue of command management of the union would be at stake in the implementation of the Meidner plan. It is an issue similar to one faced by workers in the British steel industry. The difference is only in command management by the state.

Great Britain: The Regional and National Organization of the Steel Industry

Industries in Great Britain that have been nationalized from the top down have become large bureaucracies. Political economists of different persuasions have noted that the publicly owned industries in coal, gas, electricity, and railways have developed complicated command systems. The workers' earnings and workers' participation in these industries often compare unfavorably with private industry. The role of trade unions in these industries is confined to such matters as joint production committees. The industrial boards have one or two trade unionists on them in minority positions relatively remote from the rank-and-file membership. The social issues involved in the organization of self-managed industries in England cannot all be raised here; but they can be suggested in brief fashion in this case of the steel industry in England.

In 1963 a group of production workers and craftsmen in Sheffield and Rotherham began discussing the possibilities of a "down up" process of organizing the steel industry.[22] They developed a plan that would begin to reverse the typical pattern of command administration. It would offer the opportunity of a greater measure of participation of rank-and-file workers in management. The Sheffield-Rotherham group had seen how the mining industry in Britain had been organized largely by a top-down appointed management with many unsatisfactory results. The group decided that a basic principle in planning for the nationalization of steel should be that all "worker representatives are accountable to the workers." This meant that they must not only be elected but must continue working, if only part-time, among the workers they represent. The results of the German experiments with codetermination suggested to them that the full-time workers on the supervisory boards soon ceased to have any contact with their former rank-and-file members.

They designed a plan for the steel industry, therefore, in which the pyramid of trade union representation would correspond to the pyramid of management. Their design showed power *flowing down from the top through the management pyramid* and *flowing up from the bottom in the union pyramid*. The management side then follows the line of command from Parliament and the Minister down to the shop floor. (See Figure 6.) On the union side, direct election to shop committees provides members for plant workers' councils, and thus by delegation to regional and national councils for the industry. It was proposed that the *existing structure of unions' local, regional, and national officials should be integrated* into the organization by forming councils at each level consisting partly of elected and delegated members, partly of union officials. This would avoid the difficulty of developing a new trade union structure, and it would not imply a threat to displace existing full-time officials at district and national levels. The union could nominate its own officials to a certain number of places. Also, the workers' councils at the plants might be left free to choose full-time officials to represent them at higher levels along with their own chosen delegates. The balance of membership of different unions on the workers' councils could then be expected to ensure a fair mix of full-time union officials at higher levels.

The planning group at Sheffield and Rotherham had difficulty determining how workers' councils could be assured a fair and balanced representation of the

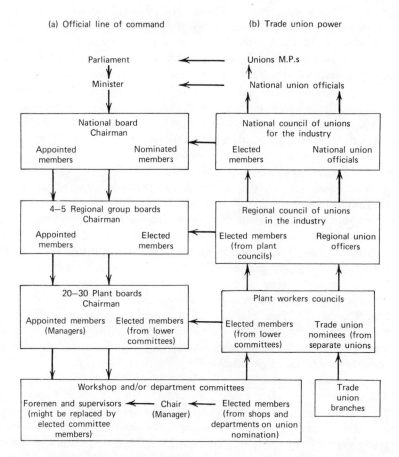

Figure 6. A Model for Developing Workers' Control in a Nationalized Industry. Source: William Meade, "Nationalized Steel," in Ken Coates (ed.) *Can the Workers Run Industry?* (Nottingham, England: The Bertrand Russell Peace Foundation, 1968).

different sections of the plant, especially with the involvement of many different sized unions. The solution reached was that half the members of the councils should be elected directly by each shop or department from candidates nominated by the unions and half should be chosen by the union branches in rough proportion to their membership in the plant. This system would not only have the advantage of ensuring representation both for the smaller shops and the smaller unions, but it would also provide the larger unions with a freedom they might wish to retain, to disown decisions of the workers' councils.

The next crucial step for the group was to consider the possibility and advisability of integrating the trade union pyramid with the management pyramid, so that negotiation would be transformed into joint management. Figure 6 indicates that elected worker members at each level function equally with appointed managerial members. Management has its own line of command originating from the Ministry. The chairman is appointed from above but with veto power from the workers. Some members of the group felt that some future modification might be made at the level of the top board. They realized that the minister "could not be expected to be responsible for a board one half of whose members, apart from the chairman, were delegates sent from below." The group therefore suggested that "the delegates from all the Unions at national level should jointly submit a list of acceptable full-time and part-time candidates from which the Minister could choose one half of the board members, and that the National Board chairman should also be subject to ratification by the national delegates of the unions."

A similar set of proposals was put forward in April, 1967 for discussion among the twelve unions that make up the National Craftsmens' Co-ordinating Committee for the Iron and Steel Industry. In both cases the organizational principles that the steelworkers felt to be mandatory included the following:

1. All corporate information should be made available to workers' representatives. . . .
2. A purposive national plan should make available the provision of alternative work opportunities if steel production is phased out. . . .
3. Senior management officials should be appointed at each level subject to ratification by the workers' delegates. . . .

Key areas of dispute between management proposals by the National Steel Corporation and this model have rested on the degree of participation and responsibility permitted union members. Management has responded to demands advanced by the steel unions for "worker directors," but it has placed the workers in a minority position. Management has proposed four or five group (regional) Boards for the industry. Each Board would have 14 to 16 members but only up to three would be worker representatives.

Where industries have been nationalized in Great Britain the economic motive has usually been "to facilitate rationalization of activity and a more intensive programme of investment than the industry concerned might be able to achieve under private, fragmented ownership."[23] Government takeovers therefore have generally involved the entire industry, as in the case of the coal, gas, and electricity industries. The steel industry has been nationalized twice for this reason, but subsequently a significant proportion of the total iron and steel capacity remained in private hands. In all these cases, however, *the degree of competition between firms was small or nonexistent before the government takeover.* The takeovers, therefore, simply continued the existing trends toward concentration and the limited competition in these industries.

The real question raised in these cases is the extent to which initiative and leadership may develop among rank-and-file workers who must labor in the public interest as well as their own interest. How can an industry be organized to raise the quality of work life and at the same time stimulate personal incentives among employees in the industry? These types of questions are confronted paradoxically by both business executives in trade associations and military leaders in socialist regimes seeking to coordinate enterprises. The answer in both cases may rest in a "bottom-up process" of creating human resources and establishing authority in the economic enterprises.

Peru: Federations of Corporations in Democratic Regional Assemblies

In 1968 a military government was established in Peru and declared its intention of transforming the social and economic structures of the country in the direction of "social democracy based on full participation." Large sectors of agricultural land were expropriated through a Land Reform Law, and new forms of collective enterprises were created in the countryside. In 1970 labor communities were created in major sectors of the economy, and a number of "nationalizations" followed. During this time the government stressed that its principal aim was the creation of "social property" which would become the "preponderant" principle of development. The idea was that a social sector of property would be created wherein workers would have the opportunity to manage and direct the firms in which they worked.[24]

On May 2, 1974, the Peruvian Government, under the leadership of President Juan Velasco Alvarado, formulated the "Law of Social-Property Firms." It remains today as a Peruvian model for social development within the economy. The current President, Francisco Morales Bermudez, has indicated his full commitment to the law, which he has called "Peruvian socialism" as distinct from capitalism or communism.[25]

The reforms creating the labor communities had, by the end of 1975, involved about 300,000 workers, or eight percent of Peru's economically active population. The first social property firms were constituted in April, 1975 and included only about 4000 workers by September, 1976. The new laws have only begun to be implemented, but by mid-1976, the government was completing a radical agrarian reform, redistributing the best pasturelands and croplands into the hands of collective enterprises. They represent the principal direction of development within the economy. The intent of the government is to provide incentives to "nurture" the new economic order into existence in the coming decades.

The Social Property Law defines a corporation as one composed exclusively

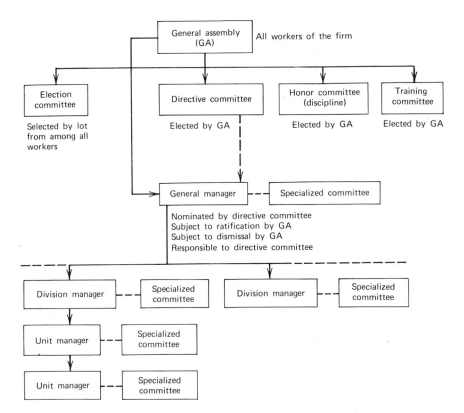

Figure 7. Organization of the social-property firm. No elected position may be occupied for two consecutive terms by the same person. Specialized committees have only advisory powers, and are elected by the workers of the corresponding division, unit, etc. The number and nature of specialized committees is specified in the statute of each social-property firm. Source: Peter Knight, "Social Property in Peru," in *Economic Analysis and Workers' Management* (Belgrade), Fall, 1976.

of workers. Corporations in the social sector are legally defined by certain characteristics including the "full participation of the workers in the direction, management and economic benefits of the firm." The "social accumulation" of income of firms is to be used in part to expand the sector as a whole by expanding existing firms and creating new ones. A "permanent training" for workers in self-management is encouraged through educational expenses treated as "production costs" in accounting. A Social Property Corporation or Firm (in Spanish, EPS) may be organized by private individuals or by institutions. But converting to an EPS from an existing firm is permitted only by agreement of two-thirds of the shareholders.

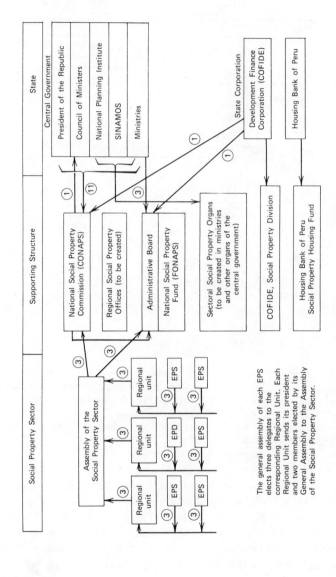

Figure 8. Organization of the social property sector. Arrows indicate representation or appointment of personnel. Numbers indicate number of representatives. Source: Peter Knight, "Social Property in Peru," in *Economic Analysis and Workers' Management* (Belgrade), Fall, 1976.

The capital for organizing the EPS comes from several sources. It may come from the Development Finance Corporation (COFIDE) or the National Social Property Fund (FONAPS). It may also come from the issuance of securities sold to financial institutions. The securities would provide economic returns but would offer no voting rights in the corporation.

The corporation or firm organized in the "Social Property Sector" bases its ultimate authority in a General Assembly of Workers. The assembly approves plans and policies and decides about the distribution of profits. It also elects a (Directive Management) Committee, an Honor Committee and a Training Committee (Figure 7).

The Directive Committee oversees daily operations. It submits plans and policies of the firm to the General Assembly for approval. A General Manager implements the committee's decisions. The appointment of a manager must be approved by the General Assembly. The Honor Committee acts as a judiciary, hearing grievances and imposing disciplinary penalities on the employees of the firm. Specialized committees are organized to help manage day-to-day operations.

The Social Property Firms belong to regional units. The regions are composed of assemblies formed by two representatives from each firm of each region plus the president of each firm. The regional assemblies determine whether all the firms are working according to the principles of the Social Property Firm Law. They approve any modification in the statute and act as a judiciary for workers fired from an individual firm (Figure 8).

The grand assembly of the Social Property Sector is formed by two representatives plus the president of each region. The representatives are elected by the region's assembly.

The National Social Property Commission (CONAPS) is the government's "support structure." It is composed of three representatives elected by the grand assembly of the Social Property Sector plus 12 members to be named by various ministries, the president of the republic, and other state agencies.

The National Social Property Fund (FONAPS) is governed by an eight-member Administrative Board. Three members are workers elected by the grand assembly of the Social Property Sector. The other five members are representatives of the Ministry of Finance, CONAPS, and CONFIDE. The chairperson must be an appointee of the Minister of Finance, and has the tie-breaking vote.

The Housing Fund for Social Property Workers is to be managed by the Housing Bank of Peru, a state-controlled institution. Resources of the Housing Fund include a percentage of the economic surplus of each firm fixed annually by CONAPS plus additional voluntary deposits by firms from their distributable surplus or by individual workers.

Through the government's initiative, new social federations have already developed and gained political force. The National Confederation of Industrial

Communities and the National Agrarian Confederation, for example, have emerged as a result of the government's political agency called the National System for the Support of Social Mobilization (SINAMOS). The federations appear at this point to be developing their own dynamic.

This rough sketch cannot tell the full story of the very complicated development taking place in the Peruvian economy, but it shows part of the model that is guiding the political leadership. It is impossible to tell at this point what future directions it will take. It could lead toward a modernization of Peru's capitalist economy. It could result in a state bourgeoisie consolidating power and becoming closely associated with international capital. In the context of Latin America, with its political pressures, it is possible that another bureaucratic ruling class could arise.

Nevertheless, the government has submitted a social plan of development intending to increase worker autonomy. The present regime has publicly rejected "the political institutionalization of the Revolution itself as a party." It seeks publicly to defend "the autonomy of social organization against all attempts at outside control." But whether the government achieves its social objectives will depend very much on the way in which the leadership becomes involved in supporting and guiding the development of the Social Property Sector.[25]

One of the questions it raises for us is how the power of "producer associations" described here as Social Property Firms are balanced with the power of "consumer associations." The issue is whether the democratic organization of the producer without the democratic organization of the consumer will not automatically require state controls and regulatory powers in the larger society.

Northern Spain: The Mondragón Network of Producer Consumer Cooperatives

Mondragón is a small manufacturing town in Northern Spain that initiated a worker and consumer ownership movement twenty years ago. The movement spread through the Basque provinces and now represents one of the few places in the world where both producer and consumer cooperatives have developed side by side to represent a major portion of the economic order.

The idea for a cooperative movement began with an educational program. In 1943 a Basque Spanish priest by the name of Father José María Arizmendi founded a Technical College in Mondragón. Students were taught that people in industry should work together for mutual benefit through democratic worker ownership. In 1956 five young men who graduated from the college organized a worker-owner enterprise making paraffin cookers. By 1959 the enterprise had increased its employees to 170 and was producing gas cookers. The spirit and good will of the workers led others in the community to create similar enterprises. By the end of 1972, the industrial enterprises numbered 47, with a membership of 10,055 worker owner-managers.[26] Today 55 producer cooperatives employ 15,000 people directly and over 40,000 indirectly through schools, hospitals, and other institutions supported by the cooperative movement.[27]

The cooperative movement has expanded rapidly in a short time, but the policy has been to keep manufacturing units within a maximum of 800 to 1000 workers. The different enterprises have included foundries, machine tools, household durables, and construction. Some enterprises are known throughout Europe and Africa for making high quality household items including mixers, toasters, waffle irons, washing machines, stoves, and refrigerators.

The cooperative system also includes four agriculture cooperatives and one fishery cooperative with a total of 1719 members. In addition, there are consumer cooperatives numbering over 26,383 members. Some of the members of these consumer co-ops, however, are also officially workers as well as customers. The dividends are therefore not simply returned to the customers of the retail outlets. They are instead divided between the workers and the social purposes of the community.

In 1968 the largest industrial firm, Ulgor, spun off five separately owned enterprises. They then combined into a single federation called Ularco. This federation of relatively independent firms, which manufacturers mainly refrigerators, now has over 6000 worker-members. The workers in these enterprises had originally formed the federation to improve their finances, sales transport, and personnel selection. They decided together to pool incomes and democratically elect a coordinating authority. It worked; each firm now nominates two members of its own "control board" to form the "control board" of the federation. The federation board in turn nominates a general manager and staff to handle planning and coordination.

The ultimate authority of each enterprise is vested in a general assembly of workers who have an equal vote in determining general policy. All new workers must become members with voting status after a qualifying period. Suppliers of capital do not have voting powers and are limited to the receipt of fixed interest.

The income of each worker is divided on a points system of job ratings. Workers know their income depends on the earnings of the enterprise. This is a positive motivating factor for work. At the same time, the maximum differential rate of pay for all cooperative enterprises is *three to one*. This is said to reduce the tendency of workers to compete for status and power inside the enterprise. There are no big differences in pay among the employees in the whole system.[28]

Workers' Bank was created in 1959 with the help of one consumer and three industrial cooperatives. The bank quickly became effective because the Basque people were willing to deposit their savings in it to advance the cooperative movement. The bank could then begin financing more industrial enterprises based on the principle of worker ownership and management. It was soon able to open branches in adjacent districts; it now has 54 branches with a staff of over 250. The bank has a democratically elected control board that appoints a general manager on the same principle as the industrial enterprises it helps finance.

The network of democratically organized producer and consumer cooperatives, which function together outside the state within a region of provinces, where people maintain a relative sense of community, is a rare phenomenon of the world scene. It may be perhaps compared only to the kibbutzim in Israel in its nonstatist character. But these examples of democratic federations are also still an interdependent part of the larger capitalist state. This fact leads us back to our interest in how whole societies develop toward decentralized federated economies.

Summary: Currents of Economic Democracy Among Nations

The amount of effective participation workers have in economic enterprises varies markedly from nation to nation. Workers councils, for example, are required by law in Belgium, Finland, France, Luxembourg, the Netherlands, and Austria, but a number of them are endowed with only consultative powers. Workers councils operate on a voluntary basis in Britain, Ireland, and Switzerland, but they do not exist at all in Greece and Spain. In Belgium, Denmark, Britain, Ireland, and Norway, the councils function on a parity with managment representatives. In Finland and Sweden they operate with a two-thirds membership of workers. In Italy, Austria, Switzerland, and Germany, they are composed of workers alone.[29]

Different nations excel in effective participation at certain levels. Sweden, for example, has an outstanding record at the job level of creating relatively autonomous working conditions. Swedish enterprises have been experimenting with increasing the variety of choices for workers on individual tasks. They have been involved in abandoning the assembly line and experimenting extensively with autonomous work groups as at Volvo and Saab. They have explored new consultative methods and ways of integrating workers from abroad such as at Kockums, the shipbuilders. At the same time, Sweden has experimented with a relatively effective national collective bargaining system at the national level. Federated unions and federated companies discuss a whole range of social problems that extend beyond simply wages and benefits.

Nations in other regions of the world have also been experimenting with democratic participation in economic enterprise. Pakistan has required, since 1972, that a workers' representative participate on the management board of all firms employing more than 50 people. Tanzania has a three-tier structure, consisting of a workers' consultation committee as well as representation on the executive and supervisory boards. In South America, Venezuela has experimented with codetermination in nationalized industries. Peru, of course, has introduced social property legislation that could lead workers toward increased participation in the economy.

The trade unions in different countries are sometimes more reluctant than the management of an enterprise to participate in higher levels of decision-making. The British motor industry (British Leyland, Chrysler), for example, has put forth propositions for some forms of participation backed by management, but the relevant unions have been slow to answer. In some countries, the resistance is based on a reluctance to change traditional roles; in others it is because of a radical demand for full control over the company rather than codetermination.

Some companies have gone beyond federated labor and management and sought participation from outside authorities. Companies in Scandinavia, for example, have taken a step toward allowing municipal councillors on their board as representatives of the public interest.

In the light of these worldwide trends, it behooves us to develop some general theory about the development of social federations in the economic order of modern society.

NOTES

1. Merle Fainsod, "The Structure of Development Administration," in Irving Swerdlow (ed), *Development Administration: Concepts and Problems* (Syracuse: Syracuse University Press, 1963), p. 1.

2. Despite this failure to add unionists to the board of directors, both sides emerged from the negotiations with plans for new experiments in worker participation at plant levels. Douglas Fraser, UAW Vice President, said that these steps toward board representation fall in the category of planting a seed. A. H. Raskin, "The Labor Scene," *The New York Times,* November 15, 1976, p. 47.

3. Michael Maccoby, "Changing Work: The Bolivar Project," *Working Papers,* Vol. III, No. 2 (Summer, 1975); cf. Agis Salpukis, "Bolivar: A Reporter's View," *New York Times,* April 9, 1975.

4. Since $1 billion in government guarenteed loans is authorized, this suggests a potential $25 million in stock for employees' accounts in ESOP under The Trade Act of 1974. I am indebted in this review of ESOP to Katrina Berman, "Employee Stock Ownership Plans and Implementation of Worker Management," unpublished paper presented to the Third International Conference on Self-Management, Washington, D. C., 1976.

5. George McManus, "I'm Giving the Workers My Company," *Iron Age,* July 8, 1974.

6. *Maple Flooring Manufacturing Association* v *United States,* 268 U. S. 563, 586 (1925).

7. *Appalachian Coals, Inc.* v *United States,* 288 U. S. 344, 373, 374 (1933).

8. *American Column and Lumber Company* v *United States,* 257 U. S. 377 (1921).

9. *United States* v *American Linseed Oil Company,* 262 U. S. 563 (1925).

10. "Of all trade associations in the United States less than five percent have ever had a charge brought against them by the United States Department of Justice or the Federal Trade Commission. Many associations among this five percent signed 'nolo contendere'

decrees because the amount of money and time involved in an antitrust action is tremendous." Kenneth Hence, *Association Management* (Washington, D. C.: U. S. Chamber of Commerce), pp. 3–4.

11. Larry Finkelstein, "Some Tough Questions About Trade Associations" in *Business and Society Review/Innovation,* 6 (Summer 1973) 23.

12. U. S. Chamber of Commerce, *Business and the Consumer—A Program for the Seventies* (Washington, D. C., 1970), p. 3.

13. *Ibid,* p. 10.

14. Friedrich Ressler, "Products Liability," *Yale Law Journal,* 76 (1967): 900–901.

15. Stewart E. Perry, *Federal Support for CDCs: Some of the History and Issues of Community Control* (Cambridge, Mass.: Center for Community Economic Development, 1973).

16. Geoffrey Faux, *CDCs: New Hope for the Inner City* (New York: The Twentieth Century Fund, 1971).

17. U. S. 90th Congress, 2nd Session, *Congressional Record* (July 24, 1968), Vol. 114, No. 129 S9269-9295.

18. James P. Warbasse, *Co-operative Democracy: Through Voluntary Association of the People as Consumers* (New York: Harper & Bros., 1936). The inherent conflict between the producer and the consumer began with the cooperative movement in England during the nineteenth century. In 1844 twenty-eight Rochdale weavers met to create a producers' cooperative during the worst conditions of capitalist industry. The weavers, out of work, formulated the basic cooperative principles that have remained a lasting part of the movement in both England and the United States. These principles included "unlimited membership," "voluntary activity," religious and political neutrality, a percentage of the profits devoted to education in the subject of "cooperation," and "uniting with neighbor cooperatives" in federations. The original Rochdale Pioneers did not have consumer interests in mind so much as worker interests. Nevertheless, consumer interests came to dominate the movement in England. The cooperative movement gained momentum around the retail store rather than the factory. Today only about 20 producer cooperatives have survived (one example is Equity Shoes of Leicester, which has 200 employees). The consumer cooperative movement, on the other hand, has prospered. It continues to have a significant impact on the retail sector of the British economy.

19. South Bend Lathe is an example where ESOP was used to make a company "employee owned" in a divestiture. In this case, a conglomerate planned to liquidate an unprofitable plant. Here an ESOP received direct federal financing through the Economic Development Administration (Title IX of the Public Works and Economic Development Act) to prevent loss of 500 jobs. The Lathe Company's ESO trust bought the plant for cash, with $5 million at 3 percent interest loaned by EDA through the City of South Bend, plus another $5 million in loans from private banking sources. The EDA loan to the city set up an industrial revolving fund, which can be used to finance other area businesses in the same way as the Lathe Company repays its loan. The Company ESO trust owns all the company stock. Shares are allocated to employees on the trust's books after their retirement or death. At the present time, the shift in ownership has had only a slight change in management. The company's board of directors is composed of holdover top managers, plus two Steelworkers Union local officials and two outsiders, a local manufacturer and an ESOP specialist banker. It is important to note, however, that this local producer-owned enterprise *does not* become a CDC until its ownership and management extends to people in the community area of its operation. Local citizens then participate and begin to affect the direction of the production and the profits in the broader interests of the community. Only then does the role of the consumer become significant to the organization.

20. "Consumer Offices in State, County, and City Governments," Executive Office of the President, Office of Consumer Affairs, May 4, 1971; cf. "State and Local Voluntary Consumer Organizations" (mimeograph, May 3, 1971).

21. Leonard Silk, "Swedish Labor Plan," *New York Times,* May 26, 1976, p. 45; cf. "Business Perspectives" *Sweden Now,* No. 2, Vol. 10 (1976), pp. 11, 12.

22. William Meade, "Nationalized Steel," in Ken Coates (ed), *Can the Workers Run Industry?* (Nottingham, England: The Bertrand Russell Peace Foundation, 1968), p. 147ff.

23. Terrence C. Daintith, "Public and Private Enterprise in the United Kingdom," in Wolfgang Friedman (ed), *Public and Private Enterprise in Mixed Economies* (New York: Columbia University Press, 1974), p. 198.

24. This section draws from Peter Knight, "Social Property in Peru: The Political Economy of Predominance," in *Economic Analysis and Workers' Management* (Belgrade), 10: 3–4, (Fall, 1976). Cf A. Covarrubias and J. Vanek, "Self-Management in Peruvian Law of Social Property," Sept. 1974, No. 78, Program on Participation and Labor-Managed Systems Center for International Studies, Cornell University; Abraham F. Lowenthal (ed), *The Peruvian Experiment* (Princeton, N. J.: Princeton University Press, 1975).

25. The formal goal of the government was eloquently expressed in the new laws by former President Velasco as follows: "a system based on a moral order of solidarity rather than individualism; on a fundamentally self-managed economy, in which the means of production are predominantly social property, under the direct control of those who by their work generate wealth; and on a political order where the power of decision, far from being the monopoly of political or economic oligarchies, is diffused and rooted essentially in social, economic, and political institutions managed, without intermediation or with a minimum of it, by the men and women who form them." Speech to the inaugural sessions of the Second Ministerial Meeting of the Group of the 77, October 28, 1971, in Velasco: *La voz de la revolucion* (Lima: Ediciones Participacion, 1972, Vol. 2, p. 285. Quoted in Peter Knight, op. cit. Cf. Luis Pasara, Jorge Santistevan, Alberto Bustamante, and Diego Garcia-Sayan, *Dinamica de la comunidad industrial* (Lima: DESCO, 1974).

26. Alastair Campbell and Blair Foster, *The Mondragon Movement* (London: ICOM), 1974.

27. Based on discussions with Rene Rodriguez, who studied in the Guipuscoa Province. Cf. doctoral dissertation in process by Ana Gutierrez Johnson under the supervision of Professor William Whyte, Cornell University; R. Oakeshott, "Mondragon: Spain's Oasis of Democracy," *Observer,* Colour Supplement, 21, January 21, 1973.

28. The surplus (profit) is divided into three parts. Ten to 15 percent goes for social purposes to benefit the community (including support of the educational system). Fifteen to 20 percent goes to a reserve fund held by the firm. The remaining 65 to 70 percent is distributed to the members in proportion to hours worked during the year and the rate of pay received. But this fund is treated by the firm as a debt or bond to members that pays about 13 percent interest. A member in good standing who leaves the firm with proper notice can take 80 percent of this deposit while the firm retains 20 percent. See Ana Gutierrez Johnson and William Foote Whyte, "The Mondragon System of Worker Production Cooperatives," an unpublished paper, September, 1976.

29. Brian Hammond, "Participation: All Over Europe, Workers and Employers Begin to get Together," *Vision,* March, 1976.

SEVEN

TOWARD A GENERAL THEORY OF FEDERATIONS:
Themes for Research

Political theorists in the West have tended either to praise the liberal business-oriented society by their theories of pluralism or to condemn all modern nations by their theories of "mass society." Their theories have been helpful in stimulating research and orienting us to major political issues. But they fail to be comprehensive and thus do not grasp the essential problem of social change and development in modern societies.

Richard Hamilton, Professor of Sociology at McGill University, has pointed to an element of truth in each theory, even while he says each of them fails to be adequate or comprehensive. He reminds us first of how formulations of "pluralism" have a special thrust. This thrust can most easily be seen in advocate Robert Dahl's fundamental axiom: "Instead of a single center of sovereign power, there must be multiple centers of power, none of which is or can be wholly sovereign." Pluralist theory then sees a wide variety of units in the business society, each with its own resources for influencing policy. Pluralist researchers focus on the role of voluntary associations and emphasize the importance of associational freedom in modern society. On the other hand, Hamilton claims that the theory of mass society "is the pathological inverse of the pluralist theory. The mass society is one in which the voluntary associations never developed or have disappeared, or have come to be politically irrelevant, engaging in a round of activity with little or no serious content." This theory points to the forms of oligarchy and dominance in the society. And these forms appear in both capitalist and socialist nations.[1]

Both theories together have contributed in some measure to our understanding of what is happening in modern nations, but they each fall short of giving us the whole picture. Pluralist theory fails to deal adequately with the problem of order. It does not explain how sovereignty is created in the matrix of enterprises and economic associations that shape the society. It does not tell us how free enterprise can function in an environment of competition and conflict without ending in oligopoly or monopoly. It cannot explain the cause for a breakdown of the business system nor the cause for modern revolution. The mass-society theory, on the other hand, neglects to establish the conditions of freedom. It ignores the large segment of "free association" in society. It does not, therefore, provide us with the social base for development and self-directing change. In sum, both theories are caught without an answer to the dilemma of modern nations. Pluralist theory idealizes the free enterprise system, whereas mass society theory, reacts against the rising corporate state. Neither theory, pluralism or mass society, identifies the key problem facing nations of the late twentieth century.

The key problem involves creating a social order of economy that yields the conditions for individual freedom. Individual freedom is not simply a problem of "the state" as these theories would have us believe. It is not simply a problem of creating civil rights and democracy in the government. It is rather a problem of the economic order, a problem of creating civil rights and democracy within the economy.

The concept of pluralism by itself, therefore, is no better than the concept of laissez-faire. It does not show how small enterprise becomes swallowed whole by more powerful conglomerates. It leads us inevitably toward more government controls. Without a concept of civil order in the economy, it leads only to economic instabilities. It leads finally to its "pathological opposite," the mass society.

The emergence of a new social order of economy can be seen, nevertheless, in the social federations that cut across the domestic life of both capitalist and socialist nations. The central issue is how these federations generate freedom and lead toward the sovereignty of the individual in society.

DECENTRALIZED FEDERALISM

The concept of a decentralized federal economy offers an important alternative to the mass society. It offers a direction toward the pluralist ideal of individual freedom in society.[2]

Economic federalism does not mean another "extreme" whereby the whole economy comes under the dominion of federations. It means only that the main body of economic life is characterized by democratic associations. These democratic associations then engage in a development process of promoting the well-being of their individual members. This includes sponsoring and encouraging independent enterprises. It is a process in which enterprises are individualized and strengthened in association with one another so that the real conditions for freedom can be established.

Social federations have already begun to "build" a foundation in the economy. The nonprofit federations in the areas of production, distribution, and consumption are coming to determine much of the viability of the U. S. economy. Federated unions, trade associations, and consumer groups are increasing the capacity of self-governance of the private sector. They have been developing relatively stable forms of social governance at local, state, regional, and national levels. Their separate growth is admittedly not all even or equitable, but collectively they manage a large segment of economic life. I have suggested that they serve together as a social foundation upon which the private economy is beginning to function in the public interest.

With this picture in mind, let us now formulate theoretical guidelines for research into the development of a decentralized federal economy. We open our discussion to sociological, political, psychological, socioeconomic, and anthropological perspectives that can help guide studies of the economy becoming federated outside the state.

Sociological Studies

A key research problem in sociology involves determining how the different independent companies and federations in an industry connect with one another to enhance their own interest and to form a self-governing unit of the economy. The private companies, the unions, the trade and consumer groups are organized differently at local, state, and national levels in each industry; they show various degrees of democratic decentralization of authority. Our research is guided by an interest in the extent to which these different groups may develop human resources, encourage an optimum degree of freedom for workers, and still function in the public interest. We are interested in tracing the organization of *production, distribution,* and *consumption,* to determine the extent to which it is decentralized and federally organized as a social sector outside the state.

Our research problem is not unique to sociology. One of the first American theorists studying "functional representation" after the turn of the twentieth century was the institutional economist John R. Commons. Commons advocated direct election of representatives for all major interest groups in American society. He had in mind the representation of such associations as major universities and churches as well as labor and business associations. The representatives of these "interest groups," he said, could become the first effective legislature of the country.[3]

G. D. H. Cole and other Guild socialists in England also advocated a functional system of representation as opposed to geographic representation. Cole argued that it was nonsense to think of representing individuals in geographic areas since it is in the very nature of persons that they cannot be represented. True representation is based on the purposes that people hold in common. Any real representation in politics, then, should be functional representation.[4]

Political theory about "functional representation" of interest groups is often set against "territorial representation" of states in a democratic republic. But we are concerned here only with the polity of the federations most closely linked to the corporate economy. We are therefore interested in both *function* and *territory* in assessing the distribution of power within unions, trade associations, and cooperative federations. The object of sociological research is to identify the changing territorial balance of power in each industry, looking for the links developing between organized production, distribution, and consumption. These links are made through union federations and business corporations (production), trade associations (distribution), and consumer organizations (consumption).

The textile and apparel industries, for example, have been changing their territorial base. The textile unions have a functional interest in production; the textile trade associations have a functional interest in distribution; and the consumer groups have a functional interest in the use of textiles. Let us look briefly at changes taking place in this industry to illustrate our guidelines for research.

Production

Recently the Textile Workers Union of America merged with the Amalgamated Clothing Workers of America. Their new combined membership amounted to more than 500,000 workers. They merged in order to build a more effective instrumentality for organizing workers. In this merger the separate purposes of each union were united. The functional identity of union workers was broadened. Murray H. Finley, president of the Amalgamated, told 3000 delegates at the Washington Hilton that "the people who weave the cloth and the people who cut it and sew it and press it" were tied together inexorably.[5]

A major purpose of the textile and apparel workers' merger in this case was to organize workers better in the South. Their main targets were the big textile corporations such as J. P. Stevens & Company, Burlington Mills, and Cannon Mills. The unions had been concentrated in the Eastern Seaboard region. The territorial movement of the corporations had weakened their organization.

The Textile Workers consist of about 160,000 persons. The union has 80,000 members located in New York, New Jersey, Pennsylvania, and New England. The Amalgamated, in turn, has about 350,000 in men's apparel. They have 48,000 in the metropolitan area of New York, New Jersey, and Connecticut. They have 70,000 altogether in New York State and 30,000 more in Pennsylvania. The growing edge of these labor federations then is toward the South and especially in the Southern Piedmont region, where a large segment of the textile industry has moved. Here we see the development of power and authority in the union federation at local and regional levels of organization. The research question is: Where are new links developing to control the "forces of production"?

The Textile Workers Union of America (TWUA) chose the annual stockholder meeting of J. P. Stevens in 1975 as a battleground for union organizing. Armed with only 12 votes at the beginning, the TWUA was later able to muster 800,000 votes in favor of one proposal and 500,000 votes on another. Their first proposal would have required the Stevens board of directors to appoint a committee of outside directors to submit a report detailing the cost of the company's ongoing labor dispute with the TWUA including legal fees, fines, and back wages. The other proposal concerned what was said to be an unfair pension plan. The two proposals had entered the agenda on a Securities and Exchange Commission ruling over the objection of Stevens' management. Some backing for the proposals came from institutional investors such as the Carnegie Corporation of New York.[6] Here we note a significant shift in union tactics. We observe a new connection in the line of attack of union leaders (as well as outside investors) as they seek a measure of control over production.

Distribution

The American Textile Manufacturers Institute (ATMI) is a trade association of textile mill firms with a budget of over $1 million. It has 300 members and about 55 full-time staff. Among its recent joiners have been the National Federation of Textiles (1958), National Association of Finishers of Textiles (1965), Textile Data Processing Association (1969), and the National Association of Wool Manufacturers (1971).[7] A sociological study here would show the extent that information is available for the development of technology in the industry as well as the extent of *knowledge about pricing and the distribution of products within regions of the United States.*

The ATMI has committees on Consumer Affairs, Environmental Preservation, Employee Benefits, and many others. The common problems and issues of the industry are discussed here. They are also published in the trade journal *Textile World.* Recently, the vice president of Towers, Perrin, Forster & Co. wrote about the need to establish new communication systems with employees of the textile industry. He said management had come a long way from considering "the employee group as a necessary commodity." In this journal and in these committees we observe the new social consciousness of management toward labor and consumer groups.[8] The research question is: What new links are developing here between labor and management?

The Saratoga Knitting Mill, Inc. is an example of how management and labor are beginning to collaborate through joint management. For the last three years, the managers and workers in this firm have jointly owned it. The firm had been a subsidiary of Cluett-Peabody for many years. But Cluett-Peabody began negotiating to sell it to another company because of its low profitability. Hearing of this, the employees began talking in jest to themselves about buying the firm.

Later, they began to talk more seriously with local bankers. Finally, with the help of the Adirondack Trust Co., the New York Business Development Corp., and the U. S. Small Business Administration, the employees cleared loans to buy the company. The transaction was a boon to the business. In 1974 its sales to Cluett-Peabody had been $3.7 million. In 1975, the self-owned company made $7.5 million in sales. The new management then announced a 5 percent Christmas bonus and a general 5 percent wage increase for all its employees. It has not yet joined the trade association, and it stands by itself among the textile giants. Here our research focuses on the *shift in employee attitudes* which permits *worker self-management.*[9]

Consumption

Consumers Research is an "independent, nonprofit, scientific, technical, and educational nongovernmental public service organization" that investigates the utility, durability, and value of textile products as well as many other types of products. Here the public learns about the FTC regulations requiring labels on all wearing apparel that must disclose information to the buyers. Our research here shows the extent to which *consumer groups* are organizing around the *problems of pricing* as well as the *quality of the products.*[10]

Our sociological research then is directed first toward the way in which union organization parallels textile corporations in terms of members and territory. We are interested in the potential link between the unions and their interest in self-management at different levels of corporate governance. Our focus then turns toward the textile trade association to determine the extent to which corporations are working together to share information of commerce and the distribution of products. The research focus finally turns toward the endpoints of product distribution. Here we are interested in the organization of retail outlets and the extent to which consumer groups are organized around the opportunity to purchase textiles and apparel of their choice. At this point we have completed a sociological unit of study in the production, distribution, and consumption of textiles.

Political Studies

The political scientist Earl Latham once argued that economic associations were the basic political forms of society. "It has been pointed out, and repeated," he said, "that the structure of society is associational. . . . What is true of society is true of the . . . economic community."[11] Seen in this light, the development of economic associations is an essential part of the political development of the society. The growth of the cooperative federation, the trade federation, and the union federation is a long-range political process. It should lead at least theoretically to the creation of a viable economic community within the larger society.

All federations have both a structure and a function. The study of the political structures and functions of federations within the economic order should enlighten us about their common problems. Research is needed on the similarities of the federations in the areas of production, distribution, and consumption. In this kind of research we can begin to see the places where coordination and integration can take place among them.

Structure and Function

An overview of all three federation zones suggests that the following structural traits are held in common:

1. A *voting structure* in which decisions are made and the opinions of members are expressed.
2. A *representative structure* in which each member association is given an equitable place in the whole.
3. An *administrative structure* (generally related to localities) through which the operations are carried out.
4. A *finance structure* in which income is created, distributed, and invested.
5. A *juridical structure* in which members seek redress or equity for breeches in administrative operations.
6. A *meeting structure* in which members confer on matters of common interest and convene to conduct business.
7. A *service structure* through which the central body relates to both members and external associations of the federation.

These structures in the three federated zones of production, distribution, and consumption have yet to be studied together. In the light of developmental changes affecting all three zones, what kinds of research questions about these structures can be posed?

It is clear, for example, that the *finance structure* in each federated zone varies markedly and would be affected differently by development policy. The creation of income for the cooperative federation is often a function of its customers' purchases. Its finance structure is like a business except that portions of the profits are returned to each member. The income of trade and union federations, on the other hand, is largely based on dues and fees charged to members. Union dues are also collected by the company before the receipt of wages by the worker. (Otherwise, it is said, the union would have difficulty collecting them from individual workers.) Both types of dues, however, emanate from a need to protect the members in each type of federation against outside threats. The outside threats are other managements, other unions, and the government. If these threats were reduced in development programs, what would happen to the "income structure" of each federation?

Each federation has certain *functions* generally associated with the maintenance of any large-scale organization. These include:

1. Integration of the members' interests and purposes
2. Coordination of the members' activities
3. Representation of members in the main body of the organization
4. Mediation of conflict
5. Formulation of administrative rules and policy
6. Expansion and growth of the organization
7. Creation of incentives for members
8. Provision for security among the membership
9. Development of communication among members and the public.

The specific nature of these functions can be judged only in the light of the goals, special interests, and norms of each federation. Each function is closely interdependent with the structure of each federation.

The "integration of the members' interests and purposes," for example, is partly dependent upon the size and power of its membership. The size and power of a corporation like the Bank of America will have a definite effect on the "democratic functioning" of the federation to which it belongs. One study suggests that the Bank of America pays approximately $90,000 in dues to the American Bankers Association. This same bank also pays approximately $150,000 to the California Bankers Association. In addition, it belongs to other associations such as Bank Administration Institute, Bank Marketing Association, Robert Morris Associates, Consumer Banking Association, Association of Registered Bank Holding Companies, Industrial Bankers Association of the U. S., Bankers Association for Free Trade, Association of Reserve City Bankers, and the American Institute of Banking. The bank's power is substantial in each of these associations apart from formal democratic practices.[12]

The adequacy of democratic practices in any federation is closely related to both the size of its members and its structure. The state of New York, for example, is more influential than is Rhode Island in determining policy in the House of Representatives. But the power of New York is checked in the Senate where it has only two representatives along with every other state regardless of size. Likewise, the structure of a union or a business federation is important to examine for its political checks and balances.

The big unions or big corporations within federations may be studied for the degree to which they are decentralized in relation to a federal structure. We have noted how unions vary in their tendencies to "decentralize," but big corporations also vary in this sense. The pharmaceutical firm of Johnson and Johnson at New Brunswick, New Jersey, for example, is a highly decentralized organization according to its chief executive, General Robert Wood Johnson. Johnson himself presided over the division of the firm into "a number of autonomous subsidiaries which are actually legal entities of their own."[13] On the other hand, large companies like General Motors and General Electric show intermediate patterns of decentralization. It follows that in the more centralized federation, members like a GM or a GE would take a more dominant role in the federation of which they are a part.

The expression of these functions in each federation can be studied in the light of a plan for social development. If federal chartering of the large corporation were part of that plan, the federation could be studied first in terms of corporate charter purposes. If the national corporation is no longer chartered solely in its own private interests and now has a public purpose, this raises basic questions about the formerly private purposes of each *federation*.

In a plan for social development, how, then, do the functions of the trade union join with the function of the trade association?

Special studies can be made in this regard guided by research questions such as the following:

How do the purposes of the Automobile Manufacturers Association connect with the purposes of the United Auto Workers in the public interest? How can these public purposes connect in joint programs? For example, how can the two associations join to improve the field of public transportation? How can they combine efforts to improve the working conditions of automobile employees across the country? How then do the federation purposes of the auto manufacturers and auto workers connect with the purposes of the Consumer Federation of America and the Center for Auto Safety?

A whole new relationship between federation zones can develop in the process of federal chartering, which also changes corporate and tax law. In 1974 the Industrial Union Department of the AFL-CIO gave $7500 to the Consumer Federation, which is the only national consumer organization that lobbies Congress on a broad spectrum of consumer issues. The Consumers Union, which tests consumer products and publishes *Consumer Reports* magazine, was the Federation's largest contributor at $33,000. Contributions to the Federation, however, are not deductible. This contrasts with contributions to the Chamber of Commerce by its membership, which are deductible. Questions for study could be raised such as:

How do such legal differences between business and consumer groups change with a development plan? How can voluntary consumer federations be given legal incentives to develop more power in the public interest? How does the federated Chamber of Commerce develop a public purpose that gives strong reasons for it to respond to the interests of the Consumer Federation?

Such questions may seem inappropriate to a society composed of competing and conflicting interest groups, but the logic of social development points in this direction. The trade union, the trade association, and the consumer federation have a joint public interest in advancing *technical* and *social* research on a national scale. Indeed, there is as much technical research to be done in redesigning transportation systems on a national scale as there is social research to be done in redesigning the corporate system that creates nationwide transportation problems.

Social and technical research now enters all phases of economic organization with a public purpose. Trade unions and trade associations can both examine methods of employee participation in corporate decision-making. They can study the problem of effective union representation on top boards of directors. They can jointly create employee courts in the private sector in the manner of European federations of employers and employees. And thereby take steps to reduce the need for the government to arbitrate disputes for them in the public interest.

Psychological Studies

A basic premise guiding the psychological study of these federations is that *they affect and involve the individual.* We are concerned here especially with the concept of the "self."

Social psychological theory, in the tradition of George Herbert Mead and Charles Cooley, suggests that the structure of society is mirrored in the structure of the self.[14] The child growing up in the family becomes socialized into the structure of society by playing the role of the mother, father, doctor, nurse, "cops," and "robbers," etc. Taking these roles in games helps the child develop the collective attitudes of society within himself or herself. The game thus cultivates the attitudes of society in children who then become prepared to take the roles "assigned" to them in society. The society determines much of the "self" through this socialization process.

The notion that the society is *the* determinant of the individual, however, is often challenged by theorists in this tradition. People are observed to act back on the society that in effect created them. The assumption is that people generate their own powers to change society. *People can see themselves in the creation of society as well as created by society.* It is this latter process of self-determination that interests us. How do individuals achieve a greater power of self-expression in the organization of the society?

The Self and Society

The concept of the self is inherent in our theory of economic governance. We have said that "self-governance" refers broadly to different levels of autonomous management in the economy. It refers scientifically to the economy as a whole and is applicable to the autonomous management of federations, enterprises, work teams, and finally to the individual in the workplace. We may now assert that the power and expression of the individual is expressed or denied *at each level of governance* depending upon the governing form of organization. Individuals express themselves creatively in organizations according to the form of social governance.

Over twenty years ago field studies in group dynamics and education were conducted with this in mind. In democratically organized groups, individuals showed greater originality, individuality, and personal motivation than groups organized along more authoritarian and laissez-faire lines.[15] Since that time, many experiments in enterprises have continued this tradition of looking for ways of increasing the "actualizing" powers of the self.[16] But now we are suggesting that the powers of each individual are extended with others in the governance of large enterprises and federations. Some part of the self is expressed either directly or through others at each interacting level of the economy: the work team, the enterprise, the federation, and the industry.

The extent to which people express and determine their own lot in the economic order depends on the form of participatory activity at each level of governance. The capacity for individuals to act back on the economic system that determines their roles is a function of their opportunity to participate in levels of economic organization. Without that participation of people in organizations, individuals become subject to the impersonal forces of the market.

David Truman suggests as much in his book *The Governmental Process:*

There are, undoubtedly, a number of reasons for the prevalence of associations growing out of economic institutions . . . There has been a series of disturbances, and dislocations consequent upon the utopian attempt, as Polanyi calls it, to set up a completely self-regulating market system. This attempt involved a policy of treating the fictitious factors of land, labor, and capital as if they were real, ignoring the fact that they stood for human beings or influences closely affecting the welfare of humans. Application of this policy inevitably meant suffering and dislocation—unemployment, wide fluctuation in prices, waste, and so forth. These disturbances inevitably produced associations—of owners, of workers, of farmers—operating upon government to mitigate and control the ravages of the system through tariffs, subsidies, wage guarantees, social insurance and the like.[17]

The *real* factors determining the life of the social economy are individual human beings. The extent to which individuals participate in the governance of the work team, the work team in the governance of the enterprise, the enterprise in the governance of the trade association, and the trade association in the governance of the economy, is a measure of the extent to which individuals count in determining the course of their own lives in the economic order.

But this theory of participation is extended further into the federations of production, distribution, and consumption. The roles of the workers, managers, and consumers in effect represent different organized "zones" where conflicts of interest arise.

The *producers* of goods, for example, are not primarily concerned with the effects of these goods on the *consumers*. The New York managers of a paper company are not primarily concerned with the spoilage of a river caused by their company's plant in Maine. They are primarily interested in company earnings. The *workers* of an automobile plant are not *primarily* concerned about the fact that 55,000 people are killed each year by the autos they produce. They are primarily interested in their wages and in maintaining their jobs. The economic roles we take in society force us to become separated from one another in the larger social whole. A part of ourselves remains unexpressed in our singular role as worker or manager or consumer.

We may now see the psychological significance of social policies leading toward the coordination and integration of these three federation zones. The three zones, in effect, express extensions of ourselves as workers, managers, and consumers. The linking of these three zones represents a joining of the divided parts of ourselves that are writ large in society.

This may seem to be a philosophical notion until we look carefully at what the social psychologist George Herbert Mead calls the development of the "generalized other." The generalized other refers to the expanding concept of the self that grows outward to incorporate larger and more complex roles. These roles continue to become integrated in the development of the self. The generalized other refers to the gradual incorporation of the roles of others in an expanding sense of community. It involves a growing capacity to act empathically and knowledgeably toward others at different levels of society. Furthermore, the individual self strains to see itself as a harmonious whole in the context of society.

The coordination and integration of economic zones of production, distribution, and consumption therefore represent a strain toward the development of a more complete self. A more complete self is created when the collective representations of the consumer, manager, and worker are represented equitably in the political economy of society. It follows that the individual is then more effectively *determining the shape of the society* instead of being so much determined by that society.

Put another way, the roles of the consumer, the manager, and the worker are learned universally in childhood. Every child learns the meaning of working, consuming, and managing to some degree while growing up in the household. Every-one is a worker, a consumer, a manager. But the economic organization of society separates these basic functions of the self into conflicting roles in the "human community." These roles become suppressed partly by an unequal dis-tribution of power. The unequal distribution of power in turn fails to communi-cate the nature of each role to others, preventing the development of an ade-quate "generalized other" within the adult.

It would be too much to assume that an instinct or "inherent tendency" for all individuals to seek a consistent and harmonious self is the cause for nations to seek a consistent and harmonious relationship between production, distribu-tion, and consumption. That kind of postulate is like arguing that wars between nations are caused by "instincts for aggression" that develop within the self. A relationship may exist, but it is not that simple. The tendency for federational zones to link their activities in the "general interest" may be related to the need for self-harmony but not wholly explained by it. The development of a balance of control in federation zones is a sociological and political phenomenon under-stood in its own level of collective dynamics.

Nevertheless, Mead's theory does lead us to suggest research on the connec-tions between the development of the self and these different federation zones. For example, the extent to which individual workers in factories can take account of the needs of consumers who use their products is an important matter for research. The extent to which individual consumers can likewise take account of the needs of workers who make the products they purchase is equally of interest. We would assume that the ability for each one to "take the role of the other," empathically and knowledgeably, would not be easy today. The hypothesis here is that a very low level of empathy for the needs of people in other federations would become evident through psychological research.

Social Needs of the Self

The early Guild Socialists like S. G. Hobson and A. R. Orage were writing in England before World War I about the fulfillment of human needs through the development of federations. Today Graham Wooten, looking back on this tradi-tion, suggests how Abraham Maslow's theory of motivation could be set against their concept of the Guild:

Under the Guild Socialist model, man's physiological (or biogenic) needs would be (in principle) better served: workers would get more than their current wages, perhaps three times more . . . Safety needs would be better cared for because the fear of unemployment would disappear . . . Workers, too, would be cared for in sickness, distress, and old age . . . Affiliative needs would be served because help-ing one's neighbour in distress is the mark of belonging, or, in their language, of fellowship. The Guild was to be essentially a fellowship as well as an economic organization. Esteem, would come through self-fulfillment (or achievement). The tradition of craftsmanship, still kept alive, despite 'intense specialization,' by the companionable nature of the workers', would flourish again.[18]

Guild Socialism did not come to flourish in England. Wooten is therefore drawn to suggest that the autonomous groups developing within the factory is the contemporary foundation upon which to study the original ideals of the Guild movement. It is here that Maslow's concept of self-actualization and self-fulfillment may be tested.

But Wooten raises new questions about how the *needs of workers are defined by the social roles* people take in the federations of society. He speaks of people as "citizen," "worker," and "unionist." He suggests that we should formulate a new concept of how people function through their *role in society*. He chooses to talk about "civic obligations" and the "civic role" of people beyond the trappings of our separate federational roles. Wooten is really asking for a new integrative concept, carrying us beyond our identity with the state, the union, or the business. He is coining a concept needed to develop an adequate concept of the "generalized other."

In sum, social psychological theory suggests that social roles determine the way we behave in everyday life but that we also generate our own independent powers to act back creatively according to the form of governance in our associations. Associations can be studied to determine how individuals can increase their power to act back and determine the course of their lives. These associations, for our purposes, begin in the workplace and extend through the enterprise to the federation. *Social development in the economy then becomes measured by the degree to which we are able to reshape the associations within society to meet our needs as human beings.*

In theory the coordination of "producer and consumer associations," which are designed to represent everyone in the economy, should lead toward a more unified sense of the self expressed in the "generalized other." The associations themselves may then express something of the humanity of their members by the nature of their articulation in society.

Socioeconomic Studies

Let us now carry this theoretical notion of socioeconomic roles one step further. We have said that these roles of working, managing, and consuming, are universal expressions of the individual in everyday life, and yet in the organization of society they are separated and at times in conflict. We may now add that the consumer in the marketplace, the laborer in the workplace, and the manager in the corporation compete heavily with each other for economic gains. The laborer seeks higher wages; the manager seeks higher profits; the consumer seeks lower prices. The consumer is a weak link in the chain of federations, however, and the consequences are more than psychological. They are social and economic. We can now propose a social cause for the economic problem of price inflation.

Price inflation is caused by the fact that consumers are not represented in strong organizations at the national level as are laborers and managers. Consumers cannot exercise control over prices in the manner that union leaders and executives exercise control over wages and profits. The conflict in economic interests between the consumer and the producer (laborers and managers) cannot be resolved within the private system in the same way that wages and profits can be resolved through collective bargaining.

Put another way, the lack of a balance of power between the consumer and the "producer" leads toward price inflation for the consumer. The lack of fair economic competition and collective bargaining between the producer and the consumer leads toward a demand for federal price stabilization. The federal government then becomes a surrogate for the consumer. Out of necessity the state becomes an entity that grows in this respect above and beyond the self-expression of individuals unorganized in the marketplace.

A balance in the organized power of these conflicting economic interests should result in an economic balance in prices, profits, and wages. It should lead toward what may be called an "economic republic" within the social sector of the economy. (See Figure 9.)

It follows logically that the growth of consumer organizations concerned about pricing could begin to stop the trend of price inflation. A process of price stabilization could take place through the well-known patterns of collective bargaining, mediation, and conciliation. Consumers could withhold the purchase of goods through federation decisions because of unfair pricing. Consumer retail

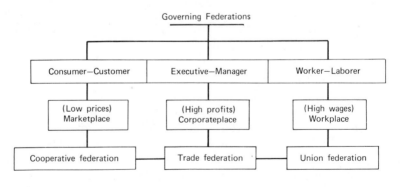

Figure 9.

stores, federated nationally, could negotiate a fair price with manufacturers on products whose prices are inflated because of monopolistic advantage.

The consequences of this development would be twofold. First, the relatively hidden conflict between the needs of the consumer and the needs of the producer would come into public focus. The consumer in this case would begin to exert a stronger collective influence over the processes of production and distribution. Second, a trend would develop toward the standardization of wages and profits across the industry. The collective pressure to hold down pricing would result in the development of formulas emphasizing equity in wages in all industries and formulas guiding percentages of profits appropriate to industry.

These are only speculative issues at the present stage of economic formation. They are nevertheless important in applying research to the direction of social development. Social research in this case may precede public policy in conceiving the developmental directions of a social economy.

Anthropological Studies

Anthropologists who study primitive societies talk about "growth without development" in a community. An example would be the case where a community's cash income grows because of its enlarged sales of crops but basic changes in the technology and culture are not forthcoming. The cash income grows while the old culture with its folkviews and values remains unchanged. No new lines of production, technology, or vocations are introduced, and literacy remains the same. The use of the new cash income goes for old status prerogatives or traditions such as the dowry. In other words, growth in cash income or in productivity can occur without community development. But the question of what constitutes community development is difficult to answer.[19]

The question of what constitutes community development is no less difficult to answer in the study of modern societies, because they have their own complicated frontier. No society has ever been "post-modern" before in history. For the study of post-modern development we need a new taxonomy to explain the new forms of transformation taking place among developing nations. The old concepts of capitalist and socialist or "private and public sector," do not always catch the subtleties of change in a nation in the process of transition.

We begin here with what Theodore Levitt describes as the three sectors of the modern capitalist society and then show how these lines are changing through current developments in the United States:

The conventional taxonomy divides society into two sectors—private and public. Private is business. Public is presumed to be all else. But "all else" is too broad; it covers so much that it means nothing. In terms of how society's work gets done, the most relevant component of "all else" is government. Its activities, influence, and power are so salient, even in the least governmentalized of nations, that it qualifies at least as well as business as a special sector unto itself. In common parlance, "the public sector" refers to those things that the government does, can do, or ought to do. But that leaves an enormous residuum, which itself is divisible in many ways.[20]

This "residuum" is a third sector, which is composed of a "bewildering variety of organizations and institutions with differing degrees of visibility, power, and activeness." Levitt notes that the United States in 1970 had some 3000 voluntary *national organizations* devoted to the performance of tasks that altogether involved annual expenditures in excess of $2 billion.

The problem with this three-sector model is that it is changing dramatically with the development of the social economy. The third sector would include trade unions, cooperative federations, and business associations such as the Chamber of Commerce and yet it would be difficult to distinguish them from the business sector. Also, we have seen the business sector itself becoming increasingly oriented to social interests in line with the purposes of many nonprofit corporations in the third sector. Furthermore, all major associations organized at the national level are assuming a public character because of their impact on so many people outside their own membership.

Instead of devising a new taxonomy, we may devise a method of looking at the matrix of social federations developing with many diverse purposes and a complex cultural character.

Latent versus Manifest Economy

It is convenient to distinguish two types of economic organization in studies of social economy. One type is manifest or overt, and the other type is latent or covert. The *manifest economy* refers to all those forms of economic organization that are legally designed especially for monetary gain. This includes corporations, companies, partnerships, retail and wholesale stores, and development groups that are organized primarily to make a profit. The *latent economy* refers to those forms of social organization that are ancillary to this manifest economic system and yet where economic activity remains significant and essential for survival. This includes churches, schools, voluntary associations, and the government. The latent economy also refers to those activities that are often unorganized and irregular and yet where economic factors still play an important role. This includes hobbies, forms of recreation, and domestic chores in the household.

An intricate relationship exists between the latent and manifest dimensions of the economy, which has yet to be understood for its meaning in the evolutionary scheme of things. We do not yet know enough about the impact of osmotic interchanges between "corporations" federated for different purposes. For example, we do not know the full effects of the National Council of Churches (a nonprofit federation) acting on the business sector when it appoints a Corporate Information Center for monitoring business activity, nor the effect of its separate corporate denominations taking joint action on stockholder issues. We do not know the real effects of changes in curriculum and text use among business and management schools across the country acting on the direction of the business economy. We do not know the full effects of shaping new models of business law from within committees of the American Bar Association (a nonprofit federation) for Congressional action. The churches, the universities, and the bar associations are all federations acting in the so-called third sector having an impact on the so-called business sector.

We can formulate a few theoretical propositions regarding the social evolution of these federations with their diverse purposes and a complex character.

First, the latent side of business organizations—their social character—is becoming increasingly manifest or public. The hidden social life of business is becoming conscious to the public. Second, the latent side of the voluntary third sector—its economic character—is also becoming increasingly manifest or public. In this case we are beginning to see the *economic dimensions* of private universities, schools, hospitals, churches, theatres, etc. as part of the public domain. A sense of general responsibility for the support of these diverse expressions of the latent economy is becoming evident.

The summative judgment about this evolutionary process is that American society is developing a system of interrelated federations whose foundations are social *and* economic but whose primary purposes lie ultimately in the cultural domain. We are seeing the development of human values realistically expressed in this large variety of associations that are federally related around such subjects as religion, art, science, and education as well as economic productivity. All these federations are grounded in the social economy.

In the broad scope of societal theory, there is a substantial literature suggesting that the latent dimensions of an evolving society eventually become manifest in the process of development. This process of development, however, is not easy to evaluate. It goes beyond any facile opinion of being good or bad. It requires continued study to see how it happens and then what it means.

What does it mean, for example, when the *latent social dimensions* of the corporate economy become manifest and public? The professional interests of the bar association or the religious values of the church may emerge to humanize the economic system or they might even dehumanize it. They could dehumanize it if the economic order were to gradually acquire a *singular emphasis* on law or morality. In place of the domination of economic interests, we could become dominated by a particular set of statutes or moral codes of conduct. Such legal and moral tones are dominant in some state socialist nations. The latent motives of social jurisprudence or a special theology can become institutionalized and *become as repressive as the profit motive* in the developmental process. On the other hand, a new legality and morality that becomes manifest in the business economy could be liberating, depending upon how it is introduced into the system.

For this reason, social research that becomes connected to planning at the national level should follow the professional practice of community development grounded in self-studies. Self-studies permit people to examine their institutions collectively and introduce their measures of change on a scale that can be understood and generally accepted by members of the community.

LOOKING BOTH BACKWARD AND FORWARD

In the first decades of the twentieth century, federations of business, labor, and consumer cooperatives were beginning to develop in the private sector of the U. S. economy. It was a time of incubation for many federations as the business system was heading for major trouble. The Great Depression followed, with the federal government seeking some nationwide basis for "recovery" beyond the aegis of the single business enterprise. The business federations were looked upon for the answer. They were given the power to set codes of conduct and pricing under official counsel with union and consumer groups. The union federations were given formal recognition from the government for their right to bargain collectively with business and to join with them to help in recovering from the Depression. But the experiment in private federalism was only in its infancy. The balance of power among managers, workers, and consumers had not reached the point where they could by joint authority assume the responsibility for regulating these key problems in the economy outside the state.

In the latter third of the twentieth century, the economy is still not organized to solve its own problems, but it has shown strong signs of moving in that direction. It still faces endemic inflation and economic instabilities as well as environmental pollution and consumer exploitation, which require federal agencies to monitor and correct. But at the same time the developmental process is continuing. Labor federations have been gaining strength, and there are nationally organized consumer organizations with state and local affiliations. New policies based on "creative federalism" have begun to appear.[21] While this concept has so far been applied to the state system, it may also be a signal for developing a new system of accountability in the economy. It may become the basis for creating a new policy of federalism in the political economy.

The notion of federalism, however, goes beyond the United States in its expression and significance. It is today a world concept. The concept applies importantly to socialist nations in the throes of their own development. It applies to the federal organization of communes in China and to the provinces in Cuba as much as to corporate life in the United States. It is a concept of as much world significance today as democracy was in the nineteenth and early twentieth century.

The twentieth century has become an age of federalism for nations around the world. William Riker notes that by 1964, well over half the land mass of the world was ruled by governments calling themselves federations.[22] Grouped by continents; these nations included:

North America: Canada, Mexico, United States
South America: Argentina, Brazil, Venezuela
Europe: Austria, Soviet Union, Switzerland
South Asia: Australia, India, Malaysia, and Pakistan
Africa: Congo, Ethiopia, Nigeria

Federalism is now an issue of world order. The succession of efforts to create world peace through "world federalism" is a twentieth century phenomenon.[23] The League of Nations was created after World War I, but it was not quite strong enough to stop violent international aggression. The League broke down and World War II erupted. The United Nations was then created as a type of federation in which nations placed new authority and confidence. Yet its focus has been largely on state diplomacy treating political issues between nations while many of the underlying problems originate in the world economy. It is therefore facing its own political crises to maintain a viable federal structure.

Nations today often act as capitalist corporations seeking their own self-interests and profits in a competitive world economy. Ministers of socialist nations and executives of transnational corporations both roam through developing countries seeking new types of investments. Developing nations become a market for both ideological and capital investment.

But the United Nations has begun to observe the critical relation between the world economy and world peace, and has created a Commission on Transnational Corporations. Member nations are calling today for a *new international economic order*. International economists are asking the basic question: What kind of economic order allows working people in diverse cultures to survive and flourish at the world level? Here our study of social federalism continues as we examine the way nations and global corporations govern themselves in a world economy.

NOTES

1. Hamilton shows us the problems associated with such theories in his own analysis of data in the national surveys, but he does not himself completely fill the vacuum in political

thought. He discusses a "social-bases-group pressures" theory as "the most appropriate for the understanding of contemporary political orientations." Richard Hamilton, *Class and Politics in the United States* (New York: Wiley, 1972), p. 555.

2. Researchers can find inspiration for theory in Mancur Olson, *The Logic of Collective Action* (Cambridge: Harvard University Press, 1965).

3. John R. Commons, *Representative Democracy* (New York: Bureau of Economic Research n.d.); cf. *Institutional Economics* (Madison, Wisc.: Univ. of Wisconsin Press, 1959).

4. G. D. H. Cole, *Self-Government in Industry* (London: G. Bell & Sons, 1917).

5. Damon Stetson, "Textile Unions Vote to Merge and Plan to Organize the South," *New York Times,* June 1, 1976, p. 1.

6. *Textile World,* April, 1976, pp. 23–24.

7. Margaret Fisk, Editor, *Encyclopedia of Associations,* 10th ed., Vol. 1, *National Organizations of the U. S.* (Detroit, Mich.: Gale Research Co., 1976).

8. Roy Foltz, "Why You Must Talk Up to Employees," *Textile World,* November, 1975, pp. 153–154.

9. The local newspaper describes the crisis stemming from the commencement of layoffs of millworkers under Cluett-Peabody. "The problem was, then, what do you do for a man who had been in this plant for 30 years, he's got five kids, he's still paying on his home and buying his automobile and his plant suddenly disappears. You're in a job area where there's no place else to go. This really was the initial thought of over 100 people in the plant." Greg McGarry, "Saratoga Millworkers Reap Success," *Post Star,* Glen Falls, N. Y., July 20, 1975. Cf. *Times Union,* Dec. 21, 1975, C-12; *Industry Week,* Feb. 2, 1976, p. 30ff; *Clothes,* June 1, 1975, p. 17. At the end of April, 1976, the company was making "a profit margin above the average for our industry." Personal letter from Donald M. Cox, President, Saratoga Knitting Mill, Inc. (July 6, 1976).

10. *Consumers' Research Magazine,* No. 10, Vol. 58, October, 1975.

11. Earl Latham, *The Group Basis for Politics* (Ithaca, N. Y.: Cornell Univ. Press, 1958).

12. Larry Finkelstein, "Some Tough Questions about Trade Associations," in *Business and Society Review/Innovation,* 6, (Summer, 1973): 25.

13. John Chamberlain, "Industrial Firms Explore Diverse Forms of Organization," *Wall Street Journal,* Dec. 17, 1956. Noted in Richard Eells and Clarence Walton, op. cit.

14. George Herbert Mead, *Mind, Self and Society* (Chicago: Univ. of Chicago Press, 1934); *The Philosophy of the Act* (Chicago: Univ. of Chicago Press, 1938); cf. Charles Horton Cooley, *Social Organization* (New York: Schocken, 1962); *Human Nature and the Social Order* (New York: Schocken, 1964).

15. Ronald Lippitt and Ralph White, "Leader Behavior and Member Reaction in Three 'Social Climates'," in Dorwin Cartwright and Alvin Zander (eds), *Group Dynamics* (New York: Row Peterson and Co., 1953).

16. Roy P. Fairfield (ed), *Humanizing the Workplace* (Buffalo, N. Y.: Prometheus Books, 1974).

17. David Truman, *The Governmental Process* (New York: Knopf, 1958), p. 61.

18. Graham Wooten, *Workers, Unions, and the State* (New York: Schocken, 1966), p. 107.

19. George Dalton, *Economic Development and Social Change* (New York: Natural History Press, 1971), p. 217ff; In studying the development of primitive societies, anthropologists have sometimes followed the examples set by the so-called modern nations as "models." But modern nations have patterns of dominance and exploitation in their organization that

these models often reflect. Many nations have called instead for their own "authentic development."

20. Theodore Levitt, *The Third Sector* (New York: AMACON, 1973), p. 49.

21. Cf. James L. Sundquist, *Making Federalism Work: A Study of Program Coordination at the Community Level* (Washington, D. C.: The Brookings Institution, 1969).

22. William H. Riker, *Federalism, Origin, Operation, Significance* (Boston: Little, Brown, 1964). Cf. Thomas M. Franck, *Why Federations Fail* (New York: New York University Press, 1968).

23. Cf. Norman Cousins, *In Place of Folly* (New York: Harpers, 1961); see also reports of *The United World Federalists.*

PART III

The International Economy

KARL MARX. Capitals invested in foreign trade can yield a higher rate of profit, because, in the first place, there is competition with the commodities produced in other countries with inferior production facilities, so that the more advanced country sells its goods above their value even though cheaper than the competing countries. In so far as the labour of the more advanced country is here realized as labour of a higher specific weight, the rate of profit rises, because labour which has not been paid as being of a higher quality is sold as such. . . . We have thus seen in a general way that the same influences which produce a tendency in the general rate of profit to fall, also call forth counter-effects, which hamper, retard, and partly paralyse this fall. The latter do not do away with the law, but impair its effect.

EMILE DURKHEIM. Only one collective form survived the tempest: the State. By the nature of things this therefore tended to absorb all forms of activity which had a social character, and was henceforth confronted by nothing but an unstable flux of individuals. But then, by this very fact, it was compelled to assume functions for which it was unfitted and which it has not been able to discharge satisfactorily. It has often been said that the State is as intrusive as it is impotent. It makes a sickly attempt to extend itself over all sorts of things which do not belong to it, or which it grasps only by doing them violence . . .

To remedy this evil, the restitution to local groups of something of their old autonomy is periodically suggested. This is called decentralization. But the only really useful decentralization is one which would simultaneously produce a greater concentration of social energies. Without loosening the bonds uniting each part of society with the State, moral powers must be created with an influence, which the State cannot have, over the multitude of individuals . . .

Only after a special study of the corporative regime and the laws of its development would it be possible to make the above conclusions more precise.

MAX WEBER. The universal revival of "imperialist" capitalism which had always been the normal form in which capitalist interests have influenced politics, and the revival of political drives for expansion are thus not accidental. For the predictable future, the prognosis will have to be made in its favor.

This situation would hardly change fundamentally if for a moment we were to make the mental experiment of assuming the individual polities to be somehow "state-socialist" communities, that is, organizations supplying a maximum amount of their needs through a collective economy. They would seek to buy as cheaply as possible indispensable goods from others that have natural monopolies and would seek to exploit them. It is probable that force would be used where it would lead easily to favorable conditions for exchange; the weaker party would thereby be obligated to pay tribute, if not formally then at least actually. For the rest, one cannot see why the strong state-socialist communities should disdain to squeeze tribute out of the weaker communities for their own partners where they could do so, just as happened everywhere during early history.

EIGHT

SOCIAL MODELS OF ECONOMIC DEVELOPMENT AMONG NATIONS

The Transnational Corporation as a Democratic Institution

Many developing nations in regions around the world today are in a state of political unrest seeking to build a new order of life. The socialist revolution in Cuba and the social property legislation in Peru are examples of struggles in the region of Latin America. The recent socialist movements in Vietnam, Cambodia, and Laos are dramatic examples in the Far East. Similar currents of change are evident in countries of the Pacific region, the Middle East, and Africa. They point toward a type of social change of major significance at the world level, suggesting a trend toward a new order of political economy.

The underlying character of this change is complex and has yet to be charted carefully in sociological research. The change clearly expresses a deep interest among small nations in achieving independence from outside controls and powers. It speaks vividly of a struggle for autonomy and self-direction. At the same time it expresses a deep desire to create a new social and political economy that breaks significantly with the past. The concern is especially to create a new democratically based political economy that fundamentally alters past patterns of corporate hierarchy, profit-making, competition, and monopoly. Many developing countries today are in transition from old systems of semifeudalism or capitalism to new systems of socialism.

The changes are disrupting the classic forms of international business. Transnational corporations no longer operate easily in their traditional manner of power and authority; they are undergoing a vast systemic change in their relationships with nations. Their existence has been threatened by new movements for national independence, and they have been attempting to adjust to the change. They are more and more required to release their exclusive controls over

241

host-nations industries. They are being forced to become accountable in new ways to people at all levels of their operations. This process of becoming accountable can be considered part of the development of a new order of political economy among nations.

Studies have not kept pace with these changes in international trade and production. We do not have sufficient facts about the new economic order among nations standing on the border between capitalism and socialism. We need new theory, new models, and new indicators of the social change. We have traditional economic indicators measuring changes in productivity and income, but we do not have indicators measuring changes in the social development of the economic order. We have statistical measures of income distribution, employment, and housing, but we do not have statistical measures of the social change in the organization of the economy at the national level.[1] We have social indicators of democratic development of the state but we do not have comparable measures of democratic development in the economy.[2]

My purpose here is to suggest a theoretical framework for designing indicators of social democratic development within the corporate economy of developing nations. I begin by reviewing theories of imperialism and modernization in order to assess the progress in modeling studies of Third World development. The review will show a lack of modeling of social alternatives to imperialism and straitjacket forms of economic modernization. To fill that gap we examine the concept of social development through self-governance and mutual governance. These alternatives are described as nonstatist economic governance and distinguished from state governance.

Here social development means increasing human resources within the economic order. By human resources I mean such attributes as social authority, power, imagination, sensitivity, and leadership. The problem is how to optimize these resources in the widest population sectors of the economic order. This research design leads in that direction.

We will suggest scientific variables of development whose optimization can be studied empirically through social indicators.[3] We can then make special reference to global corporations as they detract from or contribute to social development defined in terms of self-governance in the economic order of nations.

THEORIES OF IMPERIALISM AND MODERNIZATION: A MISSING FACTOR

Social scientists have tended to study development either in the negative terms of "imperialism" or in the generally positive terms of "modernization." But neither approach has supplied us with models that lead toward the kind of alternatives many small nations are seeking today.

Studies of imperialism emphasize a *theory of dependency* based upon the types of relationships between a big nation like the United States with small developing nations such as those in Latin America. Dependency theorists organize data in different ways.[4] Chase-Dunn suggests indices of "exploitation," "distortion," and "suppression" existing in the relationship between the core nation and the small nations of its periphery.[5] We want to look carefully at this theory, since it provides the foil for modeling new research in this field of study.

Dependency theorists argue that capitalist development shows exploitation because it drains limited "economic surplus" from developing nations. The drain is toward the core nation through the repatriation of profits and interests on loan capital. This happens because world loan companies and transnational corporations in the core nation are controlled by profit motives. Transnationals gain special positions of advantage over small developing countries through their power to accumulate profits under the protective wing of domestic elites.[6] Some theorists argue that exploitation is rooted especially in the unequal pricing that occurs in the exchange between core and periphery countries. This inequality is also expressed in unequal wage structures; low wages in developing countries provide high market returns on goods sold in the home nations of transnational corporations.[7] Other theorists point to the capacity of transnationals to engage in transfer pricing between subsidiaries located in countries with different tax bases, thus hiding profits that otherwise might be taxed where production takes place.[8]

Dependency theorists also argue that the economy of developing countries becomes "distorted" through outside trade that prevents genuine domestic development.[9] An outward-oriented economy specializing in a limited number of products for export does not as a rule diversify its own production to its own advantage and its own needs. The developing economy becomes built around "ports of exit." Railroads, roads, and port cities are constructed for the purposes of exporting goods to the core nation. This strong link with transnational corporations then retards internal development.[10] The multiplier effect, which is normal to capitalist growth, cannot operate under these conditions. (A copper mining industry that exports copper ore through a transnational corporation, for example, does not then "multiply" the number of copper enterprises making copper products for domestic distribution and sale in the host nation.) One economic sector does not stimulate another economic sector.[11] Studies suggest further that any national economy that remains specialized and undifferentiated will then suffer from changes in the world market.[12] Adding to this dilemma is the fact that dependence of a developing nation on foreign credit reduces the propensity of people to save money, thus retarding the economic growth by lowering domestic capital formation.[13] The organization of the domestic economy is thus distorted in these ways and kept from normal development.

Dependency theorists also argue that domestic efforts to stimulate autonomous growth within developing nations are suppressed by this system of transnational trade and production. A national bourgeosie is formed in developing nations that is oriented to export-import trade in ways that lead it to curtail the growth of local enterprise.[14] Domestic elites prevent the creation of tariffs that would protect new enterprises against the competition from transnational corporations. Furthermore, they encourage domestic banks to loan money to transnational companies rather than to local companies because they have more confidence in foreign enterprise and more personal ties to foreign executives. This suppression of local development occurs through a "bridgehead" created between domestic bourgeois elites and foreign executives that blocks local leaders from mobilizing for new manufacture and production.[15] International loan companies also support this bridgehead, because they believe it is necessary to maintain a good climate for development.[16] Finally, the ruling elite actively helps to keep wages low in the host nation in order to maintain "stable development" through international business.[17]

A vicious circle of exploitation, distortion, and suppression then keeps developing nations from experiencing genuine independent development under alternative systems of economic organization.

The problem in this research tradition is that economic alternatives for development are seldom clearly outlined. The thesis of dependency theorists is supported empirically in many instances, but alternative models of transnational trade and production are not fully formulated.

Economic alternatives are also missing in modernization theory, which tends to focus on the positive side of development. Modernists take their point of departure from classic interpretations of *Gemeinschaft* and *Gesellschaft*, refining them into categories called "traditional" and "modern." In the traditional society, people are organized in small villages and produce subsistence level economies. In modern societies, people live in urban areas that are industrialized and commercialized. The early society was closed, custom-bound, commensalistic, and sacred while the modern society is open, contractual, symbiotic, and secular. Modernization theorists have concentrated their studies on many positive effects of development, but they do not generally focus their attention on the critical issues of political economy and dependency. They show how periphery nations tend to follow the model of the core nation, pointing to an increase in educational services, labor organization, managerial skills, literacy, voluntary groups, radios, television sets, and so forth. They show how the characteristics of core nations become reflected in the development goals of periphery nations.[18] The studies measure many important changes based on capitalist development, but they do not offer any new economic models.

As a rule, the missing factor in these international studies is alternative models of autonomous economic development. We need, therefore, a research design open to the varieties of economic self-governance and the possibilities of innovative change. For that we need a wider social perspective; we need to formulate *generic categories that allow for maximum possible social change in every direction of economic development.* We can then begin to narrow these categories into more specific alternative models.

A HOLISTIC MODEL: THE SEARCH FOR A SOCIAL PERSPECTIVE

The problems of economic development at the level of the nation show many similarities to the problems of economic development at the level of the community. The issue of power and its expressions in forms of dependency between large and small "living units" are similar. The problem of small nations growing in the shadow of large nations is not unlike the problem of small towns growing in the shadow of the metropolis. The small town and the small nation both must play "host" to outside corporations and governmental units. They both must deal with outside controls that can lead to exploitation, structural distortion, and suppression in the social development of the economy. They both face the consequences of dependency on external authorities. They both must find ways to confront outside powers so that they can maintain a degree of autonomy and self-direction.

This similarity in problems leads us to look to the field of community development for models applicable to the study of national development. The field of community development has treated the subject more holistically than the field of national development, where studies have been more specialized. We are interested in models that take into account noneconomic values that can be applied with an overall perspective to the development of economies at the national level.

An approach to model-building in this sense has been suggested by Roland Warren in the field of community development. Warren takes account of social norms he calls autonomy, viability, and the distribution of power (polity) and treats them as independent variables of community development. He suggests that it is possible to formulate models of development based on social norms and study them from an empirical standpoint. This means treating these norms as desiderata along which certain loadings can be studied in empirical instances.[19]

We shall work with these desiderata as the theoretical basis for constructing a model of self-governance that offers alternatives to exploitation, distortion, and suppression. Here it is possible to suggest the formulation of socioeconomic indicators of a "nonstatist model" of democratic self-government within developing countries and then to indicate how variables in this model can be maximized within limits. We conclude by noting how self-governance is not a sufficient goal by itself; in the final analysis, we must look at how nations can share resources through the development of social federations.

Theoretical Orientation

Let us begin with a model orientation of social development in the economic order of nations called "self-governance." This model orientation is applicable at different political levels of "community," such as the nation, the state, the city, and the neighborhood. It is a grand model with subvariables that allow us to anticipate major directions of social development within an economic order. Drawing upon Warren's method of assessing community development, we concentrate our attention at the level of the nation while making occasional reference to applications of the model at the level of the city and the neighborhood.

Self-Governance

The measures of economic self-governance are found in the three desiderata: autonomy, viability, and polity. *Autonomy* refers to the degree of formal control that each political community (host society, region, city) maintains over its economic life. *Viability* refers to the degree of self-sufficiency of each community, that is, the degree to which the community can solve its own economic problems regardless of who controls it. *Polity* refers to the distribution of power, that is, the degree to which democratic practices exist within the economy. Each of the three desiderata can be operationalized on a continuum according to the extent that its value is "optimized" or "diminished."

The measures of each desideratum of self-governance can first be observed as "diminished" on a continuum leading toward its categorical opposite: *external governance*. (See Table 8.) First, at the far right of the continuum, following the category "Autonomy," we can observe a complete lack of economic control for the host society, which means a total dependency on outside controls. This leads to outside exploitation and is generally described as imperialism.[20] Second, following "Viability," we can observe at the far right a complete lack of self-sufficiency in the host society. This implies that resources are totally supplied by an external government. It generally means the economy has become distorted. The host society will likely suffer when external economic government leaves; the host society may then become dependent upon another outside government to survive. This is the classic form of dependency.[21] Third, following "Polity," we can observe at the far right a complete lack of internal democracy. This leads to suppression and implies some form of oligarchy.[22] The oligarchy is

Table 8. Types of Socioeconomic Governance

Political Desiderata	Self-Government		External Government Effects
Autonomy (Independence)	Host control	(continuum)	Imperial control (exploitation)
Viability (Resources)	Host sufficiency	(continuum)	Host insufficiency (distortion)
Polity (Power)	Host democracy	(continuum)	Host oligarchy (suppression)

generally found in the national bourgeoisie forming a bridgehead to officers in the external economic government.

The extreme endpoints of this theoretical continuum are of course fictions. No form of total self-government or total external government exists at the level of the modern nation. We simply measure where a nation falls on the continuum of the model. Each variable (desideratum) exists on a continuum, making it possible to "operationalize" and measure their changes. Each variable changes somewhat independently of the others. I note later, for example, how the economic order of a developing nation can show a large degree of autonomy without showing too much viability and democracy; a large degree of viability without much autonomy and democracy; and a large degree of democracy without much viability. Each variable is maximized by degree and is only partly dependent upon the other two variables.

A system of democracy inside a political community, however, requires a high degree of autonomy, that is, independence from outside controls. A high degree of internal democracy cannot exist without a correlative high degree of autonomy. But a high degree of autonomy can exist without a high degree of democracy, as we shall see. A nation can be free from outside controls and be a dictatorship.

The governance of an economic order can be observed among corporations in industry, commerce, agriculture, and finance at different levels of political community: the locality, region, province, nation.[23]

With this rather complex picture in mind, we now want to look in more detail at a model of democratic self-governance yielding indicators of nonstatist social change in the economic development of small nations. We do not concentrate here on types of command governance in socialist state systems that also may or may not lead to economic self-governance.[24] We concentrate instead on a model of *nonstatist economic self-governance*. This then allows us to examine the intersection of transnational corporations and their command systems in relation to the growing democratic aspirations of people in developing countries.

THE ISSUES OF SOCIAL GOVERNANCE

A self-governance model and a command model express contrasting forms of corporate economy at the world level. We begin with democratic self-governance and look at the desiderata of development. We then pose them against the command orientations of global business.

Self-Governance Model: Democratic Orientation

Autonomy (Domestic Control)

The desideratum of autonomy requires quantitative indicators of the degree of outside control over the economy of a host society. Such measures would indicate the *percent of foreign control over domestic land, building, sales, investments, labor, debts, and business firms.* Other measures would include the *percent of outside contributions to political parties* relative to total contributions, *the percent of domestic investment in the economy* relative to total outside investment, *the percent of domestic bank loans made to outside companies* relative to bank loans to domestic companies, the *percent of foreign bank loans to foreign corporations operating in the host society* relative to the foreign loans to host companies, the *percent of local companies purchased by foreign companies* relative to the total number of domestic companies.

Significance of Measures. These statistical measures point to vital concerns of people interested in self-governance. The measure of foreign ownership of host corporations, for example, was a major issue in the tragic case of Chile. In pre-Allende Chile, for instance, 51 percent of the 160 largest companies were controlled by global corporations. In each of the seven key industries of the economy, one to three foreign companies controlled at least 51 percent of the production. Of the top 22 global corporations, 19 operated free of all competition or shared the market with other oligopolists. Other countries show comparable figures of *low economic autonomy.* In Argentina, global corporations control more than 50 percent of each company in the top 50. The pattern of foreign ownership is more pervasive in Brazil. In 1961 global companies owned all the nation's automobile and tire production, 59 percent of the machinery industry, and approximately 50 percent of electrical appliance manufacturing.

Ten years later, foreign ownership in the latter two industries increased to 67 percent and 68 percent, respectively.

Recent studies indicate that a measure of the degree to which outside companies can purchase local companies is an important variable of the desideratum of autonomy. According to Barnet and Müller, there were 716 "new" manufacturing subsidiaries established in Latin America by the top 187 global corporations based in the United States during 1958 through 1967. Of these new subsidiaries, 331 (45 percent) were established by purchasing an existing local company. A study by the Harvard Business School of the 187 largest U. S. corporations, which account for 70 percent of all American investment in Latin America, shows that in the years from 1958 to 1967 these U. S. corporations used almost half of their investment to buy up local companies. About 46 percent of all manufacturing operations established in the period were takeovers of existing domestic industry.[25]

The percent of external debt measured against total debt-service costs is another indicator of autonomy. Barnet and Müller report that in the mid-1960s in Latin America, service on foreign debt exceeded the value of new loans. By the end of the 1960s, Latin America's external debt had doubled. This action increases the dependency of these countries on economic resources outside themselves.

Viability (Domestic Resources)

Viability refers to the capacity of people in the host society to solve their own problems. We are concerned with measuring the degree of economic self-sufficiency that exists within a society. The organization of the economy cannot be deemed wholly viable unless it can operate the primary industries that provide sustenance and survival to its people.

Criteria for *economic self-sufficiency* are in part subjectively determined. They are determined by social expectations and the culture of a society. Among the Andean Pact nations in Latin America, for example, foreign investments are prohibited within certain strategic areas of the economy which we will note later. The domestic capacity to resolve problems in strategic areas is thus considered an indicator of viability.[26]

The desideratum of viability is measured here by signs of domestic leadership and practical skills developing in these strategic areas. These "resources" constitute an important measure of self-sufficiency. They may develop in the host nation even though outside legal control is retained by an imperial power.

The degree of *economic diversification* is another measure. Global corporations in the past have concentrated production in single industries such as coffee, sugar, or petroleum within host nations. But this has generally increased levels of dependency on the outside. The alternative is to increase the diversity of domestic investments in these strategic areas. This stimulates a more effective use of resources and becomes, therefore, a sign of "viability."

The *length of time* people have been actively managing strategic areas of the economy is another measure of viability. Other measures include the extent to which educational institutions in the host nation provide its citizens with the skills and professional knowledge essential to corporate management and the maintenance of important industries. Finally, the degree of interorganizational cooperation (horizontal relations) that host leaders have experienced in strategic areas of domestic production and distribution is important. Such interorganizational measures of viability include the proportion of workers in federations and the proportions of economic enterprises in trade association activities in key sectors of the economy.

Polity (Domestic Democracy)

The desideratum of polity refers to the way that power is distributed equitably within the corporate economy. It is expressed first in the degree to which major corporations are functioning in the public interest.

Corporations in a business society have been moving steadily toward new measures of social accountability. The new measures of social accountability in the corporation take account of such categories as the following:

Product line (e.g., dangerous products), Marketing practices (e.g., misleading advertising), Employee education and training, Corporate philanthropy, Environmental control, External relations (including community development, government relations, disclosure of information, and international operations), Employee relations (benefits and satisfaction with work), Minority and women employment and advancement, and Employee safety and health.[27]

These categories have been subclassified so that some social statisticians argue it is now possible to develop indicators to measure the extent to which corporations are approximating them as "normative values."

At the same time, they are mainly secondary indicators of polity in the corporate system. They do not directly measure the extent to which the local community, consumers, and employees may actually participate in the responsible management of the corporation. Our primary interest here is on employee representation in corporate management, since the labor sector has experienced significant advances in power within Western European countries as well as in many socialist countries.[28]

The norm of democratic polity is measured by the extent to which the participation of workers is legally permissible and also a reality among workers at all levels of the corporate system. The democratization of the economic system can be studied in three areas of social life: policy, execution, and regulation. These three areas intersect with what actually happens at three organizational levels of the corporation: top management (boards of directors), middle management (workers councils), and shop-floor management (job-design committees). David Garson describes succinctly how these three areas and levels intersect in different European countries.[29]

Democratic polity at top management levels is measurable in those countries where workers are legally permitted, encouraged, or required to serve on the board of directors of major corporations. Sweden, for example, permits unions to choose two worker representatives on the boards of all companies having over 100 employees. Democratic polity at middle management levels is also measurable in many countries that allow for "works councils." In Denmark works councils must be established in all companies with more than 50 employees. Management and labor may each name half the members. Councils have the right of "codetermination" in personnel matters (local wage systems, safety, health, and the organization of work) as well as to "co-influence" production plans and new capital investments. Democratic polity can be measured finally at the shop-floor level in still other countries, where major corporations arrange for self-management on the job. Specific opportunities for job enrichment, job rotation, job enlargement, and job redesign are found variously through shop-floor committees.[30]

The democratic corporate polity can thus be measured by many variables, which combine with many variables of viability and autonomy in the larger study of self-governance in the corporate economy of the host society. (See Table 9.)

Table 9. Social Indicators of Development Toward Self-Governance: A Normative Model of Social Development in the Economic Order of Communities

I. **Economic Autonomy.** Degree of host-community (nation or locality) control over economic activities as opposed to outside control.

A. Legal specifications of percentages of host-controls.
B. Actual host controls measured in specified economic areas.

Percentage of host-community:
1. Stock in industries versus outside stock ownership in industries.
2. Land versus outside ownership of land.
3. Employment of labor force versus outside control over labor force.

Table 9.   Continued

4. Government revenue versus revenue supplied by outside corporations.
5. Foreign exchange receipts versus receipts of outside corporations.
6. Total value of production versus value supplied by outside corporations.
7. Products sold locally versus products of outside corporations sold locally.
8. Bank loans to outside corporations versus host community loans to domestic companies.
9. Bank loans to domestic companies versus loans by international banks.
10. Supplies (costs) to foreign companies versus supplies (costs) from outside in key trade areas.
11. Investments by trade areas versus outside company investments in these areas.
12. Financial deposits in domestic banks versus financial deposits by outside corporations.
13. Contributions to domestic political parties versus outside corporation contributions.

II. **Economic Viability.** Degree to which people in the host community (nation or locality) can resolve problems in the economic order by themselves.

A. *Self-Sufficiency.*   Degree to which material resources needed for survival are produced and distributed from within the host community.

1. Extent of production and distribution (domestic versus foreign controls) in such strategic areas as (a) agriculture, (b) housing, (c) transportation, (d) fuel, (e) communications, (f) clothing, (g) strategic materials, (h) banking and finance.
2. Extent of domestic diversity of investment within each strategic area.

B. *Organizational Effectiveness.*   Degree to which people can fulfill tasks essential to survival in a skillful and efficient fashion.

1. *Time.* Length of years during which domestic associations have operated in strategic sectors of the economy.
2. *Knowledge.* Percent of college-vocational graduates in domestic schools relative to occupational needs in strategic sectors (e.g., agriculture, engineering)
3. *Organization.* Percent of host leaders (e.g., presidents of companies) in strategic sectors relative to outside leaders. Proportion of workers active in unions; proportion of domestic business people in trade associations.

III. **Economic Polity.** Degree to which people in the host community share power in the corporate economy.

A. *Corporate Internal Administration* (social power)

1. *Top Management* (percent of worker representation relative to other constituencies on the Board of Directors)
   Areas of decision-making: major capital investments, mergers, charter revisions, taxation issues, etc.
2. *Middle Management* (percent of workers represented in Councils relative to management)
   Areas of decision-making: wage levels, hiring and firing, job evaluation procedures, new construction, etc.
3. *Lower Management* (percent of workers on shop-floor committees relative to management)
   Areas of decision-making: grievance committee procedures, job control, job rotation and enrichment, accident prevention, etc.

B. *Employee Bill of Rights* (social authority)

1. Right to corporate information
2. Right to elect supervisors
3. Right to "appeal" for workers accused of corporate offenses
4. Right to free speech
5. Right to a jury of peers judging unfair dismissal
6. Right to a retraining program upon dismissal
7. Right to free assembly of workers

C. *Corporate Relations* (social accountability)

1. Marketing practices
2. Employee education and training
3. Corporate philanthropy
4. Environmental relations
5. External relations
6. Employee human relations
7. Minority relations
8. Employee safety and health

D. *Intercorporate Relations* (not explored here)
(Democratic representation in trade areas; corporate industries, commerce, banking, agriculture).

Command System Model: Business Orientation

The command system of transnational business contrasts with this self-governance model. The global corporation is a vertical "external government" in the private economy of a developing nation.

The *autonomy* of the corporate system does not lie within the host society but rather within the home nations of the global companies. The corporate command model requires an integrated administrative system, an integrated accounting system, communications system, managerial system, and marketing system. Administrative integration is essential to the viability of business that is foreign to the developing country. The economic interests of the foreign corporation are of primary concern. The corporation operates for the production of capital in its own interest while sharing certain by-products of its operation. The by-products include an increased knowledge of business management and an increase in capital income for the developing country. The increase in knowledge, however, is in "command management," and the increase in capital remains largely at the top of the command administration. The increase in resources is won largely by the bourgeoisie of the developing country.

The *viability* of production and marketing operations of the transnational are generally determined by the needs of a foreign market rather than by the domestic market. The methods for solving problems are largely foreign. This does not detract from the fact that they may be helpful in many ways, but it does limit the extent to which innovation develops within the culture of the host society.

The *polity* of the global firm contrasts markedly with the democratic model. A form of corporate democracy generally exists among shareholders of the corporation in the foreign nation, but the "vote" is determined by capital investors in stocks rather than by individual persons. Executive management generally controls the real administration of the company in a pyramid of command leading down to the subsidiary of the corporation in the developing country. The work done by people locally is generally supervised first by foreigners and then later by domestic personnel who have been trained for "supervision." (See Table 10.)

The *values* associated with these models differ markedly. The values are complicated as they become part of beliefs and actual systems of economic organization. They require careful study through participant observation, public opinion surveys, and other modes of inquiry.

The command model of business enterprise emphasizes competition more than cooperation, efficiency and status advancement more than equality and the sharing of resources, economic incentives more than social incentives in work, and employee obedience to authority more than the participatory authority of the employees themselves. These differences in value emphases, however, show

Table 10.   Nonstatist Corporate Models in the Economic Order
            of Developing Nations

Self-Governance (Domestic Corporations)	External Governance (Transnational Corporations)
Opposing Needs	
1. Corporate Autonomy (Host controls) A. Domestic legal authority B. Domestic organization: owner-ship, management, markets, finance	1. Corporate Autonomy (Foreign controls) A. Foreign legal authority B. Foreign organization: owner-ship, management, markets, finance
2. Corporate Viability (Host resources and needs) A. Domestic self-sufficiency B. Domestic trade diversity C. Domestic solutions to problems	2. Corporate Viability (Foreign resources and needs) A. Foreign markets B. Foreign trade integration C. Foreign solutions to problems
3. Corporate Polity (Host democracy) A. Corporate democracy (top level) B. Workers councils (middle level) C. Self-management (shop-floor level)	3. Corporate Polity (Foreign command) A. Foreign stockholders (top level) B. Executive councils (middle level) C. Supervision (shop-floor level)
4. Corporate Orientation (Host values) A. Cooperation B. Equality (sharing) C. Social incentives D. Employee authority	4. Corporate Orientation (Foreign values) A. Competition B. Hierarchy (efficiency) C. Economic incentives D. Employee obedience

great complexities when they become "actualized" in the attitudes of people
in different corporate organizations. For our purposes they point toward important phenomenological research as these different corporate models are
studied in the context of everyday life.

We are interested in where specific conflict exists between the models of command and self-governance and in how the desiderata of self-governance in such
nations as Portugal or Peru are maximized in their social development.

MAXIMIZING DESIDERATA:
The Command System Versus Self-Governance

The Limitations of the Command System as a Method of Governance

The command system in both capitalist and socialist nations is in conflict with the model for self-governance based on the desiderata of autonomy, viability, and democratic polity. Let us look first at the capitalist nation.

The business system seeks to increase its own autonomy and viability through the auspices of transnational corporations, but it faces serious problems.[31] We described one general problem in tendencies of private corporations to produce "exploitation, distortion, and suppression" in the economic order of the host nation. We also know that global companies can produce instabilities in the world money market, become instruments of their home nation's intelligence operations, engage in illegal arms traffic, refuse to accept exclusive jurisdiction of domestic law in cases of litigation, contribute to the maintainance of racist and dictatorial regimes, super-impose imported technology and thus cause distortions in local economies, and interfere directly in domestic politics.[32] These conditions lead eventually to the destruction of "private corporations" as autonomous and viable entities in developing nations.[33]

The transnational corporation also conflicts with the economic viability and autonomy of *its own home nation* through its private command system. It reduces economic viability at home to the extent that it seeks cheap employment in foreign lands and leaves empty plants in communities of its home nation; it can also avoid taxes by juggling accounts in subsidiaries in low-tax developing nations. On the other hand, it reduces economic autonomy in its home nation to the extent that it develops strategic raw materials in other countries, rather than researching new products at home. Studies show that the United States as a core nation has become dependent upon its periphery of small nations for a great many strategic materials. Harry Magdoff carefully documents this growing dependency in the corporate acquisition of key raw materials overseas that are then used in military production.[34]

Global corporations further reduce economic autonomy by placing their assets in foreign nations. In 1971, for example, about a quarter of the assets of the U. S. chemical industry, about 40 percent of the assets of the U. S. electrical industry, and a quarter of the assets of the U. S. pharmaceutical industry were located outside U. S. boundaries.[35]

The global command system of business can thus lead to its own demise in developing nations and at the same time reduce economic viability and the autonomy in the core nation as companies strive after profits overseas.

The command system of the communist party in socialist countries does not fair much better in maximizing the desiderata of democratic polity. Yugoslavia, for example, found that it could not easily "command" rapid democratization of the corporate economy. The rapid movement of the Party led to inefficiencies in companies, because workers could not always assume the role of managers without training. Elected labor representatives in key factory positions had to be replaced at times by technical experts in order to maintain efficiency and productivity.[36]

The Soviet Union and Cuba could not "command" democratic polity on other counts. The Soviet Union found it necessary to reintroduce economic incentives and competition after top-down command decisions to institute "social incentives" and formal modes of "cooperation."[37] Cuba likewise had problems with the formal introduction of democratic values through the command system.[38]

Progress has been made toward democratizing the economic order in socialist nations but not directly through the command system. *Advances have been made through group example, group self-criticism, collective demonstrations, individual consultation, emulation, and the creation of mutual governing systems replacing the command system.* The command system that aims to democratize the corporate economy by obedience clearly defeats itself. It expresses high oligarchy, and low autonomy.

In the light of what we now know about the complicated social transition from corporate command systems, how can we best study the way the desiderata of self-governance are maximized?

The Possibilities of Self-Governance as a Model of Development

The way in which desiderata can be maximized can be seen first by the degree to which they become independently developed in actual nations. First, we know that people in a developing nation can *maximize autonomy* by gaining control over the economic order and yet not be able to manage it effectively and democratically by themselves. A nation may expropriate (nationalize) industries managed by transnationals and then later not be able to operate them effectively. The nation then expresses high autonomy with low viability and very likely low democracy. Second, a nation may *maximize viability* in the economy and yet not have much autonomy or democratic polity. People may develop the training and skills for handling their own economic problems, but with ultimate control remaining outside. Furthermore, domestic leaders may diversify the corporate economy to protect the nation from economic crisis, but by means of a dictatorship or an oligarchy. Third, a nation may *maximize a democratic polity*

Table 11. Self-Governing Variables

Autonomy (Control)	Viability (Sufficiency)	Polity (Democracy)
High or low	High or low	High or low

but without much economic viability. A nation may be democratically organized in a system of economic enterprises but not be able to operate the industries skillfully and effectively. It may achieve internal democracy without the skills of good self-management. Note these variable dimensions in Table 11.

Our proposition now is that self-governance develops in the economic order through systems of mutual governance. Here we see how subtle changes in the command system of global corporations help to develop self-governance in the host nation.

OPTIMIZING SELF-GOVERNANCE THROUGH MUTUAL GOVERNANCE

Moving from a corporate command orientation based on capital production to a democratic orientation based on "self-governance" is a complicated social process. Many new types of organizational relationships are required to encourage self-reliance. These new relationships are found in patterns of divestment and development.

Global corporations show innovative patterns of "divestiture" that indicate a basic change from the old external command authority to new forms of economic self-governance. The movement is from "foreigners giving orders" toward outside consultants providing guides to policy; from outsiders enforcing rules toward "outsiders and insiders" jointly making rules; from outside management making demands toward outside management offering suggestions to domestic managers; from outsiders creating strict regulations toward outsiders helping insiders establish principles of corporate operation. Let us examine some basic types of mutual economic governance developing on the continuum between outside command systems and democratic self-governance. The transition begins with the divestment of foreign stock.

Divestment of Stock Ownership (Development of Joint Ventures)

Economic divestment is the withdrawal of investments from one location for the purpose of reinvestment in another location. It becomes a key factor in decentralized economic development. Divestment in this instance is the release of outside controls over stock ownership in the corporate affairs of a nation. Stock is generally released for sale to agencies and individuals in the host nation. The action is significant as a step on the continuum toward self-governance, but it also increases the strength of the domestic elite who can buy the stock. *The action increases autonomy but does not as a rule contribute toward democratic polity.*

Divestment of stock has been a trend in transnational business for many years. It has led to what investors call "joint ventures," in which foreign and domestic investors participate in the ownership and management of domestic enterprise. These ventures have been developing for many reasons:

The motives of investor companies for participating in joint ventures in less developed countries may be analyzed in various ways—usually with considerable overlap. The advantages usually mentioned are: (1) the achievement of capital savings and the reduction of business risks; (2) the obtaining of management skills and the maintenance of employee morale; (3) the facilitating of sales; (4) the improvement of governmental relations; and (5) the achievement of good public relations.[39]

Governments are also interested in joint ventures. For the host nation joint ventures increase autonomy. For the transnational's home government they can improve the balance-of-payments position. For these business and governmental reasons, the traditional pattern of foreign stock ownership appears to be changing today in favor of joint ventures.

Pan American World Airways, for example, began enterprises abroad in the early 1930s on a wholly owned subsidiary basis. The pressure of growing nationalism, intensifying around World War II, moved the corporation to admit domestic minority positions in its stock. Today it has itself become a minority owner in Brazil. The process was incremental. From 1929 to 1943, Panair to Brazil was wholly owned by Pan American; in 1943, 42 percent of stock was transfered to Brazilian ownership; between 1943 and 1947, the domestic share was increased to a majority of 52 percent along with considerable financial assistance in loans and grants.[40]

Many other examples of transnational companies holding only a minority participation in foreign companies illustrate a direction in the divestment process. These companies include American Steel Foundaries (15 percent of Cobrasina in Brazil), Willys Motor Company (in Willys do Brasil), and Celanese Corporation of America (in Celanese Mexicana). There are a few cases of 50-50 stock participation. In Atic Industries, Ltd., for example, Imperial Chemical Industries of the British Isles has joined on a 50-50 basis with Atul Products of India. A British and an Indian company in this case have equal representation on the corporate board. The partners alternately appoint the chair.

Intercontinental Hotels Corporation (IHC) is a special case. It has no equity in the Brazilian Hotel Tequendama, but it does have a management contract with it. On this basis it retains considerable leverage in policy but does not have the direct controls of ownership. IHC also was instrumental in obtaining the financing for the Brazilian hotel from the Export-Import Bank in Washington. The financing of the project covers a 20-year term that coincides with the management contract. This additional tie adds strong controls but is nevertheless different from ownership. As the financing nears completion, the hotel may take an independent course free of outside controls.

Divestment of Private Stock Options (Development of Public Stock)

When transnational corporations enter into joint ventures, it is often done under special stock options offered to host corporations. It can be a part of other special business deals. Corporations then remain closed to investment by others on the open market. Nevertheless, a trend toward placing stock on the open market has been developing.

Many cases of companies on the open market abroad can be found in the studies of Friedman and Kalmanoff. Willys Overland do Brasil, for example, was organized in 1952 by Willys Motor Company in the United States to assemble vehicles. When the Brazilian government developed the National Automobile Industry Plan, it "opened" the corporation through public offerings. There are now over 40,000 Brazilian shareholders who hold a majority of the voting shares.

Divestment of Foreign Management
(Development of Host Management)

In most transnational subsidiaries, host management participates in all lower levels of the domestic administration of the company. But there are signs that multinational corporations are increasing their emphasis on host management in their foreign enterprises. In Bristol de Mexico, for example, the multinational American partner has a majority control in stock but has divested itself entirely of its own external management. It now operates the enterprise under a local management contract. Other companies illustrate a similar trend. In Industria Electrica de Mexico, the minority partner in stock is Westinghouse. It now exercises managerial control jointly through an operating committee with seven American "foreigners" out of a total of 1800 employees.

Divestment of Permanent Foreign Controls
(Development of Temporary Cooperative Assistance)

While transnational management does not generally plan for long-range divestment of foreign ownership and controls, it appears to be moving in that direction. As traditional controls are released, new types of contractual relationships appear on different political grounds. New relationships include technical assistance agreements; patent right agreements; distribution rights access to loans, supplies, auditing rights, and legal franchises. Let us look at some of these relationships, which express increasing autonomy for host enterprises and host nations.

Development of Technical Assistance and Management by Contract

Goodrich International Rubber Company holds only minority stock in its Phillipine enterprise. Its investment is partly protected by a technical assistance agreement. This keeps a consulting relationship active between the transnational company and the Phillipine company. More significantly, it is also protected by special voting rights in its foreign company. Goodrich holds only 43 percent interest in this domestic enterprise, but its consent is required to change the articles of incorporation or to dissolve the company. These actions require a two-thirds majority vote over which Goodrich control is maintained. In addition, Goodrich manages the enterprise under contract. So its formal divestment of ownership means only a slight shift in terms of a loss of control over its foreign enterprise.

But this slight shift is still significant as a step toward corporate autonomy in the host nation. Following the termination of a contract with Goodrich, the Phillipine company can technically sign a new contract with another corporation. If there is domestic leadership and there are any signs of undue dominance or exploitation of the domestic enterprise, this arrangement permits independent action. It places checks on the power of Goodrich. The Phillipine company may then move toward full autonomy with only a technical assistance agreement remaining with Goodrich. That agreement can be written for a specific time period in which both sides foresee an equitable and productive relationship.

Development of Loan Systems in Place of Ownership

The divestment of ownership is sometimes associated with the provision of large loans, which may constitute the major operating costs of a host company. The Bethlehem Steel Corporation entered into a loan arrangement with Icomi do Brasil with a 49 percent equity participation. It extended a loan to the domestic enterprise of close to $2 million. The bulk of the financing was then provided by the Export-Import Bank in Washington to the amount of $55 million. The presence of Bethlehem Steel is therefore highly influential to the enterprise. But the gradual development of capital within the domestic enterprise permits it to become independent of Bethlehem. It can set its own goals for capital development, since Bethlehem remains the minority partner. For the time being, Bethlehem remains to guide the development of the steel industry in Brazil.

Development of Franchises, Joint Auditing Systems,
and Alternative Supply Sources

Foreign companies can exercise special controls over domestic enterprises when they provide scarce supplies necessary to the successful operation of the enterprises. The development of alternative sources of supply then becomes fundamental to the movement toward autonomy.

The private auditing of accounts in the domestic enterprise by the multinational corporation is another control factor. The alternative is found in joint auditing by foreign and host accountants. Joint auditing arrangements develop especially under *franchise contracts* with domestic companies. These mutual franchise arrangements can offer a greater autonomy in auditing to the domestic enterprise than is customary. They can lead toward complete self-governance as each firm develops social accountability to the other.

H. G. Henares & Sons of the Phillipines, for example, had franchise agreements with a half dozen U. S. manufacturers for distribution and sale of goods. At one time conflict between the foreign companies and Henares developed over pricing policies. In an effort to exert some on-the-spot control over Henares, the foreign companies were given certain audit powers over the domestic firm. After a period of legal conflict, however, the foreign controls were abandoned.

THE GENERAL PATTERN AND DIRECTION
OF SOCIAL CHANGE

These patterns of development toward autonomy suggest the complexity of the change that is taking place in the transnational system. The change from one set of external controls can introduce another set of equally dominating external controls, or it can lead toward new levels of host autonomy. The new types of freedom appear to develop from mutuality. The hidden ideals are mutual influence and mutual autonomy. In the process, a new pattern of responsibilities, incentives, interests, skills, sensibilities, and technical knowledge emerges. Each shift of relationship involves a delicate change in social interaction.

The terms most appropriate to explain social development in the economic order of transnational enterprise are *divestment* and *decentralization.* But they cannot serve alone to explain development without counterpart terms we shall call *reinvestment* and *recentralization.* Each act of divestment requires a new act of investment, and each act of decentralization involves a new act of centralization in the local enterprise.

Divestment means a withdrawal from a former invested relationship. By itself, however, divestment could lead to new forms of domination, including the formation of a host oligarchy or new outside controls by another transnational company. Developmental divestment does not mean cutting off all relationships with the former subsidiary. It means a reinvestment for both parties in a new relationship. It could mean training local people in management skills. It could mean new funding for construction, with the assurance of fair economic returns to the new investors. Reinvestment includes reestablishing trust and confidence on both sides in a new relationship based on mutual governance.

Decentralization means a transfer of authority to people who did not have it in the old hierarchy of command. Decentralization cannot occur, however, without a desire on the part of those people who assume the new authority. People must want to take the authority and the responsibility that goes with it. The process thus involves a centering of decision-making power in people who take it upon themselves. Developmental decentralization involves acknowledging a new center of autonomy in the economic unit where people assume new controls. This in turn means that the new managers may begin to introduce experimental patterns of work and organization that break entirely with past management patterns.

The new local directors may issue voting stock to employees as one step toward "self-management" of the company. They may organize a board of citizen advisors to keep an eye on environmental pollution and to help distribute profits.[41] New shareholders may elect professional "public directors" to replace the old board, and these directors in turn may decide the enterprise should be chartered as nonprofit in the public interest. New directors may help "inventory" the nation's economic needs.[42] In such ways a decentralized democratic orientation may develop through the initiative of host leaders.

Future Research Questions: The Transition from Command to Democratic Systems

When types of command bureaucracy "pass through the transition" to become types of democratic self-governance, we can theorize a breakdown in "verticality," that is, a shift from social relationships based upon corporate hierarchy toward social relationships based more upon equality. Theoretically, we should see an increase in the social authority, responsibility, and autonomy of member units at the bottom of the former command bureaucracy. This means that these qualities of resourcefulness should also become more evident in the lives of larger numbers of people who participate in the self-governing member units of economic federations.

The fulfillment of the desiderata of self-governance is a highly complicated process that reaches into the divisions of corporations in both capitalist and socialist nations. The production contract of a state socialist agency with a small factory, for example, carries a level of self-governance with it that is comparable to production contracts negotiated by General Electric with a small factory. The big corporate unit can in some cases encourage a *high degree of self-governance in the smaller unit; it can thus serve as an agent of social development in the economic order.*

We have more to learn empirically about what happens when economic incentives shift to social incentives. We need to ask: Does striving for power and status then replace striving for wages and profits? Are the standard forms of economic competition replaced by social competition?

The trends of social development among small nations today suggests that a transition is taking place from command orientations based on competition, profit motives, and hierarchy to new democratic orientations based on the model of self-governance. In Table 12 we outline some details of this historical transition and add what is possible to project experimentally in the future.[43]

Table 12.   Indexes of Social Change in the System of Transnational
            Corporations—A Study Guide on Stages of Socioeconomic
            Development

1. Public and Private Interest Patterns

   A. *Corporations*

   Command Orientation
   1. Corporations battle for power and supremacy over one another.
   2. Corporations develop oligopolistic positions in society.

   Transition
   3. Corporations join in developing social interests such as giving to charities, universities, and art museums.

   Democratic Orientation
   4. Corporations become chartered at the national level to operate in the public interest as well as their own self-interest.

   Experimental Area
   5. Corporations collaborate in different economic sectors to promote the public interest by reducing unemployment, protecting the environment, encouraging small enterprise, improving the quality of their products.

B. *Federations (Trade Sectors)*

Command Orientation

1. Corporations organize trade associations to protect themselves from workers organizing unions.
2. Trade associations lobby in Congress to keep consumers from introducing legislation against injurious products and false advertising.

Transition

3. Trade associations develop common accounting systems, establish rules in trade areas that protect consumers, create uniform standards in the public interest.

Democratic Orientation

4. Trade associations begin to operate in the public interest with employee and consumer representation.

Experimental Area

5. Trade associations organize consulting groups to aid large corporations to decentralize authority within their subsidiary systems thus encouraging types of mutual governance in marketing franchises and new production contracts with community development corporations.

2. Organizational Patterns

A. *Corporate Ownership*

Command Orientation

1. Host society holds no stock in multinational corporations.
2. Host society shares less than 50 percent stock.

Transition

3. Host society and foreign nationals both own 50 percent stock.

Democratic Orientation

4. Host society owns over 50 percent of stock.
5. Host society owns total stock and introduces employee stock ownership plans.

Experimental Area

6. Educational programs are introduced to prepare employees for new responsibilities in self-management.

7. Host nation changes the nature of corporate holdings from dividend stock for purchasers to voting stock based on one vote per person.
8. Employees own the former "subsidiary" and cannot sell it for a profit because of public law.

B. *Labor*

Command Orientation

1. No labor unions exist in the multinational subsidiary and there is no worker participation in management.
2. Labor unions are organized along with personnel departments and grievance committees.
3. Agencies for conciliation, mediation, and arbitration are established.

Transition

4. Contracts are signed, with recourse to independent professional arbitration jointly agreed by labor and management.

Democratic Orientation

5. Trade unions and management provide nonstatist agencies for joint resolution of problems through arbitrations (e.g., Denmark and Norway).

Experimental Area

6. Corporate democracies created through factory councils and representation on the board of directors (e.g., English, Swedish, and German companies).

C. *Management and Language Usage*

Command Orientation

1. Management is composed largely of foreigners at top levels of industry. (Language is foreign in top-level communications.)
2. Management includes host but under 50 percent (host language broadens in usage).

Transition

3. Management is 50 percent host and 50 percent foreign. (Language usage alternates.)

Democratic Orientation

4. Management is wholly host with foreign consultants. (Host language predominates.)

Experimental Area

5. Workers exchange jobs and residences between nations for limited periods of time for purposes of intercultural education.

3. Physical Development

A. *Land*

Command Orientation

1. Host land is excavated for foreign use and then is returned to host in worse condition than before (e.g., copper mines).
2. Host land is developed for host government use in indefinite future (e.g., permanent irrigation canals and power stations), yet remains under foreign control.
3. Host land is developed by foreign company and sold to local citizens for their private company use.

Transition

4. Host land developed by foreign company and sold for use by public corporation in host nation.

Democratic Orientation

5. Land developed by multinational corporation and purchased by a community development corporation in host nation.

Experimental Area

6. Community development corporations join in a cooperative federation to assume democratic authority over a geographic sector of economic life in the host nation.

B. *Construction*

Command Orientation

1. Construction of physical facilities by multinational corporation is of no future use by host nation (e.g., complicated machinery with supplies from foreign nation, foreign ships and planes).
2. Construction of facilities whose control is totally foreign and rented by host companies (e.g., railroads, buildings, roads).

Transition

3. Construction by foreign company of facilities whose control is mutually shared (e.g., port facilities).

Democratic Orientation

4. Construction of facilities (e.g., schools and hospitals) by multinational corporation through mutually beneficial contracts with a local community whose members learn the art of design and skills of the building trade.

Experimental Area

5. Construction of production facilities by local people with the help of a multinational corporation contracting with community development corporations.

4. *Loans and Gifts*

A. *Loans*

Command Orientation

1. Loans to host nation from world banks and foreign agencies with excessive interest rates or with restrictions to invest only in the private sector.
2. Loans to host nation with low interest rates, with flexible requirements of expenditure in either the private cooperative, or public sector.

Transition

3. Loans to host companies seeking to build housing cooperatives in poverty areas of host nation, without stipulations regarding profit or non-profit objectives.

Democratic Orientation

4. Loans to host companies seeking to enlist the participation of local residents in a cooperative enterprise in which citizens plan for housing or land reform.

Experimental Area

5. Loans to cooperative *federations* that indicate plans to organize democratically within regions.

B. *Gifts*

Command Orientation

1. Gifts from foreign governments or companies that lead to concessions or limit host autonomy (e.g., political concessions to build roads near land owned by foreign enterprise).
2. Gifts that provide basis for perpetuating elite interests in the host nation and protect the status quo (e.g., military arms and ammunition).

Transition

3. Gifts provided without major concessions and in the interest of development (e.g., construction of vocational schools).

Democratic Orientation

4. Gifts that encourage independent technical research within the host nation.

Experimental Area

5. Gifts of technical information leading toward the elimination of private patent rights at the international level.

In Retrospect: A Theory of Social Development

We began by examining social models of economic development among nations based on theories of dependency and modernization. Theorists in these traditions have pointed to the need for changes in the current systems of dependency but have not formulated a complete picture of the problem from a social (nonstatist) standpoint. George Beckwith, for example, has pointed to "independence" as an essential but not sufficient condition for development among peripheral nations.[44] Samuel Morley has suggested controlling the economic investments made by core nations to the peripheral nations to ensure more balanced development.[45] Norman Girvan has pointed to regional agreements among nations as a way to control the global investments of private corporations.[46] But a systematic outlook on socioeconomic alternatives has not been evident within a scientific framework.[47]

In retrospect, it is possible to suggest the direction of a "systematic outlook" based on the notion of self-governance. It begins with the proposition that self-governance is inhibited or advanced according to different types of common governance between different communities of work. Let us trace this key notion a little further by reviewing what we have said so far and where it leads us in future research.

We have discussed the command system as one type of common governance bridging different communities of work. The corporate command system extends from one nation into trade areas of other national communities. The corporation has functioned with some measure of efficiency, but it has also been riddled with problems. I noted that this type of governing system exists in tension and conflict with a system of self-governance. Its traditional forms of command are today being broken down through "nationalization" and various forms of host governance. Host governance is being optimized as a goal in contradiction to the traditions of command. This process is occurring through various means, among them, a gradual shift toward host stock ownership, and increased use of host language in the transnational subsidiary, and increasing numbers of host executives. We can take this notion of developing self-governance one step further by introducing alternative models of common governance between nations.

We can propose that the optimization of self-governance cannot serve alone as a general model of development. Breaking away from the command system may encourage greater degrees of autonomy and self-sufficiency, but new goals of social governance are needed between work communities. The model of self-governance by itself implies that the goal is simply to be wholly self-sufficient and possibly isolated from the outside world. It does not include new types of outside relationships that help nations share resources in the process of development.

The real goal of social development is not "isolation" through the elimination of the command system. It is self-direction in the context of mutual aid and trade with other nations. What is needed here is a model of "outside relations" for nations that no longer want or need an outside command system. The alternative can be found in the federation.

The alternative models of federation and confederation represent the broad dimensions of socioeconomic development that extend research and policy beyond the command system. (See Figure 10.) They are alternative forms of mutual governance over economic activity between national communities of work. Putting together these different models of governance, we can see theoretically how new patterns of self-governance can emerge among nations. Self-governance can develop in the transformation of the command system into systems of international federation.

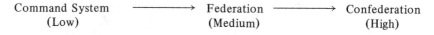

Command System   ⟶   Federation   ⟶   Confederation
(Low)   (Medium)   (High)

Figure 10.   Direction for Increasing Authority in Self-Governing Member-Units.

Our theory is that, as a rule, human resources increase within wider sectors of the working population as the governance changes from command to federation. The federated model, therefore, offers new directions for socioeconomic research and public policy. Let us look summarily at these three models, making some reference now to state socialist systems.

A *command system* is an association in which the final authority rests at the top of the organizational hierarchy. All economic units in this case are stratified so that lower units must obey the orders of the higher units. A command system exists in the business corporation and the revolutionary communist party even though their purposes are very different. In stable modern societies, however, a command system generally obtains its authority in association with some democratic institution. A business corporation like General Motors, for example, obtains its authority from its stockholders, who vote for a board of directors. The board, in turn, appoints top executives, who assume command over the corporate administration. The communist party in the Soviet Union receives its authority from a residential electorate. Elected officials then assume command over the state economy. Lower economic units in the corporate system are granted certain powers, but none are inherent in the command organization. In a state administration, likewise, cities are granted certain powers of home rule, but they have no inherent rights of their own since they do not participate in electing the state congress. Likewise, the subsidiary of an economic enterprise in a capitalist or socialist nation may be granted certain powers of "home rule," but it has no electoral privileges in the central administration. When the separate units of an economic administration are given electoral privileges to determine their own affairs through a common body of representatives, they become a federation. Their authority and power increases.

A *federation* is an association in which independent members participate democratically in a central body to administer their common affairs. The members are considered independent, but they all participate equally in regulating areas of common interest. Each member unit retains certain powers over its own jurisdiction defined jointly through the central representative body. The polity of the United States or the Soviet Union is a state form of federation. A nonstate economic federation is illustrated by business cooperatives in the United States. In towns of the Midwest, for example, 4300 farm-supply and general-store cooperatives are linked to regional wholesale cooperatives, guaranteeing them supplies of fertilizer, seeds, feed, and farm machinery. Cooperative businesses express a social federalism through joint ownership and control between local, regional, and national associations.

A *confederation* is an association in which all member units have the final authority over their own affairs. A central body of an economic confederation exists only to serve its relatively independent and self-sufficient members. It does not exert strong powers over its membership as does a federation. Thus a confederation confers still greater authority and power on its member units than either a federation or a command system. The members in this case have achieved a high degree of self-governance.

These three types of economic associations stand in theoretical order representing low to medium to high degrees of authority and power for member units of the working population. The command system allows members the least amount of authority, while the federation and the confederation offer members increasing amounts of authority. The latter forms of economic governance, then, represent target areas of social development where modeling is important.

The term "mutual governance" can be used to represent the two types of federation. They base their authority on the democratic participation of economic member units. These models of economic federation may be studied for the degree to which they express equal rights, equal control, and equal exchange among their member units.

The orientation toward self-governance in this scheme of development is measured by *the degree to which resources are increased in one nation.* The orientation toward mutual governance is measured by *the degree to which resources are shared between nations.* The actual development of a nation in the direction of self-governance may be either complementary or in opposition to mutual governance with other nations depending upon how the actual changes are made and how the models are specified in each instance.

Here we cannot specify the attributes of federal models at the world level. This belongs to future research and development. Such emergent federations as the Organization of Petroleum Exporting Countries (OPEC), the European Economic Community, and the Andean Pact are signs of new directions in this type of development. These organizations require extensive study for the way they advance or inhibit self-governance. Their authority at present is grounded ultimately in the nation-state. But these new economic federations are also beginning to extend their authority beyond the nation-state, as we shall see in Chapter Nine.

We have examined social models of economic development that stress norms of corporate self-governance and common governance in nations today. The models offer a framework for formulating social indicators of development in the movement toward a new economic order in the Third World. The models indicate alternatives to exploitation, distortion, and suppression between what is called the core nation and the periphery of developing nations. They also offer a direction for social development of economic organization, which begins with the model of the command system and moves toward new corporate forms of mutual governance in democratic federations.[48]

Social theory can thus offer a direction in the formulation of social policy at the level of nations. Social policy, at this level, is not normally generated from scientific theory. It is formulated in the meeting rooms of international diplomats, politicians, corporate executives, labor leaders, and economists who must respond to the daily needs and interests of international groups. But it is possible to bring theory into the places where policies are made. Indeed, it is crucial to make the effort to search for connections between the universal maxims of science and the practical interests of nations.

In the next chapter, therefore, we bring theory to bear on the practical concerns of policy-making in world organizations. Here theory would connect with the pressures of political life and be discussed against the practical problems faced by policy-makers. Theory may then become a part of the real drama of creating a self-governing world economy.

NOTES

1. John Walton, "Political Development and Economic Development: A Regional Assessment of Contemporary Theories," *Studies in Comparative International Development,* Vol. 7, No. 1, 1972.

2. Gabriel Almond and G. B. Powell, *Comparative Politics: A Developmental Approach* (Boston: Little, Brown, 1966).

3. N. Ruggles and R. Ruggles, "A Proposal for a System of Economic and Social Accounts," in M. Moss (ed), *The Measurement of Social and Economic Performance* (New York: National Bureau of Economic Research, 1973), pp. 111-162.

4. Charles C. Moskos and Wendell Bell, "Emerging Nations and Ideologies of American Social Scientists," *The American Sociologist* 2 (May 1967): 67-72.

5. Christopher Chase-Dunn, "The Effects of International Economic Dependence on Development and Inequality: A Cross-National Study," *American Sociological Review,* 40 (December 1975): 720-738.

6. Andre Gunder Frank, *Latin America: Underdevelopment or Revolution* (New York: Monthly Review Press, 1969); Samir Amin, *Accumulation on a World Scale* (New York: Monthly Review Press, 1974).

7. Arghiri Emmanuel, *Unequal Exchange: A Study of the Imperialism of Trade* (New York: Monthly Review Press, 1972).

8. John Gerassi, *The Great Fear* (New York: Macmillan, 1963).

9. Teotonio Dos Santos, "The Structure of Dependence," *Papers and Proceedings American Economic Review,* 60 (1970): 231-236.

10. Philip Ehrensaft, "Semi-industrial Capitalism in the Third World," *Africa Today,* 18 (1971): 40-67.

11. Hans Singer, "The Distribution of Gains Between Investing and Borrowing Countries," in George Dalton (ed), *Economic Development and Social Change* (Garden City, N. Y.: Natural History Press, 1971).

12. Paul Prebisch, *The Economic Development of Latin America and its Principal Problems* (New York: United Nations Department of Social and Economic Affairs, 1950).

13. Keith Griffin and J. L. Enos, "Foreign Assistance: Objectives and Consequences," *Economic Development and Cultural Change,* 18 (1970): 313-327.

14. Dale L. Johnson, "Dependence and the International System," in J. D. Cockroft, A. G. Frank, and D. L. Johnson (eds), *Dependence and Underdevelopment* (New York: Anchor, 1972).

15. Johan Galtung, "A Structural Theory of Imperialism," *Journal of Peace Research,* 8 (1971): 77-81.

16. Denis Goulet and Michael Hudson, *The Myth of Aid* (New York: Orbis, 1971); Teresa Hayter, *Aid as Imperialism* (Baltimore: Penguin, 1971).

17. Osvaldo Sunkel, "Transnational Capitalism and National Disintegration in Latin America," *Social and Economic Studies,* 22 (1973): 132-176.

18. David Smith, *Becoming Modern* (Cambridge: Harvard Univ. Press, 1974); Everett Hagen, *On the Theory of Social Change* (Homewood, Ill.: Dorsey Press, 1962).

19. Roland Warren, "Toward a Non-Utopian Normative Model of the Community," in Roland Warren (ed), *Truth, Love, Social Change* (Chicago: Rand McNally, 1971).

20. Benjamin Cohen, *The Question of Imperialism* (New York: Basic Books, 1973).

21. Hans J. Morgenthau, *Politics Among Nations* (New York: Knopf, 1960), p. 51.

22. Robert Michels, *Political Parties* (New York: The Free Press, 1962).

23. Richard Eells and Clarence Walton, *Conceptual Foundations of Business* (Homewood, Ill.: Irwin, 1961), p. 393.

24. Robert Solo, *Economic Organizations and Social Systems* (New York: Bobbs-Merrill, 1967).

25. Richard Barnet and Ronald Müller, *Global Reach* (New York: Simon and Schuster, 1975).

26. La Comision del Acuerdo de Cartagene, *"Regimen comun de tratamiento a los capitales extranjeros y sobre marcas, patentes y regalias,"* Tercer Periodo de Sesiones Extraordinarias de la Comision, 24 Lima, Peru, December, 1970, pp. 12–14.

27. Terry McAdam, "How to Put Corporate Responsibility into Practice," *Business and Society Review/Innovation,* 6 (Summer 1973): 8; David Blake, William Frederick and Mildred Meyers, *Social Auditing: Evaluating the Impact of Corporate Programs,* (New York: Praeger Publishers, 1976).

28. David Jenkins, *Industrial Democracy in Europe: The Challenge and Management Response* (Geneva, Switzerland: Business International, 1974).

29. David Garson, "Recent Developments in Worker Participation in Eastern Europe," in Jaroslav Vanek (ed), *Self-Management: Liberation of Man* (New York: Penguin Books, 1975).

30. David Jenkins, *Job Power* (New York: Doubleday, 1973); Gerry Hunnius, David Garson, and John Case, *Workers' Control* (New York: Random House, 1973).

31. J. N. Bhagwati, *Economics and the World Order From the 1970's to the 1990s* (New York: MacMillan, 1972).

32. Cf. Hearings before the Subcommittee on Multinational Corporations of the Committee on Foreign Relations, U. S. Senate, Ninety-Third Congress; Hearing before the Subcommittee on International Trade of the Committee on Finance, U. S. Senate, Ninety-Third Congress, (Washington, D. C.: U. S. Govt. Printing Office, 1971–74).

33. David Morris, *We Must Make Haste Slowly* (New York: Vintage Books, 1973); Paul Sigmund, "Allende in Retrospect," *Problems of Communism* (Washington, D. C.: U. S. Information Agency, 1974); Gary MacEoin, *No Peaceful Way* (New York: Sheet and Ward, 1974).

34. Harry Magdoff, *The Age of Imperialism* (New York: The Monthly Review Press, 1969).

35. Barnet and Müller, op. cit.

36. Ichak Adizes, *Self Management: The Yugoslav Post-Reform Experience* (New York: The Free Press, 1970).

37. Roy Medvedev, *On Socialist Democracy* (New York: Knopf, 1975).

38. Robert Hernandez and Carmelo Mesa-Lago, "Labor Organization and Wages," in Carmelo Mesa-Lago, *Revolutionary Change in Cuba* (Pittsburgh: Univ. Pittsburgh Press, 1971), p. 235ff.

39. Wolfgang Friedman and George Kalmanoff, *Joint International Business Ventures* (New York: Columbia Univ. Press, 1961), p. 134.

40. *Ibid.*, pp. 167–170.

41. E. F. Schumacher, *Small Is Beautiful* (New York: Harper Torchbooks, 1973).

42. Hartmut Eisenhans, "Overcoming Underdevelopment, A Research Paradigm," *Journal of Peace Research,* 12, No. 4 (1975).

43. Some writers use the term "global corporation," others use "multinational corporation," and others use "transnational corporation." Each term suggests a slightly different

interpretation of the same thing. I am using all three expressions equally here referring to those economic enterprises engaged significantly in world trade, production, and commerce.

44. George Beckwith, *Persistent Poverty: Underdevelopment in Plantation Regions of the Third World* (New York: Oxford University Press, 1971).

45. Samuel Morley, "What To Do about Foreign Direct Investments: A Host Country Perspective," *Studies in Comparative International Development,* 10 (1975): 45–66.

46. Norman Girvan, "The Development of Dependency Economics in the Caribbean and Latin America," *Social and Economic Studies,* 22 (1973): 1–33.

47. For the most recent overall approach to alternatives, see Karl P. Sauvant and Farid G. Lavipour (ed), *Controlling Multinational Enterprises: Problems, Strategies, and Counterstrategies* (Boulder, Colo.: Westview Press, 1976).

48. The model of self-governance stands in tension with the model of federation as its member units continue to strive toward independence and self-sufficiency. This independent strain then leads toward the development of the economic confederation where member units have gained a greater degree of authority and power in their economic operations. The confederation represents the ultimate social stage of resource development in the evolution of economic orders.

NINE

INTERNATIONAL POLICIES OF ECONOMIC DEVELOPMENT

The Social Sector

The traditional norms of business are challenged today by world leaders who seek to establish international standards for economic development. The traditional free-wheeling notion of commerce and industry is giving way to the idea of international control based on social and legal concepts. At the world level, social concepts of justice, freedom, and self-determination enter into discussions on how to guide and direct national business. Discussions of methods of public control within nations often turn to strategies and structures of development at regional and world levels.[1]

The large business corporation is coming to be recognized as a public institution even though it functions in the private sector. Its policies on such matters as national pricing and plant relocation are public in character even though the corporation is not managed by the state. Corporations like General Motors are being required more and more often to function in the public interest through statutory commissions and agencies; and executives today realize that private decisions that affect whole communities and the society at large become matters of public policy. Public policy, then, is coming to include decisions within all large associations that affect the public interest even when the associations are not governmental.

It is within this vaguely defined area of public policy that we now search for strategies and structures that speak to the problems created by multinational corporations. There are no government regulatory agencies at the world level to guide business activities. There is no public policy at the world level that sets limits on the activities of multinational companies. The limits are set complexly by the balance of power between nations and corporations without the benefit of direction from international agencies. It is therefore in the interest of finding firmer foundations for policy within the multinational system that we now search for alternatives.

We look especially for directions that corporations and states are capable of taking in the coming decades. We seek a new philosophy of values within the corporate order. But it is not only the broad human values that would guide our considerations of international control. It is also the norms or standards guiding business reorganization that we have been discussing so far.

We have noted how administrative standards are being formulated within corporations with the purpose of maximizing human resources as well as material resources. We have noted how these standards began to develop at the turn of the century with the human relations movement in industry and how they continued to develop more clearly through applied social research in corporations. The experiments have progressed to the point that they suggest the possible elimination of bureaucracy in corporate life. They indicate the beginning of the end of corporate hierarchy. Even though the standards are still being tested in small-scale experiments, they give us a sense of direction and a basis for studying principles at higher policy levels of decision-making. The standards are based upon the notion of decentralizing authority and maximizing responsibility within administrative levels of decision-making.

This general direction of reorganization within corporations can be applied in principle to the operation of multinational business at the world level. The strategies of decentralization apply at all levels of corporate administration: the locality, the nation, the international region, the world. At each of these levels we will first describe "organizing principles" and second, a "prototype of organization," as examples of new directions. The principles indicate a way in which excessive practices of multinational corporations can be changed so that social (as well as economic) resources can be developed. The prototypes are specific examples of how new models are actually being developed. The problem is to determine how the multinational system can be guided toward fulfilling those human values that extend beyond material gain.

THE LOCAL FACTORY LEVEL: ORGANIZING PRINCIPLES

We have said that current principles and norms of business organizations tend to locate the greatest power and authority at the top of the business hierarchy. The organization of a business generally requires *social inequality* expressed through a *hierarchy of administrative offices* involving the *supervision* of employees by *formal rules* in a *competitive* context. These organizing elements have been the basis for administrative development at local, regional, and international levels of business.

The process of organizing business with the democratic values we have been discussing, however, requires different principles of administration. These principles emphasize *social equality* through *autonomous work groups* involving *self-management* guided by *informal rules* in a *cooperative* context. These administrative principles are applicable to the organization of local plants and factories as well as "higher levels" of organization. But since multinational corporations organize plants at the local level in host nations, it is important to begin our discussion of strategies at this level.

We have noted that the movement toward decentralizing authority is beginning in U. S. corporations. Furthermore, labor leaders as well as executives in other countries have been proving the viability of decentralization through worker councils and self-management. Corporate executives have made decisions to move in this democratic direction when constructing new plants, and also within plants already operating on the old principles of administration.

In the old plants it has meant introducing an educational program through which general managers and union leaders familiarize themselves with the experiments that have already been implemented. Principles of self-management are introduced immediately into old plants as part of the job training for new employees. They are also introduced gradually as part of job enlargement for old employees through a process of self-education. New training programs can then provide incentives for workers and managers to develop the skills, knowledge, and sense of responsibility that is part of the pattern of participatory management.

The purpose of the program is to enable employees to organize themselves in a manner that reduces the need for supervision and competition. The goal is to increase the possibilities for self-management and cooperation among workers throughout the entire production cycle. The new direction of administrative principles then follows the lines indicated in the diagram below:

Command Incentives		*Democratic Incentives*
Competition	⟶	Cooperation
Hierarchy	⟶	Equality
Supervision	⟶	Self-management
Principal Direction of Organization		
⟶		

The purpose of the new emphasis in industrial organization is to develop human resources in greater depth while at the same time developing material resources at the plant level of operation. The purpose is not simply to train people for a specialized work task such as tightening bolts on a car fender, but to elicit a greater intelligence and consciousness among workers for the larger operation of the plant. The objective is to release human potential through educational processes and practice. Experiments have shown that the movement toward industrial democracy is most effective with joint planning by management and unions. The focal concern is the creation of new "sociotechnical" systems of work.[2]

The Community Development Corporation: A Local Prototype

We have noted that the community development corporation (CDC) is one model that multinational corporations and community leaders can encourage in local plant operations. The CDC is a form of business enterprise in which workers fully participate in management and corporate policy. Residents in the area are invited to purchase stock in the enterprise, although various modifications in this practice are possible. The direct participation of residents is not always feasible in certain areas of plant organization, but through educational programs in many locations it becomes a practical operation that is integrated with worker control and management.[3]

As the managerial authority over local operations increases among local workers, so does their responsibility. Local workers now become responsible for implementing contractual arrangements with outside corporations. The multinational corporation in this case would become a marketing agency for the CDC or would contract with the CDC for new lines of production. In the United States, for example, General Electric has contracted with numerous CDCs organized locally across the country. Many CDCs are organized specifically to contract with large corporations for special production.[4]

In the United States the CDC has a state charter authorizing it to do business and at the same time a private constitution that delineates the spheres of responsibility and authority for workers and area residents. Workers are concerned about the environment of the workplace, and residents are concerned about the environment within the community in which the plant operates. In other words, the CDC is the type of corporation that appears most able in its external form to express the values of social justice, freedom, and self-determination.

We noted earlier that the CDC is a mix of social and economic principles that guide its administration. In some cases, for example, CDCs have attempted to provide work for people in the community who appear unemployable or who have been discriminated against in employment because of a past criminal record. The CDC may develop housing in the locality and provide day-care centers for working mothers. These development programs are thus blended with a concern for maintaining efficiency of plant operations and a concern for building capital for the limited expansion and growth of the community corporation. The growth and development of this type of community-oriented business, however, has taken place at best only within a larger corporate environment that gives it economic support. This is why it is essential to examine the principles of corporate administration at the national level, which supply the incentives for community-oriented enterprise.

THE NATIONAL LEVEL: ORGANIZING PRINCIPLES

We have stated that some multinational corporations have sought to maximize returns by gaining and keeping a market monopoly within the host nation. In this way, they have retarded the development of host-owned businesses. In some cases, multinational corporations have sought special concessions and tax advantages from the host government, giving them an unfair advantage over local firms. In other cases, multinational corporations have financially aided politicians sympathetic to their interests in the election processes of host nations. In extreme cases, there is evidence that corporations have assisted in the violent overthrow of hostile host governments. Finally, in small nations, the multinational company may be a major contributor to a political party or restrict economic life to a single industry, such as sugar, bananas, coffee, or oil. As a consequence of this large involvement, the well-being of the small nation can become highly dependent upon the operations of the foreign corporation and inevitably the host nation becomes subject to its outside control.

It is possible, nevertheless, for multinational enterprise to adhere to a concept of national autonomy and still maintain productive exchange and commerce within the host nation. In such a case, the host nation establishes its own priorities for development, and the multinational company refrains from establishing priorities solely in its own interest. If the right to establish these priorities is respected, then the principles of self-determination that operate at the national level can be seen as akin to the principle of self-management at the level of the local plant and factory. The community development corporation is simply another level of self-determination no less important than national autonomy. Indeed, local self-management may be basic to the autonomous development of a host nation.

The principle of self-determination at this level means respecting the cultural traditions of the host nation. This principle runs deeper than the rhetoric of public relations, which celebrates a united plan for development made by the needs of the corporation and the bourgeoisie of the host nation. It also means more than simply refusing to own large tracts of land or to engage in large private construction in a host nation. It is more significantly a matter of respecting human autonomy that begins in the life of people in the host nation culture. It involves recognizing the autonomy of people in localities as well as the heads of state in commencing an economic enterprise. The principle of self-determination recognizes everyone's need for personal meaning through self-direction—a need that can be fulfilled only in an environment free from outside coercion. People require personal meaning in their daily work perhaps as much as they require the basic goods and services of a multinational business.

The principle of self-determination, then, requires that corporations recognize the cultural diversity of people in such a way that the transfer of skills and knowledge can occur in response to basic values indigenous to the region of corporate work. This principle leads to the conclusion that all foreign technicans and managers should live in a manner that promotes sensitivity to local interests and an appreciation of the needs and aspirations of the citizens in the host country. In the past, special hotels and elite accommodations have been provided for outside managers. This practice, however, has placed managers in a position of residential isolation that has often been provocative and has led to social unrest. If managerial personnel live under local domestic conditions, whatever problems of disease that arise from local water or food supplies will probably be corrected before the industry or agribusiness is developed. If foreign personnel are to be housed according to local living conditions, they need to be protected from disease along with the residents in the area. The multinational company is then not solely interested in profits in the traditional form of foreign enterprise. The enterprise is truly a joint venture—people of two nations working together to develop the area's human and material resources.

These prescriptive principles of development, however, cannot be fully realized within the current structure of corporations at the national level. New principles of incorporation are necessary. A new charter at the national level is needed to enable executives, managers, and workers to develop policy in accordance with these principles of self-determination and self-management. The implementation of these principles begins with federal chartering of multinational corporations in their home country.

A Constitutional Charter: A National Prototype

We have noted that U. S. corporations are normally chartered at the state level rather than the federal level. This practice has encouraged the corporation to design its operations primarily for the pursuit of private profits. But in the process, the corporation has incurred considerable social costs that require government protection and regulation in the public interest. The unregulated pursuit of private profits has resulted in government commissions, regulatory agencies, and myriad bureaus for the protection of consumers, employees, small business, and the physical environment. This fact has stimulated new thinking about the necessity for federal charters enabling the corporation to regulate itself in the public interest as well as its own interest. It would regulate itself through democratic processes allowing its constituencies a voice in policy and an opportunity for redress of grievances.[5]

The economist Walter Adams has suggested federal charters for U. S. corporations with assets in excess of $250 million. Walter Mueller, another economist, has suggested charters for corporations with assets exceeding $1 billion. Ralph Nader has suggested federal chartering for the top 700 interstate corporations. Most U. S. corporations in these brackets have multinational interests and investments. Federal chartering for these domestic corporations is a legal alternative in the United States and stands as a very real possibility for host nations as well. Experimentation with charters for global corporations at the national level is the first step toward chartering at the international level, but it cannot be accomplished by unilateral action.

If the international enterprise system is to be based on principles of responsible free trade and social justice, then codes of conduct and "systems of accountability" must be developed through international agreements. The Organization for Economic Cooperation and Development (OECD) has already formulated an International Code of Conduct for transnational corporations. The Centre on Transnational Corporations at the United Nations is in the process of doing the same thing. An International Code is the first step. It then requires an enforcement agency to become effective. But such a code and systems of accountability must apply to state socialist enterprises as well as to private corporations operating abroad.

To build a free, effective, and responsible international system of trade, all global economic enterprises must be accountable within a code of conduct established at each level of its operations: the locality, the nation, and the world. An illustration of problems at each level may be helpful here. Let us say that Anaconda Copper is supervising trucks carrying copper-laden rock excavated near a Chilean community, and dust blowing off the trucks seriously affects the environment of local citizens. This offense may require local monitoring and local action. Or let us say that Russian engineers from a state ministry in the Soviet Union are professionally negligent in helping to construct a sugar granary in Cuba, and many workers in the province are seriously injured because of it. This offense may require compensation and correction at the national level. Or let us say that global corporations are engaged in "transfer pricing" between subsidiaries as a technique to avoid paying taxes in the nation where their production takes place. This may require an international agency to inspect the accounting system and to recommend corrective actions in the United Nations. In other words, effective systems of accountability and codes of conduct must be present at the level where the offense occurs. It is important to charter global enterprises at local, national, and world levels, since each case involves a different level of accountability.

Charters are necessary at the national level of the home nation because global corporations often cause problems that can only be treated there. For example, global corporations may create a great deal of unemployment in the home nation by leaving it and going to foreign nations where wages are lower. Also, they can engage in techniques of tax evasion by complicated overseas accounting systems. They may even provoke conditions in other countries that plunge their home country into war. Global corporations, therefore, require chartering at the federal level in the national interest.

Arguments for national charters for global corporations have centered on the need for certain *prohibitions, obligations,* and *requirements for disclosure* of information in the public interest. Examples of specific charter requirements that need serious study as to their effectiveness and applicability for federal charters follow:[6]

Charter of the Global Corporation

A. *Prohibitions against:*
1. Acquiring stock, assets, or property of a host company overseas.
2. Granting or receiving any privileges in services, or allowances except justified publicly by the host nation.
3. Engaging in exclusive dealerships in the host nation.
4. Participating in interlocking controls over other corporations in the host nation.
5. Exceeding permissible limits on market percentage of products sold in the host nation.
6. Providing corporate loans to officers and directors.

B. *Obligations for:*
1. Licensing patents and know-how to other firms on a reasonable royalty basis.
2. Serving all customers on nondiscriminatory terms in the manner of a common carrier.
3. Pursuing pricing and product policies calculated to achieve capacity employment and production.
4. Permitting stockholders to make proposals at annual meetings in the social interest.
5. Permitting free speech by employees even when critical of the corporation.

C. *Disclosure of:*
1. Volume of various products manufactured and distributed.
2. Corporate income and tax returns.
3. Nature of holdings in other corporations, including all subsidiaries.
4. Nature of holdings of major stockholders who have controlling interest.
5. Extent and nature of facilities operated for or leased from the host government.
6. Extent and nature of foreign operations, including the identity of board members of foreign-based subsidiaries and financial interests that subsidiaries have with other foreign corporations.
7. Special social costs (e.g., pollution) and improvements (e.g., safety) in the host community.

While the recent discussion of federal chartering has focused primarily on the national conduct of U. S. corporations, the issues are directly connected to the world conduct of multinationals. It is not simply that most big corporations are multinational but rather that chartering for them is part of the logic for developing systems of accountability on the world scene. National legislation is part of the process of opening the door for world chartering of multinational corporations.

National legislation providing for the chartering of multinational corporations in the United States can provide a model for similar legislation in other nations. It would then be possible for small countries to exercise a greater measure of self-determination. Through their own efforts they could begin to place limits on foreign corporations and at the same time develop social control over their own economic development by following charter guidelines. Our assumption is that the more control is exercised through "public accountability" at the national level, the less political control is necessary at the world level. Put another way, the more big corporations create a pattern of social responsibility in their own national settings, the fewer external controls and requirements will need to be implemented in the future through world organizations. In accord with our "organizing principles," the assumption is that maximum social authority and responsibility should be created at the lower levels of corporate administration. In this case the lower level of control is a national chartering agency, while the higher level of control is a world chartering agency.

Host nations have begun to exercise control over the domestic activities of the multinational corporation through their own political bodies. Mexico, for example, has a constitutional provision excluding foreigners from holding more than 49 percent of the shares in agricultural operations, radio broadcasting, television, motion pictures, publishing, advertising, fishing, transportation, and manufacturing. Some host nations also require that top management be residents. In Colombia, the labor code requires at least 80 percent of the specialized or executive personnel of foreign firms be Colombian. In pre-socialist Burma, the foreign investor was under obligation to rapidly pass on technical and management skills to Burmese nationals. This is part of the pattern of self-determination that is developing in small nations to control the growing power of multinational corporations.[7]

Yet with all the legislation possible within the host nation and the home nations, *regional controls* are still necessary to check tendencies toward monopoly and exploitation. It is possible for corporations to set up headquarters in competing nations, thus making it necessary for neighbor nations to "bend the law" to accommodate corporate interests because of their larger national interest of economic development. There are still strong inducements offered to political elites to make unfair "concessions" and for citizens in the host nation to sit on local boards of directors "on behalf" of foreign interests. There are still foreign banks that exercise powerful controls over host-nation enterprises and strong market controls of multinationals over domestic production in underdeveloped nations. The road to self-determination and freedom is still being mapped, and its "contours" are partly visible within a higher level of world organization.

THE REGIONAL LEVEL: ORGANIZING PRINCIPLES

The redirection of multinational companies is possible regionally through such strategic structures as international alliances, international labor, divestment agencies, and international banks. The first two structures are external checks over corporate power. The latter two are internal to business itself. They are significant because they provide opportunities for corporate executives and world leaders to reconstitute the corporate pattern of development.

Important organizing principles or goals of development to recall here are (a) increasing the autonomy of people in the workplace and (b) enhancing the quality of work life. To achieve these goals, regional organization is often essential. Small nations need to strengthen their position in the world market so that in turn they can contribute more to the autonomy and work life of individuals in the local community.

Nations today are organizing regional alliances to gain strength to exercise clout against exploitation and to develop international standards for economic development. The alliance protects small nations from attempts by multinational corporations to play nation against nation in the competitive process of developing resources. Development is thus controlled and redirected through a broader political authority. In this way, the principles of self-interest guiding business administration are increasingly shifted toward a philosophy of mutual benefit at all levels of geographic organization.

Major examples of regional alliances are the Organization of Petroleum Exporting Countries (OPEC), the European Economic Community, and the Andean Pact. The regional organization in each case is politically complex, but the Andean Pact serves as an important prototype for this kind of strategy among small nations.

The Andean Pact: A Regional Prototype

Nations in the Andean Region of South America have formulated common norms and goals for economic development that affect corporate policies of multinational investment and exchange. The goals include (a) the encouragement of foreign investors to contribute to the achievement of economic objectives established in the national plans of member states, (b) the protection of national firms against discriminatory practices and laws favoring foreign investment within the region, (c) the strengthening of national firms, (d) the deterrence of "foreignization" of domestic economies arising from excessive penetration and economic strength of foreign enterprise, (e) the opening to national firms, both public and private, of greater access to the developed nations' modern technology and administrative know-how through the creation of efficient and comprehensive procedures for technology transfer, (f) the upgrading of the Andean countries' negotiating position in relation to multinational corporations and international organizations that control capital and technology.

The Andean Pact represents the first effort undertaken by a group of Latin American nations to develop procedures requiring signatory nations to pursue a course of action challenging multinational corporations to follow specific guidelines for development. The Pact recognizes the merits of multinational corporations and the role of foreign investment in the integration of the political economy in Latin America. It seeks to stimulate capital development, facilitate national participation, speed technology transfers, and coordinate foreign investment flows. It recognizes the basic sovereign right of each nation to develop its own natural resources. It favors giving preference to domestic investors while recognizing that foreign investment constitutes a positive contribution toward this end.[8]

But norms governing foreign ownership and profit remittance were subjects of careful consideration among the Andean nations. Norms were set for the reexportation of capital, the utilization of external and internal credit, and technology transfers involving licenses, patents, trademarks, and royalty arrangements. Foreign investments were expressly prohibited in important segments of the region's economies. These prohibitory sectors include:

(a) the primary resource sector, including the exploration for and/or exploitation of minerals and timber as well as the development of gas and oil pipelines; (b) public service industries, which include water, electric power and light, sanitation, telephones, telegraph, and mail; (c) the banking and insurance sectors (carefully excluded previously); (d) the advertising industry; and (e) others, including internal transportation, commercial radio and television stations, and newspapers and magazines.[9]

These commitments are accepted at the highest levels of the contracting governments and theoretically carry the force of law in signatory countries. In reality, an agreement involving a controversial issue of foreign investment policy for the region cannot possess the force of law until the particulars are fully sanctioned by congressional mandate. But the significance of the Pact rests in its meaning for the creation of future regional organizations and the implementation of legislation supporting the standards of operation. Further development of standards within nations may then bring about the decentralization of authority for industrial organization within the locality and the firm.

Other Regional Structures

International Labor Unions

Multinational companies have considerable bargaining leverage against local unions in negotiating situations partly because they are able to shift their investments at will across national borders. International unions, however, are beginning to take action against unfair bargaining positions and power. The principal unions dealing with multinationals are the secretariats of the International Metalworkers Federation, the International Federation of Chemical General Workers' Unions, and the International Union of Food and Allied Workers' Associations. These three secretariats are based in Geneva, but other organizations are making claims to challenge the multinational companies.

The power of international labor became evident when a hundred French computer repairmen struck Cie. Honeywell Bull in Paris in January 1973 and the company sought to break the strike by bringing in repairmen from Britain and Germany. The Geneva headquarters of the International Metalworkers Federation circulated the word that Honeywell was attempting to break the strike, and other workers refused to go to Paris in spite of special incentives put forward by the Company. Labor's power advantage is in the fact that it is organized internationally in the same manner as the multinational company and therefore can act on comparable grounds. International labor unions can provide their affiliates information on the tactics and techniques of multinational subsidiaries. In this way Shell Oil Co. workers who were on strike in the United States over the worker's right to a voice in establishing health and safety conditions were able to quote to American management those provisions covering the subject in other operations of the Royal Dutch Shell group around the world.

In the United States, the United Auto Workers has offered proposals designed to check policies of multinational corporations that adversely affect the interests of labor. These proposals include an effective full-employment policy with real adjustment assistance for workers laid off because of international trade shifts, an international legal code to protect workers' rights, compensation for American workers laid off by overseas investment, improvement of minimum wage standards abroad, restrictions against currency speculation by multinational companies, and requirements that American oligopolies compete when foreign importers invade United States markets. This may be only the beginning of a wider concern of American labor unions for limiting the power of multinational companies when they clearly affect employment and the conditions of work on the home front.

The AFL-CIO has been lobbying for the Burke-Hartke bill, which contains provisions to repeal corporate income tax credits on payments of foreign income taxes. It would also require stricter guidelines for depreciation on machinery in foreign plants and put an end to tax-free treatment on income from licensing and transferring patents to foreign corporations. The bill is controversial for many reasons, including the fact that it gives the U. S. President full power to regulate the transfer of capital from company headquarters to foreign subsidiaries. It concentrates power in Washington, where it is already concentrated. But the rising consciousness of the international role of unions is part of the process of divesting multinational companies of excessive control over vulnerable local unions.

International Divestment Agencies

Once a multinational corporation has invested heavily in a foreign nation it tends to consolidate its position as a permanent institution within the host country. Over the years it normally tends to expand and grow in power. Most multinational executives would not think of divestment unless the prospects of expropriation became real. For multinational companies facing the prospects of expropriation, Harvard economist Albert O. Hirschman offers a way to divest economic interests and reestablish new relationships with the host nation. Hirschman argues that a time limit be considered on foreign investments. He recognizes that the time can arrive when economic gains from foreign investment are outweighed by the social fact that the multinational corporation has come to dominate local enterprise. It is then important to encourage local development through a planned process of divestment. He stresses this as a practical matter for corporate executives, since expropriation has become a more popular alternative for nations than has been the case in the past.[10]

Hirschman recommends that new foreign ventures in Latin America should have a built-in mechanism for transferring ownership to host nation investors. He proposes that an Inter-American Divestment Corporation be established, possibly within the Inter-American Development Bank as a means to help foreign companies leave localities in which they are no longer welcome. Such a corporation could be funded by contributions from citizens who were interested in enabling the process to take place. Governments might provide a reduction in income tax returns as an incentive for making gifts to the international divestment corporation. This concept then introduces an important mechanism through which executives can direct their own corporate policy in conjunction with the principle of self-determination.

International Loan Agencies

Major strategies for reshaping corporate policy can also be designed within the loaning practices of international banks. The principal international agency for financing economic development since World War II has been the World Bank, or more properly, the International Bank for Reconstruction and Development. The chief foreign lending agency of the U. S. government has been the Export-

Import Bank of Washington and the Development Loan Fund established in 1957. Such agencies could adopt policies favoring applications that include plans to decentralize authority within the corporate system of the host nation. They could *announce plans to give priority to those loan applications from concerns who intend to humanize economic enterprise by democratizing and decentralizing its administrative structure.* They could encourage planning to experiment with codetermination and community development corporations to determine their effectiveness in different cultural environments. In this way, the business community can encourage corporate policies that enhance the development of human resources in the host country.

The Limitations of Regional Structures

Since no agencies exist at the world level to prescribe standards regulating development, multinational corporations operate in a delicate balance of power with regions of nation-states. The regional organizations that are counterbalancing the power of multinationals are now a force to be reckoned with at the world level. Regional organizations can act in a cartel-like manner in their own interest to exploit and dominate world resources in the same manner as some multinational corporations in the past.

The European Economic Community and the Organization of Petroleum Exporting Countries are powerful political groups. Their control over certain markets and industries is beginning to have international repercussions. In the interest of Arab development, for example, OPEC nations can control the supply of oil and increase prices for political reprisal against multinationals and "unfriendly nations." They can behave together as states much as the seven major international oil companies do; they can participate in regulating the supply and price of oil in the world.

Social planning therefore must now take account of this fact with all its implications for other regions of the world. World pricing and market controls can emerge on a regional level among like-minded governments in either a democratic or a cartel-like fashion. This means, of course, that more broadly based international agencies are needed to set standards for a world economy. It also means that tribunal systems are necessary to adjudicate disputes within an international framework of nations.

The fact that regional controls have political implications as well as economic implications is important to note in a world that is both capitalist and socialist. While the multinational company is defined as an economic organization, it is clearly a political organization in its international decisions.

Whereas the proposed strategies for divestment agencies and "soft loan" organizations are really efforts to humanize capitalist institutions, the problem at the world level is to humanize socialist institutions as well when they show signs of dominance and exploitation. This leads to a concentrated effort within a world organization to find new methods for introducing human values into the international economy, which today includes worldwide economic activities of both capitalist and socialist nations.

THE WORLD LEVEL: ORGANIZING PRINCIPLES

The strategies for development at the world level are comparable to those we have discussed at the national and regional levels if we take into account the more complex political economy. International law, international corporate charters, international tribunal systems, and international development agencies are subject to the same principles as their regional and national counterparts. International agencies can guide development toward an emphasis on authority and responsibility at the level of the individual, the firm, and the locality. Let us examine briefly how these concepts bear on social policies of international development starting with a decentralized court system.

A System of Courts: An International Prototype

According to some legal scholars, the expropriation of foreign property in host countries is a violation of international law if a contractual agreement exists against expropriation or if the expropriating state fails to adhere to a promise of compensation. International law, however, is not enforceable by any world court except by agreement of the participating parties. Therefore, action to correct claimed abuses must be based on consensus among affected parties. After the property of Kennecott Copper was expropriated in Chile, for example, Kennecott lawyers sought to block the sale of Chilean copper in France and Sweden through their domestic court systems. Kennecott's argument was that the expropriation was actually "confiscation" of their property, since prompt and adequate compensation was not forthcoming. A favorable decision of the domestic courts would stop copper purchases and thus punish the Chilean government. Since these events, however, discussion in the United Nations has led to the idea that host-nation decisions should be binding on all parties.

Although the International Court of Justice is an integral part of the United Nations, its authority is limited. Its main purpose is the adjustment of international disputes that might lead to a breach of the peace. The court has authority to determine the extent of its own jurisdiction, but the number and variety of cases brought to it are restricted by certain factors. For example, parties must convince their state to sue on their behalf on the legal grounds that the state itself has been injured. They must also be willing to accept the state's full handling of the litigation, including any compromises made by the state in the process. Consequently, the court handles only a limited number of cases in the field of multinational investments and securities.

Clark and Sohn have suggested a much broader and more authoritative regional organization of courts within a reconstituted structure of the United Nations.[11] They suggest a revision of the U. N. charter that would allow for the organization of 20 to 40 regional courts whose jurisdiction would be specified by the General Assembly. The unanswered question in the Clark-Sohn proposal, however, is whether the United Nations could be reconstituted in such a way that the new charter organization would eliminate the possibility of great injustices in the implementation of the law. The plan includes the creation of world law and the organization of an international peace force with limited rights to legal enforcement. The question is whether the regional court system might not stabilize and regulate patterns of domination that currently exist in the corporate state system.

The Clark-Sohn suggestions, nevertheless, are important to consider, because a pattern of world courts and a system of international law appears to be inevitable in view of the increasingly complex movement toward multinational investment, production, and marketing. It is therefore highly important to consider the nature of international law with respect to world corporations and a regional court system established in a framework of social values guiding international development.[12]

Other World Structures

World Charters

The chartering of world corporations must take account of the problem of legitimation in the same manner as the nation-state. We have said that the nationally chartered corporation is one that operates in the public interest as well as in its own interest. We have noted that chartering raises questions about such matters as limits on the purchase of stock in other corporations, specification of fair practices, and proper disclosure of corporate information. We have suggested further that chartered corporations would demonstrate intent to organize in a manner that *promotes democratic involvement of their constitutencies*. This may include such matters as a charter statement about a public review board, a bill of rights for employees, an internal tribunal system, and a plan for decentralizing authority in the corporation. The emphasis in a national charter may be on the systemic principles of work, which emphasize the participation of employees at the base of the organization. The chartering of a world corporation, however, may take many of these factors for granted, since its focus is more on the relations between nation-states.

The charter of a world corporation would still have to take account of certain questions comparable to those raised at the national level. At the international level it would seem of critical importance to require a charter statement about internal appelate systems that could respond to complaints from constituencies within the multinational network. It would seem of considerable importance to establish a world review board capable of investigating the international operations of the corporation. The complexity of the standards for chartering at the world level, however, are so great that it would seem most important at the present time to support a research agency that can begin to specify the conditions of chartering in more detail. For the present we can only argue the need to determine these standards.

An International Research Agency

The Commission on Transnational Corporations was established by the Economic and Social Council of the United Nations in December, 1974 to create a "detailed program of work" concerning the issues related to global corporations. The Commission is now the main forum within the United Nations for the comprehensive and in-depth consideration of these issues. It has already set up an Information and Research Centre.

The Centre itself has begun to identify the vast range of studies on the problems we have discussed.[13] Many studies, for example, have focused on the economic impact of global corporations on host nations. Impact studies have been made in Australia, Brazil, Jamaica, the United Kingdom, and dozens of other countries.[14] Some important studies have concentrated on foreign direct investment in special industries such as computers, pharmaceuticals, and automobiles.[15] Various governments are carrying out their own studies on global corporations operating in their territory. Norway, for example, has undertaken research on the foreign ownership of Norwegian mining and manufacturing enterprises and its effect on economic growth and the society. The United Kingdom has sponsored research on the impact of foreign investment on industrial relations and regional development. Canada has been making an empirical analysis of the takeover of local firms.[16] A significant amount of research has also developed concerning restrictive business practices on exports, through "tied purchases," payments of minimum royalties, and restrictions on sales.[17] Studies have been made on transfer pricing, which shifts profits between nations and distorts local competition. Attempts have been made to identify the methods by which transnationals move funds among different countries as well as the internal and external inducements to do so.[18] A series of studies have focused on labor problems. The International Labor Organization, for example, has published findings on the conditions of work life in global corporations and the relevance of world labor standards for corporations.[19] A whole variety of studies have been initiated on the relationships created between global corporations and governments. This includes the actual process of negotiation between government officials and corporate managers as well as the type of contractual arrangements that are concluded.[20] A number of research projects have attempted to assess the sociocultural impact of the presence of foreign affiliates on host societies, including their consumption patterns and attitudes toward political issues.[21]

These studies may now serve as the background for designing international programs of consultation between governments and corporations seeking to combine efforts in socioeconomic development. These programs would then consider both divestment and decentralization as part of that development. They would also consider self-study programs that encourage nations and corporations to look at the development of human resources as well as material resources at the world level.

A Divestment and Development Agency: Socioeconomic Research and Consultation

What has yet to be created is an international agency with support from socialist and capitalist nations to carry out investigations across national boundaries. Such an agency would need to be staffed through international professional organizations and would also need authority to act as a consultative force for social development in the world economy. It would have authority to initiate experimental studies of the problems precipitated by economic investments on the part of both socialist and capitalist countries. Its power would exist only in its investigative authority to study socioeconomic conditions of international investment. By international agreement it would have the right to gather and to disclose information on the effects of such investments. It would be authorized to report its conclusions through the mass media of member nations. One of its charges would be to recommend basic changes in political practices of global corporations, socialist ministries, and the actions of regional organizations. Its purpose would be to gather facts for the promotion of social and economic conditions leading toward a decentralized world economy.

A particular mandate for such a world agency would be to make a comparative study of the pattern of capitalist and socialist investments at the local, regional, and national levels of economic development. This would imply searching for a model of international organization that can most effectively decentralize authority and cultivate local responsibility among individuals while still maintaining productivity within its total organization. It means the kind of corporate administration that can be efficient and at the same time be able to meet basic standards of justice, freedom, self-determination, and quality of life in the environment.

The research agency would also be especially designed to study the issues of corporate charters and international law. This process can begin by examining the social conditions under which human resources are cultivated without ignoring the development of material resources. Thus research begins ideally by reversing the current priorities of multinational corporations, which stress the development of material resources without emphasing the development of human resources. The agency would direct its attention to the kind of corporate organization that can produce goods and services while maximizing human sensitivities, skills, authority, and knowledge of the total social context of the corporation. The research process then would conclude by defining the specific requirements of a world charter that can meet the realistic conditions already created by multinational activities.

Research into the standards of world charters for major international investments can include the study of proportionate economic returns and tax requirements for people at the various levels of organization: the locality, the host nation, and the home nation. Research can include the review of appropriate public agencies to investigate the nature and extent of corporate accounting and organization.

The accounting books of any global enterprise—socialist or capitalist—should be open for inspection by its constituencies in different parts of the world. The facts regarding the nature of its ownership and the extent of its subsidiary organization should be available to the citizens of any nation in which it operates. The books of an open enterprise are available to the citizens of nations in which it operates. If the economic enterprise is open and publically oriented, then its activities are more likely to be in the interests of the people it serves. A closed corporation, on the other hand, is more likely to serve the private advantage of a select few, exploiting a large number of people at the bottom of the organization. Furthermore, if the operations of the corporation are subject to public review, it is more likely to be interested in the equitable development of resources in its area of operations and serve as a model for development in other areas.

Following the principles of development we are proposing, an international research agency would study the strategies that ultimately enrich the lives of people in the work organization. The various structures we have suggested are designed to lead toward social (not merely state) controls and inner incentives for self-management. They are designed to create a sense of responsibility in work organization that contributes to the larger community. The structures of social accountability within the economic enterprise are designed to eliminate the necessity for adding state controls. At the same time, all structures of control, such as autonomous work groups, public review boards, and tribunal systems are themselves only interim strategies. They are designed to create corporate conditions that increase individual responsibilities in the larger community of work. They are intended to elicit the basis for people to develop social controls that eliminate the necessity for state supervision and management.

In this sense, then, there is reason to suggest the world registration of all major socialist and capitalist investors in developing nations. All investors would then be required to operate in the open with a public orientation. Both socialist ministries and transnational corporations are in effect "investment enterprises." The registration of investments at the world level could provide the information essential to determine the extent of financial involvement of one nation in the economic affairs of another nation. World registration of investments would reduce the tendencies for both socialist and capitalist states to engage in unfair competition to gain the allegiance of small nations.

Summary

The purpose of this type of development policy is to create social controls within the corporate economy at the world level. The corporate economy of both capitalist and socialist nations may then be encouraged to operate more democratically, publicly, and effectively outside the command system of the state.

The growing tendency toward the expropriation of foreign property can be attributed in part to the privacy of operations that lead to the special interests of a privileged few at the top. The new strategies for multinational organization would require operations that are open to inspection by democratically constituted agencies. These agencies would have the authority for public review of all international enterprise without enforcement powers from a world state. Violations of a world charter would then be adjudicated through a tribunal system organized within the corporate system to hear complaints from corporate constituencies. If the private adjudicative process did not operate fairly, the offended parties would still have recourse to domestic court systems.

An investment agency which helps decentralize authority is more likely in the long run to be socially and economically effective on the world scene. The decentralized enterprise is more likely to respond to the diverse cultural life of people. Indeed, a pattern of democratic corporate development should lead eventually to the elimination of pressure to create state enforcement agencies at the world level.

An international research agency, following the principles we have been discussing, would examine those strategies and structures that are designed to move multinational enterprise toward decentralized controls of administration, taking account of the cultural context of the locality within which it operates. The general purpose of its research would be to determine the standards of operation that enrich the cultural life of the workers and determine the optimum levels of productivity within the local and regional environment.

There are fundamental reasons for the establishment of international policies for divestment and development. They are part of the broader purposes of creating human societies that will help to maintain a self-governing world economy.

NOTES

1. Cf. Paul M. Goldberg and Charles P. Kindelberger, "Toward a GATT for Investment: A Proposal for Supervision of the International Corporation," *Law and Policy in International Business,* 2 (1970): 295; Harry G. Johnson, "The Multinational Corporation as a Development Agent," *Columbia Journal of World Business,* No. 3 (May-June, 1970): 25-30; "The Role of Foreign Private Investment in the ECFE Region," *Economic Commission for the Far East,* UN, March 18, 1971; Frank Church, "Why I Voted No," *New Republic,* Nov. 13, 1971.

2. Eric L. Trist, "A Socio-Technical Critique of Scientific Management," a paper contributed to the Edinburgh Conference on the Impact of Science and Technology, Edinburgh University, May 24-26, 1970.

3. Geoffrey Faux, "CDCs: New Hope for the Inner City," Report of the Twentieth Century Fund Task Force on Community Development Corporations (Twentieth Century Fund, 1971).

4. General Electric has contracted with the following CDCs:
EG&G Roxbury, Inc. This is a diversified instrumentation firm in Boston's Roxbury district. GE did not take an equity stake in the project. Instead, they gave free managerial, marketing, and technical assistance. A community group raised the seed money and organized a management team.
Progress Enterprises, Inc. This is a group of subsidiaries under Zion Investment Associates, Philadelphia, Pennsylvania. The Missiles and Space Division of GE played an important part in the planning and design of an aerospace plant and continues to lend technical assistance. GE committed itself to a $2.6 million purchasing agreement for the plant's first 18 months of operation. The aerospace company has a policy of employing hard-core unemployed residents recruited from the Opportunities Industrialization Center.
Southwest Virginia Community Development Fund This development effort brings together rural whites and urban blacks as part of one community corporation. Its primary purpose has been to build housing. An electrical assembly plant is to be opened in Roanoke. It will do light assembly work. GE has offered to subcontract one-third of its electrical harness assembly work and to train the firm's manager.
For other cases of corporate links to community-owned enterprises, see Jules Cohn, *The Conscience of the Corporations: Business and Urban Affairs, 1967-1970* (Baltimore: The Johns Hopkins Press, 1971).

5. Richard Eells, *Global Corporations* (New York: The Free Press, 1972); Severyn T. Bruyn, Norman J. Faramelli, and Dennis A. Yates, *An Ethical Primer on the Multinational Corporation,* (New York: IDOC, 1973).

6. Most of these charter requirements are discussed in Ralph Nader and Mark Green, *Corporate Power in America* (New York: Grossman, 1973).

7. "The Americas in a Changing World," Report by the Commission on United States Latin American Relations, Center for Inter-American Relations, 680 Park Ave., New York, N. Y., 10021, 1974.

8. The Andean Pact came into being in 1969, when the representatives of Bolivia, Chile, Colombia, Ecuador, and Peru signed the Cartagena Agreement. Venezuela refrained from joining then, while seeking clarification on provisions relating to industrial and agricultural production, tariffs, veto use, devaluation, and certain national safeguards. With the entry of Venezuela in 1973, the six-nation group is potentially the strongest active economic organization among these developing countries. Their combined foreign trade is larger than that

of Brazil, Mexico, or India. For a summary of the recent steps of Venezuela in joining the Pact, see *Venezuela Up-to-Date,* Vol. XIV, No. 2, Spring, 1973.

For a detailed presentation of the Andean Region's policy governing foreign investments, see La Comision del Acuerdo de Cartagena, "Regimen comun de tratamiento a los capitales extranjeros y sobre marcas, patentes, licencias y regalias," *Tercer Periodo de Sesiones Extraordinarias de la Comision,* Decision No. 24 (Lima, Peru, December 14-31, 1970).

9. Stephen F. Lau, *The Chilean Response to Foreign Investment* (New York: Praeger, 1970), p. 26.

10. Albert Hirschman, "How to Divest in Latin America and Why," *International Essay* 76: Princeton University Press, 1969.

11. Granville Clark and Louis B. Sohn, *World Peace Through World Law* (Cambridge: Harvard University Press, 1966).

12. For related articles, see Detley F. Vagts, "The Multinational Enterprise: Power Versus Sovereignty," *Foreign Affairs,* 49, No. 3-4, (July, 1971): 736-751; Hedley Bull, "International Law and International Order," in Richard Falk and Cyril Black (eds), *The Future of the International Legal Order* (New Jersey: Princeton Univ. Press, 1970).

13. What follows are examples of studies identified by the Centre. See United Nations, "Research on Transnational Corporations," Commission on Transnational Corporations, Jan. 28, 1976; "Research on Transnational Corporations," March, 1976; "Information on Transnational Corporations," March, 1976.

14. Cf. Australian Commonwealth Treasury, *Overseas Investment in Australia,* Treasury Economic Papers No. 1 (Canberra: Australian Govt. Publ. Service, 1972); Teotonio Dos Santos, "Foreign Investment and the Large Enterprise in Latin America: The Brazilian Case," in J. Petras and M. Zeitlin (eds), *Latin America: Reform or Revolution?* (Greenwich, Conn.: Fawcett, 1968), pp. 431-453; Norman Girvan, *Foreign Capital and Economic Underdevelopment in Jamaica* (Kingston, Jamaica: Institute of Social and Economic Research, 1972); P. J. Buckley and John H. Dunning, "The Industrial Structure of U. S. Direct Investment in the U. K.," Reading University Discussion Papers in *International Investment and Business Studies,* No. 12, mimeographed (Reading: Reading Univ., 1974).

15. Cf. Jack Baranson, "Automotive Industries in Developing Countries," World Bank Staff, *Occasional Papers,* No. 8 (Baltimore: Johns Hopkins Press, 1969); Y. S. Chang, "The Transfer of Technology: Economics of Offshore Assembly, The Case of Semiconductor Industry," *UNITAR Research Report* No. 11 (New York: United Nations Institute of Training and Research, 1971); J. Wilner Sundelson, "U. S. Automotive Investments Abroad," in *The International Corporation,* Charles P. Kindleberger (ed) (Cambridge, Mass: M.I.T. Press, 1970).

16. Cf. Grant L. Reuber, "Antitrust and the Takeover Activity of American Firms in Canada: A Further Analysis," *Journal of Law and Economics,* 12 (Oct. 1969): 405-417; Grant L. Reuber, with H. Crookel, M. Emerson, and H. Gallais, *Private Foreign Investment in Development* (Oxford: Clarendon Press, 1973).

17. United Nations Conference on Trade and Development (UNCTAD), "Review of Major Developments in the Area of Restrictive Business Practices: Report by the UNCTAD Secretariat," April 29, 1975.

18. Cf. Jeffrey Arpan, *International Intracorporate Pricing: Non-American Systems and Views* (New York: Praeger, 1972).

19. International Labor Orgainzation (ILO), *Multinational Enterprises and Social Policy* (Geneva: ILO, 1973).

20. Cf. Raymond F. Mikesell (ed), *Foreign Investment in the Petroleum and Mineral Indus-*

tries: Case Studies of Investor-Host Country Relations (Baltimore: Johns Hopkins Press, 1971).

21. Cf. Robert Angell, *Peace on the March: Transnational Participation* (New York: Van Nostrand-Reinhold, 1969); John Fayerweather, "Elite Attitudes Toward Multinational Firms: A Study of Britain, Canada, and France," *International Studies Quarterly,* 16 (December 1972): 472–490.

PART IV

The Social Economy

KARL MARX. As far as the present cooperative societies are concerned, they are *only* valuable if they are independent creations of the workers, and not the protégés either of governments or of the bourgeoisie . . . . Freedom consists in converting the state from an organ superimposed on society into one thoroughly subordinate to it.

EMILE DURKHEIM. Here in broad outlines, is what corporations should be in order to render the services rightly to be expected of them. When their present state is considered, of course, it is somewhat hard to conceive of their ever being elevated to the dignity of moral powers . . . .

This restoration, the need of which is universally felt, unfortunately has to contend with the bad name left in history by the corporations of the ancient regime . . . The old, narrowly local corporation, closed to all outside influence, had become an anomaly in a morally and politically unified nation; the excessive autonomy it enjoyed, making it a State within a State, could not be retained while the governmental organ, ramifying itself in all directions, was more and more subordinating all secondary organs of society to itself. So the base on which the institution rested had to be enlarged and the institution itself reconnected with the whole of national life. But if similar corporations of different localities had been connected with one another, instead of remaining isolated, so as to form a single system, if all these systems had been subject to the general influence of the State and thus kept in constant awareness of their solidarity, bureaucratic despotism and occupational egoism would have been kept within proper limits.

MAX WEBER. Within a social relationship, whether it is traditional or enacted, certain kinds of action of *each* participant may be imputed to *all* others, in which case we speak of "mutually responsible members;" or the action of certain members (the "representatives") may be attributed to the others (the "represented"). In both cases, the members will share the resulting advantages as well as the disadvantages.

TEN

CONCLUDING NOTES ON SOCIAL PLANNING:

A Public Agenda for Policy Research

Social economy encompasses such subjects as business history, corporate research, institutional problems, economic federations, and international relations. It consists of a body of research and theory based on facts about society. But it is also a field based on human values that give us direction into the area of planning. In this last chapter we look at planning and add perspectives to the concept of self-governance. The discussion then serves to summarize essential arguments in the book.

We have seen features of social planning in each of the preceding chapters. In Chapter One, for example, we saw how historic changes have been made in business law and labor-management relations as well as in the formation of post-industrial enterprises. These changes have been broadening the system of accountability of business in the American economy. It was also noted most importantly that a growth in social consciousness has taken place among corporate lawyers, business executives, labor leaders, and professional scientists. History shows how leaders in political and economic life have taken the initiative to increase the degree of social responsibility within the business system. Thus, through planning, the system has begun to function more intentionally in the public interest.

In Chapter Two we saw how professional scientists have created a variety of models for studying business firms. These research models, however, can also be seen as a basis for planning new directions for corporate administration and development. They give new perspectives on the purposes of the corporation and the function of the business enterprise in American society.

In Chapter Three we saw how the economy functions as a human institution.

We saw it expressing social and economic problems that have threatened to destroy its viability as a self-governing system. But we also saw how these problems have latent solutions within the enterprise system itself. In fact, some of these solutions have already been implemented through planning. Hence we saw how a complex macro system can be altered intentionally at certain junctures so that it will operate more directly in the interest of the people it affects in the larger society.

In succeeding chapters we looked at how a system of social federations has been developing to govern the macro system. The federation was seen as a democratic means for developing human resources, and I noted its potential for helping to empower people in wide sectors of the economy. Now we can see how it offers a social base for planning the development of human resources in the economic order. The federation offers important opportunities for the self-governance of economic enterprises within the nation.

The development of the social economy therefore is dependent upon planning. We know now that social and economic problems are not solved merely through the operation of a traditional laissez-faire policy. Indeed, we have seen the consequences of trying to maintain laissez-faire in the traditional sense. It leads to its own eventual destruction as a nonplanning philosophy: More and more government bureaucracy is required to solve the problems of the private economy.

In this final chapter, then, we are led to examine methods of social planning more carefully. To do this we begin with the scientific paradigm of social economy because its assertions tell us something about the planning process. They provide the framework for treating the fundamental problems facing the American economy.

Here we will also examine the problems themselves. I have already described "bureaucracy" as a central problem, but there are other problems to face in the field of planning. One is the growing fiscal crisis of the state. Another has to do with the effective management of a complex corporate economy outside the command bureaucracy of the state. We have seen historically how a large bureaucratic state can dominate people. But we have also seen how the private sector of business has had difficulty governing itself without planning; it seems to require the growth of a bureaucratic state. There appears to be no exit from what Max Weber once described as the "iron cage."

We will therefore look at the efforts of Western European nations to solve the problems of the business system through state planning. This brief review is essential to distinguish state planning from what we will call social planning. State planning remains one important way to deal with the problems of business. But here we discuss its difficulties and raise questions about its success. One criticism of state planning is drawn from the logic of assertions in the scientific paradigm. If all economies operate essentially on a social foundation according to our paradigm, it follows that an emphasis on state planning cannot by itself provide the real solution.

The most critical question then follows: What is the alternative to state planning? What is social planning? The answer to this question occupies our attention for the remainder of the book. It speaks directly to our basic theme of *decentralizing authority through the cultivation of human resources.* This means developing a new sensitivity to the quality of work life and to the productive capabilities of people. It means looking at specific ways to realize the value of the economy as a self-governing institution.

THE SCIENTIFIC PARADIGM

Thomas Kuhn proposed a thesis in *The Structure of Scientific Revolutions* that the major advances in the natural sciences have been made when an old theoretical paradigm is abandoned in favor of a new one. He noted that the shift to a new paradigm seems at first to appear suddenly but in reality it is preceded by a long period in which scientists have tried to modify the old paradigm in the face of contrary evidence. Kuhn's concept of a revolutionary shift in paradigms shows some similarities to the social sciences even though it is not directly applicable to them. These similarities are most marked today in the field of economics, which has drawn its model from the natural sciences. We know now that the economy cannot be studied as though it were primarily a physical phenomenon. A new paradigm has been developing for many years around the concept of the economy as a human institution.[1]

The old theory of competition and the free market has been defended and revised for many decades, but it can no longer account for the empirical facts. The facts are that the so-called free market is largely regulated by state and federal agencies or by private oligopolies. But more significantly substantial evidence reveals that the whole economy is regulated by complex patterns of social action. These patterns of social action involve collective attitudes, public opinion, customs, conventions, contracts, charters, company rules, political pressures, and many types of organizations that are based ultimately in human decision-making. The facts are that *the economy exists on a social foundation.*

The nineteenth century concept of the economy as grounded essentially in *nature* may still be argued among philosophers, but we know that the economy today can only be understood through society. The philosophical problem is to find what is natural to people living in a particular society. The popular concept of the self-regulating economy in the old paradigm must be translated into the terms of social organization in the new paradigm. Self-regulation must now be understood in terms of self-governance.

The concept of competition has also been undergoing a shift in meaning. It has been losing its former place of centrality in the old paradigm. Competition still remains a fact of modern society, but its role and significance has changed; it is more complex than the old paradigm allows. Competition appears now to be grounded in deeper patterns of cooperation. And these deeper patterns may be the natural order that has been suppressed by the modern design of the economy.[2]

Peter Kropotkin first began to see this as a fact when he studied the life of nature under the influence of Darwin's *Origin of Species* (1859). Kropotkin states that he eagerly looked for "that bitter struggle for the means of existence, *among animals belonging to the same species,* which was considered by most Darwinists (though not always by Darwin himself) as the dominant characteristic of struggle for life, and the main factor of evolution." What Kropotkin saw with his own eyes in the field caused him to develop grave doubts concerning Darwinian theory. He suggested on the contrary that the concepts of cooperation and mutual aid were more fundamental to explain the natural order.[3]

Competition today is generally seen as a necessary reality, while cooperation is often seen as a hidden ideal. This tells us something important about a planning model. A planning model takes seriously the interplay between the real and the ideal. It is not so important in planning to postulate what is the essential nature of the social economy in metaphysical terms as it is to take seriously what people see as the real and the ideal in their lives. Both the real and the ideal determine our behavior. They both must be counted important in social planning.

We have seen that economic imperialism, for example, is real as a social fact. It is a fact that can be observed existing not only in international relations but also within a nation. It is a form of dominance that exists interstitially among provinces, states, municipalities, and neighborhoods as well as between big nations and their satellite countries. Imperialism is a reality we can observe within economic organization.

The command organization of business in the United States has the attributes of imperial control over sectors of the population and even at times over whole localities. It differs from socialist state imperialism in many respects, but it exists nonetheless in the business society. It finds root in the power to hire and fire large numbers of employees, the authority of an absentee owner to relocate a factory from one community to the next, the capacity of a corporation president to finance politicians and political parties, and the privilege of monopoly or oligopoly in the marketplace. We can say realistically that the capitalist economy is a system of imperial enterprise as much as we can say idealistically that it is a system of free enterprise.[4]

It is this interplay between the real and the ideal that becomes the focal point of good planning. Planning must account for both "facts" in guiding the social development of the economy. The practical question is whether a transition can be made from a system of command bureaucracies to a system of relatively nonbureaucratic organizations where authority is more widely and efficiently distributed in the social organization of the economy.

Social planning in this paradigm is a process that implies decentralized economic development. It means creating incentives for community enterprise, independent enterprise, and economic federations with a public purpose. It means creating a new technology to help decentralize work systems. It means forming common purposes at the national level to engage in both social and economic development. In the final analysis it seeks to combine the ends with the means—to increase the capacity of people to govern their own lives at every level of society.

THE PROBLEM: THE STATE IN A FISCAL AND MANAGEMENT CRISIS

James O'Connor has set forth a new thesis in the Marxian tradition that the capitalist state is in a fiscal crisis. He claims that the modern state must try to fulfill two mutually contradictory functions he calls *accumulation* and *legitimation*. The state must maintain and "legitimate" a business system that "accumulates" profits and thus provides the sources of revenue for state expenditures. State expenditures are required to meet social needs that develop in a special way within the business society. The state in effect takes taxable profits from corporations to invest in the social sector to finance programs the business sector does not finance. The government must finance urban renewal, highway construction, higher education, welfare, pollution prevention, etc. These state expenditures then do two things simultaneously. They legitimate the business system, while at the same time they subsidize it to keep it going. The state and big business then support each other and together expand their institutional power in society. We have, then, the continued growth of a corporate state.

The hitch is that a "fiscal crisis" develops in this growth process. The crisis occurs in the gap that develops between state expenditures and state revenues. State expenditures increase more rapidly than state revenues; the federal debt continues to grow, burdening the state with its own legitimacy as an institution. Special interests continue to make claims on the government budget for increasing social (noneconomic) expenditures. The expenditures thus build bureaucracies based on welfare and warfare. The "welfare state" expands because a growing populace of the unemployed require financial support to live. The "warfare state" expands because surplus capital cannot continue to be created and disposed of at home; corporations invest overseas where labor is cheaper and profits are greater. These investments must then be protected by foreign aid and military bases overseas. In other words, welfare expenditures expand while keeping people poor; at the same time, transnational corporations, foreign aid, and military bases expand while inhibiting authentic social development both at home and overseas. According to O'Connor, in the long run it is a losing battle for the capitalist state.[5]

Put another way, social problems are created by the business system faster than the state can pay for them. The problems are legion, but the environmental field can serve as one example of what happens. Here we see agribusiness using chemicals harmful to crops in its pursuit of profits. This pursuit in turn requires state health departments to spend money to correct or monitor the problem. At the same time we see big corporations making nonbiogradable goods like plastic containers to reduce their production costs. This pursuit in turn requires the taxpayer and municipalities to pay the costs of burning or burying the used containers. Then the corporations, which make a profit by causing pollution, are subsidized by the state to make more profits solving the problems they originally created. (About two dozen pollution-control companies are subsidiaries or divisions of big corporations including Dow Chemical Co., Monsanto Chemical, W. R. Grace, and Du Pont.) California provides a special five-year tax write-off, and Connecticut gives a 5 percent tax credit for antipollution efforts.[6] Then add the federal tax loopholes for the biggest corporations that make it impossible to obtain government revenues needed to pay for the corporate subsidies or the state rehabilitation that should have been treated directly by the corporation in the first place. Each case may be disputed on its own merits, but adding them all up spells "fiscal crisis" for James O'Connor.[7]

One way to treat the fiscal and management problems of a business society is to increase state controls. By increasing state controls it is believed that social accountability can be introduced directly into the organization of the economy. Social responsibility can be enforced more immediately when it is seen to be lacking in the corporate system. The system will then pay the social costs directly and the fiscal crisis will be resolved.

This type of planning has been growing steadily in Western European nations, and many political economists have said that this is the only alternative for the United States. We must therefore give it our attention to obtain a sense of what it means as a mode of top-down planning. Although the total context of planning in Western Europe is, of course, much more complex than can be suggested in a brief sketch, it is nevertheless important to record how certain aspects of state planning differ from social planning.

THE EUROPEAN SOLUTION: COORDINATION OF PLANNING AT THE TOP

Roy Bennett argues that the solution to the problems of the business economy is to be found in a greater degree of state planning in conjunction with business leaders. This proposal in effect advances a trend that has been in the making for some time in all capitalist countries. The trend toward state planning began most significantly during the Great Depression. It then continued to develop most markedly in European countries after World War II.[8] Let us look briefly at these trends.

France

After World War II, the French government nationalized a large part of the "economic infrastructure" of the nation. In the following decades it continued in this direction so that today the public sector now includes railroads, coal, power, oil, airlines, the three largest banks, the largest insurance companies, the largest automobile company (Renault), and half the aircraft industry. About 25 percent of industry and nearly all public services are publicly owned. The economic system is managed by the Commissariat au Plan, an organization of about 300 specialists in commissions with a staff of around 3000. The plan involves computing the "basic input-output" of 28 broad sectors of the economy. The planners engage in detailed negotiations with about 20 percent of the French firms, which produce 80 percent of the nation's output. In other words, the central planners deal with a relatively small number of big public and private firms that make the key decisions. It is assumed that their decisions will largely shape the conditions of the rest of the economy.

The plan is formally intended to be "indicative" rather than "imperative." The planning agreements do not carry the force of contract law. But at the same time the plan exerts a great leverage over the big enterprises. The enterprises are backed by government credit supports, the availability of long- and short-term capital, and public opinion.

Italy

Italy has the highest level of public ownership of any European nation. It approaches 40 percent—some say over 50 percent, depending upon what proportion of government stock in private firms defines them as "public." Public enterprise includes steel, engineering, fuel, power, transport, communications, insurance, and banking.

Italy is unique in having two "public conglomerates" that hold enterprises operating in different industries. One conglomerate, The Institute for Industrial Reconstruction (IRI), is a holding company of enterprises in iron and steel, engineering, shipbuilding, telecommunication, airlines, motorways, radio, and television. The other public conglomerate owns all petroleum refining and gas production down to the gas pumps on IRI motorways. These conglomerates operate at a profit and expand into new fields, sometimes competing with private enterprise. That conglomerate organization enterprises operate in different industries is significant to note here because it is also the direction of private corporate development in the United States. It contrasts with corporate organization in socialist nations, which is administered along the lines of a single industry. The Communist Party in Italy, however, has accepted the principle of mixed industries under one corporate administration.

The direction of development for private enterprises in Italy is similar to that in France in many respects. Large enterprises are becoming integrated into the public system through "program contracts," with final oversight and guidance from the central government.

Germany

Germany is not so highly centralized in state planning enterprises, but the economy is nevertheless highly coordinated through its unions and industrial federations. The Federation of German Labor Unions in Dusseldorf, for example, has 7.4 million members and 16 industrywide unions. They own banks, insurance companies, and the largest real-estate concern in the nation. By law they hold half the seats on the boards of directors of the largest industries.

Industrial and banking management is no less organized at the national level. The 39 existing West German Industrial Associations were taken over intact from the Nazi era. The associations are centralized by the Federation of German Industry, which is built on Hitler's model of the 1930s and was referred to at that time as "guided private enterprise." The three top banks virtually control German banking, which includes investment departments handling all the private firms' share dealing. People who want to buy or to sell stock must go to a bank, because only bank officials may trade on the floor of the stock exchange. German management and labor are therefore strongly organized side by side in centralized federations. Together they help determine the direction in which the economy will develop.

Clearly the meaning of this type of development in the political economy of nations must be carefully examined.

STATE CORPORATISM AND ITS MEANING:
THE SEARCH FOR AN ALTERNATIVE

Western Europe is in a transition from state capitalism to state socialism. A new sense of unity has been developing among top corporate executives and top union leaders. They have become increasingly aware of the importance of making connections with the purposes of the larger society. Business leaders and union leaders have begun to collaborate in promoting economic development.

They have begun to form common standards for development and have taken steps to organize federations in the national interest.

At the same time, the organization of corporate enterprise is increasingly controlled from the top. The corporate state today is not too far removed from the conditions that led it to Nazism and Fascism. Another major fiscal crisis like the Great Depression or another World War could quickly turn these states into Behemoths. And they could call themselves capitalist or socialist.

Let us look further at these centralizing trends in order to know better what to avoid in social planning.

Social Planning versus State Planning

State planning in Italy illustrates many of the problems in the socialist transition. It has not led to economic development in the more impoverished regions of the nation. It has led more clearly to the absorption of private firms into the state. In this situation there appears at the moment to be no alternative.

The movement toward nationalization of enterprise began slowly and with great resistance in Italy. Two decades ago, Pignone, a medium-sized engineering firm near bankruptcy, was rescued by the publicly owned Ente Nazionale Idrocarburi (ENI). There was endless debate about it in the newspapers and the parliament. A few years later, the absorption of a large textile concern (Lanerossi) by the same ENI passed almost without comment. Other, similar moves toward state control followed. Private corporations came under the aegis of the state with similar ease in mining, shipbuilding, engineering, and food. By 1973 there was general agreement among leaders in the government, trade unions, and private industry that the public sector should take control of the mounting number of near-bankrupt firms that otherwise would fail and hurt the economy. This process of nationalization of course centralizes authority in the state.[9]

Italian leaders have differed strongly on this direction of economic development. Conservative leaders have claimed that the slow movement toward state socialism has produced a malaise, a paralysis of planning, a seeking of safe ground for executives where the risk and the venture of independent enterprise no longer exists. Communist leaders, on the other hand, have claimed that it is a stalemate of power between the Christian Democrats and themselves. They say that when the Communist Party gains full control, the situation should change.[10]

The question is, of course, how will it change? The policy of the Ministry of Industry in the meantime continues to provide state subsidies to the private sector without social planning. It continues to support command systems without regard to processes of social development from the grass roots level of the community.

The Italian city of Bologna illustrates a measure of development at the local level in the face of central government controls. The Communist Party in

Bologna won about 51 percent of the vote in the last elections and has won over half the 60 city council seats. The local government permits private enterprise and intervenes in only limited ways to protect the workers. The workers have displayed an independence by setting up factory councils in some cases apart from the old union structures. They have begun to grapple with problems of company and workplace democracy. The communist and the non-communist unions are a basic part of the local system, though they are reportedly not dominated by the local government.

The relation of the city to the central state in this case illustrates the problems of internal imperialism that are facing the Communist Party in Italy as much as it did for the Communist Party in the Soviet Union. The Soviet Union has sought to maintain strong central controls over its cities and border countries, such as Poland and Yugoslavia. The problem of internal imperialism faces all nations, but it is accented under state socialism.

We may therefore see a problem of state imperialism developing for a city like Bologna. The social services, housing, education, and transportation section of Bologna are said to be as good as or better than anywhere else in Italy. But the city itself is still strongly dominated by the central government, as noted by Andrew Kopkind:[11]

The centralization of power under the Italian Constitution keeps a loose noose around any city's neck, and the danger of strangulation is real and present in red Bologna. All tax revenue, including property taxes (and excepting pet licenses and other pittances) are collected by the central government—when they are collected. Not more than 30 percent of the estimated possible taxes are paid; wage earners have their taxes deducted from their paychecks, but many businessmen, professionals and property owners skip off free. Roman bureaucrats approve each city's budget line by line and apportion niggardly shares back to the local administrations. Those items in Bologna's budget that are ideologically or politically at odds with the ruling Christian Democrats' interests are the first to be cut.

Here we see the problems of development facing the Communist Party. State control over localities could in some ways become more total and severe than under the capitalist system, depending upon the purpose and method of planning. *The purpose of social planning is to enhance the autonomy of the locality and not to dominate it.* The method involves creating national incentives for community development, experimental programs, and community self-studies, as we shall see.

Bottom-Up Planning versus Top-Down Planning

The top-down model of state planning in which controls remain at the top has been attractive to many countries. In these countries we see what not to do as well as good reasons for moving in the opposite direction. But top-down planning may also occur outside the state.

In England during the 1960s, for example, industrial representation was vested in three organizations—the Federation of British Industries (FBI), the British Employers' Confederation, and the National Association of British Manufacturers. In 1965 these separate federations combined to form the Confederation of British Industries (CBI) so that industry could speak as one voice in the "power context" of organized trade unions and the government. The model of indicative planning in France was an important reason for organizing the industrial confederation.

I noted earlier that the model of a "confederation" is intended to be a decentralized structure of authority for member units. But it can be a centralizing force when organized by big business corporations who are organized in command bureaucracies. The members of CBI were centralized federations of businesses. The CBI was organized simply to advance national interests and had no interest in attending to internal development. So it took the initiative to declare a twelve-month limitation on prices in 1971 to help curb the rising rate of inflation. But it could take no leadership toward democratic development within its ranks. In fact, it discouraged small economic enterprise. (The Smaller Businesses Association was formed in 1968 in reaction to CBI policies.) It could not curb the movement toward business mergers and the rise of conglomerates in England. As the decade progressed, the number of corporate mergers increased. In 1961 in manufacturing, for example, the largest 28 companies held 39 percent of the net assets and by 1968 their holdings had increased to 51 percent.

Such cases tell us what not to do. Now let us examine what can be done in social planning.

THE PLANNING GOAL:
SELF-GOVERNANCE THROUGH SOCIAL GOVERNANCE
OF FREE ENTERPRISE

The concept of self-governance refers to the way people in organizations of the economy manage their own affairs. All organizations are by some measure self-governing, and by some measure they value self-direction in their management. Self-governance is then an important focus of social planning. It can be seen as a goal that is achieved by steps at different levels of the economy.

Achieving optimum levels of self-governance means planning changes in the democratic organization of the workplace, the firm, and the federation. Planning is best begun in the workplace and then extended as an educational process throughout the rest of the enterprise. It becomes a major mode of change that can increase individual and social resources. In the democratically managed firm, for example, everyone participates to some degree in determining the basic directions and policy of the company. But the changes to be made in this direction are not simple. Many factors are involved in the single enterprise, including the size, the expertise required in its technology, the existing system of ownership, the pattern of voting, the financial stability, and the attitudes of the employees. In the face of such complexity, the changes must be experimental and determined as completely as possible by the members of the firm themselves.[12]

The next step in planning occurs at the level of the federation. The issues here involve the manner and degree to which the resources of the smallest units of a federation are enhanced. The question is how federations may decentralize authority in the context of local communities. The answer involves planning, which can occur only with a change in the concept of the state and its function in economic affairs.

The Role of the State: Creating the Conditions for Self-Governance

The way out of the growing dilemma of top-down state bureaucracy requires seeing the state in a new role. The new role of the state is to set the conditions whereby it can eventually remove itself from control over the economy. The purpose of planning is to create an organizational environment that makes it unnecessary to supervise, regulate, monitor, or interfere in any way with the normal processes of economic and social development.

The role of the state in this sense is similar to that of the parent who creates the right environment for offspring to develop their own independence. The parent counsels, guides, and even intervenes at times so that the offspring may learn its limits. But the good parent seeks to instill confidence, authority, and sensitivity in the life of the child so that it can live independently and responsibly with others in the community. The state could do no better for private enterprise and federations, which must function justly in the community.

The state therefore participates in social planning in limited ways. Here we note only a few examples that require extensive socioeconomic research.

The Method: National Studies and Experimental Programs

To create the conditions within which business functions responsibly in the society while tending to its own interests requires a new perspective of the economy as a system of private enterprises with public purposes. This perspective of the economy can be created only through a series of steps that include the initiation of national studies sponsored by the U. S. Congress. Let us look at what would happen in this process.

Study Commissions are formed by the Congress at the national level with the purpose of enhancing the powers of self-regulation in the economy. The commissions would be given authority, first, to initiate professional studies of different sectors of the economy and, second, to provide financial incentives to experiment with social planning and development.

The commissions would study the basis for developing the following: *autonomous enterprises with systems of social and public accountability; a strong socio-economic base for small enterprises in the secondary market; local authority in subsidiaries of nationwide chains of business to help increase their accountability and effectiveness; and new approaches to community development to increase local autonomy.* Let us now look at these separate processes in the spirit of a Study Commission.

Developing Autonomous Enterprises with Social and Public Accountability

A Study Commission designed to examine the "public economy" begins by reviewing the organization of corporations in different economic sectors such as fuel, transportation, and food. It concludes by recommending incentive systems to guide the development of autonomous enterprise in these different sectors.

The commission looks first at the relationship between three different types of corporate organization: command systems and democratic systems of management; private and public corporations; profit and nonprofit corporations. Data about these types of corporate organization is important because its analysis makes possible enabling legislation to balance the advantages and disadvantages of these different forms of autonomous enterprise. Planning at this point seeks the successful transition between the real and the ideal.

The Transition from Command Systems to Democratic Systems of Management. Here the commission reviews attempts at the democratic self-governance of companies. It would, for example, look at the social experiments of such companies as R. G. Barry Corporation, Imperial Chemical Industries, General Electric, Cummings Engine, Xerox Corporation, Polaroid Corporation, Donnelly Mirrors, Inc., and many others.[13]

Donnelly Mirrors, for example, employs more than 400 people in the manufacture of rear-view and day-night mirrors for automobiles. It supplies 70 percent of the world market and produces glass components for other industries. In 1952 the firm instituted its own version of the Scanlon Plan, which included plantwide sharing of productivity gains and involved employees in problem-solving. Then in 1967 the company hired a director of personnel and organizational development who acted as an "internal change agent" for the next four years. In this period, major organizational changes included the creation of autonomous work teams, the elimination of time clocks, the elimination of the wage system, the introduction of the salary system for all employees, and a new level of plantwide participation of employees in decision-making. The organizational changes introduced at Donnelly are the kind that many different companies could accept and implement.

The organizational changes at the Topeka plant of General Foods, however, are still more advanced, and they present a challenge to other plants. Here the formal plant hierarchy was virtually eliminated. Equal and autonomous work teams were organized to rotate jobs throughout the plant. The transformation of the Topeka plant significantly increased the equity and the autonomy of all the workers. At the same time their productivity and work efficiency increased. The next problem for them to surmount is diffusing the idea to other plants. General Foods has 48 plants and warehouses in the United States and Canada and many more in the rest of the world. All plants are different and all have different types of management.[14]

These are steps in social planning taken independently by corporations to improve their systems of management, but such steps can also be encouraged at the national level. The Scandinavian countries have shown one way to do this.

In Norway a Joint Committee for Research and Development for Industrial Democracy was established to examine the problems of traditional management. The committee offered its services to any companies that wanted to treat problems such as monotony in assembly-line work and high turnover rates. When it found a company willing to participate in experimental changes, the committee commissioned a detailed study of the production process and wage scales. Next, action committees were formed, composed equally of company and worker representatives. These committees then engaged in a program of self-study and developed strategies to promote direct worker participation in job design, job enlargement, and autonomous work groups.

In 1968 the Swedish government appointed a Delegation for Industrial Democracy. Its principal charge was to "take the initiative and cooperate to carry out practical experiments in increased democracy in a number of nationalized enterprises" in conjunction with company management and the relevant trade unions. The purpose was to put experts at the disposal of enterprises that wished to try new forms of organization.

In the spring of 1969 the delegation carried out an experiment at the Swedish Tobacco Company. The company agreed to the idea, and its pipe tobacco factory in Arvika was chosen as the site. A preliminary study made at the factory found that the employees and the management were willing to participate. The result of the experiment showed that:

It had proved possible to introduce a number of democratic joint councils, which has meant that the individual worker has the chance to exercise greater influence in the administration of the division and over his own work—under otherwise mostly unchanged technological conditions. It is also evident that the introduction of the councils has resulted in decentralization.[15]

Social planning has thus begun effectively under government auspices as well as independently in private industry in this field. Furthermore, it has also begun to democratize and to decentralize authority in the enterprise system without increasing state ownership. But it is also important for us to see the wider implications of this process of social planning for autonomous enterprises.

The Transition from Private to Public Enterprises Outside the State. I noted earlier how a system of self-interested private enterprises actually results in a system of state-regulated enterprises. A system of state corporations emerges eventually to replace private systems that fail to exercise social responsibilities. The alternative to this development of state corporations, however, is the development of a new kind of public enterprise outside the state. This means, paradoxically, planning for the appearance of public enterprises within the private system.

Toward this end, a Study Commission must examine carefully the difference between the private corporation and the public corporation. The difference is not determined simply by state ownership. A private corporation does not become public merely by shifting its control to the state.

One difference between private and public corporations is said to be the degree to which the general populace has access to corporate records. But if public access to records were the key criterion here, some state-owned corporations would be found more protective and bureaucratically removed from people than some private firms. A private corner grocery store in a friendly neighborhood may be more "public" in this respect than a state-owned corporation.

A Study Commission can begin to develop criteria for what constitutes a public corporation by examining specific cases that involve such factors as the charter of the corporation, the duties of its top officers, its size, the extent of its market, its rules of conduct in administration, its formal purpose, and the attitude of its employees.

The answers to the following questions direct attention to the attributes of a public corporation. To what extent:

1. Is the corporation democratically managed by its members?
2. Does the corporation's constituency, including customers and subsidiaries, have an influence in determining its policies?
3. Are the corporation's accounts open to general inspection?
4. Do the corporation's products or services express the needs of the community in which it operates?
5. Does the corporation reflect the basic values of the society?

Such questions can become more specific, and the answers can take the form of public policy. The purpose of the Study Commission is to initiate such guidelines for the formation of public corporations. When these guidelines become clear, it is possible to introduce them into congressional debate and directly into formal legislation.

The first step in legislation is the provision of certain tax benefits for those private corporations that meet the test of a "public corporation." The second step is to introduce public requirements for the operation of very large corporations. If federal charters are extended to these large corporations, it means that they would operate in the public interest according to specific guidelines described in Chapters Three and Four.

An example of a tax benefit can be found in the investment reserve system established in Sweden to treat the problems of recession and unemployment. The investment reserve is a device designed to help smooth out economic fluctuations by encouraging private corporate savings in periods of unemployment. Companies are encouraged to set aside part of their pretax profits in a reserve. When there is a downturn in the business cycle, the government opens applications for investment of the reserve. The company decides how much, if any, of its investment reserve to use. The government indicates areas and industries where the rate of employment is low. The company then makes the investment and gains special tax privileges.

Martin Schnitzer, Professor of Business at Virginia Polytechnic Institute, states that the Swedish Investment Reserve has had a significant effect in creating employment in the construction industry where investments have been directed. He also claims that the Investment Reserve is more responsive and flexible than legislation-mandated spending. A powerful impact can be secured at short notice. The time lag between the government announcement of the release of funds and actual company investment is small compared with more general monetary policies.[16]

Here we can see how business investment could be directed to promote special jobs for welfare recipients. It can also help restore the health of cities and build up depressed regions of the American economy. This task then becomes one of the purposes of the public corporation.

The Transition from Profit to Nonprofit Corporations. Profit and nonprofit corporations are beginning to look alike in many ways. This is frustrating for corporate lawyers who must keep the distinction separate, but it is instructive for a Study Commission that must examine the social transition.

The nonprofit corporation has a public character of the kind often intended by legislators in nationalizing private corporations. The nonprofit corporation, for example, cannot give money to political parties or to politicians; its charter sets limits on the extent of profit-making, and as a rule these profits must be spent for its social purposes.

We can therefore learn from the nonprofits about how to create public charters for profit corporations that direct their revenues to social purposes. Their social purposes are not to contribute to the churches and the universities. Their social purposes are rather to *improve the quality of work life for their employees, maintain employment during periods of economic slowdown or depression, create profitable jobs in poverty areas, organize job training programs for prospective young employees, and maintain respectable positions for the "unemployables"* including the handicapped, the bedridden, the delinquent, and the ex-convict. The public corporation then stays in the work it knows best and fulfills its social purposes.

At the same time, the nonprofit corporation can learn how to make profits. Many nonprofit corporations have trouble surviving without a productive base. Such nonprofit corporations as hospitals, theaters, churches, universities, orchestras, schools, and service groups are often dependent upon the good will of the profit sector or of the state. The church, for example, must invest in business corporations in order to survive. The university depends heavily upon gifts from the business sector. Yet this dependency can severely interfere with the autonomy of these institutions.

The question at stake is whether these institutions can develop their own economic base independent of the profit sector. The integrity of the church has in some cases been called into question by its corporate investments. The autonomy of the private university has been challenged by the necessity for businessmen to sit on it board of directors. But if these organizations were given incentives to develop their own productive base, then their purposes could be fulfilled, independent of the interests of the profit sector.

In the state socialist society, the church and the university fall directly under the authority of the government. Yet the values inherent in both institutions go beyond the state. Such types of organizations therefore face a period of crisis in the modern transition. The purpose of a Study Commission is to help establish new economic foundations for the nonprofit sector independent of the state.

Cultivating a Socioeconomic Foundation for Small Business in the Secondary Market

Institutional economists have shown how there are two types of business markets, which operate with different controls and privileges. There is a primary market in which big corporations operate in a chain of command from key metropolitan centers and a secondary market where millions of smaller firms operate in neighborhoods, suburbs, towns, and rural villages. The organization of the two markets contrast significantly.[17]

The *primary market area* of the big corporations is relatively protected and financially secure. The selling of corporate goods in this area is largely "administered" by monopoly or oligopoly. Here the labor market is rewarded with a fair measure of job stability. Labor has relatively high wages, reasonable opportunities for job advancement, and fair retirement and pension benefits.

The *secondary market area* of the small enterprises, on the other hand, is unprotected and financially insecure. A greater competition exists for goods, with a greater fluctuation in prices. The labor market is less stable, offers low wages, and workers are more subject to layoffs without union protection. Labor is more competitive and less productive. Working conditions are less bureaucratic and more personalized, although perhaps no less subject to dominance from employers and bosses.[18]

The Study Commission can examine the social and economic intersects within and between these two types of markets, with an eye to the development of small enterprises in the context of localities. These "intersects" consist of a variety of authority relationships between the big corporations and small businesses that keep the locality in a position of subservience to the big cities and the larger national economy. Here I mention only three types of economic intersects, which differ in the degree of empowerment created in the secondary market. These are the subsidiary, the franchise, and the local independent business.

Each successive type of business, as a rule, represents an increase in self-governance. The local independent business usually has more autonomy than the franchise or the subsidiary, although individual cases can be exceptions to the rule.

The Subsidiary. The corporation subsidiary is the least autonomous form of business operating at the local level. It functions as part of a command system of authority stemming from the top offices of the big corporation in the primary market area. This means that the subsidiary retail outlet or factory intersecting with the locality can be created or destroyed by the command of top executives who must make decisions primarily in the interest of the larger corporation. Various degrees of autonomy can be observed in subsidiary systems, since local managers are given different options in running the subsidiary, but formally the ultimate authority rests above, and generally outside, the locality.[19] It is, therefore, often less complicated and shows less variety than the franchise.

The Franchise. Franchising takes one step further toward autonomy at the local level. The franchise is a growing form of business, which may also reflect a growing interest in maintaining independence in enterprise.

In 1972 the Department of Commerce showed approximately 357,000 franchises were operating in the United States. By 1974 franchises in the retail sector accounted for approximately one-third of all retail sales. It is therefore an important intersect to study in the market economy.

The franchise encourages many types of autonomy beyond the subsidiary but always according to contractual arrangements. These arrangements generally provide for consultation and managerial training to ensure that the local business has the best chance of success. A major company, for example, may provide the franchisee with the following:

(1) location analysis and counsel; (2) store development aid, including lease negotiation; (3) store design and equipment purchasing; (4) initial employee and management training, and continuing management counseling; (5) advertising and merchandising counsel and assistance; (6) standardized procedures and operations; (7) centralized purchasing with consequent savings; and (8) financial assistance in the establishment of the business.[20]

There are many reasons why franchisors seek to reduce the degree of dependence of the franchisee, including the fact that it saves money, by reducing the costs of consultation and supervision. Local authority is therefore often encouraged on such matters as hiring, firing, record keeping, and merchandise ordering.

But the actual process is much more complicated and can also result in unnecessary patterns of dependency. Franchisors may create a high degree of dependency because of a complicated technical system or because of a lack of personal trust in the local entrepreneur. Here the franchise system needs study to determine the kind of relationships that lead toward increasing self-governance.

The process of achieving a high level of autonomy has both legal and sociological dimensions. The legal dimension involves the degree to which the franchisor may control or obligate franchisees by contract before they lose their ability to act on the basis of their own business judgment. The sociological dimension involves many other factors affecting the independence of the enterprise outside of the legal contract.[21]

Franchising is a social system of "sponsorship" in which one organization uses the facilities of another organization to reach a "target population." This same type of system develops in the nonprofit corporation. In the case of the Boy Scouts, for example, church and school organizations volunteer to sponsor local chapters under guidelines set by the central Scout organization. This permits the national organization to function effectively on the local level without a command system. It can offer a considerable degree of autonomy to a local chapter or corporation. It is in effect a replacement of the command system for achieving "direct penetration" into an area. It avoids bureaucratic expansion. In the case of a big corporation like General Motors or the Ford Motor Company, the system of franchised dealerships allows the central offices to reach a broad market through relatively nonbureaucratic channels. At the same time, it can be seen as a method of debureaucratization that conserves both capital and labor.

A Study Commission would find that franchise arrangements vary greatly in their capacity to draw forth local autonomy and responsibility in enterprise. McDonald's, a major hamburger chain, for example, is fairly centralized in its techniques while at the same time it remains more decentralized than the subsidiary system. Theodore Levitt describes how McDonald's sales rose from $51 million in 1964 to $724 million in 1974. Its "thundering success," he says, is based on many factors, but among them is the fact that "it is financed by independent local entrepreneurs who bring to their operations a quality of commitment and energy not commonly found among hired workers."[22]

Franchises vary in the amount of skills and capital equity required to commence the local enterprise. Ben Franklin Stores, for example, is a retail variety business that provides merchandise and retailing assistance to more than 2000 stores in 50 states. It generally requires $50,000 equity capital to begin operations. Kampgrounds of America, Inc., on the other hand, has different requirements and purposes. It maintains 493 sites across the country and requires about $25,000 equity to begin the business. Edie Adams Cut & Curl has 220 franchises in 33 states and offers salon training to beginners. It requires $15,000 equity but will supply the financing to "qualified applicants." And so it goes with a great number of other enterprises, including auto repair shops, accounting firms, income tax preparation agencies, "newcomer" services, furniture distributors, shoe distributors, and food stores.

In the absence of national studies, we can only guess at how human resources are developed in this system. In contrast with the subsidiary system, we would conjecture that a greater measure of self-reliance and self-determination is cultivated through the franchise contract. A greater degree of personal authority must enter into decision-making. A broader range of decisions must be involved here—including capital investments, hiring, firing, marketing, pricing, accounting, and advertising. These types of decisions must require a greater imagination and must challenge more intellectual resources.

If we hold constant the size of the subsidiary and the franchise, it should follow that a greater degree of knowledge is required to run the franchise effectively. It also would follow that the system should encourage a greater degree of personal independence. We know that some franchisees build their own businesses around their licensed establishment. National studies may determine more conclusively that these inferences are correct. And if it is true that more human resources are developed through the franchise than through the subsidiary, the franchising system then calls for social planning. It calls for incentives and guidelines for economic development based on the findings of those studies.

The Independent Enterprise. Chandler Levy is a locally owned hardware store in Newton Centre, Massachusetts. It is owned and managed by people who live in that community. Mrs. Levy handles the giftware department, and Mr. Levy oversees the general operation of the store. Its local autonomy is determined in part by the variety of choices the owners have in purchasing their goods for retail sale. In this case they buy from a large number of jobbers and manufacturers. They buy about 15 percent of their goods from local jobbers, 45 percent direct from manufacturers, and 40 percent from a national "dealer-owned wholesale distributor" by the name of Cotters. Cotters was organized nationally to help local stores compete against the big chains. Cotters has 6000 members who have voting shares and the privilege of its buying power. This allows local independent stores some leverage against chain stores like Lechmere's, Medi Mart, Caldor, and others. Local stores then buy on a cost plus basis and receive dividends on the profits at the end of the year.[23] With this power and the variety of choice in purchasing, along with its good volume of consumer trade, Chandler Levy maintains a relatively high degree of autonomy.

Other retail stores have not been so lucky as Chandler Levy. Many retail stores in Newton Centre have been wiped out by the big chain with subsidiary outlets. Local stores in less well-to-do communities suffer still more from the power of the big chains and control by the primary market. For example, the local stores in commercial sections of Roxbury, a poverty area of Boston, are most vulnerable to corporate decisions made in the primary market area. Banks will not loan money to them because the risk is too high. Insurance companies will not offer protection because it would not be profitable. Roxbury stores cannot afford expensive lawyers to fight their battles. Furthermore, state agencies do not respond as quickly to an injustice in Roxbury as they do in the more well-to-do communities. When a buyer refuses to sell an item to Chandler Levy that it sells to other stores, Mr. Levy can threaten to call the attorney general on "restraint of trade," and the buyer will most likely sell him the goods. The same measure of power does not exist in a poverty area.[24]

What can we conclude here? The next step toward the development of local autonomy appears in the independent retail store or factory owned by people in the community. But the actual situation can be complicated in different cases. The locally owned enterprise could be highly controlled by outside markets. Its autonomy might not measure much higher than that of a subsidiary or a franchise. Its autonomy is determined finally by its intersect with the primary market of big corporations. It is thus only in the overall scale of development that the independent local enterprise expresses a high degree of self-governance relative to the subsidiary and the franchise.

What can be done to increase the powers of self-governance among small businesses operating at the level of the community?

Decentralizing Nationwide Business to Increase Efficiency,
Accountability, and Human Resources

The 500 largest American corporations constitute only .002 percent of all businesses in the United States. Yet they produce over three-fourths of all American goods and services and employ a similar percentage of the work force. It appears, therefore, that business efficiency may be a factor of size. The bigger the corporation, the greater the efficiency and productivity. Many institutional economists, however, have argued that such a concentration of business is not efficient. Furthermore, it can also be exploitative, and even inhumane.

Economists have shown that corporations have become large not by increasing the size of their local establishments but rather by buying out the existing firms and bringing them under a central administration.[25] Barry Stein, for example, has shown that local establishments remain relatively small under the new management. It appears to him as though smallness is where the efficiency levels are best. Stein notes that the average employment of establishments in the United States is only 52.5 persons. He suggests that the efficiency of these plants is not changed simply by their incorporation into a big conglomerate. Stein further finds that even the biggest manufacturing firms generally consist of, relatively small local plants. The largest manufacturing companies employ on the average only 203 people per plant.[26]

Many institutional economists extend the argument for limiting the size of business by presenting evidence that the smaller plants and businesses are the more innovative and humanly sensitive to their environment. The major innovations in technology in the primary market appear in the smaller, more peripheral firms.[27] The small firms show more sensitivity to social change because they can perceive more accurately and respond faster. (Stein compares them to small ships, which can maneuver more easily than large ones.) Small firms can "track" consumer needs much better than large ones. They do not have the bureaucratic costs that encumber the conglomerate. Finally, it is said that the bigger businesses show the character of impersonal dominance and insensitivity to workers. As size increases, so too does worker dissatisfaction, strikes, physical injury, sabotage, and mental illness. Important human factors become lost in the large corporate bureaucracy.[28]

In sum, these economists argue that business efficiency is not increased simply by building a bigger organization. Most significantly, they also argue that a large portion of the multiunit manufacturing, wholesale, and retail firms could be converted into independent operations without a loss of effectiveness. Indeed, they argue that it could result in a considerable gain for everyone.

The studies of institutional economists mentioned earlier appear at first to be in conflict with these findings. The secondary market of small business on the first count shows many signs of weakness and instability relative to the primary market of big corporations. These other studies, however, show their strengths. Institutional economists generally agree that the reduction of dominance and exploitation by big corporations would only lead toward increasing the strength of business in the secondary market. The evidence is not all in, but here is where the Study Commission begins its task. It can develop more substantial evidence on these issues and then encourage experimental programs to test their conclusions.

Stated another way, the function of the Study Commission in this case is to examine the socioeconomic ties between the markets to find ways for small enterprise to gain strength in the locality. In the process, experimental methods can be devised to study the "big tradeoff" between the efficiency of enterprise and the value of self-governance.[29]

At this point we learn a great deal from the nonprofit corporations. Nonprofit corporations like the American Medical Association, the U. S. Chamber of Commerce, the Congregational Church, and the Lions Club have highly autonomous systems of local membership. The big nationwide nonprofit corporations as a rule are organized on a democratic basis. Their local corporate members, such as the neighborhood Legion Auxiliary, the town Kiwanis Club, and the village Presbyterian Church, participate in the decision-making of their common corporate bodies at regional and national levels. *The power to make decisions at the top is derived from the democratic authority of its members at the bottom.*

This pattern of corporate organization suggests two things for strengthening the secondary market. First, that big nationwide corporations can develop an effective type of decentralized organization. Second, it suggests that with proper incentives, such as loans and taxes, it is possible to invite big corporations to experiment in this direction. The nationwide industrial corporation and the nationwide department store could begin operating with a structure similar in certain ways to the nationwide professional association.

The shift toward a more decentralized organization for business would not create a great stir if it were decided voluntarily and experimentally with incentives provided for the whole industry. Let us now look briefly at two extreme types of business organization to review the issues involved in decentralization.

Federated Department Stores: A Centralized System of Enterprises. Federated Department Stores, Inc. was once a loose holding company organized simply to serve the common interests of independent merchant families. Then, in 1945, Fred Lazarus, the owner of one firm in the federated company, recommended that it become a full-fledged operating company. Under the leadership of Lazarus, the federated company was then centralized in Cincinnati. Today, Federated operates 262 stores in 18 states, including a multimillion dollar discount operation and a supermarket chain (Ralphs, in California) as well as 15 department stores such as Filene's in New England, Bloomingdale's and Abraham & Straus on the East Coast, I. Magnin and Bullock's on the West Coast, Burdine's in Florida, Foley's and Sanger-Harris in Texas, Shillito's in the Midwest, and Goldsmith's in the Memphis area.

Management decisions in this chain of stores continue to favor centralization through the establishment of a new computer system for inventory and financial controls. Managerial uniformities are being introduced into the various stores. Yet autonomy still remains in some measure. The separate federated store divisions still do their own buying and merchandising and make their own managerial appointments. Headquarters simply makes the key decisions. It names the divisions' top executives, passes on division budgets, and approves any new store openings.[30]

If we evaluate the performance of this enterprise on traditional terms, it appears to be a great success. But if we look at the broader problems of centralized enterprise, we must come to other conclusions. The decision of the government to encourage decentralization through loans and tax incentives rests in part on whether or not thousands of such nationwide firms—many of them far greater in size than Federated Stores—do not in the final analysis add to the costs of central government. The history of big corporations has shown that the government eventually assumes their social costs through consumer agencies, regulatory agencies, welfare, manpower programs, environmental protection, and small business bureaus. At the same time, the government becomes subject to their rising power. It then provides tax loopholes and state subsidies only in turn to face its own fiscal crisis and mounting debt. It cannot raise the revenue essential to pay the social costs.

The decision of corporate executives to decentralize their nationwide enterprises, given the incentives, is not easy. But a decision can be based on whether *the efficiency of the firm would be increased* by decentralization; whether it would *increase diversity in the style and management* of the stores; whether the stores would become *more responsive to their local customers and environments;* whether a *greater degree of responsibility, independence, and imagination* could be forthcoming in the life of lower-level managers in a decentralized federation. These are all important reasons, which must be weighed by members of the firm on the basis of the available evidence. Then the capacity of the executives to maintain confidence in the process is no less important than the capacity of the store to maintain the profit level deemed important to continue developing the enterprise.

The adventure and risk in private enterprise does not disappear in this developmental process. It simply assumes a new dimension.

The government's role in planning is to offer incentives for large chains to decentralize and at the same time to become socially accountable. It can do this in ways that are compatible with business law. The traditional incentives of tax benefits, loans, free legal advice, and so forth must be offered competitively to a whole industry or to all corporations of a certain size. In the case of Federated Stores, the incentives would be available to all of its competitors, including May Department Stores, Allied Stores, Dayton Hudson, and Associated Dry Goods. The concept of competition is then applied in the interest of social accountability and local development. If the decentralized experiments of companies prove to be effective, other companies are bound to follow.

Washington Food Federation: A Decentralized System of Enterprises. A Study Commission also focuses its attention on the seedling enterprises and federations that have no real power. The small business ventures are important to observe because they show the problems of staying alive in the secondary market.

Here we look at a deviant case in business. The social economist is interested in deviant cases for the same reasons as the agricultural scientist. In agriculture, a new hybrid corn may remain unnoticed by the farmer, who sees only the vast harvest of ordinary corn. Ordinary corn provides his income and profits. But the scientist looks carefully at the hybrid for its long-range productive value. It could be the beginning of a new "agricultural revolution." In the long run, it could pay off to the farmer. And so the Study Commission cannot ignore the "hybrid business" that struggles to survive in a centralized competitive market.

In Washington, D. C., a food-buying cooperative called Glut was organized in 1969. It continued to grow, and by the fall of 1971 it was supplying 70 buying clubs. The business continued to grow in spite of the competition from two big supermarkets in the neighborhood. It soon formed another small store called Stone Soup, which did not seem to have much hope of surviving. Then suddenly the two nearby supermarkets, Safeway and Giant Food, experienced a citywide checkers' strike. It was just what Stone Soup needed. Supermarket shoppers moved temporarily to Stone Soup, which then generated $30,000 a week in sales. Its sales leveled off later at about $20,000, but the local cooperative was on its way. Another affiliated cooperative store, Fields of Plenty, then opened down the street. It began selling at about $11,500 a week. By 1974 the three stores were generating enough business income among themselves to support a small trucking collective, a small dry goods warehouse, and two small restaurants. They then formed a Washington Food Federation to support their movement.

The Commission could see in this case how the primary market affects the kinds of goods that local enterprises can sell on their shelves. Del Monte decides what size cans will be made for them regardless of what Stone Soup and its customers want or need. The Washington Food Federation finds it almost impossible to stock "cereals without lots of sugar, refined wheat, or artificial flavoring; canned fruits without heavy surgared syrup; inexpensive cottage cheese without emulsifiers; or vegetables produced without synthetic fertilizers, pesticides, fungicides, and shiny wax."[31] The big corporations determine what goes into the local stores without authority from below.

The Commission could also see how the big supermarkets can influence the fate of the local stores. At the present time, Safeway and Giant Foods have found it too unprofitable to operate in the low-income areas of the inner city and have begun to pull out. But Giant Foods has begun to lobby for city subsidies to lure it back into the city. If the city decides to vote for a food subsidy, it will probably mean that the supermarkets will regain their power and control over the distribution of food in the local environment.

Finally, the Study Commission can observe most importantly how human resources are developed and increased in this mode of democratic planning at the community level. This Federation has been experimenting with new kinds of decentralized decision-making. Here we see a mix of "decision structures," which range from democratic worker-management (Stone Soup and Fields of

Plenty) to worker management combined with a limited amount of consumer influence in decision-making (Glut), to a store with equal worker and consumer representation (Bethesda Avenue), to a wholly consumer-managed store (Arlington Cooperative Organization).[32] Such a variety of decision-making arrangements is rare and important to study in a local federation.

Social planning includes continued observation of such local experiments. But such experiments also require support if they are to survive. At the present time, a legislative bill for a National Co-op Development Bank is pending in the U. S. Congress. This legislation would provide long-term low-interest loans to cooperatives. Its passage, of course, would be one more measure helping to stimulate such experiments in local enterprise.[33]

Encouraging Community Development Programs

The aim of social planning in the last analysis is community development. The real purpose of planning from the top levels of administration is to cultivate a capacity for self-governance in community life.

Planning for community development involves treating the national institutions that perpetuate bigness while at the same time building new communities with relatively self-governing economies. This requires community-oriented technology, new forms of community planning. In the final analysis, it requires a new method for monitoring the results of planning at each stage of development. Let us now look at the key principles underlying this planning process.

Decentralizing Political Organization Through New Technology. A self-governing local economy can be conceived only with a supporting system of technology that permits it to develop. At the present time we can say objectively that all communities are highly dependent upon outside economic powers and outside sources of supply. They do not function with any degree of that self-sufficiency dreamed of by social philosophers. They are highly vulnerable to the forces of technological and organizational change in the larger society.

This extreme dependency, however, leads to excessive nationalism and then quickly moves to Fascism. It can be corrected first by changing those contemporary modes of technology that centralize organization. The subject is not treated as a rule in public policy, but we know that technology can powerfully affect the whole way of life of people in society. The invention of the automobile, for example, changed the entire structure of the American community. It helped to draw people from the inner city and created a vast system of suburbia. It helped change courtship patterns and family life styles, and produced a whole new set of organizations and occupations in American society.

The question is: How can we govern technology instead of letting technology govern us? E. F. Schumacher, the British economist, suggests that we could design technology with a social purpose; technology could help reverse the centralizing forces of society. He notes in his book *Small Is Beautiful* how Third World countries demanded that international oil companies operating on their territories construct small petroleum refineries with low capital investment per unit output for their own uses. In spite of expert opinion to the contrary, these units have proven to be as efficient and low cost as the much bigger and more capital-intensive refineries. He also reports on how small "package plants" for ammonia production have been designed especially for small markets. The investment cost per ton in these plants with a 60-ton-a-day capacity is about $30,000, whereas a conventionally designed unit with a daily capacity of 100 tons requires an investment of approximately $50,000 per ton. It pays in such cases to remain small.[34]

The decentralizing power of technology is important to consider because it permits the planning of a rounded economic base for the local community. It permits planning for decreasing the economic dependency of small towns and cities.[35]

Balancing Production and Consumption in Community Organization. Barry Stein and Mark Hodax have raised questions about the extent to which economic dependency can be reduced in the face of the corporate networks of interdependence at the national level today. They found that almost 70 percent of U. S. industry would "use plants with less than 250 employees; 44 percent of them need less than 100 employees." They also found that if automobile products were excluded, "71 percent of all consumer goods (by value) could be locally produced for an area containing 1 million persons. Twenty percent could be produced even for a market of 200,000."[36]

Stein and Hodax are talking about the possibilities of planning a relatively self-sufficient region of cities and towns given contemporary modes of technology. If the design of technology were different, however, the area of self-sufficiency could be smaller. We know that technology can be designed instead to favor decentralization without necessarily increasing costs. This fact argues further that it is possible to work toward the planning of a relatively self-governing region of communities.

Social planning in this sense, then, means helping localities create a balance in the production, distribution, and consumption of goods and services, at least within regions. It means helping "production communities" find markets for their goods within the region. It means helping "consumer communities" build production plants that provide them with a sound economic base. A sound economic base is essential for building a rich institutional life. This means encouraging communities to produce goods they need themselves as well as technical goods for outsiders.

It is often possible to build the technology that is suitable to small areas even though such planning has not been common. James Ridgeway and Bettina

Conner at the Institute for Policy Studies, for example, suggest that it is possible to decentralize public energy systems within small districts. A workable model, they say, can be seen in the public utility district (PUD) of the state of Washington. Here public agencies are responsible for the production and distribution of electric power. The PUD mechanism in this case has achieved "spectacular results" in economically poor Wahsington counties. Ridgeway and Conner suggest that the PUD mechanism could expand into "public energy districts" and then operate on a regional level.[37] The Tennessee Valley Authority, of course, offers the clearest example of how regional planning can develop while at the same time reinforcing the power of local governments. Our point would be that the whole process of decentralization can be done on the basis of what we have called the "public corporation" operating in the private sector.

Building Self-Governing Towns. The concept of the self-sufficient community does not as a rule guide modern economic planning, and it has a dubious place today in social planning. It leads some social planners into thoughts of Utopia and other planners into nightmares. The first set of planners see a place where people know each other well and care about one another. It is a place where individual freedom reigns and human values are realized. The second set of planners see a place where people know each other *too* well. Individuals are trapped by local prejudice, bigotry, and rumor. It is a place to avoid in social planning.

The fact is that the small community stands somewhere between these extremes. Here again, planning seeks the ideal within the real. The reality is that the community has been "eclipsed" in the mass society. The problem in this case is to offer localities some measure of identity and economic stability. One way to do this is through legislation enabling corporations to decentralize some of their power to localities through their subsidiaries, and another way is through the creation of new towns.

Edward Kirshner and James Morey have conceived a design for constructing a "new town" of 100,000 (31,000 families) that is relatively "self-contained" over a fifteen-year period. They have calculated the cost based on the "nonprofit model" as opposed to the "profit model" of development. They find that the "total savings due to nonprofit ownership of a reasonable portion of commercial and industrial enterprises, in addition to real estate and utilities, may cut capital costs to families roughly in half." Put another way, the common ownership of enterprises in the new town built on the nonprofit method of incorporation is more profitable to individual members. The way in which common ownership yields individual responsibility in enterprise and the way subcommunities develop within the "new town" then become important aspects of this planning. The plan in general encourages self-governance based on equitable sharing of revenue in the planning process.[38]

The aim of such planning is not to create an isolated or wholly self-contained community. The aim is to achieve a balance between self-governance and mutual governance of the economy with outside enterprises. Mutual governance means maintaining some measure of economic autonomy for enterprises in the locality through federated relationships with regional and national enterprises. The aim is not a reduction in the number of outside ties but rather the development of democratic forms. Outside ties are essential in reducing tendencies toward local oligarchy; democratic relationships outside the community help especially to increase the likelihood of democracy and freedom developing within the local community.[39]

IN CONCLUSION: MEASURING THE PROGRESS

One of the most important undertakings of contemporary social science has been research on social indicators.[40] This undertaking offers the promise that researchers and scholars can begin to deal directly with the broader changes taking place in society. In this undertaking we see how socioeconomic development can be monitored. The results of social planning can be observed and new plans formed in accordance with the findings.

Many different models and definitions of social indicators have been formulated since the movement first gained its impetus in the 1960s. A "social indicator," for example, has been defined by the government as "a statistic of direct normative interest which facilitates concise, comprehensive and balanced judgments about the condition of major aspects of society."[41] According to this definition, statistics on the number of physicians or small businesses would not be social indicators. They are simply raw statistics that must be connected to a norm or goal. Figures on health or economic self-governance, however, would be "indicators," because they point in a direction of development.

The national income statistics are one kind of social indicator insofar as they indicate the amount of available goods and services in society. They do not, however, indicate the amount of pollution in the environment or the extent of economic dependency in regions, states, and cities.

A program of social accounting in the nation is clearly in accord with research, theory, and planning in social economy. Its focus in this case is on the well-being of individuals in localities within states and regions. Citizens who are not professionals can participate in the process. Social accounting then becomes a system of guidance that contributes toward self-governance. A system of social accounts can be developed in ways that advance the quality of work life. People at local levels can participate in determining their own accounts and thus control them; they can use them to guide their own planning.

Communities can be helped in this process of self-monitoring and development by the organization of state and regional training centers for self-management and institutes for studying "appropriate technology." They can also be helped by adult education programs in business schools and consulting services in professional firms that aid federations seeking to decentralize their resources in communities. The social economy then develops by citizen participation and planning at different levels of political organization.

National planning is based on a continuous review of—not direct control over—the development process. It is based on empirical facts as much as on social ideals. It assumes that "economic forces" and "bureaucracy" need not rule society. People can rule their own society on the principles of self-direction and self-governance. Through our own planning efforts we can avoid the Behemoths of the past.

With national studies of the economy leading directly toward incentive systems and experimental programs, we begin to formulate an economics "as if people mattered." We introduce the novel idea that human values belong in the economic order. Perhaps we may then also begin to fulfill those dreams of the nineteenth century writers responding to the world of Adam Smith—Robert Owens, Charles Fourier, Karl Marx, Pierre Proudhon, and Peter Kropotkin—who all believed, in their contradictory ways, that a new era was in the making.

NOTES

1. Thomas Kuhn, *The Structure of Scientific Revolution,* 2nd ed. (Chicago: University of Chicago Press, 1970); for a discussion of this book's relevance to sociology, see Ritchie Lowry, *Social Problems* (Lexington, Mass.: D. C. Heath, 1974).

2. Some theorists would claim here that the suppression of cooperation only results in its reappearance as an illegal activity defined as "collusion" or "conflict of interest." These are classic issues. Karl Marx's *Critique of Political Economy* should make it clear that the alternative paradigm is Social Economy.

3. Petr Kropotkin, *Mutual Aid: A Factor of Evolution* (Boston: Extending Horizons Books, n.d.; o.d. 1902); also *Fields, Factories, and Workshops Tomorrow* (London: George Allen & Unwin, 1974; o.d. 1898).

4. Cf. Pablo Gonzalez Casanova, "Internal Colonialism and National Development," *Studies in Comparative International Development,* Vol. 1, No. 4 (1965): 27-37.

5. James O'Connor, *The Fiscal Crisis of the State* (New York: St. Martin's Press, 1973); *The Corporations and the State* (New York: Harper & Row, 1974).

6. Paul Ehrlich, *Eco-Catastrophe* (San Francisco: City Lights, 1969).

7. The alternative is to decentralize management and introduce social accountability into the system. In this way the payment of the social costs occur where they arise in the first place. It is not then necessary to pass the money back up through a centralized corporation, which in turn pays limited taxes to a centralized government bureaucracy, which then sends it back down through the government hierarchy again in state expenditures to support new corporate subsidiaries or through revenue sharing to cover local pollution agencies. The best solution is to respond to the problem where and when it arises.

8. Roy Bennett, "National Economic Planning in Western Europe and Japan," *Social Policy*, Vol. 5, No. 6 (March/April, 1975). For more details on the European scene, see Raymond Vernon (ed), *Big Business and the State: Changing Relations in Western Europe* (Cambridge: Harvard Univ. Press, 1974); for details on the original indicative planning in France, see Vera Lutz, *Central Planning for the Market Economy* (London: Longman's, Green, 1969).

9. In the early 1970s, for example, many firms faced a precarious financial situation. This led to the creation of a financial organization called *Gestioni e Partecipazione Industriale* designed to help rescue ailing firms. But in the political climate, it led instead to repeated state takeovers.

10. Alberto Martinelli, "The Economic Policy of the Italian Communist Party," *Challenge*, September-October, 1976, pp. 35–40; for a criticism, see Walter Laqueit, "Eurocommunism and Its Friends," *Commentary*, Vol. 62, No. 2 (August, 1976).

11. Andrew Kopkind, "Bologna: Socialism in One City," *Working Papers*, Vol. 4, No. 2 (Summer, 1976).

12. Louis Davis and Albert Cherns (eds), *The Quality of Working Life*, Vols. I and II (New York: The Free Press, 1975); cf. Michael Pooley, *Workers' Participation in Industry* (London: Routledge & Kegan Paul, 1975); Peter Bowen, *Social Control* (London: Routledge & Kegan Paul, 1976).

13. Other "experimenting companies" include Proctor & Gamble, Overnite Transportation Co., McCormick & Co., Lincoln Electric, Questar Corp., Syntex Corp., and PPG industries. See Report of a Special Task Force to the Secretary of H.E.W., *Work in America* (Cambridge: M.I.T. Press, 1973).

14. Lyman Ketchum, organizational specialist at General Foods, brought in an outside team to help plan a "total systems approach." The problem now is "diffusion" to other plants. See Lyman Ketchum, "A Case Study in Diffusion," in Louis Davis, op. cit., Vol. II, p. 138ff.

15. Mogens Agervold, "Swedish Experiments in Industrial Democracy," in Louis Davis, Vol. II, p. 53.

16. This study was drawn to my attention by Professor Martin Lowenthal of Boston College. Martin Schnitzer, *The Swedish Investment Reserve: A Device for Economic Stabilization?* (Washington, D. C.: American Enterprise Institute for Public Policy Research, 1967).

17. The economist Robert Averitt distinguishes between "center firms" and "periphery firms." The center firm is large by its number of employees, total assets, and yearly sales. It tends toward "vertical integration." It excels in managerial talent and financial resources. The periphery firm is small and "may be an economic satellite of a center firm." Robert J. Averitt, *The Dual Economy* (New York: W. W. Norton & Co., 1968). John K. Galbraith describes the sector of big corporations as the "planning system" as opposed to the "market system" of small firms that must adjust to it. The "market system," however, includes about 12,000,000 small firms including 3,000,000 farmers; "just under" 3,000,000 garages, service stations, repair firms, laundries, and restaurants; 2,000,000 retail establishments; 900,000 construction firms; 200,000 small manufacturers; and an "unspecified number of multivariate interests in what is called vice." Galbraith calls for a "public planning authority" under close "legislative supervision." See John Kenneth Galbraith, *Economics and the Public Purpose* (Boston: Houghton-Mifflin, 1973).

18. Some institutional economists argue that these markets recruit workers with basically different skills and personality traits and provide them with different rewards. See D. Gordon, *Theories of Poverty and Underdevelopment* (Lexington, Mass.: D. C. Heath, 1972); Benjamin Harrison, *Education, Training, and the Urban Ghetto* (Baltimore: Johns Hopkins

University Press, 1972), Chapter Five; P. Osterman, "An Empirical Study of Labor Market Segmentation," *Industrial and Labor Relations Review,* 28 (July, 1975): 508-523.

19. Thorstein Veblen discusses the moral-legal grounds for the subsidiary system of ownership with his unmatchable satire. He states that "The established order of law and custom which safeguards absentee ownership in recent times and among civilized nations is, in the main, a modern creation . . . ." Absentee ownership gains its legitimacy by operating within the larger national community. The system continues only as it is closely tied with national identity. Thorstein Veblen, *Absentee Ownership* (Boston: Beacon Press, 1967, o.d. 1923), p. 13.

20. *A Business of Your Own* (New York: Drake Publishers, 1974), p. xiv.

21. Fred Sklar, "Franchises and Independence," unpublished paper, no date, drawn from the author's doctoral dissertation, "Franchises, Independence, and Action," University of California at Davis, 1973, p. 3.

22. Theodore Levitt, "Management and the 'Post-Industrial' Society," *The Public Interest,* 44 (Summer, 1976): 86.

23. This information is based on interviews with Mr. and Mrs. Levy.

24. The alternatives developing in poverty areas cannot be detailed here. But the fight against discriminatory practices by big banks is important to note. It has led to new types of "customer influence," state controls, and the notion of a decentralized public bank. Cf. Ron Dorfman, "Greenlining Chicago," in *Working Papers,* Vol. III, No. 2, Summer, 1972; Derek Shearer, *Public Control of Public Money* (Washington, D. C.: Institute for Policy Studies, 1976).

25. John M. Blair, *Economic Concentration* (New York: Harcourt Brace Jovanovich, 1972).

26. Barry A. Stein, "Decentralizing the American Economy," in Harold S. Williams (ed), *The Uses of Smallness* (Emmans, Pa.: Rodale Press, 1977).

27. J. Jewkes et al., *The Sources of Invention* (New York: W. W. Norton, 1969).

28. *Work in America,* op. cit.

29. Arthur M. Okun, *Equality and Efficiency: The Big Trade Off* (Washington, D. C.: The Brookings Institution, 1975).

30. The name "Federated Stores" is of course a misnomer under its present organization. "Federated: The Most Happy Retailer Grows Faster and Better," *Business Week,* Oct. 18, 1976, p. 74ff.

31. Daniel Zwerdling, "Shopping Around: Nonprofit Food," *Working Papers,* 3 No. 2 (Summer, 1975): 29.

32. "Community-Worker Control," *D. C. Democratic Economics,* 2, No. 1 (Summer, 1976): 5.

33. The National Consumer Cooperative Bank Act (S.2631) is a bill "to provide for consumers a further means of minimizing the impact of inflation and economic depression . . . through the development and funding of specialized credit sources for . . . self-help, not-for-profit cooperatives, and for other purposes."

34. E. F. Schumacher, *Small Is Beautiful: Economics as If People Mattered* (New York: Harper Torchbooks, 1973), pp. 175-176; cf. David Morris and Karl Hess, *Neighborhood Power: The New Localism* (Washington, D. C.: The Institute for Policy Studies, 1975).

35. Robert Swann, Director of the International Independence Institute, tells me the following story of how a critical decision on technology maintained a decentralized system of villages in a North African nation. Government leaders in this nation had planned to build

a large nuclear plant to desalinate ocean water for village use. The construction of the nuclear plant, however, would have added greatly to the power of the central government in the administration of water supplies. It would have made all local villages dependent on a top bureaucratic agency for this scarce resource. It was discovered, however, that a new bituminous mix would provide the basis for adequate cachements of water from normal rainfall. Such cachements had existed in the past but they had been subject to leeching and cracking, thus making them unpotable. The application of this bituminous mix to local cachement basins, then, kept political power relatively decentralized in the local villages.

36. Barry Stein and Mark Hodaz, *Competitive Scale in Manufacturing: The Case of Consumer Goods* (Cambridge, Mass.: Center for Community Economic Development, 1976).

37. James Ridgeway and Bettina Conner, "Public Energy: Notes Toward a New System," *Working Papers,* Winter, 1975, Vol. II, No. 4, p. 45ff.

38. Peter Bass, *New Town Development: Costs;* Edward Kirshner, *New Town Development;* Master of City Planning Theses (Berkeley: University of California, 1971).

39. A literature has developed around the concept of Urban Economics, but only recently have studies begun to focus on the social organization of the city economy. See Gary Gappert and Harold M. Rose, *The Social Economy of Cities* (Beverly Hills: Sage Publications, 1975).

40. Kenneth C. Land and Seymour Spilerman, *Social Indicator Models* (New York: Russell Sage Foundation, 1974).

41. U. S. Department of Health, Education, and Welfare, *Toward a Social Report* (Washington, D. C.: U. S. Govt. Printing Office, 1969); the phrase "social indicators" apparently appeared originally as a reflection of the title *Economic Indicators,* a compendium of economic statistics compiled by the Council of Economic Advisors.

The Social Economy of Copper Mining: A Case Study in Puerto Rico

PART ONE

INTRODUCTION:

A Field Trip to the Hills

In the late months of 1970 I was meeting regularly with staff members of the Boston Industrial Mission (BIM) and the Center for the Study of Social Change and Development in Cambridge, Massachusetts, helping to conduct a Seminar on Technology and Values. It was an informal affair where seminar members discussed the impact of corporate technology on society.

The issue of copper mining in Puerto Rico was introduced by Norman Faramelli, Associate Director of BIM. He had recieved information from Richard Gillette, the Mission Director in Puerto Rico, that major environmental questions were involved in a corporate proposal to excavate copper on the island.

We learned that Kennecott Copper and American Metal Climax (Amax) had been negotiating for a number of years with the Puerto Rican government to arrive at a contract to mine copper, and the settlement seemed to be drawing near. The churches were uniquely concerned, and a public hearing was being sponsored in Puerto Rico to determine the feasibility of influencing the government to postpone the agreement.

Our Seminar on Technology and Values became interested in the problem. We gathered more information about it and inquired into how we might assist the Mission in Puerto Rico. In pursuit of a Seminar relationship to the problem, I was asked to make a trip to Puerto Rico with Rafael Rodriguez, a Puerto Rican living in the Boston area. Our purpose would be to determine the grounds for supporting the inquiry further from stateside.

I decided to begin the inquiry by traveling to the countryside where the copper companies were planning to make their excavations. I had just completed a study of the country operations of The United Fruit Company, which had taught me about the importance of beginning the inquiry in a context independent of the "interested" corporations. My study of the United Fruit Company had begun by talking with top officials before moving to live for a summer on the banana plantations in Central America. The sequence of steps taken in that inquiry made it difficult to talk with country people in the hills around the plantation. They quickly identified me with the company, and I found it virtually impossible to talk with people in the resistance movement.[1] I could not, therefore, round out my picture of corporate operations and their effects on people. For this reason I decided that in Puerto Rico I would begin in the hills surrounding the proposed copper sites. I could talk later with company officials who were far removed from the local situation.

This brief case study reveals that original fieldwork emphasis. The documents help explain some of the reasons for the resistance to transnational corporations. The report also records my own response to that resistance. It was in the hills talking to *independentistas* that I found it important to design a new type of organization for copper mining in the area. That design is included as the last document in this Appendix.

THE FIELD EXPERIENCE: PERSONAL DIMENSIONS

Rafael Rodriguez was a native to Puerto Rico. He had grown up in a slum in Mayaguez and personally experienced the effects of exploitation. He knew the towns in the mining area. Our combined roles and knowledge provided a basis for the kind of research needed for the Seminar in August 1971. We went first to the Industrial Mission in Rio Piedras to obtain accommodations. Then we rented a Volkswagen and headed for the hill towns where the proposed mining venture would take place. We wanted to talk directly with people who would be affected by the mining.

Our contacts began with people in Utuado, a community six miles from the proposed excavation area. We talked first with Pedro Matos Matos, a resident of the town who was opposed to the mining venture and active in the movement for Puerto Rican independence. I spent several days with Matos obtaining his perspective of copper mining on the island.

We then went to visit with members of the Student Brigade. The brigade was an organization of young people who were also opposed to the mining proposal and associated with the independence movement. Brigade members distributed the socialist newspaper *Claridad* to people in the area. They regularly distributed 300 copies in Utuado and 100 copies in Adjuntas, a neighboring town.

The brigade members had established their headquarters in Judea, a crowded slum in Utuado. Rafael and I stayed there during our time in the community. We learned that the landlord was worried that his building would be burned down because of the students' association with the leftist movement. Only pedestrian traffic was permitted in the court street on which we lived. The density of living quarters increased the drama and the risks in the students' work.

The houses in the neighborhood were "tossed together," with floors and walls made of wooden planks with sizable cracks between them. Electricity was available, but wires dropped down the walls from the ceiling. The bathroom was separated by a curtain from the living room. The shower consisted of a bare iron pipe and stood next to the toilet in an undivided room. The toilet had no seat on it. The walls of the main room had posters of Che Guevara and signs left over from past celebrations. The signs read: "Imperialismo Yanqui, fuera inmediatamente de corea del sur." Another: "Julio Roldan, Young Lord, Asessinado por la policia." Still another: "Gran Concentración obrera, Internacional de los Trabajadores." On one wall was a large sign emblazoned "El Cobre es Nuestro." (The Copper is Ours.) It had a picture of an arm with a hand reaching for gold ore. The cuffed arm was designed with blue and white stripes and a star.

There was a typewriter on a table in one room and two bunk beds in another room where Rafael and I slept. Old copies of *Claridad* were scattered about. The rooms cost $45 a month, which was too much for the students; they were broke.

I mention these matters because the work of the brigade was open and was having an effect. There was no special effort to hide activities. The purpose of the brigade in the area was to distribute information on copper mining along with socialist literature on independence. Their efforts were threatening to the more established families in the area.

Rafael and I decided to visit the proposed excavation site with a brigade member as our guide. We spent a day in a torrent of rain gathering rock and copper samples, taking pictures, and listening to our guide tell us the facts as he saw them.

Our guide was a high school student in a neighboring village. He said the land should be used for agriculture instead of mining. The abandonment of farming in Puerto Rico had placed the island in complete dependence upon the United States. The economy now rests on manufacture, he said, and 70 percent of all factories belong to American companies.[2] The copper companies will only exploit the land and the environment and the people in the area. Local citizens will have no power to act back on the problems except through revolution.

We traveled next to Lares, a neighboring community bordering on another proposed mining area. Lares is the town where patriots revolted against Spain in 1868. The revolt was silenced, but the story and symbol of Lares survived. In 1930, Don Pedro Albizu Campos, a poet rebel, inaugurated annual pilgrimages to Lares. Later, Albizu himself set up a shadow government in Lares to proclaim the continuation of the independent republic. Albizu died, but the revolutionary movement continued.

In Lares we talked with a man who claimed that the mining explorations had already begun to exploit people. When I asked him for specific examples, he told me of a boy who had been burned about the chest and neck four years earlier while playing around a hole dug by one of the copper companies. The boy had dropped a match in the hole and was burned by an explosion of the fumes. The company offered no medical compensation for the boy. The man said that people in the area were afraid to protest such matters. The boy recovered and had since moved to New York, but the family was still in the area.

I insisted that we talk with the family to confirm the report. We spent the next day traveling into the hills. We went as far as our Volkswagen would carry us over the rough roads. We found a friendly farmer who took us further with his jeep, but the road again became too rough. We parked the jeep and walked the remaining several miles to find the family.

The father of the boy verified the incident for us. There was apparently no medical compensation provided, but the father was not angry. He had been told that his land would become valuable if the mining venture took place and that he would be able to live well by selling his land to the company. He spoke honestly with neighbors and with Rafael, although I was looked upon with some suspicion. One farmer said later that he thought at first I was an FBI agent from the United States.

A wide range of feeling and attitudes about the mining venture existed among farmers and townspeople. The full meaning could be assessed accurately only by extensive residence and study. It was clear, however, that the ambiguity of opinion and the tension that existed could easily be swept in any direction by the government or other organizers of information. Our purpose, however, was not to obtain a sampling of opinion but rather to sense the potential.

We traveled further into the hills and stayed overnight in an old cabin that was used by the opposition. There were preparations for resistance on a larger scale. Maps hanging on the cabin walls pinpointed the locations of company sites. It was obvious that the decision to proceed with the mining would lead to rebellion and violence.

Bombs had already been exploded on company construction sites. No one has yet discovered who planted them. The resistance disclaimed responsibility and accused the company itself of setting the explosives. They said the company wanted to turn the townspeople against the resistance movement. The jeep used by the Student Brigade had been burned twice in the months before our visit. The brigade claimed it was done by the "rightists." The lives of *independentistas* had been threatened.

We went back to San Juan to talk with officials about the copper proposal. I made the rounds talking to university economists, chemists, sociologists, and agriculturalists, the Executive Secretary of the Mining Commission, and the General Manager of the Amax subsidiary. Our purpose was simply to gather further information on the nature of the proposal and develop a perspective from which to assess the need for research in the seminar.

The larger picture of mining as a social (as well as business) venture began to fall into place in these talks.

NOTES

1. A monograph is being prepared on this research. A brief description can be found in: Severyn T. Bruyn, "The Multinational Corporation and Social Research: The Case of the United Fruit Company," *Social Theory and Practice,* Vol. 1, No. 4, Fall 1971.

2. A monograph is now being prepared on corporate investments and their social consequences on the Puerto Rican political economy. For a brief picture of social and economic history, see Severyn T. Bruyn, "Puerto Rico: Self-Determination in an Interdependent World," *Peace and Change,* Vol. IV. No. 1, Fall, 1976.

PART TWO

A SHORT HISTORY:

Facts, Negotiations, and Resistance

Kennecott's subsidiary, Bear Creek Mining Company, obtained exploration rights in the mid-1950s after a British entrepreneur had discovered copper and molybdenum in the hills. In 1960 Amax became interested and in 1962 sought leases for exploratory work. Amax drilled 27 miles of hole for samples under the direction of its wholly owned Puerto Rican subsidiary, Ponce Mining Company.

Kennecott and Amax together spent 10 million dollars on exploration, and early in 1965 a contract seemed imminent. But the agreement was halted by a succession of governors and public criticism of the negotiations.

Governor Munõz Marin was succeeded in the office by Sanchez Vilella. At the same time a critical article was published "exposing" the secret discussions on the mining proposal. The contract was postponed during Sanchez Vilella's administration, although discussions did take place. The profits from the mining were to be split three ways between the two companies and the government. The actual income for the government would be delayed, however, until profits could be realized.

In January, 1969 a new Administration took office under Governor Luis Ferré. The New Progressive Party overcame the incumbent Popular Party, signalling a time for a new approach to the mining interests.

The Ferré administration wanted an immediate income from the mining operations. On December 5, 1969 (following the Ferré election) the two companies submitted a proposal to the Mining Commission, which took account of these interests. The companies agreed to undertake the mining and smelting as a joint venture. They would mine the ore over a longer period of time. The mines could pay half as much taxes for twice the period of time and begin payments the first year of operation. The plan called for extracting ore from Amax's Rio Vivi project first (near Utuado) and Kennecott's Tanama project (near Lares) later.

341

One concentrator would be built. The construction period would employ 1600 men. At full production there would be about 800 people earning about $9 million a year.

FACTS

The Mining Process

Four major areas of extraction and processing operate with environmental and social risks: the pit, the milling and transportation of tailings, the smelting, and the refining.

Copper pits are dug deep into the ground. For each vertical foot the miners dig one horizontal foot. Therefore, a pit a quarter mile deep will be at least a quarter mile in diameter. The ore is drilled, blasted, and removed from the ground and placed in a mill or concentrator. The environmental problems around the pit itself include acid draining into the ground water, rock dust, the unsightly condition of the pit, and the removal of residents from the area.

The mill takes the rock and "concentrates" it. In Puerto Rico, the rock is about .75 percent copper. An organic foam separates out the "heads," a concentrate about 30–40 percent copper.

A major environmental problem exists in the disposal of "tailings," the waste rock containing less than .05 percent copper. The tailings represent the bulk (95 percent) of the rock dug out of the ground. This rock must be transported away from the mill and dumped. In the Puerto Rican project, tailings must be dumped at the rate of about 19,000 tons a day.

Another environmental problem is posed by the mining operation's water requirements, which are estimated at 3700 gallons per minute. Eighty percent of this water need arises in the tailings disposal process.

The smelter is like a great blast furnace. Its tremendous heat turns the concentrate into a liquid. Waste gases and slag rise to the top. The slag is removed while the gases go up the smokestack. The leftover ore, called "blister," is 99 percent pure copper. Since the gases escape into the atmosphere, they represent a major hazard to the environment. Estimates differ on how much of the sulfur escapes. Amax claims that 92 percent of the gases will be recovered and made into sulfuric acid.

The refinery is the next stage of processing, since the blister is not pure enough to be used as an electrical conductor—the primary use of copper today. The companies did not plan to build a refinery in Puerto Rico at first because their own refineries stateside were not working at full capacity and they claimed it would be too costly to build another refinery on the island. As we shall see, the Mining Commission insisted that a refinery be built on the island in order

to aid in the development of a copper industry. The matter is still under negotiation.

Public Hearings: Church Panel

In the fall of 1970 the Right Reverend Francisco Reus Foylan, Episcopal Bishop
of Puerto Rico, proposed that the General Convention of the Episcopal Church
evaluate the negotiations of the mining companies. The Church had considerable
stockholding interests in the two companies, and since the Church was a part
owner of the companies, the bishop said it had a responsibility for the action of
the companies.

The Standing Committee on Social Criteria for Investments was authorized
by the Episcopal Executive Council to consult with executives in the concerned
companies to conduct public hearings on the matter, but the companies did not
respond. The hearings were held subsequently under the joint sponsorship of
The United Church of Christ, the United Church Foundation, the American
Baptist Home Mission Society, Women's Division and National Division of the
Board of Missions, United Methodist Church, Coordinating Committee on Inter-
American Affairs, United Presbyterian Church, U.S.A., Committee on Social
Criteria for Investments of the Executive Council of the Episcopal Church, and
the Board of Social Ministry of the Lutheran Church in America. *The six
churches held a total of 963,000 shares of Amax (out of a total of 23,000,000)
and 143,000 shares of Kennecott (out of a total of 33,000,000).*

These churches formed the panel that reviewed the evidence and issued
recommendations. Experts on the mining proposal were invited to the hearings.
Amax and Kennecott refused to appear, but a representative of the Mining Commission did appear.

Key recommendations of the Panel were that:

the companies disclose to the public their complete current and future proposals
to the Government . . . the companies be conscious of the social impact of the
proposed mining of copper in Puerto Rico and not enter into copper mining
without the expressed, uncoerced consent of the people of Puerto Rico and particularly those in the area where the mining is projected to occur . . . the agencies of the churches prepare and support appropriate stockholder resolutions
that implement the recommendations and findings of the panel . . . the (corporations) postpone mining in the island of Puerto Rico because of the danger such
mining will be to the health and well-being of the people . . .

In February and March, 1971, the Mining Commission held its own hearings
in San Juan, Mayaguez, and Utuado to clarify the nature of the copper proposal
from the standpoint of the government. It concluded that the majority of its
witnesses favored the extraction of copper reserves.

Stockholder Resolutions

The Committee on Social Criteria for Investments in the Episcopal Church felt it important to take one more step. It introduced stockholder resolutions to both companies. The resolutions were presented as follows:

Stockholder Resolutions
for American Metal Climax and Kennecott Copper

#1 RESOLVED, that the shareholders declare it to be the policy of this corporation that henceforth the corporation shall not enter into new mining ventures unless it undertakes to indemnify those upon whom its operations will impose costs in terms of environmental damage.

#2 RESOLVED, that the corporation shall publish in its annual report each year a reasonably detailed description of what steps it has taken to guard against ecological damage from its operations and the amount expended during the most recent fiscal year in taking these steps.

Statement of Security Holder

The rise of ecological concern poses a serious threat to the future prosperity of the company. There have been calls for the complete cessation of mining operations, for strict governmental regulation, and for government ownership. In the past, various mining costs of the type which economists call "externalities," such as pollution from operations and non-rehabilitation of land following cessation of operations, have not been paid for by the company but by the larger community. Enlightened self-interest demands that to prevent over-reaction by those now bearing these costs, we bear the full economic cost of new mining ventures.

THE VIEWS OF PRINCIPAL PARTICIPANTS

The views of various people related to the contract proposal have been voiced at different times stateside and on the island. The following are quotations from corporate personnel and concerned Puerto Rican citizenry. They indicate the range of opinion regarding the mining proposal.

PEDRO A. GELABERT, Executive Secretary of the Mining Commission (the governmental agency responsible for the regulation and supervision of all activities related with the exploration, extraction, production, and conservation of fuels and mineral resources in Puerto Rico). *The environmental pollution is not negotiable! The companies must comply with the standards we set up. Yet the* *importance of developing an extractive mining industry in Puerto Rico is vital to our complete economy because it will serve as a backbone to the creation of an extensive metallurgical complex, based upon a local raw material. Puerto Rico could become the mining and metallurgical center of the Caribbean Region. Ores and concentrates from nearby islands or lands so far as the South American continent could be processed into final products here. An appraisal in terms of dollars and cents for the potentialities of such a complex could surpass our greatest expectations.* (Statement to Ecumenical Panel, January 19, (1971)

FRANK R. MILLIKEN, President of Kennecott Copper Corp. *We will deal in openness and frankness with the Puerto Rican government. We can tell them what we can contribute . . . jobs, housing . . . tax money that can be used for whatever purpose the government decrees . . . It is up to the Puerto Rican people themselves to make a judgment in this case, and we will abide by their decision.* (Annual meeting of Stockholders held May 4, 1971)

DAVID ACKERMAN, Vice President of Amax. *Our primary business is the discovery, extraction and refining of minerals. We have discovered two ore deposits in Puerto Rico, very near each other, with a total ore content of 104 million tons of ore averaging 0.82 percent copper. Kennecott has found a deposit of 139 million tons of ore averaging 0.64 percent copper. Together, then, the joint venture has ore reserves of 243 million tons . . . Our interest has always been a stable and economically feasible supply of copper. In the Puerto Rican case, I'm surprised at the patience of our board of directors.* (Remarks to Overseas Press Club, October 22, 1970 and *Engineering and Mining Journal,* February, 1971)

MAXIMO CERAME VIVAS, Director of the Department of Marine Sciences of the University of Puerto Rico. *We have sustained and continue to sustain that Puerto Rico, due to its climate, its very limited territorial extension, its population and its natural attributes, will not tolerate the ecological impact which is the consequence of copper mining, no matter the nationality of the company nor the origin of the capital.* (Statement at Mining Commission Public Hearing, Mayaguez, February 25, 1971)

JOHN WHELAN, President of the Natural History Society (concerned citizen group, composed of environmentalists and professional scientists). *We see serious problems arising from (1) the smelter, (2) tailings disposal and (3) land and water reclamation. As a group of private citizens we want to bring our concerns to the appropriate authorities.* (Interview March 6, 1972)

CRUZ MATOS, Executive Secretary of the Environmental Quality Control Board of Puerto Rico. *The Mining Commission and the EQB will develop an Environmental Impact Statement. The companies are obliged to adhere to these* *standards and we have the authority to stop the operation of the mines if need be. Pollution is not negotiable in Puerto Rico.* (Interview March 13, 1972)

JUAN MARI BRAS, Secretary General of the Puerto Rican Socialist Party (PSP). *The mining of copper by American Metal Climax and Kennecott Copper Corporation represents the theft of the century. Our slogan is 'Puerto Rican mines or no mines.'* (Speech October 30, 1970)

ANTONIO CAPELLA, State House Representative from the mining district. *I am totally in favor of the proposed mining operation because the mines promise to alleviate the poverty of some of my constituency. Where the mines are is a very poor, sparsely populated portion of the Island.* (Interview March 5, 1972)

RAFAEL PICO, Vice Chairman of Banco Popular de Puerto Rico. *Puerto Rico is a small, densely-populated island that during the last 30 years has struggled to uplift itself by its "bootstraps" with the great help of American capital and management wherever it was necessary. However, we still are way behind the average for the United States and consequently must continue to use all our resources, including the copper ores of Central Puerto Rico.* (Statement at Annual Meetings of Kennecott and Amax May 4 and 7, 1971)

PART THREE

A COUNTRYMAN'S VIEW OF THE SYSTEM:

Pedro Matos

Pedro Matos is the son of a countryman of limited means. He has lived in the Utuado area most of his life. He was four years old when his father died in 1916. At seven he was taken to an orphans' asylum in San Juan, where he received elementary education and military training and also learned several trades. At seventeen, after completing these elementary and vocational courses, he left the asylum where he had been for almost eleven years, never to have a chance to continue his education again. He returned to his home town early in 1930. In 1931, jobless in spite of his skill in several trades, almost destitute, he joined the U.S. Army, where he served for thirty months. In 1932 the Army sent him to the Cooks and Bakers School at Fort Slocum, New Rochelle, New York, for a six-month course. In 1933, discharged from the army, he left for New York as a stowaway aboard an army transport (U.S. *Chateau Thiery*). With five cents as his "capital" he arrived at the Brooklyn Army Base in the late spring and managed to survive in New York City for three years, without a relative or a job, during the later part of the Great Depression. In July 1936, at the age of 24, he returned to Puerto Rico, and for the last 35 years he has devoted his life to the causes of his people "who supported the orphans' asylum where I learned to read and write, . . . the poor people of Puerto Rico who paid the taxes while the rich either paid very few or did not pay any at all, just like it still happens in Puerto Rico." He has been a leader and organizer for the independent movements throughout all these years. Operating in what is now known as the *Zona Minera* (the mining zone), he has come to know the territory and the people in the four municipalities: Utuado, Lares, Adjuntas, and Jayuya.

He has four children who have grown up and have their own careers. One is a businessman in San German, on the west coast of Puerto Rico; another son works in refrigeration repairs for Penneys' Stores in San Juan; the youngest son studies business administration at the Inter-American University, at Hato Rey; and a daughter is married to a businessman settled in Utuado. All of them have had some college education. One is about to obtain a degree. Pedro Matos himself sells insurance and has an office in Utuado.

Matos first learned about copper explorations near Utuado by "foreign companies" (Kennecott and American Metal Climax) by talking to peasants during his frequent tours of the rural zone.

He began reading about the copper industry in encyclopedias and journals and ever since has been actively opposed to company proposals. He has faced officials of both the government and the companies, and has appeared in public hearings. He has given lectures to lodges (freemasons) as well as in public rallies. He keeps a map and literature display in his office for those who come to Utuado for information on the mining proposals (the mining affair, he calls it) and for students and the public. He says his children are in essential agreement with his beliefs about the proposals and in his beliefs about Puerto Rican independence, but they have not been as active as Pedro Matos himself.

We talked for two days at various locations. We sat in his office and examined maps of the area, drove to Adjuntas and looked at the area affected by the mining, enjoyed breakfast in Utuado, and reviewed together the problems of Student Brigade activities at their headquarters in Judea, a poor housing district among the several existing in Utuado.

The following record is essentially how he sees the problem. I have omitted from these notes his discussions about agriculture (the importance of the "yagurmo" tree, distinctions between "malanga" and "yautia" by the contour of their leaves, the excelsa variety of coffee) and other matters not related to copper mining. I have placed headings before sections of his discussion to make the reading easier, but the flow of ideas and facts as Pedro Matos sees them remain essentially as they were given to me.

ON EMPLOYMENT

The companies claim that they will hire one to two thousand workers for the first two or three years during the construction of the mines, and then they will drop to about 800 workers during normal operations. They claim they are helping us solve unemployment, but it is not true. The truth is that our own government will be hiring most of the people for road building, house building, and other construction such as electric power and water supply, and even telephone facilities. The companies are putting the costs of employment back on us. Then, when the mining operation becomes normal, we know that no more than 300 workers (at the uppermost) will be hired, and, as the operation mechanizes itself, there will be no more than 50 workers including specialists, field, and office, mostly from outside. The companies deny it, but we have other information about modern mines in Norway (the Aitic mines, above the Arctic circle). They are so mechanized that they started with only 100 workers, including field and office. The operation began in 1965, and it was then expected that in a short time the whole mining operation would be run with 10 to 15 people. The size, expected length, and production of the Aitic mines are similar to the mines in the Utuado-Lares-Adjuntas area in Puerto Rico. Thus we can affirm that the mines will not reduce unemployment here. Instead, they will help create it.

The same thing happened when the two lakes (dams) were built in this area some years ago to produce energy for the industrialization of Puerto Rico, in what came to be known as "Operation Bootstrap" by the Puerto Rico Reconstruction Administration, first, and later by the Puerto Rico Industrial Development Plan. This part of Puerto Rico was one of the most prosperous areas of the country. At least we had about the most sound economy and least unemployment of any. True, we were poor by the standards of industry, as always happens with agricultural economies. But still we were better off than most of the country, and our businessmen and farmers were relatively sound in their economies. We had some industry, besides, generated by our agriculture and by our local needs. Then they told us that we needed to industrialize. So they built the dams to produce electricity. Even though there was no real unemployment before this, they told us about the money that would flow in the streets if we built those dams north of here. So the first dam was built: Dos Bocas Reservoir. People came from all over Puerto Rico to work here. Contractors brought their own gangs of workers from their own home towns. Local workers hardly landed a good job. Even common laborers (unskilled) came from outside. There was a little employment boom and they built the second lake: Caonillas Reservoir, and another little boom by the token of the first one. But when the lakes were finished in about seven years, down went the jobs . . . the capital city area flourished with new industries at our expense . . . but we got none. Even rural electric service remained unattended in this area until many years later. We produced the energy, and our peasants lighted their homes at night with medieval gas [kerosene] lamps and burned wood or charcoal in their *fogones* [rudimentary cooking tables built of logs and mud with three stones to hold the cooking utensils (pots and pans) over the fire]. The added population attracted by the construction of the lakes became the source of our first unemployment problem here, and our slums swelled to their present size and number, more and more deteriorated.

So progress brought us all that. People went on relief and began to live in poverty in numbers and conditions never known before in this area. Now they are telling us the same thing again with the copper mines as they did with the lakes. Of course we know it will be the same story after the construction of the mines. More unemployment and more slums. But also, more social disaster and more social unrest due to the apocalyptic consequences of depredation of our mineral resources and forest and water reserves, aside from the political impact of the copper giants over the Puerto Rican nation. They will not only run the mines. They will run our politics like they do wherever they set foot.

The mines will use water from our streams and lakes, but there is not enough water for them and for our normal needs. So, new lakes will be necessary. More of our low-grade lands, valleys, and ravines will have to be turned to artificial lakes. Good farmland will make the bottom of the lakes. They are ruining our agriculture. People in the surrounding highlands begin to speculate to sell their land to industry. They leave their farms idle, hoping for profits. Then, lakes take away water from elsewhere, in streams, even the water table is affected. When the mines are finished here, there will be no opportunity for work in mines any more and there will be no agriculture either.

ON PROPERTY

At some time we will have to do some mining in Puerto Rico, but it must be done for the people of Puerto Rico and by the people of Puerto Rico—not for the profit of foreign corporations, or of individuals, foreign or domestic. It is true that the people who own land around these mines will make money on the sale of the land to the company and maybe on royalties paid to them by the government out of the government's share. But these people don't represent the people who will have to endure life and work in this area throughout and after the exploitation. Some landowners send their profits to their motherland (Spain) and hope to retire there with the money they make here. *There* will also go the product of their speculations with the mining companies. The family of Governor Ferré owns land around the immediate area proposed for mining. The Secretary of the Mining Commission, Pedro Gelabert, also owns land not far away. A group of lawyers and politicians associated with the Ferré family have been buying land for their Cordillera Corporation, a Ferré-owned enterprise speculating in land and mining.

We know that the companies will not limit their mining operations in Puerto Rico to this section of the island. This area will just be the beachhead to be secured for further expansion all over the country, which as you see in the map contains fifteen different kinds of mineral, besides petroleum. These as you see, are zinc, lead, copper, molybdenum, chromium, iron, nickel, gold, manganese, silver, mercury, antimony, cobalt, platinum, and uranium. From this area they will keep moving eastward and westward as they eat out deposit after deposit until they eat up the whole Central Ridge, our mountain system where all our water resources are born, that is, from where our streams flow to irrigate the coastal plains. Mind you, Puerto Rico is just 3500 square miles (100 X 35). In such a small area we have a resident population of 2,700,000 or more inhabitants. These are divided into 77 municipalities consisting each one of a city or town and a number of rural demarcations called *barrios* (rural wards). That will give you an idea of how necessary is the vital space for the future development of our Puerto Rican nation. It will further explain our stubborn opposition to the indiscriminate destruction of our vital space through mining-for-profit operations by corporations or individuals, foreign or domestic. Absentee landlords and speculators such as professional lawyers, physicians, engineers, construction contractors, and professional scientists and politicians, as well as merchants may expect to harvest money by the bushel and then scamp with it to either Spain or the continent (U.S.A.) but those very few are not the people of Puerto Rico all by themselves alone as they selfishly pretend.

Americans told us that we had to industrialize because we had a poor land and no minerals here. That was a lie. They knew much better than that. Even the Spaniards knew better than that. I have an article here published in 1902 which tells of the rich ore in Puerto Rico. A report by a governor of those days (American) to Congress tells of how our land would support a population of 8 million residents. That is, agriculture could do that. A book published in Spain in the year 1849 by a Puerto Rican physician, *El Gibaro* by Dr. Manuel Alonso, devotes some paragraphs in one of its chapters to inform of the necessity of establishing a technical school in Puerto Rico to prepare our youth for the exploitation of our "vast mineral resources." The story that is told to us in the school books from the first grade in school until we finish our degree in college is just a colonial tall tale intended to create an inferiority complex in the Puerto Rican in order to soften us down for political and economical exploitation. It is intended to produce the type of Puerto Rican of which Mr. Ferré, Mr. Duran Manzanal, Mr. Muñoz Marín, Mr. Antonio Santiago Vasquez, Mr. Rafael Hernandez Colón, Mr. Ramon Mellado, Mr. Córdova Dávila, and others of their kind are representatives. Of that mentality are also our bishops (Catholic) except Bishop Antulio Parrilla, and almost all the clergy of almost all the denominations. They all were cradled to the tune of that music by their stepmother country (or foster mother country) and eventually trained for their roles as Quislings to their own motherland. Those are our Tories. Remember your own?

ON TRANSIENT RESIDENCE AND BUSINESS

This town (Utuado) has about 9500 population (urban and suburban) and about 25,500 rural. The companies say their operation will affect only a small number of families, but in truth it will affect the whole region including three other neighboring towns adjacent to the mining pits, those of Adjuntas, Lares, and Jayuya. The combined population of the four municipalities amounts to 100,000 or more. Utuado lays 6 miles from the mining pits to the east and west of the city, rather south-east and north-west. Lares lies 6 miles north-west of the pits; Jayuya lies about 6 miles north-east of the Cala Abajo and Piedra Hueca pits; and Adjuntas is just 2 miles south-west of these same two pits. These distances are in air miles, not road miles, since with the contour of the land here, it sometimes takes many road miles to travel an air mile. Certainly new business will come to Utuado temporarily. It has already begun to come. At least four Cuban exile concerns are established here already, only very recently, in the food, hardware, and clothing and wearing apparel wholesale and retail lines. Workers will come to town to spend a few bucks, get drunk, and look for girls. But neither new business nor workers will come as permanent residents. Just for the occasion. Just transients.

For example, I knew one of the drillers who came to Utuado for exploratory work. He earned about $9000 a year. His wife took in laundry for the other Americans. They said they had come here only to save money to take home to the States. They were right. When they left they took with them everything he had earned. They had lived on the wife's washing, and babysitting for the fellow American explorers.

New stores will come around Utuado until the mine work runs out. Then it will become just another mining town. Eventually, maybe a ghost town. When new pits are opened eastward and westward near the next town, everybody will leave. Town after town, area after area will be exploited until the mines run out. It will be a matter of just a couple of centuries and then, our lands and waters ruined, exhausted, polluted, our sea and shores the same, the Puerto Ricans will only have a desert to flee from and we will become the new Jewish people wandering across the planet without a plot of land where to settle down as a nation again, a new Jewish thorn injuring the ribs of the nations of the world, a political thorn, to force a settlement of our own.

In Utuado today, many people are on pensions, social security, relief, a few mercantile jobs, or in agriculture. We have only one industry—a cigar factory—which doesn't account for much. Government provides the most jobs here—teachers, policemen, street cleaners, janitors, etc. Nurses and others. We used to have craft industries (shop industries) and farming generated its own—like tobacco stemming and cigar making—and we once had sugar cane and a sugar factory in town and two others in Adjuntas and Jayuya (Pellejas and Santa Barbara Sugar Factories), so everybody was employed. We have had no real progress in the last fifty years. The present cigar industry does not process locally grown tobacco. It just makes cigars with U.S. and other foreign tobacco. Most of our land is mortgaged to the banks. Borrowing and mortgaging whatever we have is our main source of currency. That accounts for our negligible saving habit.

We are eating and being eaten from inside out. Mining will only aggravate our predicament.

ON CORPORATE POWER

Kennecott and Amax are not going to finance this mining operation themselves. The banks are going to do it for them. All they will do is mortgage us to the banks by financing their contracts. The copper is here. It is our copper that will be used by the companies as collateral for their loans and bonds. So we do have the capital to undertake the exploitation of our ores without having to give it away to any foreign concern. If we lack any know-how we just will hire it when we need it. Or we may prepare our own people in due time. Then we would have control over what happens. As it is now, the companies are too big and powerful for us. They will run right over the country. As I said before, Puerto Rico is made up of little principalities (towns, cities, rural wards), and the companies, with the help of the government, will pick them off one by one. The companies are too big for our colonial government. If the companies have spent, as they claim, 10 million dollars already in exploration, do you think they are going to stop once they begin the exploitation? Do you think anyone on this island can stop them once they are footed on their beachhead? No! They must not be allowed to begin! There will sure be trouble if they try to force it. They know that. The administration [government] should know it too. It all began when some of us found out that secret explorations were being done. Then we found that they were ruining the land they purchased for exploration and that speculation on the surrounding land was ruining the farming. Dr. Neftali García, a professor of biochemistry from the University of Puerto Rico, began to test the water, the concentration of copper and other minerals, the effects of their exploration on water in the area. Company technicians had dug a tunnel in the hillside of Piedra Hueca and a test pit in the slope of Cala Abajo hill. They had practically a whole mining operation going in their exploration, with its railroad into the Piedra Hueca tunnel and a rock crusher and everything. When they found us looking into the matter, they closed it down. Then Garcia was fired from the university. Reasons: his investigations of the mining affair. Just like that.

A student brigade came here to help the people with information about the mines and to organize them for the defense of their national patrimony. Secret police agents, Central Intelligence Agency hounds, F.B.I. agents and all sorts of repressive media were let loose against them. Some weeks ago, their jeep was burned twice and bombs were thrown against and into the home of a member of

the opposition to the mines here. Tension has been growing, and it will continue
to grow.

ON AGRICULTURE AND MINING

When we first learned about the explorations by the companies I began to read
about the copper industry. In the encyclopedia *Technirama,* I saw that where-
ever there is copper there are also other incidental minerals—such as gold and
silver—and that these incidental minerals pay for the whole operation by themselves. I have written and spoken to people from the university and in the government. Also to the Bar Association and to masonic lodges. We try to make
clear to them what the problems are going to be. In 1965 (March), I appeared
before the House committee that was investigating the mining proposals. In
1968 I appeared before the Bar Association's Committee on Mining asking them
to take a stand on the question.

We know agriculture, even under the present conditions and lack of support
by the government, will yield more than the mining operation over a period of
30 years as planned by the companies. The idea that the land here is not good is
not true. Uncultivated land, at its worst in this area, will yield 100 lbs (or $68)
of coffee per *cuerda* [a little less than an acre]. But if it is well cultivated it will
yield three or four and even ten and fifteen times as much per *cuerda.* It is simply
a matter of government support to agriculture, well-intentioned and well-manag-
ed support, of course, I mean. It is well to point out that being a colony we lack
the sovereignty to provide our agriculture such support. You will further see.

The land here will be a mess when the companies finish with it. Mr. Faustino
Rivera Lopez, (former) head of the U.S. Department of Agriculture Soil Conservation Office in Utuado, told me that nature takes 100 years to build up one
inch of soil under the best conditions of climate and other circumstances. And
under the worst conditions (such as after mining operations), it takes 1000 years
to produce the same inch of soil. After the companies have finished mining, they
propose, the land will be returned to the possession of the government of Puerto
Rico for just $1.00 per acre, as a favor. They have not even considered to re-
claim it themselves. It would be just too costly. Thus, for $1.00 per acre we'll
be purchasing from the companies all the trouble and all the multibillion-dollar
burden of reclaiming the land that the companies have ruined and destroyed.
They will eat the duck and we'll pay for it.

ON INDUSTRIALIZATION

The Americans are industrializing themselves in Puerto Rico with our money
through Fomento. Puerto Rico sells bonds in the States, and investors there pur-

chase these bonds. We pay high rates of interest—as much as 8 percent—in millions of dollars. When the money comes here, we build for American investors who also borrow from us at lower rates than our government pays American investors who purchase our bonds.

We guarantee American companies tax exemption of all kinds, low salaries—as low as 1/3 of stateside salaries for equal production—and no labor unions. Our constitution guarantees the right of our workers to unionize, that is, to form labor unions, but the NLRB, the Puerto Rican Labor Relations Board, Fomento, and the Puerto Rican Labor Department, all have arrangements under the table. And the fact is that in spite of our right as written in our constitution all American factories in Puerto Rico go along without labor unions, or when they accept any, it is one patronized by the employer himself thus making muck of our constitution.

The tax exemption is given to American and other foreign companies of American capital for 10 years in San Juan, Ponce, and other seaside industrial developments and 17 years inland. Yet even this law is fooled. At the end of their exemption period, the companies just change names and start all over again. That's the way our money goes. Some companies claim to go back to the States after the exemption period, but in another month the same operation comes back with new exemptions.

It is funny how many government officials began their political careers poor and after just a few years retire as millionaires and jump to board ships in some American or foreign corporation which they helped before. It is the system that brings pressures on our people to overlook the law.

Fomento has been a failure for Puerto Ricans. It has only profited Americans and their stooges here. Some of the work was due to stupidity and the most to the system. For example, Fomento purchased obsolete rope-manufacturing machinery from a factory in Leavenworth, Kansas, which was remodeling its own operations. So they got good money for their remodeling while we got obsolete machinery to compete with them. Fomento provided free rent for one year in a Fomento building, loaned money to American investors, and gave them all kinds of incentives. The factory went to the rocks next year. The investor returned home happy. We lost it all.

A stocking factory was planned for Arecibo. Obsolete machinery was purchased also. The machinery was turned into scrap at the Arecibo Vocational School, and the factory never opened.

Fomento has built about 10 industrial buildings in Utuado but all remain empty except for the cigar factory and a glove factory.

Americans get tax exemptions of all kinds. Not only the corporations but even their officials go tax free. (Officials living outside of Puerto Rico and who funnel out huge salaries.) It is the price we have to pay for their only asset: know-how. So they put the know-how and we put the "how-how."

Local corporations, as well as American, established here long before the Fomento plan, also avoid paying taxes. The Ferré family owns several corporations. They avoid taxes by organizing separate corporations. The Puerto Rico Telephone Company is a franchise. They made huge profits. So they have organized several separate corporations, for repair and other operations. Then through extravagantly high salaries and high costs among themselves they dilute their profits and avoid paying high corporate taxes. If an individual gets into a too high income bracket, he incorporates or creates a foundation of some kind, and thus his capital increases but he pays no taxes or pays lesser ones if any. The Ferrés have a foundation.

People can leave the country and their profits follow them. Only the workers and common government employees are left to carry the burden of paying the bulk of the taxes with which to run an expensive government that only serves the interests of those who avoid paying taxes.

Libby's produces tomatoes and other truck garden crops on land they rent from the government in the south (Lajas Valley). They funnel their profits abroad while they operate here. Their main source of business, capital, and production is in the States. When they deem it convenient they'll leave. Their low-paid workers will return to unemployment again. Libby's will have funneled home huge profits containing within them the salaries they did not pay to our workers that they would have had to pay stateside during the time they operated here. That is the true meaning of being a colony.

Corporations are not supposed to own more than 500 acres, but there are many ways to get around this. Companies find local friends and lawyers who they pay to own the land for them. There is no limit to individual land holdings.

When Muñoz came to power in 1941 he tried to enforce the 500 acres law. It worked until he touched American interests. Then he was "persuaded" by U.S. corporations, more or less like this: "Stop it or your government will fall." He decided not to fall. The writs of *quo warranto* are still in the drawers of the Supreme Court—all cases have been stopped from prosecution and the law is dead.

There is no way out for our government. It is a puppet of Washington. The U.S. Congress, the President of the United States, any congressman, any bureaucrat, civilian or military, or any millionaire in the United States can do his will here. According to the Treaty of Paris it is Congress that should have the only say about Puerto Rico. It was (and is) a treaty between Spain and the United States in which the Spanish domain was turned over to the victorious nation in the Spanish-American War of 1898. Puerto Rico, a nation by itself, was the object in the transaction between the warring powers, but our people did not even have a representative sitting at that table where our destiny was being disputed by two ruffians at a crap game table. There is a painting by one of our best artists that portrays a famous crap game 2000 years ago, where the robe of

Christ was disputed between two Roman soldiers, and a similar game in 1898 where our flag was the prize in dispute. It is one of the best protraits of imperialism. The U.S. Congress controls all allotments to Puerto Rico in education, health, welfare, loans, and it also controls all our commerce, communications, customs, immigration, labor laws and labor relations, social security laws, agriculture (through dumping and quarantine); allows us a limited access free of tariff to their market but in turn keeps for itself an unlimited monopoly of all our trade with the world and an unrestricted monopoly of our consumer market (local market), so if our government officials do not follow U.S. interests, our allotments are cut, our trade is ruined, our agriculture is ruined, we are choked until we have to beg for mercy. If opposition is too strong here, you go to jail. Pedro Albizu Campos opposed U.S. policy, and he spent his life in jail. There are several other political prisoners in Puerto Rican jails and in jails abroad—Atlanta, Leavenworth, etc.

In the midst of all that evil, something good must come—something less exploitative—such as home building for farmers away from cities or big towns by the Farmers Home Administration. That accounts for the beautiful concrete houses that you observed during your tour of the country areas. The U.S. investors have lots of money lying idle. They want that money to move within the flow of investments so that it may bring home more profits, direct and indirect. But it must be guaranteed on its returns. Thus they lend that money to the U.S. Government, at a low rate of interest, for investment by the U.S. Department of Agriculture with the guarantee of the land, in the construction of homes for farmers, and more recently it also applies to persons who, not having a house of their own, may have a lot somewhere outside of the areas where banks (commercial) may lend money for home construction. The Farmers Home Administration manages that plan. Yet this carries a 33-year mortgage, and the houses are built with U.S. products one way or the other, with U.S. insurance and using public utilities with U.S. stockholders. So, large benefits return with interest to the upper classes in the United States even under the best conditions.

ON FARM SURPLUS

Even welfare to Puerto Rico pays off for the upper classes in the States. In Puerto Rico, 850,000 people out of 2.7 million are dependent upon food surpluses (*mantengo* we call it) "given" by the United States. Giving away food to the 850,000 destitute raises prices for the remaining 1.85 million people in Puerto Rico. It keeps us from producing on our own farms. The food could be given to the poor who certainly need it, without boosting the market prices, but it would disrupt the system and keep profits down. The excess given to Puerto Rico safegaurds these profits in the United States. We pay for it here through increased market prices. They export the excess and the United States pruchases good relations in the same bunch, besides recovering through profits the subsidies they give. And the government presses for more industry in Puerto Rico at the expense of low salaries, no taxes, and subsidies to the rich (always high ones). No agriculture. What a bargain! We all lose except for wealthy farmers and the U.S. investors.

Before we were receiving U.S. food for the poor in Puerto Rico, butter was 15 to 18 cents per pound. Ever since, the price has gone up. Butter is $1.00 or $1.25 per pound now. They "give it away" free to us, yet we pay for it. The right thing would be to encourage our own agriculture so we can feed our own people. The United States can keep their own surplus or regulate their own production. Then people would not have to pay to keep it in storage or they could sell it, not give it away free, to other countries as part of an equitable trade between nations. We all pay for a system that keeps some people wealthy at the expense of keeping whole nations poor. And then the government wonders why we are opposed to copper mining tearing our land and more industry (foreign) ruining our agriculture.

ON DEVELOPMENT

The antitrust laws don't apply in Puerto Rico the way they do in the United States. That is why American corporations can create monopolies and exploit our resources. They call it development.

They tell us we can't develop ourselves. They tell us we don't have the power or the know-how to do it. England used to tell Egypt they couldn't run the Suez Canal. Only England knew how to do it. Yet Egypt is running it today. They said Cubans could not run their country without help from the United States. Yet Cuba is doing it. Americans say, "Look how people have to stand in line to eat at the restaurants in Cuba." But if the restaurants were open to all the people in Puerto Rico, there would be longer lines here than in Cuba, provided our poor people would have the money to buy food like Cubans have. But don't you see that long, long, 850,000-strong bread line to get the surplus food that they cannot afford to buy here? What is more pitiful, to line up in front of a restaurant to buy food with your money, or to line up in front of a commissary to get relief that you cannot afford to buy? Our poor just cannot afford to eat at *fondas* currently, least of all at restaurants.

San Juan is like Havana before the revolution. There is prostitution, drugs, gambling, high class hotels, and slums. Puerto Rico is today like Cuba was in Batista's time. But in another sense also, Puerto Rico is like Cuba. People are very much alike here. We are homogeneous in our culture. We are capable of unity. We are separated and different from the United States in culture and language. We have our own history—by the way, more than 100 years older in western civilization than the United States.

They say that Havana is not as brightly lighted today. But all the provinces are becoming lighted. Exiles forget to say that. So what if they don't make their goal of 10 million tons of sugar. They make nine. That is more than before the revolution. More important, they are at the same time diversifying the crops. It has been American monopolies that create one crop. One crop makes us dependent. But times are changing. Cuba's future is in the making. We hope to make our own.

They say that Chile cannot make it alone. But Chile cannot achieve normality in two years. Not after centuries of capitalist exploitation. It is not just building up from the foundations on an empty lot. It is like demolishing and cleaning the debris of an old archaic building and then starting all over again from the foundations upwards. But Chile will make it, no doubt. The whole world, even the United States will make it too.

In 1898 the capital in Puerto Rico was 80 percent local and 20 percent foreign. From 1898 to 1940, Americans became owners of 25 percent to 40 percent of the capital. Today it has completely reversed itself with Americans owning 80 percent of the capital of Puerto Rico. Investments here are 3 times as much as they were in Cuba before the revolution.

ON THE MILITARY

When you hear of so many millions of dollars of American investment per year in Puerto Rico, you have to understand that three-fourths of it goes to U.S. Armed Forces facilities in Puerto Rico. We are a fortress, a nuclear fortress, mind you, for the United States. The military has expropriated 13 percent of our land—of the best land, mind you.

On the island of Vieques—the only place in Puerto Rico where Bolivar set foot—there is a total of 36,000 acres of land. It had a population of 11,000 with three sugar factories and a prosperous economy. Since World War II until today, the Navy has occupied 29,000 acres and has cornered the population in the remaining 7000 acres with about 1000 people per acre.

In Culebra, the same action was taken by the Navy. The object was to eliminate Culebra from our map in order to keep the island for themselves.

ON THE DISTORTION OF VALUES

Spain came here originally and mixed with the Indians and later on with the Africans brought as slaves. That melting pot kept boiling and brewing the Puerto

Rican culture, the Puerto Rican race, the Puerto Rican nation. Then came the rich Spaniards, most of them of military ranking, fleeing from independence movements victorious in Latin America—not caring, these new immigrants, much for Spain or Puerto Rico, they just cared for their own selves. They became the masters of the mixed bloods. The mixed bloods came to be known as *jibaros* (at that time written *gibaros*), the peasants, and looked down upon by the newly created aristocracy. The exiles from South American and Central American nations (newly established) together with those from Haiti, the first sovereign nation after the United States, took over the land and the *jibaros* became *agregados.* (Millionaires in Puerto Rico today are mostly offspring of those masters.) Illiterate people were taught to be inferior, and after the invasion by the United States this became the chief norm of our educational system, with all our infancy educated to that tune. America the great, Puerto Rico the small; America the rich, Puerto Rico the poor; America the strong, Puerto Rico the weak; America the intelligent, Puerto Rico the stupid. They began to use the almighty dollar instead of the almighty God. So "Dollar" and "American" have replaced God. No longer they strive for dignity—only Americanism, moneyism.

Puerto Ricans are placed at the heads of boards of industry, but the real power is in the States. And the money goes back to the United States. The Puerto Rico Telephone Company (I.T.T.) has a board of Puerto Ricans but the profits are not Puerto Rican. In the first year of American investment, one-third of the investment goes back. By the third year they are taking our own money back to the United States. We call that "decapitalizing."

In 1920–1930, a peasant with 50 cents to $1.00 a day managed better than a peasant with $6.00 today. When he gets $8.00 a day he will be no better, because the cost of life keeps rising all the time. But the rising cost of life to the millionaire is not like it is to the poor. The poor must buy in little quantities and pay high for low quality, while the rich man can buy in big quantities and he pays less for higher quality not available to the poor man. What does this teach the Puerto Rican?

The average American also pays for the exploitation even though he may not know it. Americans fall into the hands of the wolf; so the world gets the wrong impression. That is, the average American is exploited by the imperialists within their nation just like we are by their system, but they, particularly the elite of the working and professional classes, have been trained to be happy as far as they can enjoy three square meals a day and some pleasure at night or over the weekend, without consideration of the rest of the world. They come to be exploited exploiters. The world tends to identify all Americans as imperialists, and thus all Americans are ugly Americans. Until the common American becomes aware of this reality the world will be cursing all Americans for what only the imperialist American is responsible.

ON CORPORATE POWER AND
PUERTO RICAN INDEPENDENCE

Leadership in Puerto Rico is stored away by the government. The government has become the main source of employment. Universities and colleges prepare the students for government employment almost only. Physicians, lawyers, engineers, scientists, professional people go into the establishment. Most of them are paid for doing little or nothing at all. The government has money, the taxpayers' money coming from two sources. Local taxpayers' money is intended to run our government for us. U.S. taxpayers' money is funneled through Congress to have our government run for them. But anyway, the government has money and the educated is the merchandise to buy with it so that any prospective leader in sight may not go to the peoples' side. It is a virtual auction of intelligence. The government is like a storage tank of brains. In government jobs they make a lot of money and get a lot of habits. They buy a lot of things and get entangled in debts and mortgages. Soon they become bellied and clumsy, and like old mares are set aside on pensions. Free at last but worthless. Thus the people lose prospective leaders and men of action that would have been. It is a well-designed plan to castrate the people of any opportunity of redemption. Nature nevertheless is wiser and more powerful than all the imperialists put together. So out of every class the best few are saved for the people by nature first and by the conscious education obtained out of experience in life and at home. That is the reason why the people's cause always has the best brains and the best hearts. Empty skulls and empty chests always turn to imperialism, and to colonialism.

Once automobiles were assembled in Puerto Rico, and it was a good source of employment for Puerto Rican labor besides being an excellent source of technical education for mechanics and craftsmen. That no longer exists. Now we bring the cars wholly assembled and ready to be driven. We not only lost the wages that our workers used to earn. Now we also pay transportation charges aboard American ships for the car and for the empty space under, above, and within the car from the bottom to the top of the hatch and on the sides between one car and the other. Formerly, a crate containing the parts to form an automobile here was just small—as large parts were packed together for a number of cars. That way the freight charges were small by comparison with today's. Now a car pays $200 to $350 to come to Puerto Rico. Formerly it must have been a matter of $25 or may be $50 unassembled. See how much we have lost by losing our own assembly shops? If we weren't a suffering country we would have our own plants. We are quite a big market for cars. All we can do now is repair them when they break down. How many millions of dollars do Americans make just by selling us autos made in the United States? A jeep is just a can of sardines with four wheels—no comforts, luxuries, except a four-wheel drive. A small jeep costs us $4,000—it used to be $1700 back in 1948-52. Do you think a Puerto Rican farmer can make money when he must buy a jeep at that price and then maintain it? Think of 10,000 pounds of coffee collected by an average farmer and sold for $6800, and then think of that farmer paying $4000 for a jeep that will last him at most five years but an average of only three. Out of the $6800 he has to pay a full year of operating expenses, and his profit may end being some $2000. The purchase of the jeep plus the purchase of gas, grease, tires, spare parts, etc. during the lifetime of the jeep will eat up by themselves more than the profits accumulated during the same time. So the farmer is working only to support the automobile industry in the United States. Meantime he eats his own land and farm, chunk after chunk through mortgaging it to American money lenders (banks). Result? Dispair, agony, a family headed for the slums, who knows what else?

You say that Puerto Rico has an export market, but I say it is American products we are exporting. The product of cheaply paid labor. For example. We have a cigar factory and we plant tobacco. But our tobacco does not go into our cigars. They buy our tobacco for export to the States and they bring their tobacco for their cigars from the States. Maybe our tobacco is blended there into their own tobacco to make it better and cheaper. That must be. Then they ship it back to us—that is, to their factories here—to be made into cigars with our cheap labor. Then they ship it back to their distribution centers in the States and sell it with enormous profits (for them). Is it our market? Or theirs?

All that shipping, back and forth, of the raw material and the finished goods pays freight charges to American steamship companies, and all that handling by American workers increases the cost of those goods when they reach our homes. Because you must understand that we are distributing our own production not from our factories but from *their* distribution centers in the United States. In other words, our commerce, stores, have to import from the United States what our factory workers manufacture here. It's all for the sake of profits to the Americans!

We are kept not a part but a possession of the United States to pay more costs than we draw benefits. Americans pay Spain, England, France, Turkey, Israel, various African and Asian nations, billions of dollars for having American military bases within those countries. In Puerto Rico, they have even nuclear bases, real complexes, and they just don't pay a penny.

Our trade balance with the United States shows a red $800 million against Puerto Rico. And that's where the real money is. The United States then returns, say, $125 million dollars for road building, education, etc., while U.S. corporations go tax free and the military bases go rent free. How much money would that mean to us if we had the power to change all that properly? But we have no power.

Of course we wouldn't allow it anyway if we were independent and sovereign as a nation.

We can't even put prices on what we sell. Americans decide on everything—on how much salary our workers will be paid and how much they (U.S.) want to pay us for our products. Americans decide how many automobiles they'll pour into the island. And also decide how much sugar or any other product we may be allowed to put into their market in the States or into their world market (we have no world market of ours). And they still levy taxes on our exports to their market, a tariff to protect themselves from our competition while we are not allowed to do the same to them. They impose on us their Sugar Law—we have no say about that.

Hawaii became a state because Americans owned all of the land there and the native Hawaiian people had been reduced, in a century, from 600,000 to only 10,000 the year they were admitted as a state of the Union.

That is what American corporations like Kennecott and Amax are trying to do here. But Puerto Rico is not Hawaii. Some day Puerto Rico will have its independence.

ON THE RUM INDUSTRY

We had the world's largest rum industry. Now it is almost all foreign. Like the milk industry. To protect their own whiskey, they levy a tax on every gallon of rum we export to the United States. It is clearly a protective tariff. After it has been collected and it has had the effect of raising the price of our rum in their market, they reimburse the product of the tax collected in the States by the federal government, to our treasury. But by that trick they have reduced the demand for our rum stateside while we cannot do the same to their beer, for instance, or to their food shipments to us. It is a one-sided proposition. They are the masters. We are their colony. You get it?

FINAL COMMENTARY

When we discuss here how we could negotiate with the banks just as the companies will do if given the green light, we just try to point out that we have the capital because the copper is ours and it is here. Since it would be the collateral security to be given to investors in securing loans for the operation, copper is the capital itself. But, be it very clear, we would not allow any exploitation of our mines for profit to either foreign or domestic corporations or individuals. They must be, if ever exploited, for the benefit of the people of Puerto Rico, as a socialist nation and provided then that all the vertical industrialization and marketing of our minerals are done here and by us as a socialist nation, for the ultimate benefit of our people.

By no means it may go to boost foreign or local bank accounts while our people are kept poor and exploited. All the product would have to go to the development of our socialist society in all aspects of life, and to reclaim the land to normal use again after the exploitation, because the vital space is more important to our people than a short-sighted, roughly done mining operation, regardless of how much it may yield.

PART FOUR

THE SOCIAL ECONOMY OF COPPER MINING:

An Alternative

I wrote the following outline on the social economy of copper mining in Puerto Rico after talks with government and company officials in 1972. It offers an alternative to the formal proposals under discussion between the government and the multinational companies. The outline was reproduced and distributed by the Misión Industrial de Puerto Rico and submitted to local officials. It remains in limited circulation on the island; the contract between the companies and the government has not yet been signed.

The following document, then, offers a basis for discussion about how a foreign extractor of raw ore might enter a host country with a minimum of exploitation and a maximum of benefits distributed equitably to all concerned parties. It stresses two basic areas of concern: (1) the environmental and socio-economic costs of the mining venture and (2) the kind of social organization of the mining project that would achieve maximum return in benefits to employees, consumers, the government, the companies, and the residents in the mining area.

THE ECONOMICS OF COPPER MINING IN PUERTO RICO:
COST-BENEFIT ANALYSIS AND CORPORATE ORGANIZATION

The Kennecott and Amax proposals to extract copper in Puerto Rico do not anticipate any social and economic damages on the Island that cannot be corrected. The present contract negotiations indicate that the Commonwealth government will be largely responsible for protecting the physical environment.

Certain social problems can be anticipated in the extraction, smelting, and refining process, however, due to the limited development planning that has preceded the contract proposal.

First, no cost-benefit plan has been formulated that specifies the overall gains and losses on both sides. Economic cost estimates have been made in certain phases of the plan, but many other phases have been omitted. Further specification of social and economic costs is essential if we are to comprehend the full consequence of copper extraction on the Island. Second, no plan for social development accompanies plans for economic development. No social controls outside the government are offered to ensure that standards of environmental quality and social justice will be maintained in the development process. This makes future government officials vulnerable to pressures from outside companies when differences of opinion occur over environmental protection. While present government officials are fully determined to set standards and "regulate" the extraction process, this does not guarantee that future officials will be equally determined once the multimillion dollar operation has been started. It is important, therefore, to examine methods for assuring continued protection of the physical and human environment over the planned 30-year period of business development.

The missing factors in the full assessment of a contract for copper extraction can be determined in a cost-benefit plan and a plan for social development. The factors to be considered in these two plans are discussed in the following pages.

COST-BENEFIT PLAN

In the field of microeconomics, cost-benefit analysis has been extremely useful in anticipating problems involved in corporate operations. Cost-benefit analysis is only beginning to be applied to wider spheres of intercorporate activity, and so the tools are not fully applicable to the complex mining operations. Yet it is important to approximate the costs in each phase of the mining impact on the island in order to judge better its overall public effects. Carefully prepared cost estimates are essential to effective multinational investment and planning. Cost estimates in both the social and economic spheres of corporate operations enable host-nation officials to negotiate contracts with multinational corporations on a sound basis.

Definitions for our immediate purposes are as follows. A *social cost* is a description of the way people see the problems created by the implementation of economic policies. A *socioeconomic cost* is the estimated amount of money required to correct the problems created by economic policies. An *economic cost* is the amount of money required to fulfill an economic goal based upon the maximization of return in an entrepreneurial context. In order to simulate a model of social accounting I have drawn from only a few references in the controversy. A full statement of costs would be much more inclusive. My emphasis is on "social costs" since no information was available on socioeconomic costs.

The following outline suggests the kind of goals that could be projected and the kind of cost problems that need to be resolved. References to the facts submitted here are included in the bibliography, p. 371.

Goals

Society

1. Create jobs for the unemployed and development for the community.
2. Provide income for island institutions: education, government, arts, housing, etc.
3. Provide a satisfactory income for all working people.
4. Strive to become a less dependent society.

Corporation

1. Create profits for employee salaries, pension benefits, environmental protection, and research.
2. Provide a satisfactory work experience including opportunities for personal growth and self-management.
3. Contribute to a healthy working environment.
4. Seek optimum levels of efficiency in work life and a high level of quality in the items of production.

Social and Economic Costs

Sociophysical Environment

1. *Tailings (Waste Rock)* Mining Requirements
   a. Waste rock will be discharged at the rate of 19,000 tons per day in the ocean near Punta Cuchara on the South Coast. (Ackerman)
   b. Mining operations will feed 135 million tons of waste into an ocean canyon by clear water pipeline and cover 125 billion square feet, at 2.2 pounds per square foot after 25 years of operation. (Ackerman)

2. *Sulfuric Gas*
   a. Mining Requirements
      1. Generally 85–90 percent of smelter emissions of sulfurous gases can be recovered. (Ackerman)

2. In this case, 94 percent of emissions can be recovered. (Mining Commission Interview)
3. Improved smelters exist to reach 95–98 percent recovery.

b. Social Costs

1. In Sudbury, Canada, the company had to build a chimney 1250 feet high (height of the Empire State Building) because previous emissions had harmed 3200 square miles of forests, yet it was still insufficient to reestablish vegetation in the area. It would no longer destroy existing vegetation but new vegetation could not be established with a new chimney. (Cerame Vivas). Percent of original emisions unknown.
2. Highest possible recovery by smelting is 98 percent, and yet 3 percent of gases are lethal to coniferous vegetation. (Cerame Vivas).
3. Winds from the east on the coast will carry toxic gases to the Guanica Forest. They will likely form rain clouds and come back to the smelter area in the form of rain. No clear data exists on the direction and movement of wind currents.
4. Water mixed with sulfuric gases produces a highly corrosive sulfuric acid. (Levins)
5. Incidence of lung cancer is "excessive" in areas where there are emanations of sulfur dioxide in the atmosphere, as in mining areas. Increments in sulfur dioxide are accompanied by an increase in mortality rate of illness: Annual rates reveal an increase in frequency of respiratory symptoms and lung illnesses. (Cerame Vivas)

c. Socioeconomic Costs
No estimates (Company claims no costs involved.)

3. *Extraction*
a. Mining Requirements: Trucks must transport ore from pit.
b. Social Costs: Dust from uncovered trucks will cover area. Even though covers for trucks can be utilized, it is likely they will not be used because of inconvenience in the operations. (Francisco Cadilla)
c. Socioeconomic Costs: No costs estimated by Company.

4. *Climate and Land*
a. In Puerto Rico, 70 percent of urban sewer waters go into the sea without adequate treatment. Damage done to coasts in proportion to population is much greater than in other countries.
b. Social Costs
1. There is no precipice canyon at the ocean site for dumping; it is a slope less exaggerated in its decline than suggested by the company description of the ocean floor. This fact increases the likelihood of trouble. (Cerame Vivas)

2. Cyanide might be dumped into the sea with tailings. (Cerame Vivas). (Denied by Company—in any case, pyrite added in pipeline would neutralize sodium cyanide).

3. Tiny amounts of copper will be dumped into the sea. According to Robins (*Pollution and Puerto Rico*), copper concentrations as low as .013 milligram per liter kill many species of blue-green algae, and copper tailings will be over .10 milligram per liter. (Francisco Cadilla)

4. No studies exist on the effect of tailings on sea organisms. (Cerame Vivas)

5. Physical turbidity of active tailings in sea could kill bentonic forms of marine life and seriously disrupt the ecological equilibrium. (Francisco Cadilla)

c. Socioeconomic Costs: No estimates exist.

5. *Water (Regional)*
   a. Mining Requirements: Water consumption of 3700 gallons per minute is required. 80 percent of the water is used for tailing disposal. (Ackerman)
   b. Social Costs (Supply)
      1. Half of the volume of the rivers in the area will be taken for water; as this flow is diminished it will affect organic life (e.g., the bilharzia snail may change in number of its species). (Levins)
      2. No water problem
         (a) By the year 2000, only 24 percent of water available will be needed by local municipalities and mining adds no more than 10 percent. (Natural History Society).
         (b) Water resources are adequate. (Government)
      3. History
         Ponce Mining Co. (Amax affiliate) caused a drought in farms during its drilling operations and were forced to pay damages to farmers. Only by submitting the case to the court were citizens able to obtain reparations from the Company.
   c. Social Costs (Pollution)
      1. Rain on exposed rock oxidizes it, causing sulfurous acid to form, going to the bottom of the pit.
         (a) It must be pumped out and may go into the regional drainage system, thus polluting it.
         (b) It may seep into the water table if some cracks exist at the bottom of the pit.
      2. Tailings will be spread over an ocean area 1.4 times the size of Puerto Rico.
      3. Standards of the United States do not apply to the environment of Puerto Rico.

Community Development Costs

Community development costs were not specified in initial negotiations.
1. Land reclamation costs
2. Social surveys and cultural studies of area (current and projected costs).
3. Relocation and community development program (projected estimates of six-month training program in community corporation management, locally and island-wide).
4. Transportation (public ways, electricity, easements, etc.)
5. Employment (location of personnel, training, etc.)
6. Community construction and administration (housing, schools, hospitals, recreation)
7. Land value lost

Commonwealth Supervision and Oversight
(Mining Agency costs, current and projected)

1. Cost of accounting offices and investigatory work to determine
   a. Whether the Company is following regulations.
   b. Measurement of extraction for judging extent of royalties.
   c. Costs of arbitrating company vs community problems.
2. Costs for arbitration between the Commonwealth and the companies.
3. Contingency cost estimated on basis of errors calculating pollution protection (e.g., tidal movements relocating tailings, special insurance against accidental damages, etc.)

Socioeconomic Benefits

Assessment includes following categories:
1. Commonwealth Income (e.g., estimated millions of dollars per year)
2. Commonwealth Gains from company provisions of:
   a. Materials for construction
   b. Production
   c. Transportation
3. Wages (direct and indirect computed separately)
4. Land Value Added (E.g., constructing a highway to site from surrounding towns is "value added.")
5. Community Institutions: schools, hospitals, recreation facilities, etc.

References

David Ackerman, "Environmental Planning in Modern Mineral Development," *Mining Congress Journal,* April, 1970.

David Ackerman, "Mining and the Environment," *Industrial Puerto Rico,* February–March, 1970.

Dr. Maximo Cerame Vivas, "Interview" in *The Mining of Copper in Puerto Rico,* p. 6; (Translation by Allen Pripps; Ponce Mining, August, 1971). Industrial Mission of Puerto Rico, pp. 11, 10, 21.

Ibid., Dr. Francisco Cadilla, pp. 62, 41, 50, 61.

Ibid., Dr. Richard Levins, pp. 1–2.

Statement of Natural History Society (140 members) of the University of Puerto Rico.

Water Resources Division, Puerto Rican Government.

Remarks of David H. Ackerman, Vice President, Ponce Mining Company, delivered before the Overseas Press Club, Oct. 22, 1970.

Other related readings:

"Control of Potential Sources of Pollution Due to Proposed Copper Mining Commission, Oct. 1967).

"Surface Mining and Our Environment," A Special Report to the Nation, U.S. Department of Interior, August, 1967.

George P. Lutjen, "The Curious Case of the Puerto Rican Copper Mines," *Engineering and Mining Journal,* February, 1971.

William Effros, "Copper Exploitation Bids in Puerto Rico by American Metal Climax and Kennecott," *Economic Priorities Report,* Council on Economic Priorities, 1127 Connecticut Ave., N.W., Washington, D.C. June–July, 1971.

MODERN INDUSTRIAL ORGANIZATION: SOCIAL PLANNING

In planning copper mining and refining, it is important to consider not only the most advanced techniques in industrial engineering to protect the environment of the island, but also the most advanced organization in business administration, which includes the interests of workers and the consumers. The interests of workers and consumers are an essential part of the social cost-benefit evaluation of copper development in Puerto Rico.

Research in industrial organization within both capitalist and socialist countries is relevant to planning in this case. The principal direction in the social organization of industry today is toward the decentralization of authority and responsibility in the field of work. The problem is how to make it possible in a corporation for persons to be masters of their own work and at the same time for consumers to participate responsibly and efficiently in the life of the larger organization of work.

Considerable administrative thought and practical research is being devoted to this problem. For example, Ralph Nader and associates have developed the legal concepts essential for what he describes as "constitutionalizing" the business corporation. This concept simply means chartering a corporation in the interests of workers and consumers as well as managers and owners. The aim is to find ways of organizing the administration of business on a "self-governing" democratic basis.[1]

Business corporations have been successfully organized on a democratic basis in numerous countries and serve as an example of what is becoming possible for the future of business administration. In other words, it is possible today to decentralize authority within an industry and still retain or increase the efficiency and productivity of a business.[2]

In the United States, many large companies have begun basic changes in organization with the purpose of eliminating the classic forms of supervision, competition, and bureaucratic hierarchy. The process includes replacing these forms of administration with other forms based upon principles of cooperation, equity, and self-management.

Multinational corporations have begun to initiate new types of contract relations with domestically oriented companies in overseas business. These contracts respect the rights of property and the distinct culture of the nation in which multinational business is transacted. Contracts are written today, for example, to train local people in specialized areas and technical work. In this manner, the whole process of industrial organization remains in the hands of people in the host nation.

These various advances in administrative thought and organizational research suggest a new course of action for the industrial organization of copper on the island. The following outline takes into account these considerations as a basis for contracting with outside copper companies on a competitive basis. An outside company that contracts to train people in the mining and refining of copper must be prepared to meet organizational expectations, as well as engineering and financial expectations, in the development process.

AN OUTLINE OF CORPORATE DEVELOPMENT: FOCUS ON COMMUNITY PARTICIPATION THROUGH COPPER MINING

An organizational plan for copper development takes account of how people are living today in towns and neighborhoods of the Utuado-Lares-Adjuntas area. It takes into account how they will be living during mining operations.

A development plan, therefore, must include an explanation of how people can determine the direction of their own lives in the process of community development. The importance of this principle of planning lies in the fact that new industry can disrupt and destroy important cultural patterns of life. The consequences are social rebellion and revolutionary activity. There must be serious account taken of local institutions, interests, values, and cultural life. In the past, the search for an expression of such cultural values has been lost or subordinated in the effort to industrialize. At the present time, there are no plans for community studies in housing, recreation, church life, or schooling in the area. The potential is great for village self-development, and yet all planning is centralized outside the site area. A community development plan anticipates community needs and sets forth a philosophy of industrial and economic life.

Community Planning Studies of Socioeconomic and Cultural Settings

1. *Past and Present Settings*
   a. Cultural Study: Beliefs, customs, mores, folkways, language, cultural origins.
   b. Social Study: Description of religion, education, housing, political life of people in the area.
   c. Demographic Study: Vital statistics, sex ratio, migratory facts.
   d. Economic Study: Average income, skills and talents, land costs, productivity of land, etc.
2. *Future Settings: Community Development Planning*
   a. Plans for building new industry involves local residents. (No "company community" allowed.)
   b. Plans for housing conservation and renewal in Utuado, Lares, Adjuntas; a description of location and type of housing in community additions.
   c. Description of new schooling, church life, recreation.
3. Relationship between Past Community Life and Future Institutions. Assumptions:
   a. Continuity in cultural life is examined between past and future by people in the area.
   b. Community life is respected in the context of work life during the extraction of copper locally.
4. A regional educational program on the nature of a *community development corporation* is instituted.

The Business Contract—Includes Plans for Community and Islandwide Controls

1. *Premises*
   a. Land in the mining area under the plan will be owned by local people through a community corporation based upon cooperative principles (one person, one vote).

b. During the early mining operation the land will be owned jointly by a Community Corporation and an island-wide "public" corporation while outside copper companies help develop the area.

(By utilizing public and community corporations under contract with foreign firms, the people who benefit on the island can be closer to controls over a major industrial operation affecting their local communities.)

2. *Overview: Planning Distribution of Income and Authority*
   a. A percentage of income from mining operations is specified to return to the *community corporations* for reclamation and town development.
      1. The local corporation selects a board of directors having contract authority over local mining developments.
      2. Additional land is purchased by the community corporation for mining but limited by the authority of
         (a) The Environmental Quality Control Board seeking overall protection of the region from excessive mining exploitation.
         (b) Zoning powers of the local government.
   b. A percentage of income is specified to return to the island-wide *public corporation* for purposes of commonwealth planning of copper development.
      1. The public corporation cooperates with the Department of Natural Resources in the island-wide search for copper development balanced with social development.
      2. The public corporation negotiates with external firms on production and marketing contracts.
      3. The public corporation works with CDCs and the copper refinery in coordinating the overall production and distribution of copper on the island.
   c. A percentage of income returns to the copper refinery on the basis of its output and needs, and a program for training employees in worker councils is initiated.

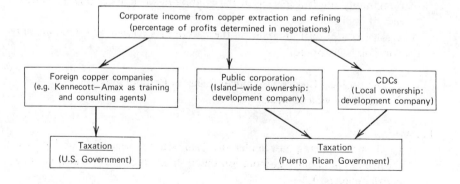

Figure A.1.

1. The refinery is codetermined by labor and management and after a period of training and development of personnel, it becomes completely self-managed.
2. Experts on the forms of management known as "codetermination" in West Germany and self-management in Sweden or Northern Spain are consulted on the social organization of the refinery plant. Consultation begins with companies that are experimenting with self-management.
3. Experts from the copper company (e.g., Kennecott) train island personnel in refining copper.

d. A percentage of income returns to the outside copper company whose employment, training skills, and equipment are utilized in the process of copper development. (See Figure A.1.)

The Nature of Public and Community Corporations

The rationale for public and community corporations established in Puerto Rico is based on the need to correct existing deficiencies in the multinational business system. These corporations represent ways to organize effectively in the public interest without government controls. They decentralize business domestically and institute host-nation controls over multinational corporate development.

The Public Corporation

The function of the public corporation is to help initiate community corporations, adjust problems in corporate–community relations, locate investment money, negotiate with outside copper corporations on terms of development.

1. *Public Initiation*
   a. The public corporation is organized with legal counsel by interorganizational officials including, for example, a representative from the government, the church council, the university, labor unions and the Chamber of Commerce. Each organization contributes to a public fund to initiate the public corporation.
   b. Stock is issued and sold in the corporation with legal limits on dividend returns and the amount of stock that can be held by any single person. (In the cooperative sector of England, the law restricts the amount of dividend returns and investment to keep one person or institution from gaining undue influence.) Each stockholder has one vote regardless of the number of shares owned. Anyone on the island can own stock at the purchase of a $5.00 stock certificate.
   c. A *plan of development* is formulated.
   d. Efforts to find *capital* for copper development are made. Sources of capital are:
      1. Government revenue bonds

2. The World Bank
3. Inter-American Bank
4. Capital reserves of major copper companies who agree to work with certain phases of the regional community development plan

2. *Public Organization*

a. A *board of directors* is elected annually and is constitutionally responsible to report to the stockholders.

b. A *constitution* and by-laws are written to account for the rules of membership, responsibilities of officers, principles by which the corporation operates in the public interest, a juridical board to consider offenses, a public review board to consider effectiveness and fairness of operations.

c. A *public review board* is organized separately from the public corporation, yet working in liaison with it. The public review board has the responsibility of monitoring corporate operations. The activity and purpose of the board is written into the constitution of the corporation, but its members are appointed or elected outside the body of corporate stockholders.

The review board consists of an accountant, an economist, a chemist, a social scientist, and a lawyer, who are appointed (or elected) independently through their respective professional associations. Their function is to study the continuous operations of the corporation on the island.

The board has legal access to all corporate information pertinent to the public interest. The board has legal responsibility to publish annual reviews of the progress of the corporation in its various fiscal, economic, scientific, and social operations.

The board has no powers of coercion. It has rights only to corporate *investigation* and *reporting* on corporate activities relevant to the public interest.

d. A *juridical board* is composed of five respected members of the Commonwealth from various walks of life. Two members would be selected by the board of directors of the public corporation; one member would be jointly agreed upon by the community corporations and the public corporation. The latter person selected would chair the session.

The responsibility of the board is to hear cases from corporate personnel and people in the communities affected by the mining relative to development operations. People who are offended by "development" or "working conditions" can appeal directly to the Board. Board decisions are final. The public corporation and the community corporations are constitutionally required to act according to the judgment of the board. In case of deadlock (failure of corporate action), the issue would be taken to the Commonwealth court system. The Commonwealth decision then would be based upon the charter constitution of the corporation and the public interest of Puerto Rico. Each community development corporation has the option of organizing its own juridical board to handle minor cases of dispute and grievance.

The Community Development Corporation

The function of "community corporations" is to help develop the mining area. One corporation in the Utuado community and the other in the Lares community could be created. Everybody living in the geographic area of each corporation is free to join the corporation, but no one can join who is living outside each resident-corporate boundary. Each person must pay $5.00 for one share and one vote in the corporation.

1. These community corporations are nonprofit entities with a constitution and by-laws. The purposes of the corporations are to develop the area (educationally, economically, socially) and to operate in the public interest. Profits are annually channeled into local research and development.
2. *These corporations are the beneficiaries of a percentage of the income (royalties) now under negotiation to be paid to landholders.*
   a. Landholders are compensated for their property at just prices.
   b. A court of equity can be established to make adjustments on past contracts (respecting royalty agreements for land purchased). The land in the mining area becomes owned by the community corporations, which contract with the Island-wide public corporation for ore extraction over a specified period.

A Copper Refinery

The refinery is organized in a manner similar to the community corporation located in the site area of copper extraction.
1. People in a limited geographical area of the refinery have the option to purchase stock in it at $5.00 per share with limited dividend returns and one vote per person. They elect a board of directors in conjunction with personnel of the corporation. The board of directors has final responsibility over the operation of the refinery in the community area.
2. The constitution of the refinery defines the division of responsibility and authority of the members of the corporation, including the principles guiding the hiring and firing of personnel.
   a. The board of directors meets semiannually to consider:
      1. Distribution of revenue for improving working conditions, community development projects, plant expansion, major marketing problems relative to contracts with the public corporation.

2. Reports from the general manager on company policy.

b. The organization of the refinery company is determined initially by the public corporation with the purpose of developing a worker council wherein personnel participate in company management in a responsible and effective manner.

c. Representatives from the employees are admitted to the board of directors of the refinery. A proportionate authority is determined between employees (worker council) and the local community with the advantage given eventually to locally residing employees.

Social Design

1. Development is proposed for a 30-year period. During that period, other development sites are contemplated, which involve the organization of new CDCs. A regional development board then becomes necessary to (a) supervise the initiation of new CDCs and (b) open avenues for old CDCs to develop new industry for their locality after their site has been exploited and renovated.

2. The social organization of copper mining in Puerto Rico would then have the schematic organization illustrated in Figure A.2.

The Puerto Rican Government through its Quality Control Board, Planning Authority, and Natural Resources Department, retains final jurisdictional authority. The government agencies work in cooperation with the public corporation. But, if environmental standards are not being enforced by newly elected government officials who are less sympathetic to the people of Utuado and Lares, officials will have to contend with a local corporation having significant authority over the development of their community.

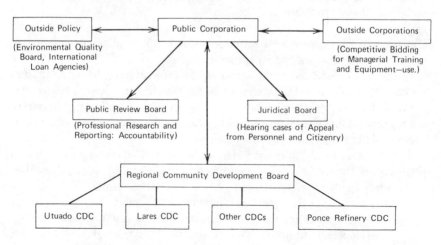

Figure A.2.

3. Ponce Mining and Cobre Caribe (Amax and Kennecott subsidiaries) contract with the public corporation and subcontract with community corporations for management, engineering, and site development. The outside subsidiaries, then, no longer own the land. But they train local management and help develop the area under contract with the public and community corporations with a designated percentage of the profits.

Comment

The need to decentralize economic operations into community corporations is coming to be recognized as important in the United States. A "community self-determination act" has been under consideration by the U.S. Congress. If passed by Congress, the law will provide money at the federal level for people in economically deprived localities to incorporate themselves to improve community life. Puerto Rico has an opportunity to develop a similar model in this case of copper development.

AGRICULTURAL DEVELOPMENT

No copper-mining program of any magnitude seems justified in Puerto Rico under present economic conditions without guaranteeing comparable (or superior) efforts in the field of agriculture.

No major Puerto Rican authority doubts the significance of mineral development for the future of the economy. Indeed, a number of experts have pointed to the uncontrollable movement to excavate copper all over the island. That movement may be unleashed by this first encounter with Amax and Kennecott, especially with the incentive of an island refinery. But the emphasis given to industrial development can no longer continue without destroying the rural-urban balance. Any new industrial ventures must link with agricultural plans or suffer the decay of rural life.

Rural towns, supported in part by agriculture, can be supplied with incentives for young people in recreation, cultural life, and good jobs. The establishment of community development corporations in conjunction with an overall island plan will increase the likelihood that a balanced program can be formulated in rural areas of Puerto Rico.

In the case of copper mining in the Utuado-Lares-Adjuntas area, three facts should be considered in the organizing process:

1. Many laborers are required in the "construction phase" who will not be needed in the "administration phase."
2. These workers will be laid off after construction, creating unemployment.

This could worsen slum conditions of the area. Unemployment in Utuado is already over 30 percent.

3. Agriculture is in need of development in the area.

A coordinate plan can be developed in which *construction workers are given the opportunity of participating in an agricultural program planned to be initiated at the time of layoff. A program of alternating industrial work (mining and refining) with agricultural work in the fields can become a part of the plans for community development in the area.*

In the Boimondeau watch-case factory in France, workers organized themselves into a cooperative in which 8 months of the year are spent working in the factory and 3 months are spent working on a farm owned by the factory. Educational programs have been introduced into factory life. Thus, workers have opportunities to hear lectures from the university and to take courses in literacy, English, history, and mathematics. At the same time, clubs and interest groups have been organized within such areas as drama, photography, dance, and basketball in the factory. In this way, industrial organization has raised the cultural life of the workers.[4]

In sum, a social plan could be initiated in the industrial organization of copper in Puerto Rico. A balance in the development of agriculture and industry can be a goal in the area of Utuado-Lares-Adjuntas. And new educational and cultural activities can be planned and encouraged among workers and others in the region. Puerto Ricans can then move ahead in social development as well as in economic development on the Island.

NOTES

1. Ralph Nader, *Corporate Power in America* (New York: Grossman, 1973).

2. Seymour Melman, Professor of Industrial Engineering at Columbia University, conducted a comparative study of Israeli industrial firms in six different fields, six at kibbutz and six privately owned. The jointly owned and jointly managed firms in the kibbutzim outperformed the privately owned companies in productivity of labor, productivity of capital, and net profit per worker. Administrative costs were 8 percent lower in the kibbutz. The kibbutzim paid normal taxes, obtained no subsidies, and competed on relatively equal terms with private industry. S. Melman, "Industrial Efficiency under Managerial vs. Cooperative Decision-Making," Report published by Hakibutz Ha'artzi Hashomer Hatzair, Tel Aviv (no date). For other studies, see David Jenkins, *Job Power* (New York: Doubleday, 1973).

3. U.S. companies experimenting with worker participation include Proctor & Gamble, Overnite Transportation Co., McCormick & Co. Lincoln Electric, Questor Corp., Syntex Corp., PPG Industries, Barry Shoe, and Imperial Chemical. See Report of a Special Task Force to the Secretary of H.E.W., *Work in America* (Cambridge: M.I.T. Press, 1973). Cf. Federick C. Taylor, *An End to Hierarchy! An End to Competition!* (New York: New Viewpoints, Franklin Watts, 1973).

4. Claire Bishop, *All Things Common* (New York: Harper & Bros., 1950).

Author Index

Ackerman, David, 345, 371
Adams, Walter, 149, 281
Adizes, Ichak, 274
Almond, Gabriel, 273
Althusius, Johannes, 157
Amin, Samir, 273
Angell, Robert, 298
Arggris, Chris, 50
Aristotle, 4, 156
Arpan, Jeffrey, 297
Averitt, Robert, 331

Babchuk, N., 120
Baker, Ralph J., 40
Baldwin, William, 120
Baranson, Jack, 297
Barker, Ernest, 40
Barnet, Richard, 249, 274
Bass, Peter, 333
Batten, T.R., 119
Baumol, William J., 41
Beckwith, George, 269, 275
Behrens, William, 150
Behrman, Jack N., 36
Bell, Daniel, 13, 38, 43
Bell, Wendell, 273
Benello, George, 149
Bennett, Roy, 306, 331
Berger, Joseph, 44, 85
Berle, Adolf, 40, 102, 103, 120
Berman, Katrina, 149, 213
Bernstein, Paul, 149
Bhagwati, J.N., 43, 274
Black, Cyril, 297
Blake, David, 274
Bluestone, Irving, 192

Blum, Fred, 86
Blumberg, Paul, 120
Blumenthal, W. Michael, 120
Bodin, Jean, 157
Bowditch, J.L., 43
Bowen, Peter, 331
Bradley, Joseph, 188
Brandeis, Louis, 21, 160
Bras, Juan Mari, 346
Brooke, Michael, 149
Brown, Michael, 120
Bruyn, Severyn T., 43, 119, 296
Buckley, P.J., 297
Bull, Hedley, 297

Cadilla, Francisco, 37
Calhoun, John, 159
Campbell, Alastair, 215
Capella, Antonio, 346
Cartwright, Dorwin, 50
Cary, William, 40
Casanova, Pablo Gonzales, 330
Chamberlain, John, 236
Chamberlain, Neil, 46, 85
Chandler, Alfred, 85, 126, 149
Chang, Y.S., 297
Chase-Dunn, Christopher, 243-273
Cherns, Albert, 331
Church, Frank, 296
Clark, Granville, 291, 297
Coates, Ken, 120
Cockroft, J.D., 273
Cohen, Benjamin, 273
Cole, G.D.H., 61, 218, 236
Coleman, James, 187
Commons, John R., 42, 218, 236

Subject Index